UNDERSTANDING CHINA

A Guide to China's Economy, History, and Political Culture

Fourth Edition

by

JOHN BRYAN STARR

Table of Contents

LIST OF TABLES

LIST OF TABLES

LIST OF MAPS

LIST OF GRAPHS

LIST OF DIAGRAMS

Preface

This book began as a seminar on issue in contemporary Chinese politics that I offered at Yale University for seventeen years beginning in 1978. I am grateful to my Yale students for what I learned with and from them. Originally published in 1997, the book was revised and reissued in 2001 and again in 2010. Given the substantial changes China has experienced over the past fifteen years, this fourth edition was clearly needed if the book were to continue to serve its original purpose—that of introducing to contemporary China those who have had no prior exposure to it.

Because the intended audience for this book is primary American, there are numerous comparisons in it between China and the United States. Some Chinese readers of earlier editions of the book have complained that these comparisons serve to underscore how China falls short of the United States. This could not be further from my intent. Indeed, I believe that we Americans tend to take our ideal of American experience and measure the reality of Chinese experience against that ideal, often ignoring how far American practice falls short of American ideals. Thus, the comparisons I make between Chinese and American data are intended to serve the same function as the small ruler in a scientific drawing—an indication of scale based upon something with which most of us are familiar.

Lastly, I want to acknowledge with my thanks individuals who contributed significantly to this volume. First, my longtime colleague and friend, Bradley Farnsworth, made use of his recent experience working in and with contemporary China to help familiarize me with the changes the country has undergone in the years since I last spent time travelling and working there. Next, Janet Millar has my particular thanks for her careful editing of the manuscript and her shepherding of it to final publication. Finally, I am indebted to Joel Conti, whose splendid maps adorn this fourth edition of the book.

Chapter 1: Introduction

To the limited extent that Westerners pay attention to what is going on beyond their shores, China commands a disproportionate share of that attention. Moreover, those of us who have some knowledge of what is going on in China tend to have strong feelings about the country, acting as cheerleaders for its successes and as harsh critics of its failings. We find it difficult to be indifferent.

There has been a great deal of good news coming out of China in recent years. China has one of the world's fastest-growing economies. Indeed, there are those who predict that at its current rate of growth, China will be the world's largest economy by 2035, surpassing that of the United States. Economic growth has substantially improved the standard of living for most, if not all.

Chinese people. In nominal terms, per capita income is significantly greater than it was in 1978, the beginning of the current period of economic reform, though income in the cities is close to three times that in the countryside. Economic liberalization has been accompanied by some relaxation of the Chinese government's tight control over its population. Most Chinese people are enjoying substantially more freedom from government interference in their lives than they did before reform began.

There is also bad news. American enthusiasm for an opening and reforming China in the 1980s had the unintended effect of filtering out much of the bad news, but that filter ceased to function when, on the night of 3 June 1989, tanks clattered through Beijing, clearing the streets of demonstrators and killing many hundreds of them in the process. Since then, we have been attentive to the repressive measures taken against its own people by a government deeply concerned about the consequences of political instability.

Our attentiveness to China's shortcomings in governance was amplified with the collapse of the Soviet Union in 1991. The demise of what Ronald Reagan had called the "evil empire" and the emergence of a new democratic state from its ashes made the resilience of authoritarianism in China all the more repugnant. To those with a Manichean streak who see the world as a conflict between the forces of light and those of darkness, the shoes just shed by the Soviet Union seemed to fit China perfectly.

Economic success had made the Chinese government—and perhaps the Chinese people—much less malleable and easy to deal with than they once were. China has run up a trade surplus with the United States, surpassing that with Japan. It demands full membership in the world economy but sometimes balks at playing by the rules. It has taken actions outside its borders that may be evidence of a worrisome new military expansionism on the part of Asia's largest power.

Complicating any attempt to resolve the contradictions that China presents was the fact that with the death of Deng Xiaoping, the country passed a milestone in its recent history and experienced all the uncertainties that accompany major change. In the end, China proved to be no exception to the rule that no socialist system had made a smooth transition following the death of its principal leader. There was a rocky changing of the guard when Mao Zedong, leader of the Chinese Communist Party (CCP) for forty years and of the People's Republic of China (PRC) since its founding, died in 1976. Having maneuvered his way through those rocky shoals, Deng tried twice to put in place a group of capable leaders whom he could trust to carry on his political program. He established a Central Advisory Commission in 1982, which provided elderly Party leaders such as Chen Yun and Li Xiannian a formal channel to influence the decision-making of the Politburo Standing Committee. By avoiding the top positions and by retiring early from the positions he did hold, he hoped to make himself thoroughly dispensable and thus easily and smoothly replaced. He failed on all counts; his trusted successors proved insufficient to the task. He had to abandon his efforts to retire to the distant role of *éminence grise* when student demonstrators called into question his authority and his legacy in 1989, and he disassembled the Central Advisory Commission when he fully retired from politics in 1992.

On his third attempt, Deng selected Jiang Zemin, who took on the posts of head of state, head of the party, and head of the PLA. Jiang was eager to prove that his claim to be a worthy successor was more than merely transitory, but he was of a very different caliber from his predecessors. Deng's death in 1997 marked the end of a unique political generation—the generation of the leaders of the Chinese Communist revolution and the founders of the contemporary Chinese political system. Rapid change has been a permanent feature of China for the last seventy-five years. As a result, members of each political generation after Deng's have led very different lives, careers, and experiences. The people who make up those generations differ in training, perceptions, connections, and aspirations.

Although Deng was not wholly characteristic of his generation, most members of his revolutionary cohort were born in China's hinterlands, ill-educated in a formal sense, and limited in their knowledge of and experience in the world outside China. The next generation, born too late to have been active in the revolution and civil war, grew up in a China heavily dependent on the Soviet Union. They were educated in schools modeled after Soviet schools, they learned the Russian language, and many of them spent time studying or working in the Soviet Union. They were technologically adept, ideologically cautious, and instinctively bureaucratic. At the time Mao died and reforms began, they were late-middle-aged dogs who found the new tricks somewhat difficult to master.

The third generation—the generation of Hu Jintao and Wen Jiabao, the next party and state leaders—had their lives and careers shaped by the chaos of the Cultural Revolution, launched by Mao in the 1960s. This experience rendered many of them at best skeptical, at worst highly cynical. As such, although they are significantly better educated and their opportunities to interact with the outside world are infinitely greater than those available to their elders, the new ideas they have encountered have not engendered great optimism in them. Having lost their idealism at an early age, they now find the materialism of contemporary China a comfortable fit. Although educated and trained in China, Hu and his colleagues in the highest echelons of power developed a degree of cosmopolitanism through their contacts with Japan, Europe, and the United States. They grasped, sometimes imperfectly, what China was and what it can become and proved reasonably successful in bridging the gaps that separate the generations, but they lacked the compelling stature and vision of their predecessors.

A fourth generation came to maturity after the post-Mao reform period began. Jiang Zemin was brash, hardworking, and cosmopolitan, but he was as self-interested as he was public-minded. One of his goals was to amass personal wealth, and that was best pursued in the rapidly expanding private sector. But devoting his energy to solving major problems in the public realm was his principal concern.

Xi Jinping and Li Qiang head up the current, fifth generation of Chinese leaders. Unlike his immediate predecessors, Xi has established himself as a permanent fixture in the Chinese pantheon, maintaining, like Mao and Deng, a lifetime hold on both Party and state leadership.

As China opened up to the outside world in the early 1980s, there were some assumptions about the country's future that were widely held by Western observers. The decision to allow market forces to operate in a formerly centrally controlled economy would, it was argued, require two elements to succeed: first, the absolutely free flow of information, and second, the establishment of the rule of law. And from the introduction of these two elements, political liberalization and democratization would inevitably flow. These arguments were reinforced when, in 2001, the International Olympic Committee awarded the 2008 Summer Olympics to Beijing. In the seven years leading up to that event, it was said, China would surely advance its pursuit of human rights. These assumptions proved to be wrong. As we shall see in the pages that follow, China has developed a market economy without the absolutely free flow of information and without having established the rule of law. Moreover, far from promoting the advance of human rights in China, there were some shocking violations of the rights of Chinese citizens even as the Olympics were underway in the nation's capital.

The purpose of this book is to look beyond the immediate situation and to explore four questions. First, in what way were our assumptions about the inevitable link between the free market and political liberation flawed? Second, what are the principal problems confronting China today? Third, what is the capacity of the Chinese political system to deal with these problems successfully? Finally, given the answer to these three questions, how might the political situation play itself out in the near term?

My answers to these questions, which I elaborate in the chapters that follow, are, first, that if skillfully manipulated by a purposeful authoritarian regime, economic liberalization need not inevitably lead to democratic reform. Second, the serious problems that China confronts in the near term would tax the capability of the strongest and most able of governments. But third, it is by no means clear that the capability of the Chinese government is such as to be able to address these problems. Hence, fourth, China's near-term future is bright, but far from unambiguously bright.

A scant dozen critical issues face China's leaders. Each of them threatens the nation's ability to continue on its current trajectory of economic development. Some of them threaten the viability of the state itself. Three of them affect primarily the two-thirds of the population that lives in cities. Three of them affect primarily the remaining third of the population that lives in the towns and villages of the countryside. Four are problems that affect Chinese society as a whole, and the others concern China's relations with the outside world.

The first, and thorniest, urban problem is how to accommodate the influx of new residents from the countryside. China already has more than 300 million migrant workers who have flocked to the major cities in search of more lucrative employment than they are able to find at home. But these migrants are very clearly second-class citizens in the cities; indeed, they are not urban citizens at all, their population registrations remaining in the villages they left. As a result, they are short of housing and most social services, overworked, irregularly paid at low hourly rates, and when employment is scarce, they are herded onto trains headed back to their rural homes. Over the longer term, this problem will only become more serious. Given high unemployment and underemployment in the rural economy, Chinese planners anticipate that as many as 300 million more will move into the cities, shifting the balance between rural and urban populations to something more closely resembling that in other rapidly developing economies. Expanding housing, social services, and schools for this massive influx of people will tax the capacity and the fiscal resources of most, if not all, Chinese municipal governments.

Congestion is another urban problem requiring attention. Visitors to China shortly after the country opened to tourists will recall looking out from their hotel windows at a wide river of deliberately moving bicycles as people went to and from work. With the number of cars on China's streets having increased more than twentyfold over the last twenty years, the river of bicycles has been replaced by a stagnant pool of cars scarcely moving at all. While every major city has in recent years undertaken major infrastructure projects, including subway systems in many of them, congestion is outpacing all attempts at relieving it. The influx of hundreds of millions of new urban residents will, of course, only exacerbate this problem.

A third issue that, for the moment, affects most directly the urban population is the party-state's attempt to stem the flow of information available to its citizens. More than one billion Chinese have access to the Internet, and roughly half that number make use of *Weibo*, the Chinese equivalent of Twitter, to discuss politics and news. In response, the party-state has constructed one of the world's most sophisticated systems for monitoring, filtering, and blocking information on the Web. But two countervailing forces undermine these efforts. First, China's continued economic growth depends on access to information about the global economy. All information cannot be blocked if growth is to continue. Second, China has produced a large and skilled community of hackers who very often seem to be at least one or two steps ahead of the party-state's efforts to outwit them.

There are serious problems in the countryside as well. First among them is the growing gap in the standard of living between urban and rural China. Average income in the cities has always exceeded that in the countryside, but during the early years of reform, the gap began to close. Beginning in the mid-1980s, the gap widened once again. While the ratio of urban to rural incomes remained relatively steady at 2.5:1 over the first twenty years of the reform period, it now stands at 3.3:1, and the gap in monetary terms today is forty-five times what it was in 1978. The gap is even wider if average rural per capita income is compared with per capita income in China's most prosperous cities. It is also wide if one takes into account the many social services—health care, education, and pensions—that are available to the urban dweller but not to those who live in the countryside. The difference between rural and urban incomes used to matter very little, since country people were only dimly aware of living conditions in the cities, and even if they knew that life was better there, they were prevented by the government from relocating. Neither one of these conditions prevails today.

Another source of dissatisfaction in the countryside is excessive government extractions. Although the agricultural tax was nominally restricted to five percent of household income and is in the process of being eliminated entirely across the country, local governments' need for additional revenue leads them to impose every imaginable kind of fee, fine, toll, and levy, so that peasant households regularly pay between 15 and 50 percent of their incomes to the local authorities. This would be unsatisfactory for most citizens under any circumstances, but it is especially galling here because a significant portion of that revenue ends up being used by local officials in ostentatious personal expenditures.

A third issue that has led rural residents to express their frustration in public demonstrations, some of them violent, is the wrongful appropriation of land without appropriate compensation. Only very recently has rural land come to be owned by those who live on it and farm it. But even now, what we might call eminent domain is taken to extremes. Local officials appropriate farming land to build factories and housing developments and pay peasants a fraction of the resale value of that land, ordinarily pocketing the difference. Sufficiently widespread is the problem that Premier Wen Jiabao, in his address to the National People's Congress meeting in 2006, spoke of what he called "land grabs" as a historic error that could threaten national stability.

Then there are issues that are not particular to the city or the countryside. The first is the fraught relationship between ethnic groups in China's border regions. More than 90 percent of the population consider themselves to be of the same Han ethnicity, but the remaining tenth is divided among fifty-five distinct ethnic groups. In many instances, these groups occupy territory that spans the borders with China's neighbors to the north and west. Most of them inhabit what the Chinese government calls "autonomous regions," but in fact they enjoy little if any autonomy. Increasingly, in recent years, they have come to demand genuine autonomy, often engaging in acts of violence to underscore their point and, in some instances, eliciting international support for their cause.

The seventh and eighth issues are interrelated: How will it be possible to feed a growing population on a rapidly shrinking amount of arable land? And how to solve the problem of environmental degradation. The government is dealing with a fraction, the numerator of which is agricultural production, and the denominator is population. Its task is to increase the numerator and keep the denominator from growing too large.

As we will learn in greater detail in Chapter 18, China's population growth unexpectedly peaked at 1.41 billion in 2022, having tripled in less than a hundred years. The population then began to shrink, and the government's population control program, or one-child policy, had successfully addressed the denominator. In response, that policy was modified in stages, and the limit currently stands at three children per family. But in its latter years, the one-child policy was fully effective only when draconian measures were applied—measures that further alienated a population already highly dissatisfied with its government.

As for the numerator, grain production currently stands at 706 million tons per year. That is a substantial increase over what was being produced in the 1950s, but the growth rate in production has begun to slow. Per-acre yields are already impressively high, and many observers are skeptical that they can be raised much higher. Meanwhile, arable land, already a scarce commodity in China, is being taken out of cultivation with alarming speed. China feeds 20 percent of the world's population on less than seven percent of the world's arable land. But recent economic development has resulted in substantial quantities of this land being taken out of cultivation and used for factories, roads, and houses. Finally, like that of all developing societies, the Chinese diet is evolving. As the living standard improves, consumption of meat and eggs is increasing, raising the demand for grain to feed the animals. Taking all these factors into account, pessimists some years ago forecast a grain deficit in 2030 so large that it would be impossible for world grain exporters to fill it.

The eighth issue that affects not only the Chinese but the rest of the world as well is that of environmental degradation. Nearly 60% of all factories in China are polluting the air and water in violation of the state's environmental regulations, which are as strong as those in Western countries but only sporadically enforced by local authorities. Sixty-three percent of Chinese cities do not meet the nation's clean air standards. At its current rate of economic growth, by this year, China will be producing two and a half times the amount of greenhouse gases currently produced in the United States. Seventy percent of China's bodies of freshwater are polluted, and 90 percent of the water flowing through cities is unpotable.

Finding sufficient energy to fuel China's development is a domestic problem with strong implications for its participation in the global economy. It was Deng Xiaoping's initial plan that revenue from oil exports would more than cover the cost of massive imports of technology to help China catch up with the developed world. His calculations of both China's oil reserves and the rate of growth of domestic use of oil were flawed. China became a net importer of oil in 1994. Consumption currently measures some 15 million barrels of oil per day, second in volume only to the United States. Soon, China will also be the second-largest importer of oil, and its interactions with the global economy now center on finding new sources of oil to import.

Greater China—Hong Kong (香港), Macao (澳門), and Taiwan (台湾)—and the world beyond it presents its own set of problems. Administering the special administrative regions of Hong Kong and Macao in such a way as not to disturb the delicate equilibrium on which the remarkable success of those territories rests is of particular importance. Between the time the Sino-British agreement on Hong Kong was signed in 1984 and the actual transfer of sovereignty in 1997, considerable rancor developed on both sides; reactions in Hong Kong to the Tiananmen (天安门)Square massacre in 1989 fundamentally altered China's view of that city and Hong Kong citizens' view of their future. These changes are expressed in some of the specific provisions that filled in the vague outline of Hong Kong as a special administrative region contained in the Joint Declaration of 1984. Hong Kong thrived under British administration, many argue, because of its government's light hand on the tiller of the economy. It remains an open question, even after 28 years of having Hong Kong under its control, whether the Chinese government will prove willing and able to maintain an equally light hand. It is normally heavy-handed in its own domestic affairs; even if it were willing, would it be able to lighten its touch sufficiently in dealing with Hong Kong?

The last two issues affect the world outside of China. The relationship between Taiwan and the mainland is closely related to that of Hong Kong. Hong Kong is intended to be a model of the Chinese government's ability to keep the promise of "one country, two systems" that it has extended to Taiwan as well. Continuing success in administering Hong Kong, so the argument goes, may raise confidence in Taiwan that under Beijing's rule after reunification, its political, economic, and social systems will remain unchanged.

In 1987, the Taiwan government began a process of opening contact with the mainland. That process has eventuated in a sizable amount of trade and investment closely linking the two economies. Informal talks between the two sides aimed at facilitating their relations began in 1993, but the process of coming together was interrupted in 1995 by a strong reaction on the Chinese side to what the Taiwan government calls its flexible diplomacy. What the Taiwan authorities depict as efforts at securing informal recognition of Taiwan's standing in the world as a political and economic power, the Beijing authorities construe as moves in the direction of a declaration of independence, which is absolutely unacceptable to them, and they have pledged to use force to ensure that it does not come about. Both Taiwan's then-president Lee Teng-hui's statement, in the summer of 1999, that relations across the Taiwan Strait could be conducted only on a "state-to-state" basis and the subsequent election, as his successor, of Chen Shui-bian, the candidate of a party that had earlier advocated Taiwan's independence, served to heighten the tension. With Chen's administration succeeded by that of Ma Ying-jeou, the Nationalist

Party candidate, cross-strait relations improved significantly. They cooled slightly under Tsai Ing-wen and her successor, Lai Ching-te. Nonetheless, the underlying question of sovereignty over the island remains unresolved.

All too closely intertwined with relations across the Taiwan Strait is China's relationship with the United States. With the Shanghai Communique in 1972, the United States attempted to recuse itself from this entire issue, but in the ensuing years, politicians in Beijing, Washington, and Taipei have worked to prevent that from happening. Chinese leaders have sought U.S. assistance in bringing Taiwan to accept their terms for reunification. Taiwan authorities have sought U.S. endorsement of their claim to be other than merely a province of China. And some Americans, mindful of the historical ties between the United States and the Republic of China, argue for a revival of American guarantees for Taiwan's interests.

The Taiwan question is but one of a series of conflicts between Beijing and Washington that, as the new century began, brought Sino-American relations to a low point reminiscent of the near rupture of ties following the Tiananmen massacre in 1989. Americans are repulsed by the Chinese government's violation of the human rights of its citizens and alarmed by what was until very recently the mounting deficit in U.S. trade with China. The Chinese see the United States as reviving a Cold War policy of containing China and thwarting it from taking a deserved place as a nascent world power. Two incidents reinforced this view: the NATO bombing of the Chinese embassy in Belgrade in 1999 and the collision of a U.S. reconnaissance aircraft with a Chinese fighter plane off the coast of Hainan (海南) Island in 2001. In both incidents, the Chinese government encouraged the popular view that U.S. actions were taken to harm China. During his visit to Beijing at the end of 2009, President Obama attempted to reframe the United States-China dialogue, encouraging conversation about containing global warming and accepting the necessity of taking rather than giving advice on issues of global finance and trade, a testament to the rapidly expanding position of China in the world economy.

Since then, as we shall see, China has developed to the point of threatening the American position as the sole superpower. Relations in 2025 are particularly tense given President Trump's decision to raise tariffs, even temporarily, on Chinese imports to unprecedented heights.

In addition to negotiating its relationship with Washington, Beijing must attend to its immediate neighbors—Japan, the Koreas, Southeast Asia, Pakistan, India, and Russia. What is now a complementary economic relationship with Japan is very likely to become a competitive one as China's economy expands. China's armed forces are growing and flexing their muscles, and Japan has responded in kind. Doing so has confirmed long-standing Chinese concerns about a revival of Japanese militarism, of which China was the victim in the first half of the twentieth century. In short, the two nations must come to a new strategic and economic understanding that takes into account the altered circumstances in which both find themselves in the third decade of the new millennium.

There are territorial disputes with China's neighbors in Southeast Asia that arise from Beijing's claim to sovereignty over much of the South China Sea, its island chains, and the oil that may or may not lie beneath its waters. China's relations with Pakistan, once close, have become strained, as Islamic fundamentalism has become a force within China's own Muslim population. That Pakistan and India have developed and tested nuclear weapons has complicated Beijing's approach to the South Asian peninsula.

As the United States has claimed the position of sole superpower in recent years and has acted on several occasions in ways that China regards as arbitrary and hegemonic, Beijing has begun to look toward Russia and India as potential partners in an alliance that might serve as a makeweight against unilateral actions by the United States as well as significantly strengthen its own military strength. Russia has, for some years, been a source of military hardware for China. More recently, China has initiated conversations on global strategy with both Russia and India.

It is hard to imagine a government that would have the vision, the political capital, and the tenacity to address this daunting agenda successfully. The Chinese government at present is far from that ideal. It has suffered a serious loss of credibility in the eyes of its own people. It is deeply enmeshed in corruption and seems incapable of disentangling itself from it. It is weakened by rigidity in the face of change and by its absolute refusal to countenance organized opposition of any kind. It is vying for authority, sometimes unsuccessfully, with insubordinate cities and provinces.

The CCP has as little political credibility today as it has ever had since its founding in 1921. It came to power in 1949 with a tremendous reservoir of popular support. It added to that reservoir with reforms it undertook in the early 1950s, then soon lost credibility with a series of misguided movements undertaken at Mao's insistence that had disastrous consequences for the Chinese people. The Cultural Revolution had a further devastating effect on the party's reputation. So complete was the loss of popular confidence that even a reversal of the party's policy line and a partial repudiation of its past mistakes were not enough to repair the damage.

Most Chinese people are quick to acknowledge that the reform policies put in place by Deng Xiaoping in 1978 have put contemporary China in a position to realize its great potential for the first time and have substantially improved their standard of living. Paradoxically, however, these successes have done little to bolster the party's reputation, probably because most people inseparably associate the party with the Marxist-Leninist rhetoric that they find so irrelevant to their lives. And Deng's own reputation suffered a serious blow when it became clear that it was he who had instructed that martial law be declared in Beijing in 1989, he who had ordered distant but loyal troops into the capital, and he who had determined that Tiananmen Square must be cleared of protesters at any cost.

It is also a paradox that the collapse of the Communist Party in the Soviet Union appears to have given the CCP's credibility an unanticipated boost. One might have expected the CCP, an illegitimate party with an illegitimate elder leader, to collapse of its own weight like virtually every other Communist party in the socialist bloc. Unlike those other parties, however, the CCP has been remarkably effective in ensuring that no other organization in the country could take its place. There was (and is) no Solidarity, no powerful Protestant or Catholic church, no opposition party, no nationally elected parliament. Because no other institution stood between the Chinese people and a disorder such as that which they witnessed in Eastern Europe and Russia, they accorded the party a limited vote of confidence. Living under the CCP was preferable to living in anarchy.

The current leaders of the party-state are clearly mindful of the issues I have listed and are pursuing policies designed to address them. They have ruled out political liberalization because of what they believe would be its destabilizing effect on society and have chosen instead to introduce measures of accountability to restore honesty to the single party and to win back popular respect. In effect, they have entered into a bargain with the Chinese people: do nothing to disrupt political stability, and we will provide you with the benefits of rapid economic growth—in short, prosperity in exchange for stability. In general, the bargain has held, but, as we shall see, in those cases where it has broken down and individuals and groups have come to see themselves as victims rather than beneficiaries of economic growth, instability quickly follows.

But the bureaucracy, the instrument that party leaders must use to implement their policies and uphold their bargain, is fundamentally (some would argue fatally) flawed. China's burgeoning economy has multiplied the already numerous opportunities for corrupt behavior on the part of government and party officials, and few have failed to take advantage of them. From village councils to the party's Politburo, officials have been profiting from their positions. Campaigns are launched to stamp out the pervasive corruption, but the officials put in charge of the campaigns are themselves deeply involved in corrupt behavior; the campaigns stagnate, and even the party newspaper opines that "a certain amount of corruption is inevitable." With their eyes firmly fixed on personal gain, not the public weal, officials are hardly in a position to tackle the complex problems facing them. An example of these campaigns was the "Mass Line Education and Practice Activities" launched in 2013. Its goal was to "thoroughly clean up the working style" of CCP members through "self-purifying, self-perfection, self-reformation, self-elevation, self-criticism, self-education, and self-analysis." It was extended for a second year to include cities, counties, and townships, and ended with some improvement in party members' working style and a significant decrease in the squandering of public funds. Within the PLA, three major generals were arrested, and more than 200 senior officers came under investigation for corruption. The public was supportive of the campaign, praising Xi Jinping for his courageous line of action.

The capability of China's political system is further diminished by an advanced case of arteriosclerosis. Conscious that its status is precarious, the party-state has become more and more rigid, less and less tolerant of disagreement and dissent, and more and more prone to act, often unpredictably and counterproductively, on its habits of repression. At a time of rapid economic and social change, the party has grown less flexible, less open to political reform. Always a society ruled by men, not by law, China finds itself with a group of late-middle-aged leaders who give lip service to the principle of subordinating themselves and their actions to a fully developed code of law but who, when push comes to shove, ignore the law in favor of arbitrary and often self-serving action.

Meanwhile, political power and authority have shifted noticeably from the center of the party-state to its periphery. Central government and party organs have delegated power, and provincial and local governments have gained it. The economy's market reform has been accompanied by an appropriate loosening of central control. Problems arise, however, because this loosening has occurred without a clear-cut or uniform allocation of authority between the center and the regions. Each region has negotiated its own arrangements, and none is prepared to give back what it has obtained. At the same time, regional interests have begun to diverge from those of the center, and, adding to the complications, regional interests are diverging among themselves. There is the possibility (albeit remote) that if anyone or a combination of these political problems reached a crisis stage, the center might not hold.

The glue that the party-state has come to rely on since 1989 to hold China's political system together is the PLA. It is the only organization with national scope that is capable of supporting a seriously weakened party-state or of taking its place. Given that fact, the party-state finds itself beholden to the military in a way that is unparalleled since the violent phase of the Cultural Revolution threatened to spin out of control in early 1967. China's military budget is growing, and it is acquiring substantial, new, and sophisticated equipment. At the same time, actions it has taken in Myanmar, in the South China Sea, in the Taiwan Strait, and elsewhere raise the question of the degree to which China's foreign policy is being made in the Foreign Ministry or by uniformed officers.

The PLA paid dearly for its decision to respond to Deng's orders in 1989 at Tiananmen Square. Its public image suffered, and it found all its carefully cultivated contacts with foreign military establishments suddenly severed, leaving it without the technology, training, or intelligence it had come to depend on. In exchange, it has received substantial budget increases each year, but only now is it beginning to rebuild its credibility and contacts, and it would be very reluctant to repeat this unhappy scenario. On the other hand, military officers are patriots—indeed, many are xenophobes—and unlikely to sit on the sidelines were China to begin to come apart at the seams or move toward anarchy. Whether or not their intervention into the political sphere would be successful is another question.

I begin this book with an exploration of China's geography, illustrating some of the natural constraints on the country's growth and pointing up the unevenness of the endowments of its regions. Then, in an act of almost unparalleled hubris, I devote a single chapter to China's very long and turbulent history, attempting to identify the patterns discernible in that history that influence the thinking of the Chinese people as they look at their current situation.

Then I describe the political system as a power grid, with central agencies constituting the vertical elements and regional agencies the horizontal elements. When center and region are at odds with each other, as is often the case, the grid thwarts rather than facilitates the implementation of central directives. A chapter on politics talks about political leadership, the characteristics of the political process (including preferences for consensus, bargaining, networking, saving face, and the prevalence of corruption), and the limited vehicles the Chinese population has at its disposal to make its interests known to the party-state (including elections, petitioning, protest, litigation, and nongovernmental organizations). Next, the description of China's economy in transition focuses on three questions: Who owns what? Who works where? And who is making the economic decisions?

The following three chapters are devoted to the rule of law, the People's Liberation Army, and what I call "the centrifugal forces of regionalism." Then we consider in two chapters the two spheres into which the Chinese population is divided: its cities and its countryside. Two chapters consider what we might call "the outliers" on China's map: the autonomous regions that house the majority of the country's ethnic minorities and the special administrative regions of the former colonies of Hong Kong and Macao. In the next section of the book, five chapters look at sectors of the party-state devoted to particular functions: those of education, health care, the flow of information, environmental challenges, and population pressures. The last three chapters look outside of the country, first at Taiwan, and then at China's interaction with the rest of the world, and finally, the current struggle between the two superpowers. The conclusion takes a cautious stroke or two through the dangerous waters of predicting China's future.

To aid the reader in the journey through the forest of events and players in the pages that follow, I have included as an appendix a timeline of major events in China since 1911.

Chapter 2: China's Geography

As a first step toward understanding China, one can hardly do better than to spend some time with a good atlas. It is vital that we begin by understanding China's diversity, and a key element in that diversity is its geography.

Superimposing an outline of the United States on an outline of China reveals that China, covering approximately 3.7 million square miles, is nearly the same size as the United States, which spans just over 3.6 million square miles. Both countries are situated at similar latitudes; for instance, New York and Beijing are at roughly the same latitude, as are New Orleans and Shanghai.

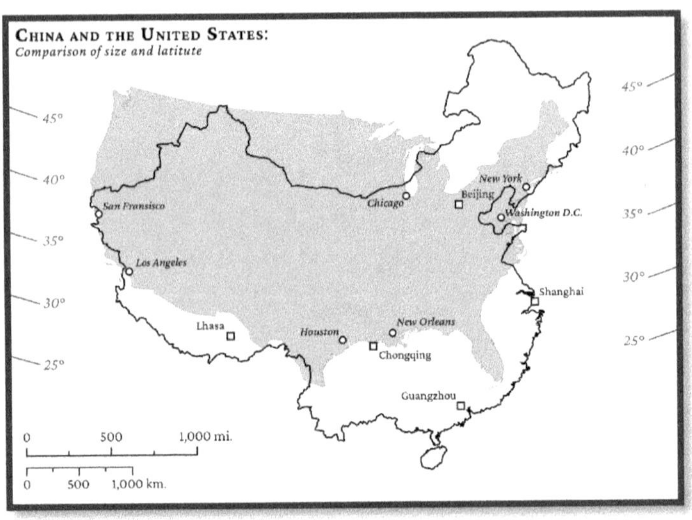

China and the United States. Comparison of Size and Latitude

A topographical map, on the other hand, shows us important geographical differences between China and the United States. Only about a third of the United States is taken up with mountains and desert, and the remainder is reasonably flat and easily habitable; but in China, these proportions are reversed. The difference in the amount of land available for cultivation in the two countries is even more striking: 40 percent in the United States versus only 10 percent in China.

In any country, rivers serve as arteries for transportation and as sources of both irrigation and energy. Silting improves the fertility of river basin fields, but flooding destroys crops and houses and often claims lives. The major river systems on the North American continent run from north to south, while China's three major river systems flow from west to east. The northernmost is the *Huang He* (黄河 Yellow River), which runs for more than three thousand miles from the western territory of Tibet (*Xīzàng 西藏) to its mouth in Shandong* (山东) Province. The river takes its name from the color of the extraordinary amount of silt it carries, deposits of which continuously raise its level; it now flows well above the level of the North China plain and is contained between high dikes.

The second major river system, the *Yangzi* (洋子)or *Changjiang* (长江 Long River), also originates in Tibet. At nearly 4,000 miles in length, it is somewhat longer than the Yellow and has ten times the discharge. It is navigable by ocean-going ships from its mouth near Shanghai (上海) as far upstream as the city of Wuhan (武汉). About three hundred miles upstream from Wuhan lies the very large and controversial Three Gorges Dam (*Sanxia Daba* **三峡大**坝). The dam extends the navigability of the river to the city of Chongqing (重慶), produces some 100-terawatt hours of hydroelectric power, and regulates the flow of the river to control downstream flooding.

The *Xi Jiang* (西江 West River) in Guangdong Province, the third of China's major river systems, is the shortest of the three, flowing 1,650 miles before merging with the *Zhu Jiang* (珠 江 Pearl River) in the delta, at the mouth of which are located

Guangzhou (广洲 once more familiarly known to Westerns as Canton), Hong Kong (*Xianggang* 香港), and Macao (*Aomen* 澳門).

China's most fertile agricultural regions are in the deltas of the Yellow, *Yangzi,* and West rivers. A fourth area of high fertility is along the upper reaches of the *Yangzi* River in *Sichuan* (四川) basin, just south of the center of the Chinese landmass.

A striking difference between the North American and the Chinese landmasses is found in the nature of their western borders. In the United States, it is an ocean coast, while in China, it is marked with mountains, plateaus, and deserts. This difference accounts for major dissimilarities in the prevailing climates of the two landmasses. America's weather is governed by the movement of the jet stream, carrying moisture-laden Pacific storms across the continent. China's weather is determined by monsoon winds that between December and March blow northwest to southeast; coming from the Siberian landmass, the air crossing the northwestern provinces is very dry and provides little rainfall. Then, during the summer months from April to November, the monsoon winds reverse themselves, and now moving across the South China Sea, they are heavily laden with moisture that descends as rainfall on China's southeastern coast; the winds are relatively dry by the time they reach the northwestern provinces. Annual rainfall on the southern coast exceeds seventy-five inches, but along the Mongolian border, it is no more than five inches.

Temperatures along the southeastern coast of China are moderate enough even in the winter that there is a year-round growing season, and as many as three crops of rice can be harvested. North of the Great Wall, by contrast, the growing season is only 140 days, and farmers consider themselves fortunate to harvest a single crop of spring wheat.

Energy resources and raw materials are somewhat more equally distributed across China than is its scant supply of agricultural land, for coal is found in substantial quantities across the eastern half of the country as well as in Xinjiang, while principal onshore oil fields are located in Gansu (甘肃), Xinjiang (新疆), Shanxi (山西), Sichuan (四川), and Heilongjiang (黑龙江)).

The distribution of China's population accords closely with the location of fertile soil and adequate growing seasons. Approximately 75 percent of the population lives on 15 percent of the landmass, being most heavily concentrated in the fertile river basins, where densities exceeding two thousand people per square mile are not uncommon. (This compares with a population density of fewer than four hundred people per square mile in the northeastern United States, its most highly populated area.) Compared with the river basins, western China is sparsely populated, but even these wide-open spaces have a fair number of people. The autonomous region of Xinjiang, China's largest province, is also the country's least densely populated, with some forty people per square mile. (By comparison, Wyoming and Alaska have five and one per square mile, respectively.)

Nearly six hundred million people—45 percent of the Chinese population—reside in China's 701 cities, and the density of the network of these cities generally conforms to the pattern of population density shown in the map. This is a more even distribution than is the case with many other countries at a comparable level of economic development, for three distinct reasons.

As the territory over which China's sovereignty extended began to expand as early as the third century B.C., the central government established administrative seats from which its officials exerted control over the populace. At the beginning of the nineteenth century, a network of some two thousand cities and towns covered all of what we now think of as Chinese territory, with, at the center of each, a walled compound housing the local representative of imperial authority. Each administrative seat was part of a hierarchy organized according to the respective ranks and positions of the imperial officials. Beijing, the imperial capital, stood at the apex of this hierarchy, provincial capitals formed its mid-levels, and county seats formed its base.

A second reason for the rise of urban aggregations in China was commercial. The exchange of agricultural goods and handicraft products and, subsequently, the exchange of both of these for manufactured items led to the rise of itinerant merchants, moving periodically from village to village, and then to a whole stratum of society devoted entirely to commerce. While some villages were centers of commercial activity only occasionally, others, by virtue of their locations, were more frequently. Eventually, the markets became permanent. Thus, a hierarchy of commercial centers was created that was integrated with, but at the same time distinguishable from, the hierarchy of administrative centers.

Whereas the administrative centers were laid out from the top down in a reasonably orderly fashion so as to exert imperial control as uniformly as possible over China's hinterlands, the network of market towns grew naturally from the bottom up. The former were called *cheng (城), a word that also means "wall" and that conjures up an image of a formally laid out and enclosed urban space; market towns were called zhen* (镇), which connotes an outpost or a garrison without a formal layout or walls. Administrative centers were large—the smallest had a population of between three and ten thousand—while the market towns were much smaller, the lowest ranking among them being mere hamlets of as few as five hundred people, half or more of whom were full-time farmers.

The third force that gave rise to urban agglomeration in China came much later in the country's history and resulted from the government's unsuccessful effort to prevent or at least to limit foreigners' commercial and cultural contact with China. One result of the series of defeats that the Chinese endured in the modern period at the hands of Westerners superior in modern armaments *and the tactics to employ them was that, for the first time in its history, China was forced open to the influx and influence of non-Chinese. Because Western nations were themselves in rivalry with one another for slices of what came to be called the "Chinese melon," the Chinese used this rivalry to their advantage to restrict the points of Sino-Western contact to a few locations called treaty ports (商埠shangbu).* Unlike administrative and market towns, treaty ports were part of neither a hierarchy nor an effective network. To the extent that the Chinese government was able to control their designation, they were situated where contact between Chinese people and nefarious foreigners would be minimal and easily controlled. To the extent that Western powers succeeded in imposing their preferences, the treaty ports sprang up where Western entrepreneurs found maximal ease of access to what they sought in China: cheap labor, cheap raw materials, cheap maritime transport, and abundant consumers.

Today, even the smallest of China's 701 cities seems very large to Americans; at the other end of the scale, 113 cities in China have more than one million people. There are only nine cities with more than a million people in the United States.

Table 1: China's Fifteen Largest Cities

	Population (in millions)	*The four largest U.S. Cities and their population (in millions)*
Chongqing	32.1	
Shanghai	29.9	
Beijing	21.9	
Chengdu	20.9	
Guangzhou	14.6	
Tianjin	14.5	
Harbin	10.0	
Nanjing	9.9	
Xian	9.0	
Wuhan	8.9	
		New York 8.2
Shenyang	7.8	
Qingdao	6.4	
Zhengzhou	6.0	
Changchun	4.8	
Nanning	4.3	
		Los Angeles 3.8
		Chicago 2.7
		Houston 2.3

China is by modern standards inadequately interconnected, with less than 3.3 million miles of highways and roads, about 88 percent of which are paved, roughly 90 percent of the highway network in the United States. Moreover, the roads are unequally distributed: dense in China's eastern provinces and sparse in the west. About three-quarters of the country's freight traffic and more than 60 percent of its passenger traffic are carried on these roads and highways, and highway construction is a high priority in the country's economic development program. Close to six thousand miles of new highway, much of it at the expense of China's limited supply of arable land, are being added annually.

The rail network covers about 100,660 miles, 60 percent of which is double-tracked. (The United States currently has a rail network nearly twice that size.) This rail system carries about 35 percent of the country's freight and passenger traffic (coal accounting for nearly half the freight). As China's economy expands, its railways are operating at or close to capacity and are meeting less than 60 percent of the demand for rail transport. Major construction has been underway to add track to the system. The largest of these projects, a second north-south rail corridor connecting Beijing and Guangzhou and paralleling the existing line to the east, was opened to traffic in 1996. Building high-speed rail lines connecting China's major cities is a current priority. Nonetheless, projections suggest that the railroad system's share of passenger and freight traffic will decline to about 30 percent each over the next fifteen years, with highways and airlines attracting away passengers and trucking absorbing the difference in freight traffic.

China's system of navigable inland waterways, both rivers and canals, is nearly twice as long as its rail network. About 12 percent of freight traffic and 1 percent of passenger traffic move on inland waterways.

The four thousand domestic commercial air routes in China (a number that shows an increase by a factor of twenty in the thirty years since the economic reforms began) now cover about a third of the distance covered by highways, though the volume of air transport remains small. Until the mid-1980s, air transport was handled by a single state-owned corporation, the Civil Air

Administration of China (CAAC). Between 1985 and 1995, CAAC was broken up into more than a dozen local companies, which have taken over domestic and some international routes; CAAC, operating under the name Air China, is now an exclusively international airline. A shortage of equipment and trained personnel has hampered the expansion of air transportation, which, in any case, has a dauntingly bad safety record.

As with the network of roads and highways, so with waterways, railways, and air routes: eastern China is well linked; western China is much less accessible.

Mountains and deserts rendered interaction with China's neighbors to the north and west problematic throughout the nation's history, and for most of that time, the ocean on the east was also a barrier to, rather than an avenue for, interaction. Capable of an autarkic existence, China cut itself off from contact with the outside world for much of its long history. Exceptions to this habit of isolation are seen with the expansion of maritime trade during the Tang and Song dynasties, in the tenth and eleventh centuries, and with the opening of the overland Silk Road, connecting China to central Asia and the Middle East, during the Yuan dynasty in the thirteenth century.

In the nineteenth century, the European nations, Japan, and the United States began to push on China's closed door. They initially came to buy tea and silk; later, they began to think of China as a potential market for Western manufactures and a source of inexpensive labor to produce those goods. Almost all the intercourse into which China was reluctantly forced took place at ports on the eastern littoral, a pattern that was revived when China rejoined the world economy in the late 1970s. The preponderance of China's now extensive interaction with the outside world occurs in the major coastal cities that were once treaty ports—Tianjin (天津), Dalian (大連), Shanghai (上海), Fuzhou (福州), Xiamen (厦

门), and Guangzhou (广州). To be sure, there is significant cross-border economic interaction with Russia and the former Soviet Central Asian republics to the north and west and with Myanmar and Vietnam in the south. But this economic activity pales by comparison with the volume of transactions initiated in the coastal provinces.

In ethnic terms, the Chinese population is unusually uniform. Despite great cultural differences among various groups, more than nine-tenths of the population consider themselves to be of the same Han ethnicity. The remaining population is divided among fifty-five distinct minority nationalities, each with its own language. This small fraction of the total population, however, inhabits nearly two-thirds of the Chinese landmass, including northern, western, and southern China.

Beneath the ethnic uniformity of the Han Chinese population lies a strong sense of local loyalty that is reinforced by language, cuisine, and a remarkably persistent regional stereotyping. The Chinese term difang guannian (地方观念), best translated as "sense of place," has great importance in the individual Chinese psyche, despite the homogenizing tendencies of a rapidly modernizing society. Ask an American where he or she is from, and you are likely to get some variation of a current zip code as an answer. Ask that same question of a Chinese, and you are likely to receive an answer that will call into question your command of the first lessons of elementary Chinese.

"Where are you from?" I have asked a new acquaintance. "I am from Shanghai," comes the answer. "Shanghai is changing very rapidly," I respond. "When was the last time you visited there?" "I've never been to Shanghai," he replies, and I wonder where my simple conversation went astray. As it turns out, my Chinese is not at fault. My new friend has, in fact, never been to

Shanghai, nor has his father. It was his grandfather who was born in Shanghai and who left at the age of twenty, never to return. Yet at some important level, my friend continues to consider himself a Shanghainese and to identify with the fortunes of his "native" place.

Local dialects are an important ingredient of this persistent sense of place. All of the Han population shares the same written language, and about three-quarters of them speak a more or less mutually intelligible version of the language that we Westerners often refer to as Mandarin. The rest of the population speaks mutually unintelligible dialects that adhere to seven major dialect groups and countless local subgroupings. The northern dialect, or Mandarin, forms the basis of what the Chinese call *putong hua* (**普通话** - 普通话–the common language), which is taught in schools throughout China, is used as the medium of spoken communication in official life, and until quite recently was the only language spoken in radio and television broadcasting.

Diet and cuisine vary by region in China, as they do in many countries, and constitute an important part of this strong regional self-identification. The most significant distinction is found between the northern provinces, where wheat is the principal grain, and the south, where rice predominates. Northern cuisine is best known for its flavorful sauces; southern cuisine features fresh ingredients with light, often sweet sauces that enhance the fresh flavors. South-central Chinese cuisine makes copious use of the red pepper. Fish and seafood figure prominently in the coastal provinces; pork and chicken predominate inland. In areas inhabited by Muslim minorities, lamb is the preferred meat. Throughout China, grain and vegetables are still the principal sources of protein, though with growing affluence, a preference for meat is increasing, a trend viewed with concern by those worried about feeding a massive population on a limited and shrinking supply of arable land.

Over the centuries, the enduring regional identities have created regional stereotypes that Chinese people never abandon. As is the case in other parts of the Northern Hemisphere, northerners in China are often thought of as reserved, formal, and aloof; southerners, by contrast, are seen as more outgoing, volatile, and spontaneous. Residents of Beijing, like those who live inside our Washington

Beltway has a reputation for being highly political and power seeking; like New Yorkers, people from Shanghai consider themselves, and are considered by others, sophisticated, cosmopolitan, and managerially capable. Residents of Guangzhou are often characterized as having a highly developed commercial sense; natives of the south-central provinces of Sichuan and Hunan (湖南), perhaps because of their peppery cuisine, are called hot-tempered and impetuous.

The People's Republic of China is divided administratively into twenty-two provinces and five so-called autonomous regions, where the majority of the population is non-Han. In addition, there are four directly administered cities—Beijing, Tianjin, Chongqing, and Shanghai—which, with their surrounding counties, are treated for administrative purposes as equivalent to provinces. Finally, there are the Hong Kong and Macao special administrative regions.

The provinces are divided into prefectures, of which there are 333, or about 10 per province. Prefectures, in turn, are divided into counties, of which there are just under 3,000 nationwide, and cities. Under the supervision of the county governments, rural political and economic administration is conducted at the level of the township or town. Each county has, on average, some two dozen townships and towns, with a national total of 41,000 townships and 20,000 town governments. There are just under 800,000 village governments, the lowest level of rural administration, or about two dozen per township. The average village population is a little over 1,000, though the villages vary significantly depending on whether they are located in densely or sparsely populated regions.

Translating China's geographical inequalities into economic terms, one begins to sense the significance of regionalism in China today. Consider the data in Table 2 on economic output in coastal, central, and western China.

They show that the significant advantages enjoyed by the coastal region are long-lived. The table also confirms that the coastal region, with a very substantial lead in foreign investment, is set to widen the gap in the years ahead. The distinction between coastal China and the rest of the country is obvious, but the lead of the west over the center is less clear-cut. The output of foreign-invested firms is significantly higher in the central provinces, and per capita gross domestic product is slightly higher. On the other hand, the average growth rates in all three regions are barely distinguishable.

Table 2: Comparative Gross Domestic Product by Region, 1952 and 2023

		Index of 1952 per capita output (national average = 100)	Rank	Index of 2023 per capita output (national average = 100)	Rank
Coastal China	Beijing, Fujian, Guangdong, Hainan, Hebei, Heilongjiang, Jiangxi, Jilin, Liaoning, Shandong, Shanghai, Tianjin, Zhejiang	215	1	139	1
Westen China	Gansu, Guangxi, Guizhou, Inner Mongolia, Ningxia, Qinghai, Tibet, Xinjiang, Yunnan	87	2	78	2
Central China	Anhui, Chongqing, Henan, Hubei, Hunan, Jiangxi, Shaanxi, Shanxi, Sichuan	77	3	74	3

Were we to disaggregate the data in Table 2 to consider individual provinces, we would see that some provinces and cities have altered their relative positions significantly between 1952 and 2023. The southern coastal provinces of Guangdong and Fujian (福建), for example, stand out as late bloomers, while provinces in China's northeastern Rust Belt have slipped significantly.

The information in Table 2 substantiates the hypothesis that the policies of the economic reform period have caused the influence of China's geographical inequalities to reemerge.

Before, development policy in China operated according to a different logic. Mao Zedong's first principle of economic development was egalitarianism. Mindful of the regional differences and geographical inequalities, he argued that resources should be preferentially allocated to the poorest regions, allowing them to develop to the level already achieved by the richest; only then would the richest regions be encouraged to move forward, and the pace of their development would be kept to a rate that could be matched by China as a whole.

The reform policies inaugurated in the late 1970s shifted away from Maoist egalitarianism. Deng Xiaoping and his like-minded colleagues believed that egalitarian development for China was inevitably development at an unacceptably slow pace. Arguing that the Chinese people could not be persuaded to delay gratification any longer, the reformers adopted a policy of building on the best. Resources once devoted to developing China's poorest regions were reallocated to its most promising regions—that is, the coastal provinces.

Moreover, the reform policies themselves, substituting market forces for central planning in the national economy, gave a significant advantage to the well-endowed coastal regions, since they favored areas that could generate capital through agricultural surpluses, or had surplus labor with skill levels appropriate to new industrial processes, or had access to domestic and foreign markets in which new products should be sold, or, finally, could develop global connections to potential source of investment capital. The coastal provinces possessed all these characteristics; some of the provinces in central China possessed some of them, and the poorest provinces in western China possessed few, if any. So, the coastal provinces, perfectly positioned to take full advantage of the policies of market reform and opening to the world economy, benefited accordingly. As we shall see, the central provinces have only recently begun to be able to take advantage of the reform policies, and the western provinces are still unable to do so. While it is useful to think of coastal China as a single, well-endowed economic region, it is important to understand that its provinces are rivals for scarce resources, particularly as regards their foreign economic relations. Foreign investment is concentrated almost exclusively on the coast, and many of the coastal provinces have been disproportionately successful in cultivating economic ties with a specific foreign nation; as a result, after two decades of growth, one sees a pattern that looks like the spheres of influence into which foreign powers carved China a century ago.

Hong Kong is the principal source of outside investment in China, contributing almost 47 percent of the $3.66 trillion placed in China by external investors to the end of 2024. These Hong Kong investments are heavily concentrated in Guangdong Province. Taiwan is contributing just under four percent, according to 2024 figures, much of it in Fujian Province. Shandong Province has been especially successful in attracting South Korean investors, while foreign investment in the northeast—in Heilongjiang, Jilin, and Liaoning provinces—is dominated by Japan. U.S. investment in China through 2024 amounted to just over $189 billion, or about 3.4 percent of the total, and is dispersed widely across the country.

These linkages differ in important ways from the spheres of influence in nineteenth-century China. First, the nations most active in "carving the Chinese melon" a century ago—Britain, Germany, and France—are not the most important investors in the Chinese economy today, nor have they concentrated in particular areas. Second, the spheres of influence were created by means of decisions made by foreign governments and firms, whereas in the current situation, Chinese economic actors are as involved in soliciting investment as the investors are involved in selecting the areas of China where they will invest.

Table 3: Utilized Foreign Direct Investment (FDI) in China in 2023, by Country

	US$ billion	%
Hong Kong	111.18	70.1
Singapore	9.78	6.2
Virgin Islands	6.86	4.3
Netherlands	5.36	3.4
Japan	3.89	2.5
Cayman Islands	3.52	2.2
South Korea	3.51	2.2
UK	3.41	2.2
US	3.36	2.1
United Arab Emirates	2.21	1.4
Germany	1.92	1.2
France	1.34	0.8
Samoa	0.86	0.5
Taiwan	0.73	0.5
Macao	0.66	0.4
Total	**158.59**	**100.0**

Source: *www.statista.com*

This brief geographical foray gives us a background for trying to understand some of the major issues with which China's political and economic systems must contend in the near term. One of them involves that critical fraction that will determine China's ability to realize its economic potential, the numerator being food and water supply, and the denominator, population. A second set of issues concerns energy resources—how they will be developed and the effect of that development on the environment of China and that of the world. A third set of issues arises from the consequences of China's very rapid economic growth: Will development result in greater equality or greater inequality in the standard of living of the country's 1.4 billion people?

Chapter 3: Patterns From the Past

The Chinese phrase *henduo yiqian* (很多以前) means "a long time ago." A literal translation reads "a long way in front of me," which suggests a very different sense of the direction one faces to look at the past from the one we are accustomed to. It calls to mind the image of a Chinese historian seated beside the stream of events looking toward its source, while behind him the stream runs on into the future.

What are the patterns Chinese people discern as they look upstream toward their past, and how do these patterns inform their understanding of the present? As in many ancient cultures, the patterns are as much myths about Chinese history as they are accurate accounts of past events. Common wisdom about the Chinese past is that China has always been a strong, unified state headed by a single, powerful individual, a minimal state with maximal reach–that is, a relatively small state apparatus that succeeded in extracting substantial revenues and labor from a large population. The bureaucratic system undergirding the state is believed to have been remarkably stable, having functioned without significant change for two millennia from its founding in the second century B.C.E. to its demise at the turn of the twentieth century. Moreover, the changes that did occur over this extraordinarily long span of history are believed to have been cyclical rather than linear; the system evolved, but it evolved through a series of deteriorations and restorations as new dynasties looked to re-create the system as it had existed in a perfect form at some point in the past, not to build a new order.

A key component in the Chinese view of their past is the idea of a unified state with a strong central government led by a single ruler exerting control over subordinate, weaker local governments and neighboring states. The geographical scope of this idealized state was very large. What the Chinese consider as having always been inalienable Chinese territory is in fact all the land inside China's borders when the reach of the empire was at its broadest–that is, during the middle years of the last dynasty in the eighteenth century. But when the contending principalities living in what is now Chinese territory were first unified under the control of the Qin emperor in 221 B.C.E., the empire occupied only a third of today's China, as far north as the Great Wall but not beyond. Its capital was in the city of Xianyang (咸阳, present-day Xi'an 西安), and its territory lay westward to the center of what is today Gansu (甘肃)Province. The first Qin (秦) emperor aspired to control all the land as far south as present-day Guangdong and Vietnam, but his armies' hold on that territory was tenuous at best.

The Chinese empire expanded and contracted, and the fluctuations were periodically interrupted by conflict and fragmentation. The Chinese may look on the latter as temporary aberrations from the unified, centralized imperial norm, but they in fact persisted a quarter of the time, five of the twenty centuries about which we are speaking. Nor were these times of regional fragmentation in the far-distant past. The century prior to 1950 was marked by a sharp decline and eventual collapse of central control and its replacement by dozens of heavily armed and contending satrapies.

Premodern China was twice overrun by foreign invaders, once by the Mongols and again in the seventeenth century by the Manchus, and in each case, the received wisdom would have it that the conquerors were engulfed and assimilated by their nominal victims. The Yuan (元) and Qing (清) dynasties, respectively, are made to fit the pattern of China's own dynasties; in fact, it was under Manchu rule that the Chinese empire reached its maximal territorial grasp. The island of Taiwan, for example, was brought under Chinese control only during the last dynasty in the late seventeenth century; Tibet, briefly under Chinese suzerainty during the Tang dynasty in the seventh century, also came under the tenuous hold of Chinese authorities at about the same time. When officials in Beijing speak of Taiwan and Tibet as "always" having been inseparable parts of China, they conveniently ignore these facts.

A dominant thread in this pattern from the past is the strong emperor. There were norms for the emperor to observe and rites to perform, but only two real constraints on his power: his personal capacity and the size of the empire under his rule, and the necessity it imposed on him to make use of others to carry out his wishes and his will. And the proof of the pudding was always in the eating. If the dikes were mended, the borders were secure, the people well fed, and commerce was thriving, the emperor was *ipso facto* doing his job. A bad harvest, a natural disaster, a foreign threat, and hard times, by contrast, were signs that there was trouble at the center, under which circumstances those adversely affected might well consider mounting a rebellion aimed at displacing the incompetent monarch. But this was an extreme solution to the problem of misrule and occurred only a dozen or so times over two millennia. Most of the time, an arbitrary emperor was restricted only by the length of his reach.

In China's traditional domestic sphere, a minimal state structure effectively controlled a massive society by making only limited demands on it, expecting society to control itself through its strong family system. The traditional order consisted of four interdependent elements: the family; the upper class, or gentry, as it is most commonly known; a group of bureaucratic officials who were recruited to office by means of a civil service examination; and the imperial throne itself. It endured for so long because it involved a carefully constructed division of labor and a finely calibrated balancing of power and authority among these four elements.

The foundation of traditional Chinese society was the family, ideally consisting of several generations united under a single roof. But this ideal was feasible only for the best off in the best of times; for most people most of the time, the family consisted of two parents and their children.

The Chinese have taken relationships within the family as paradigms for relationships within society and, indeed, for China's relationships with the world beyond its borders. They were described and subsequently canonized in the works of Confucius, the great scholar-teacher who died just a little less than a decade before the birth of Socrates. Confucius, an ethicist, not a metaphysician, argued that there were more than sufficient problems to address in this world, so he had no time to devote to issues about the next world. Comfortable in his position on the banks of the stream of events and looking upstream, Confucius, as a teacher, aimed to find a way of restoring harmony to human relations.

The paradigmatic relationship in Confucius' mind was that between father and son, and he depicted it as reciprocal. It is the responsibility of the son to obey and respect his father in all circumstances, of course, but the father, too, has obligations. The father must serve his son as a moral exemplar, to teach moral behavior by modeling rather than relying on rules and harsh punishments. Confucius then applied this model of reciprocity to other relationships within and outside the family—between siblings, between marriage partners, and, ultimately, between ruler and subject.

The father-son paradigm also informed China's sense of its relationship to the outside world, just as the father's authority is based on his superior grasp of and ability to reassert ethical principles, so China's authority among its neighbors was believed to be based on its superior grasp of ethical principles and its monopoly of a civilization that exemplified them. By these lights, the obligation of sharing its civilization by example, just as its neighbors owed it obedience and respect, which were symbolized by an elaborate ritual of bringing tribute to the emperor at various intervals. This Sinocentric worldview made for great stability in East Asian for a very long time. It also made it difficult for China to take seriously the notion that there might be value in ideas or approaches outside its own sphere of cultural influence.

The relationship between the commoner family and the gentry class was also a reciprocal one. The family was responsible for providing for its own subsistence, and beyond that, it relied on a surplus of both labor and product that could be tapped by the gentry for its private purposes and by the government for its public purposes. It was also expected to instill in its younger members a respect for order, discipline, and hard work.

Although the nuclear family was theoretically self-sufficient, in practice, there were situations in which it needed to call upon external resources. In normal times, this might take the form of mutual assistance arrangements with one's neighbors; in hard times, there was the extended family and, beyond it, the clan. Exploring the familial web far enough, one might well encounter a relative, however distant, who had secured membership in the gentry class; the resources of the extended family, especially where there were gentry connections, might be tapped for financial assistance in straitened times, for providing and education to a promising young scion, or for adjudicating a civil dispute that had turned uncivil.

Defined in narrow terms, members of the gentry class were those men who had passed a civil service examination and had thus received a degree. Degree holders numbered, on average, about half a million men. If we add the members of their immediate families, the gentry class would have numbered no more than about five million in a society that grew gradually from about fifty million to about a hundred million people. As we have seen, the gentry as a class depended on the nuclear and extended families into which all Chinese society was organized, and they, in turn, depended on the gentry. Similarly, the gentry and the bureaucracy were engaged in an interdependent and reciprocal relationship. Although gentry membership, strictly speaking, required a civil service degree, landownership and the revenues derived therefrom were the gentry's economic mainstay. The imperial bureaucracy relied on the gentry to manage the local agrarian economy in such a way as to make available to the state the revenues and labor power it needed for public works and payroll. Also, by virtue of its monopoly on knowledge of the canon on which the examination system was based, the gentry identified and instructed future recruits to the bureaucracy. Finally, for reasons we shall explore in a moment, local representatives of the bureaucracy were strangers in the territories they administered and thus depended on local gentry for the information needed to administer successfully.

But members of the gentry were equally beholden to the bureaucrats. While receipt of a degree entitled a man and his family to membership in the gentry, every degree holder aspired to hold an office. A position within the bureaucracy not only enhanced the status of the gentry family but also added significantly to its wealth. Beyond this, the bureaucracy's monopoly on political power was a necessary complement to the gentry's economic power. It was the bureaucracy that organized and supervised the public works—roads, dikes, and canals—on which the successful functioning of each local economy depended.

The bureaucracy was composed of men who had been appointed to their official positions by the throne. Its size varied substantially over time, but a reasonable figure to keep in mind is about thirty thousand officeholders. The lowest level in the bureaucratic hierarchy was the county magistrate, of whom there were some two thousand. A magistrate, assisted by a staff of clerks, runners, and personal servants would have been responsible for governing on average between 25,000 and 50,000 people. It was his responsibility to investigate crimes and prosecute criminals, adjudicate civil disputes that could not be resolved within the family system, collect taxes, mobilize a workforce for public works, and raise a temporary militia in times of civil unrest.[1]

Because he set examinations, awarded degrees, and appointed officials, the emperor legitimized and controlled the bureaucracy, but the bureaucrats were the eyes, ears, arms, and legs that made it possible for him to govern China's vast territory and to control and extract tax revenues from its large population. From the emperor's perspective, the danger lay in the possibility that the bureaucracy would come to rule in his place rather than in his name. A carefully constructed system was devised to prevent local alliances from forming that might impinge on the power and authority of the center. To be avoided at all costs was a confluence of political, economic, and military power held simultaneously by men with strong ties to a particular territory. The "law of avoidance," designed to prevent such a confluence, proscribed bureaucrats from serving as officials in their home locales. A

---

[1] A useful and entertaining example of the functioning of this system is found in the Judge Dee mysteries of Robert Van Gulick (*e.g.*, *The Chinese Maze Murders: A Judge Dee Mystery* (Chicago: University of Chicago Press, 2024).

newly appointed magistrate thus arrived at his post as a stranger. With no local ties and, more often than not, speaking a dialect different from that of the staff and clientele at his new post, the magistrate came to rely heavily on the local gentry (with whom he could communicate in Mandarin) for intelligence about the community.

State bureaucrats held a monopoly of political power within each local community. Although office holders profited from their offices through legitimate and extra-legitimate emoluments, local economic power rested securely in the hands of the gentry. And though the local magistrate was authorized to call up a militia, once the disturbance was extinguished, militia members returned to their civilian pursuits. A standing army was the exclusive purview of the throne. Political, economic, and military powers were thus controlled by three separate and independent elements of China's society.

A key ingredient in the glue that kept this carefully balanced traditional system together over so long a period was the idea that one's position in the social order was not fixed for all time. A limited amount of social mobility was endemic, but more important to the system's stability was the pervasive myth of social mobility. The fortunes of many families, whether rich or poor, in fact remained much the same across many generations. (As in our own highly mobile society, there were obstacles to overcome in moving up and advantages to being on top.) But the myth held that a family's fortunes were likely to change radically every fourth or fifth generation: a peasant's great-great-grandson might well become a bureaucrat, and the bureaucrat's great-great-grandson might well end up tilling the fields. To sort out the myth and the reality of social mobility, we need to take a close look at the rungs of what one historian called the "ladder of success in imperial China."

To begin the process of upward mobility, a commoner family needed two things: a son with intellectual promise and enough wealth and labor power to do without his work in the fields. The next step would be to find a teacher to assist the son in the torturous process of becoming literate and acquiring an introduction to the classics on which the examination system was based. Here, a family connection to the gentry, however attenuated it might be, was of great value. The teacher was, in all likelihood, himself a recent product of the examination system, a degree holder but not as yet an officeholder, who might well spend years training others before securing his own position in the bureaucracy.

The young man's education was largely a matter of modeling and memorization. One learned to write characters by reproducing perfectly and frequently examples of excellent calligraphy. One learned the classics by committing them to memory. One was prepared for the examination by repeatedly practicing the complicated, formalistic essay style in which answers were to be couched.

Examinations were given at the local level every three years. Those who passed were granted the degree that brought elevated status and respect. The top few candidates in the local examinations were then admitted to examinations administered by the central government; successful passage of these brought still higher degrees and a greater likelihood of appointment to office. Those who failed the local examination were entitled to take it again…and again. Those whose persistence exceeded their proficiency might well continue to sit for examinations into late middle age.

The successful scholar, degree in hand, would then begin what for many was a long, often tedious process of securing office. Respected for his intellectual attainments, he might find employment as a tutor or, even better for his résumé, as the secretary to an official. In this latter capacity, the scholar would encounter for the first time the practicalities of governance, which neither his education nor the examinations had been concerned with. Whatever extra income he had would be invested in buying land, for it was in his capacity as a landlord and lender that a member of the gentry who did not hold office was able to advance his family's interests.

Office holding, when it finally arrived, was the capstone to the upwardly mobile scholar's career. His status and that of his family were enhanced and their wealth augmented by the emoluments of office, both legitimate and illegitimate ones (commonly known as "squeeze"). Once again, it was additional land into which that wealth was most likely to be invested.

The reverse process, descent of the ladder of success was predicated on two important features of China's state and society: the first, a political feature, held that with the exception of that of the emperor himself, no position was hereditary; the second, a social feature, was that primogeniture was not practiced and a father's estate was divided equally among his sons. Given these facts of life, a son had to go through the same process his father had gone through–education, examination, and appointment to office–to hold onto the family's position in society. Of course, the deck was stacked in favor of the already well-endowed, and the chances of success were much greater for a scion of an elite family than for a scion of a commoner family. On the other hand, wealth and status often encouraged an effete lifestyle that dulled interest in and ability for a classical education. Failure to pass an examination puts the entire generation at risk. Without income from office holding, the family would be hard put to maintain the extravagant lifestyle of China's upper elite, and landholdings, rather than being augmented with the investment of a surplus, would be sold to make up the deficit. Also, with the passing of each succeeding generation, landholdings were equally divided among the sons; the progeny were likely to find themselves obliged to work for a living until such time as, with a combination of wit, drive, and a cash surplus, the family might begin the process of ascent once again.

Marxist historians in China have worked hard to persuade themselves that the system described here was feudal in character and thus that Chinese society was moving through the same historical stages that Marx and Engels used to describe European history. As is clear from this brief description, however, the Chinese experience differed significantly from that of feudal Europe (or feudal Japan, for that matter), where a family permanently retained its status in the social order. Though fact may have fallen far short of myth, there was mobility in the Chinese system, and status was ultimately based on achievement, not on birth, and only indirectly on wealth. Moreover, estates were more likely to be dissipated when all the sons were obliged to share the bequest with their male siblings.

In the same way that the fortunes of a Chinese family might rise and fall over time, the fortunes of an imperial dynastic house would wax and wane. To give a sense of continuity over a vast span of history, these changes were seen as fitting a cyclical, not a linear, pattern. Throughout, a Confucian set of ideas about governance, with a strong emphasis on the value of restoring an ideal system of right rule from which actual practice had slipped over time, dominated this cyclical pattern.

The idea that the imperial family had the "mandate of heaven" as its source of political legitimacy dates from as early as the Zhou (周)dynasty in the twelfth century B.C.E. The idea of an anthropomorphic deity had been dominant during the Shang (商) dynasty, which preceded the Zhou, and it gave way under the Zhou to the vaguer concept of "heaven" as a "supreme spiritual reality," as one student of Chinese philosophy describes it. It was heaven that bestowed the right to rule, and the ruler and his offspring retained that right or mandate so long as they ruled virtuously and effectively. A lapse in virtuous rule meant that the mandate would be withdrawn and placed in the hands of another, more virtuous emperor.

A corollary to the idea of the mandate of heaven was the right to rebel. Under circumstances of misrule, since the mandate was about to be withdrawn from the ruler anyway, it would not be wrong to speed up the process by mounting a rebellion. This "right," however, was granted only in retrospect–that is, if the rebellion was successful, it proved ipso facto that the mandate was about to be withdrawn, and if it failed, its very failure demonstrated that heaven was not ready to shift the mandate.

With nine major dynasties and numerous minor ones over two thousand years of Chinese history, the mandate shifted many times. Intriguingly, however, the new incumbent on the imperial throne, whether rebel or foreign invader, invariably made it his business to restore the system to the way it had existed at some better point in the past and never undertook to change it in any fundamental way. No doubt this had something to do with the strong restorationist theme in Confucianism, which served so effectively as the basis of the state ideology, but also had to do with the fact that the carefully articulated and balanced social-political system had proved such a remarkably efficient form of administration of a large, unwieldy empire.

The apex of the dynastic cycle was marked by good times, when the central government was at its strongest, taxes were collected, and the appropriate sum of tax revenue made its way to the capital. China's borders were secure, public works were undertaken and maintained, and the baneful effects of natural disasters were effectively addressed. In short, the economic health of the empire was sound, and the authority of the central government relative to that of local officials and the gentry was strong.

Conversely, at the nadir of the cycle, marked by bad times, the empire's economic health was seriously threatened, poverty was widespread, and the people were underfed, overworked, and overtaxed. The central government was weak and ineffective, tax revenues were insufficient, and a disproportionate share of them stayed in the hands of local officials and never reached the central coffers. External threats to the empire were not successfully repulsed. Natural disasters occurred with what appeared to be increasing frequency, and their devastation of the lives and livelihoods of the people went unmitigated by government action. With the authority of the central government weakened, local power holders were emboldened, and their excesses went unchecked. Superstition surged: since heaven was known to express its dissatisfaction with the unvirtuous ruler through natural signs, people anticipated floods, droughts, earthquakes, and everyone's favorite among the portents–birds flying backwards. At this point, the mandate was transferred through rebellion or invasion, and the process of restoration and rebuilding began again

Because restoration occurred with such unvarying regularity, one might have expected it to occur once again when the authority of the Qing dynasty began to wane in the mid-nineteenth century. How do we explain the fact that the Qing was replaced, not with another dynastic cycle but with a long, intensely painful period of linear change, a period that has yet to draw to a close?

One very important feature of China in the nineteenth century that had not been an issue at the time of other dynastic nadirs was the size of the population, for its population growth rate had remained constant and very low for centuries. Estimates of the population in early times are naturally subject to large errors, but historians generally agree that the population in the Han (汉) dynasty (at the beginning of the Common Era) reached about 60 million people; a thousand years later, at the time of the Song (宋) dynasty, it passed 100 million; and five hundred years thereafter, in the middle years of the Ming (明) dynasty, it stood at perhaps 150 million. During the course of the Qing dynasty, which ascended to the throne in 1644, China's population roughly trebled, and it stood at close to 450 million by the late nineteenth century.

Historians attribute this population surge from the mid-seventeenth to the mid-nineteenth century, which mirrors a growth in world population during the same period, to advances in agricultural techniques that permitted higher yields from the land. It had to do as well with the introduction of new crops from the Americas, including corn, the sweet potato, and the peanut. Whatever the cause, the result of this extraordinary spurt of growth was that China's population quickly exceeded the capacity of the land to produce an adequate food supply; the development of a transportation network lagged far behind the growing population, and a food shortage in one area could not easily be relieved by shifting surpluses from another.

A second new factor was a series of steps taken by the throne to put down a virulent rebellion that came very close to overthrowing the dynasty. Rebels, led by a group claiming to have Christian connections, proposed to replace the Qing dynasty with a "heavenly kingdom of great peace." So serious was the threat from these *Taiping* (太平) rebels that the throne agreed to undo the careful separation of political, economic, and military power that had given China such remarkable stability. Responding to the demands of a capable general, Zeng Guofan, the throne agreed to suspend the law of avoidance and the prohibition against mounting a permanent military force under local command. Zeng succeeded in defeating the Taiping threat, but in the process became the first in a long sequence of local warlords who held full political, economic, and military authority over discrete pieces of Chinese territory.

A third factor in the nineteenth century was the arrival on China's shores of Western powers intent on opening it up as a source of raw materials, labor power, and new markets and using weapons and technology that gave them significant advantages over their Chinese adversaries. The defeat of the defending forces time and time again at the hands of foreign powers discredited the central government, reminding its subjects of the foreign origins of the Manchus and sapping their authority.

Along with their guns and later their railroads and factories, Westerners brought their ideas. The first response of Chinese intellectuals was to accept the guns, railroads, and factories and reject the ideas, the scientific and philosophical systems, that had given rise to them. Maintaining a "Chinese essence" (ti 體) while borrowing "practical things" (yong 用) from the West was a last-ditch defensive stance against the threat of wholesale westernization. It was quickly overwhelmed, and Western ideas about social and political relationships soon damaged the credibility of the Confucian canon to the point that it could no longer serve to underpin the mounting of a new dynasty and the restoration of the old order. Instead, restoration gave way to a long, intensely painful process of revolution

The uniquely long history of Chinese civilization is looked on by most Chinese as a source of great pride. Much effort has been expended in an attempt to preserve this heritage in the face of changes encountered as China has entered the modern world. But more and more, others in China look at themselves and their compatriots not as enriched but rather as imprisoned by China's past. Perhaps the most vivid version of this counterview was a film series aired on Chinese television in the summer of 1988 titled *He Sheng* (河殇 River Elegy or River Dirge), which used familiar images from China's past–the Yellow River, the Great Wall, the dragon–to symbolize the restrictions and limitations imposed by tradition and juxtaposed these earth-tone images with that of the blue Pacific, symbolizing the freedom of the outside world. Only by looking beyond China and its past to the world outside, the series said, could the restrictions of that past be overcome, and the country's great potential be realized. Even those Chinese who agreed with the film's premises found the starkness of the images disturbing, and those who disagreed were vitriolic in their condemnation of such an attack on China's splendid past.

This affinity for the past causes some, both inside and outside China, to try to fit the Chinese history of the last century into this earlier pattern of dynastic cycles. In a rather Procrustean view, the cycles continued with the ascendancy of the *Guomindang* (国民党 Nationalist Party), which ruled only briefly after the fall of the last Qing emperor several decades earlier. The Chinese Communist Party (CCP) that seized power from the Nationalists in 1949 is but the last in this long series of dynasties, subject to the same cyclical forces that result in a rise to power, a period of ascendance, and then, inevitably, the signs of decline and fall.

But, as I have said, post-dynastic Chinese history is better thought of as linear rather than cyclical. Those in power in China over this century-long period have had their political, economic, and philosophical views importantly informed by modern, some would say Western, ideas of progress over time. For many reasons, China's leaders would reject the image of contemporary China as dynastic.

In recent years, some scholars have encouraged us to look beyond the image of the period between the fall of the last dynasty in 1911 and the rise to power of the Chinese Communists in 1949 as a nearly forty-year-long period of interregnum and spinning of the wheels. They point to the outburst of democratic reform that immediately followed the collapse of the Qing and to the democratic practices (however attenuated) of the so-called Nanjing Decade (1929-37). And few would dispute the degree of economic development and modernization that was achieved, with substantial foreign involvement and under the most adverse of conditions, between 1911 and 1949. Unquestionably, there is evidence of progress over time.

The Chinese Communists found their patterns from the past in the theories of Karl Marx, who, taking his lead from Hegel, found a synthesis between the contradictory ideas of history as cyclical and history as linear in the image of history as an upward-moving spiral. Through a series of revolutions, society advanced from a slave system through a feudal system and a capitalist system to a socialist system and, finally, to communism and the "end of history." As we have seen, "feudal" China looked very little like feudal Europe. Moreover, to create a socialist revolution in a feudal society, as the Chinese Communists were proposing to do, was to skip an entire (and inevitable) stage in Marx's progression. Nonetheless, difficult as they have found it to stuff modern Chinese history into rigid Marxist molds, Mao and his colleagues and successors have never stopped trying.

Yet another pattern from the past that was useful in thinking about experiences of the thirty-odd years that Mao led the Chinese party and state was informed more by his experience of guerrilla warfare than by his familiarity with Marxist historiography. Just as he had found during the course of their revolutionary struggle against the Nationalists that even obstacles that appeared to be insurmountable could be overcome if the army put its mind to the task and the populace was mobilized to contribute its assistance, so when the CCP came to tackle the enormous tasks that awaited it as it seized state power, the movement (yundong 运动) or campaign seemed an obvious method to employ. Campaigns followed a predictable pattern. People were first mobilized through the use of ideological slogans. When those slogans lost their punch, people were coerced into obedience. When coercion brought on popular alienation from the goals of the campaign, the party turned to monetary rewards to buy compliance. Looking back at the six major campaigns–the Great Leap Forward (1958) and the Cultural Revolution (1965) are the largest and best known of them- and the many minor campaigns, the Chinese could see a pattern to their recent history. By the end of Mao's lifetime, it was a pattern the Chinese people would almost unanimously seek to put behind them.

But Mao's is the portrait that still hangs, very much larger than life, over the Tiananmen, the Gate of Heavenly Peace, in Beijing. And Mao is the baby that contemporary party leaders are surprisingly loath to throw out with the destructive bathwater of his campaign style. And so, they have come to talk of "generations" as constituting the pattern of their present and immediate past. After his death in 1976, Mao was succeeded by Deng Xiaoping, who became the "core" of the second generation. After several false starts, Deng identified Jiang Zemin and Zhu Rongji as leaders of the third generation that would succeed him. Hu Jin Tao and Wen Jiabao were the fourth of these generations. Unlike the early generations, Hu and Wen were selected well in advance of their accession to power and were inaugurated without significant opposition. They thus lent credence retroactively to the founding fathers in the same way that the founding fathers lent legitimacy to their successors' positions in power. More recently, we have seen the ascendancy of a fifth generation headed by Xi Jinping, of whom we will have much more to say in subsequent chapters. Each generation is seen as having made its unique contribution to China's progress, its mistakes, some of them catastrophic, having been conveniently forgotten.

Despite the calming continuity and vision of orderly progress afforded by this generational pattern, there are still skeptics who have their eyes peeled for any sign of birds flying backwards.

Chapter 4: The Party-State

Americans like to think of the Chinese political system as the opposite of the U.S. system. Ours is a democracy; theirs is authoritarian or even totalitarian. Ours is a rule of law; theirs, a rule of men. Ours protects the rights of the individual; theirs regularly infringes on these rights. In some instances, these generalizations are supported by strong evidence, but in others, they obscure similarities and common problems. In still others, they fail to take account of the substantial changes to both systems that have occurred in the past twenty years. But in each instance, the comparison is made between an American ideal (often very different from American practice) and Chinese practice (often falling far short of Chinese ideals).

When American students learn about their political system, they are taught to think about four relationships: that among the executive, legislative, and judiciary branches of government; that between the federal government and state and local governments; that between political parties and the government; and that between civilian and military authority. Civics texts refer to the system of checks and balances that governs and regulates the relationship among the three branches of the federal government, designed to prevent any one of them from assuming an inappropriate ascendancy over the others. Laid out in our Constitution, these checks and balances have been elaborated and refined over time, with the three branches pulling and tugging, each trying to influence the other two.

The relationship between the federal government and state and local governments is still in flux. The idea of states' rights is an active political rallying point, reminding us that local governments existed before the federal one, which was created through an agreement reached among them. The terms of that agreement, spelled out in detail in the Constitution, include the important provision that what is not specifically set out as the prerogative of the federal government remains that of the states. Two hundred and fifty years of practice, a range of issues inconceivable to the framers of the Constitution, and the addition of thirty-seven new states have all served to modify the balance between federal and local power. A current case in point is the question of which level of government has which set of responsibilities with respect to our public schools.

The relationships between our political parties and the government and between (or among) the political parties themselves postdate the framing of the Constitution, and custom more than law regulates them. Though there are remnants of an ideological core in each of the two major parties, they are not particularly ideological and generally play to the middle when they are out to win elections. Also, they are not selective: voters are free to choose (and to change) their party affiliations or to participate in the electoral process as independents. Each party tries to control the government by getting its candidates elected to the presidency or to a majority in Congress, but its ability to do so is limited by the actions of the opposition party. The existence of a vital opposition is critical to our definition of an effectively functioning democracy.

As for the relationship between civilian and military authority, we accept that our system is based on the principle that military forces must always be subordinate to civilian leadership. So ingrained is this idea in our political process that, although we go through periodic bouts of concern over military spending or over the influence of the Pentagon on our foreign policy, with the exception of the Civil War, intervention by our armed forces into our political life has never been a serious threat.

Considering these four relationships in the Chinese political system, we find similarities—many superficial—and profound differences. The most important difference between the American and the Chinese political system concerns political parties. The key function of setting government policy in China since 1949 lies outside the government entirely and is monopolized by the Chinese Communist Party. There is no significant interaction among or between political parties, for while the CCP has allowed some eight so-called minor parties to continue to function, these parties have only about a million and a half members among them, have no corporate status, and are unable to raise funds or own property. Moreover, at the top of the party's current agenda is preventing the emergence of any force that could even begin to be a nucleus for an organized political opposition. For example, twenty-five years ago, more than a dozen individuals in cities across the country were given prison sentences of up to thirteen years for their roles in attempting to organize and register a new China Democratic Party (CDP).

A selective organization, the CCP chooses its members based on their suitability for leadership in its political life. Roughly one in every fourteen Chinese is a Party member, for a total membership of about ninety-nine million. (In contrast, roughly one in every four Americans is registered with a political Party, and the total number with Party affiliation is roughly eighty million.) Functioning somewhat like a board of directors for the country, the CCP defines its function as that of making all the critical decisions, which the government must then carry out. Unlike a board of directors, however, the CCP has created an organizational structure operating in parallel to that of the government bureaucracy, so that Party members oversee the work of the bureaucrats at every level, completely blurring the line separating policy making from policy implementation.

Operating under the supervision of the party, China's government, like ours, has three branches: a legislature, an executive branch, and a judiciary. But in practice, there are really two, since the Chinese judiciary functions more as a department of the executive than as an independent check on the other two arms of the government. Similarly, the legislature has only very recently come to see itself as a potential check on the operations of the executive branch and the judiciary. The branches are not equal partners, and there is no provision in the Chinese constitution for checks and balances to maintain an equality among them. Indeed, the constitution itself and its function in the political system reveal an important difference between the two systems. China has had four constitutions since the People's Republic was founded in 1949, and although the most recent constitution has been in place for more than forty years, it has been amended on five occasions, most recently in 2018. In fact, the document is probably best understood as a mission statement or policy platform with a finite duration. It was not intended, nor does it function, as a set of fixed principles against which specific laws and practices are measured and overturned if found to be at odds. Then there is the strange proclivity on the part of successive generations of party-state leaders to have their "thoughts," however banal, enshrined into the language of the constitution, rather as though, as George W. Bush completed his second term, the preamble of our Constitution was amended to incorporate the phrase "axis of evil."

In general, the Chinese system relies much less on relationships fixed by law, constitutional provisions, or regulation than on negotiated relationships between and among individuals, agencies, and organizations that dominate the political landscape, which helps account for the very different relationship between the national government and regional and local governments in China from that in the United States. China is not a federal system, and the central government deals with provincial and municipal governments by means of myriad *ad hoc* agreements made after complex bargaining negotiations.

In practice, the center-local relationship can be thought of as a kind of power grid, in which the vertical elements are the bureaucratic departments of the central systems and the horizontal elements are the provinces and cities. In many, if not most, instances, the vertical and horizontal elements work at cross-purposes, stymying rather than facilitating political activity. Emblematic of this situation is the fact that there are more than one thousand offices in Beijing run by provincial, city, county, and local governments, the function of which is to represent their interests to the central government, much as K Street lobbyists represent the interests of their clients in Washington. Recognizing their contribution to mounting corruption, the central government has ordered (not for the first time) the shuttering of some of these so-called liaison offices.

With respect to the relationship between military and civilian authority, there are, once again, substantial differences between the two political systems. Like the United States' Founding Fathers, the leaders of the newly formed Chinese state in 1949 had been active in the revolution that brought them to power, but unlike our Founding Fathers, the Chinese revolutionaries were slow to distinguish between military and civilian authority. The blurring of the lines was especially acute in regional and provincial governments, where, in most cases, the officer who had "liberated" an area stayed on as head of the new government.

As military and civilian authority gradually became differentiated, the party continued to exert control over the army in the same way that it exerted control over the government bureaucracy. Twice, though, as we shall see, the party found itself obliged to call on the army to intervene on its behalf in civilian affairs, in the aftermath of which the armed forces retained at least a temporary hand in political decision making.

Today, because of the effectiveness of the Party's efforts to eliminate any organization that might challenge its monopoly on political life, the People's Liberation Army (PLA) is the only organization in China with a nationwide reach that could pick up the pieces if the CCP should falter. For all these reasons, any account of the power grid in China must include a careful look at the PLA (to which we shall turn in Chapter 8).

Political party membership in the United States is an exclusively self-selective process involving an individual's only having to fill out a form or complete it online. The result of this process, as of 2020, is shown below:

Table 4: U.S. Voter Registration Statistics 2020

Democrat	45,512,696	38.62%
Republican	37,314,494	30.44
Other Parties	3,127,800	2.55
No Party Preference	34,798,906	28.39
Totals	122,577,294	100.00

By contrast, the Chinese Communist Party likes to think of itself, ideally, as an elite organization that selects its members from the best that Chinese society has to offer. The selection process involves six steps over a period of more than three years:

1. The candidate completes a written application and submits it to the local Party cell. The cell sends someone to explain the rest of the process.

2. After providing a CV, information on family, social connections, and the political background of the applicant's parents, he or she is accepted as a candidate.
3. There ensues a one-year preparation period during which the candidate completes a three-day course at a Party school. The candidate submits a monthly reflective report on Marxism-Leninism, the guidelines of the CCP, and current political developments. The Party cell verifies the candidate's information and political commitment by interviewing at least eight colleagues, neighbors, and acquaintances.
4. Candidates can then officially apply for Party membership. They must name two guarantors or mentors. A superior Party organization reviews the application in three to six months and interviews the candidate.
5. If the organization accepts the admission, the candidate is registered, sworn in, and begins a trial membership. Depending on income, members must pay between 0.5 and 2 percent of their net income annually as a membership fee.
6. If there is no breach of Party discipline or law, official membership is granted after one year.

Selection criteria have changed over the years, but political correctness-a knowledge of the current line and an ability to apply it to day-to-day decisions–has been a constant despite many changes in the current line. Currently, the Party also emphasizes technical competence, managerial skills, and entrepreneurial ability in its recruiting efforts. Its legitimacy is based on its monopoly of these desirable leadership qualities and of the policies that derive from them. Currently, the Communist Party of China's membership acceptance rate is on par with that of the Ivy League of American colleges

At more than ninety million, Party membership is at an all-time high. Party members, however, are unequally distributed among the population, with a substantially heavier concentration in the cities and a sparser concentration in rural communities. Moreover, the Party is having difficulty attracting China's best and brightest. For that reason, in 2002, Jiang Zemin, then serving as Party general secretary and president, advanced the idea that the Party should actively recruit new members among the growing number of successful entrepreneurs. The "Party of the proletariat" now includes capitalists as well.

Table 5: Profile of Chinese Communist Party members as of 2023 (in percents)

Gender:	Male	70.6
	Female	29.4
Age:	35 and below	25.0
	36-60	46.9
	61 and older	25.1
Education:	College or junior college degree	53.2
	High school	25.7
	Primary school	21.1
Occupation:	Farmers, herders, and fishermen	26.0
	Retirees	20.6
	Technicians	16.1
	Managers	11.4
	Party and state officials	7.7
	Industrial workers	6.6
	College students	2.8
	Other occupations	7.8

While in the past, Party membership was the exclusive avenue of upward mobility, that is no longer the case. An ambitious young Chinese with imperfectly developed entrepreneurial skills and business contacts can get a leg up in career advancement by joining the Party, thereby acquiring political clout that might be translated into economic gain. But for those with a full set of skills and contacts, Party membership is largely superfluous, and the CCP does not attract the most successful of China's young entrepreneurs.

This should be no surprise because the Party's political authority has been progressively undermined over the last hundred years by the irrationality of its policies, the corruption of its leaders, and its failure to put forward a compelling vision for China's future. It came to power in 1949 with a reputation for honesty and a promise to end inflation. It set up a government that contrasted with its predecessors in its dedication and in its young officials' freedom from corruption. Inflation had been brought under control by 1952, and prices remained largely unchanged for thirty years. The substantial changes brought about in the Chinese society and economy in the first years of the CCP regime appeared reasonable to most Chinese people and helped improve the welfare of the vast majority.

Within a decade, however, people began to question the probity of the party's leaders. The Hundred Flowers Campaign was the first of a number of events that undermined the Party's legitimacy. Confident of its achievements and its reputation, the Party called in 1957 for criticisms of its first eight years in power. "Let a hundred flowers bloom!" Mao cried. The attacks on those who responded to this invitation–imprisonment and forced labor for thousands of so-called Rightists–seemed irrational and out of proportion. Then the further excesses of the Great Leap Forward in 1958 and the destructive anarchy of the Cultural Revolution thereafter took even more of a toll on popular confidence in party leaders.

One would assume that the considerable successes of the economic reforms undertaken after Mao's death would have restored at least some of the Party's lost legitimacy. Interestingly, this does not seem to be the case. Individual party leaders–Deng Xiaoping, chief among them–are given credit for the transformation of the Chinese economy and its subsequent rapid growth. But the party does not share in this credit, perhaps because the transformation is the result of the effective abandonment of the Marxist-Leninist principles on which the party rests. At best, the party is credited with stepping out of the way and giving people with entrepreneurial skills free rein. Even this limited degree of legitimacy was all but wiped out by the party's brutal suppression of the nationwide pro-democracy movement of 1989.

Today, the party maintains its monopoly hold on the levers of power with the argument that it is the sole agency capable of maintaining the political stability that makes the country's rapid economic development possible. When economic development slowed as a result of the collapse of global financial markets, even that tenacious claim to indispensability was called into question.

According to the textbook description of the relationship between the party and the government in the Chinese political system, the party proposes, and the government disposes; the party makes policy, and the government carries it out. In real organizations, things seldom function according to the textbook, and the line separating policy making from policy implementation is often difficult to draw. Certainly, the reality of the relationship between the party and the government in China shows this confusion, since all but a few of the key party leaders also occupy senior positions in the government. Decision-making is monopolized by a handful of powerful individuals; although the party's constitution provides that the Party Congress is responsible for setting political policy, in fact, that authority rests with half a dozen or so party leaders who, at any given time, are members of the Standing Committee of the Political Bureau of the party's Central Committee. In the recent past, even this small group had to refer all major decisions to retired elder statesmen, notably to Deng Xiaoping as the *primus inter pares* of that group, and more recently to the current party chair, Xi Jinping.

The party has two means for ensuring that its policies are implemented by government officials. First, it has the power of appointments, since at each government level, appointments are the responsibility of the party organization at the level just above. (Provincial officials are appointed by the central party organization; provincial party organizations, in turn, appoint officials at the county and city levels.) Second, the performance of officials appointed by the party is then monitored by party agencies. In organizations, agencies, and enterprises at each level of the government, a party committee monitors political correctness and ensures that policies are carried out. It is thus next to impossible to separate the roles of policy making and policy implementation. Exceptions to this rule are privately-owned enterprises, a rapidly growing sector in the Chinese economy, whose owners and managers have been reluctant to set up party committees.

The party's dominance of China's political system has led some observers to favor the term "party-state." It seems useless to try to distinguish party from government when the government is so lacking in independent authority. And many in China agree, finding it futile to draw distinctions when they are so blurred in practice. On the other hand, some in China have begun to demand that the rule of law be extended and that the party and its leaders be subject to it, implying the idea that the blurring of functions is inappropriate. Indeed, one could argue that a strong state, operating with an effective legal system and set on eliminating political corruption, would have significantly greater legitimacy than the party currently enjoys. But until that goal of eradicating corruption is addressed effectively, it makes sense to continue to use the term "party-state" to describe China's system.

During the early 1980s, the goal of the political reform movement that went hand-in-hand with economic reform was to address and rectify this situation. Party and government were to be separated, and double hatting eliminated wherever possible. The functions of and relations between the two structures were to be clarified, with the government acting independently in day-to-day affairs and the party confining itself to broad policy making. But these efforts at reform came to an abrupt halt in 1989, when, in violation not only of the principles governing party-government relations but also of party rules for decision making and discipline, Deng Xiaoping moved from behind the scenes to mobilize support for the declaration of martial law in Beijing and, subsequently, to use the army to clear demonstrators from its streets.

Political reform has returned to the agenda in the ensuing thirty-five years, though the definition of reform is now confined to reforming the legal system, expanding democratic practices within the party, and attempting to curb the rampant corruption that saps the legitimacy of both party and government organs. Extending democratic reform outside the party, however, has largely stalled. Currently, there are contested elections for representative councils in about three-quarters of the country's 2.7 million villages, and for local people's congresses at the township and county levels. However, these elections are tightly controlled by the party, and genuine electoral competition is limited. Party leaders have repeatedly stated that "Western parliamentary democracy absolutely will not work" in China.

The executive branch of the Chinese government is headed by a cabinet, the State Council, whose members are the heads of the twenty-
four commissions and ministries that make up the three million-strong central bureaucracy. The Focus of about a third of the ministries and commissions is the economy, its reform, and its relations with the world economy. There are, in addition, ministries devoted to non-economic issues, such as public health and foreign affairs. In principle, commissions have a more comprehensive function than ministries, and some are intended to coordinate the work of several former ministries. The current structure of the State Council was put in place in 2023 as a result of a program of central government consolidation and simplification.

Each ministry or commission stands at the top of a system of bureaus and offices located in provincial capitals and county seats. In all, there are probably some ten million bureaucrats in these vertical systems, each of which has a specialized function, overseeing a narrow sector of the economy or society. The smooth operation of these vertical systems is complicated by the fact that bureaus and offices of central ministries and commissions report not only to them but also to the local government of which they form a part. The Shanghai Education Bureau, for example, reports both to the Shanghai municipal government and to the Ministry of Education in Beijing: its staff appointments are made by the latter, but its budget is set by the former. When push comes to shove, the interests of the local government often take precedence over those of the central ministry or commission.

In theory, communication flows smoothly and regularly up and down each system. Communication between systems, however, is often difficult or impossible to arrange except at the uppermost reaches. A construction project in a county seat, for example, requires the approval of a number of local bureaus of different systems, and the project manager will find it hard to get officials in one to talk to those in others; it seems much more effective to refer the question up one or two levels in the bureaucracy–in some cases, even as far as the central government itself–where differences between systems can be hashed out and approvals coordinated.

China's unicameral legislature, the National People's Congress (NPC), is routinely described in the Western press as a rubber-stamp parliament. In fact, until quite recently, every proposal initiated by the Party and drafted by the executive branch was given unanimous approval by the three thousand-odd delegates to the NPC at annual meetings in March. This led observers (and presumably many of the delegates as well) to wonder what purpose was served by their being regularly called together.

Early in his career, Mao was a great believer in citizen initiative. Defining what he called the "mass line," he said that correct ideas originate among the people and are then refined by those with a full command of and adherence to ideological principles. These refined ideas, now policies, must then be taken back and explained to the people, who were their original inspiration. So, legislatures in the Chinese political system embodied this principle. Congressional meetings gave leaders the chance to hear what delegates had to say, and delegates in turn could have policies explained to them by the central authorities. Rather than a group of representatives brought together to initiate laws and policies, the NPC was conceived of as a group of representatives who would learn about laws and policies. While this exercise may have been educational, it was certainly not legislative in the sense that we use the term in our own political arena.

Delegates to the NPC now seem less and less willing to accede to this narrow definition of their function. While final responsibility for drafting new laws remains in the hands of the Party, since the early days of the post-Mao reform period, the NPC, through its Standing Committee, has actively participated **in** drafting legislation needed to introduce a full-blown legal code for Chinese society. Moreover, NPC delegates have taken to speaking out during NPC meetings. At their 1998 session, close to half of them abstained or cast negative votes, once an unheard-of act of defiance, to express their disapproval of a report describing the government's handling of the mounting crime rate. Dissenting votes on actual legislation have been fewer in number. The tally on a controversial law designed to protect private property rights at the 2007 meeting of the NPC showed 2,799 delegates voting in favor of the law, 52 voting in opposition, and 37 delegates abstaining. Although these are significant steps in the development of an independent legislature, one should not overemphasize the progress made to date. Casting a vote against a government minister's annual report or against the candidacy of a new vice premier is a far cry from having the authority to initiate significant legislation or to exert routine oversight and comprehensive budgetary control over the work of the executive branch of the government.

Delegates to the NPC are elected to five-year terms but not directly by the constituents whom they represent. The process is indirect: members of village or city street-level committees are directly elected by constituents. These local committees elect delegates to county and municipal provincial congresses, and in addition to these, congress delegates are selected to represent local organizations and interest groups. County and municipal congresses, in turn, elect delegates to provincial congresses. Delegates to the NPC are elected by these provincial congresses or by national organizations and interest groups. It is important to note, however, that candidates for these positions are vetted in advance by the party, and it is a rare occurrence when non-party candidates are elected.

The trend of legislators taking their jobs seriously affects Congress at all levels. Indeed, delegates to local congresses, who are in frequent face-to-face contact with their constituents, are even more serious than their national counterparts about securing the initiative in local political battles. In this connection, a precedent was set in the fall of 1999, when the Guangdong Provincial People's Congress became the first legislative body in China to hold a public hearing on a piece of proposed legislation.

China's judicial system was not intended to serve as a check or a balance on the bureaucracy or legislature, nor does it so function. Its principal purpose is to serve as part of the apparatus of social control alongside the police and the prosecutors' offices. Verdicts are subject to review and modification by senior party leaders at each level. They are also subject to appeal, and the Supreme People's Court (and the party's Politburo, which oversees its work) is the final court of appeal. It is not the function of the Supreme People's Court or of any lower court, however, to rule on the constitutionality of the law violated by the defendant in a case. Determining whether or not a law conforms to the Constitution is the responsibility of the legislature and, by extension, the party. Hence, the court cannot serve as a check on the work of the government, the legislature, and, least of all, the party. The court system's principal function is, rather, to apply policies, laws, and regulations to specific cases.

China is divided into thirty-four governments at the provincial level (thirty-five if one chooses, as does the government in Beijing, to regard Taiwan as a province), twenty-three of which are provinces; four city governments (Beijing, Tianjin, Chongqing, and Shanghai); two special administrative regions

(Hong Kong and Macao); and five autonomous regions. The latter are province-like units, the population of which includes substantial numbers of non-Han people (there are also smaller autonomous units within several provinces), but (as we shall see in greater detail in Chapter 12) these ethnic minorities' autonomy from central control is largely fictive. Most of their local officials are drawn from the minority populations, the minority languages are used in government and education, and the populations were exempted from the one-child policy. On the other hand, though the ethnic minority population as a whole is small, the autonomous regions are strategically located, many of them contain important deposits of oil and minerals, and Beijing is worried about ethnic ties that cross China's national boundaries. Subsequently, many Han people have been moved into the autonomous regions, the regions are heavily garrisoned by the PLA, members of the ethnic minority elites are brought into China's central and coastal provinces for schooling in political orthodoxy, and Beijing is quick to suppress any expressions of genuine autonomy.

Provinces are divided into prefectures, counties, and cities. The average Chinese county, of which there are some twenty-nine hundred, is almost the same size as the average American county, of which there are approximately twenty-eight hundred. The average population of Chinese counties is something under five hundred thousand. Counties in China are administered from county seats and the area is divided into townships, each of which is made up of a number of villages. The cities are similarly divided into districts, and districts into neighborhoods.

At the lowest level of the political system is the danwei (单位), usually translated as "unit." In its heyday in the 1960s, the unit was a key element in the CCP's system of social control, and virtually every Chinese person was affiliated with a unit. The workplace was the unit for fully employed people; the school, for students; the neighborhood, for the unemployed and retired. The unit was supposedly nurturing: its function was to provide for all the needs of its members. But it was also the job of the unit to maintain biographical data, employment histories, criminal records, and information on political attitudes. Moving from one unit to another almost never happened, and when it did, approval in advance from both the old and the new units was required, and the person's file was transferred as well.

With the gradual emergence of a labor market, more and more Chinese find themselves cut loose from both the support and the watchful eyes of their units. Today, 150 million or so migrant workers are not affiliated with units, nor are the approximately 95 million who work in the private sector. Even those who remain formally enrolled in a unit find that it is much less encompassing than it once was. The weakening of the *danwei* system is a major reason that most Chinese think their government is less intrusive in their daily lives than it once was. At the same time, they find that the government is less effective in meeting their day-to-day needs.

There is no formal division of authority between the center and the provinces or between the provinces and their counties and cities. Instead, the relationship among central, provincial, and local governments is most frequently thrashed out in case-by-case agreements that are subject to renegotiation as conditions and needs change.

In theory, certain powers are vested in the superior level over its subordinates. The most important among these is the power to appoint and dismiss officials. Here, the dilemma for the central authorities is analogous to that confronted by the throne in earlier times: an outsider in a given locality is likely to be loyal to the central government officials who appointed him or her but less likely to have the connections that will make him or her effective in office, while the reverse is true of a local person.

Second, the government at each level reserves the power to draw up budgets and levy taxes in its subordinate units. The central government determines what is taxed, the rate at which it will be taxed, whether the tax will be collected by the central government or by local governments, the proportion of tax revenue that will go to the provinces, and the government expenditures for which local authorities will be responsible. Provincial governments do the same for counties and cities under their jurisdiction.

Third, the central government reserves the power to allocate and redistribute resources among the provinces; provincial governments do the same for counties and cities. Tax revenues from well-off provinces are reallocated to help less well-off regions. Certain key resources, energy important among them, are also allocated in this way. This Robin Hood function of the central authorities was used most actively under Mao Zedong, among whose first principles was that of equality of opportunity for rich and poor regions of China.

Local governments, on the other hand, are not without resources of their own. First, they have the choice of cooperating with or making life impossible for appointed officials. Second, though the central government levies taxes and determines the distribution of revenues, until very recently, local authorities actually collected the taxes and forwarded a portion to the central government.

Fourth, and most important, local officials can thwart central directives by inaction. When local officials engage in this tactic, China's power grid experiences gridlock. As those who have had dealings with Chinese bureaucrats know, no phrase comes quite so quickly to a bureaucrat's lips as *kaolu yixiazi* (考虑 一下子–

"I'll have to look into that a bit") or *yanjiu Yanji* (研究研究– "That needs some further study"). As we shall see presently, the bureaucratic style favored by the Chinese tends to result in a glacial pace of decision-making and execution

A case in point, covered by Anthony Kuhn for the *New York Times,* will help to illustrate the interaction of party and state in actual practice at the local level in Guangdong Province.[2] Fourteen years ago, the residents of Wukan (乌坎), a small rural village in Guangdong Province, chased Communist Party officials out of their hamlet and elected a new leader. Immediately after the riots broke out, Communist Party chief Wang Yang interceded. This led to free elections that resulted in the village leader being displaced as village chief and Communist Party secretary by protest leader Lin Zuluan, who then undertook to undo illegal land sales, make Wukan village financial records public, and hold new elections for village leaders. The government's response and the resulting compromise between the two sides were considered a "Wukan Model" that might be copied and applied to the thousands of similar local disputes that erupt across the country every year. The province's governor received credit for his deft handling of the protests, and he was promoted to vice premier in 2013. But he subsequently took pains to deemphasize the significance of the Wukan Model for reform. He played down the election of several protest leaders to the village committee, saying that the poll adhered to existing Chinese laws on village governance. "We merely implemented what's already on the books. That's all." Cai, a female villager who withheld her given name, had this to say: "Actually, ours is a very civilized village. If we hadn't blockaded

---

[2] Anthony Kuhn, "Protest's Success May Not Change China," *New York Times,* 4 March 2012.

the roads, the authorities would have come in and hauled people off. We were just defending ourselves."

Four years later, the village residents rose up in protest once again after their elected leader, village chief and Communist Party secretary Lin Zuluan, was detained on corruption charges. Hundreds of students in tracksuits and elderly residents, some in wheelchairs, carried Chinese and Communist Party flags as they marched through the village. They called for the release of Lin, who had been arrested and stripped of his job as party secretary. Many Wukan residents think his confession was staged and the charges were trumped up. A villager said that protests were triggered by the actions of property developers, who took village land without compensating residents. Land grabs are a common problem, especially in Guangdong, where urbanization is rapidly swallowing up farmland. Police suppressed the violence with tear gas and rubber bullets, took away dozens of village leaders, and locked down the village for days.

When Lin Zuluan was tried in Foshan in 2016, he confessed to taking $82,000 in bribes and kickbacks in relation to building projects in Wukan and other deals on behalf of the village committee. He was sentenced to 37 months' imprisonment and a $27,000 fine. During a hearing into his appeal, Lin withdrew his confession and protested his sentence.

In 2017, CCP Politburo member Hu Chunhua, then Guangdong's Communist Party boss, made his first trip to Wukan. It was he who had ordered the crackdown in 2011. He was quoted as saying, "The village has strengthened the building of the party's grass-roots organization and made progress in resolving the land disputes according to the law."

Retired University of California law professor Stanley Lubman reflected on the incident thus: "The Wukan events and the lack of progress thereafter suggest the extent to which the protests, the institutions involved, and the stark policy issues confronting the Party state present major challenges to China's leadership. The uprising in a little village symbolizes issues of law and policy that are intimately intertwined throughout Chinese society and must be unwound."

In addition to the party and the state, there is a third institution, the People's Liberation Army, that we must take into account. Writing in the middle of the Chinese Communist revolution and the war against Japan, Mao described the relationship between military power and political power: "Political power grows out of the barrel of a gun, [but] our principle is that the party commands the gun and the gun must never be allowed to command the party." Control of the PLA in China today rests in the hands of the Party's Central Military Commission. The commission's General Staff Department has operational command over the approximately three million active-duty troops via seven military regional commanders. Administrative command is exercised by the General Logistics Department. The General Armaments Department is responsible for weapons development and procurement. Finally, the General Political Department stations political officers at each level of command to ensure that "the party commands the gun."

The relationship among party, government, and army fundamentally altered on two occasions. At the height of Red Guard activity during the Cultural Revolution, the situation became anarchic, with both party and government under attack and in no position to restore order; the PLA restored order and then set up and continued to participate in new political structures —Revolutionary committees, as they were called. The year 1969 marked an apex of military involvement in China's political system, with military officers exercising political control at every level of the system, including the party's Central Committee. Some officers no doubt enjoyed their foray into politics and were reluctant to return to their barracks when, in the early 1970s, the regime tried to demilitarize the political system. But many others were eager to relinquish their political responsibilities, realizing that they were discharged at the expense of military readiness: China's poor showing in a border war with Vietnam in 1979 proved their point.

In a second moment of party weakness during two incidents of civil unrest in 1989, the armed forces again intervened in the political realm. In Lhasa (拉萨) in March, when Tibetans demonstrated against Chinese control of their region, which had been complete since 1951, and interference with their religious practices, martial law was declared and the army put down the demonstrations. Two months later, party officials, unable to respond effectively to the challenge posed by massive numbers of students and workers occupying the streets and central square of Beijing, once again ordered the army to intervene.

But the military involvement in politics that had followed the earlier episode was not repeated in the 1989 aftermath; the only evidence of a shift in the balance of power was in the military budget, which increased significantly each year thereafter. Today, however, many of China's neighbors are concerned about evidence of Chinese military expansionism and speculate that the PLA, not the Foreign Ministry, is calling many of the shots in China's foreign policy. They attribute the party's inability to control the PLA to its indebtedness to and continuing dependence on it. We will take a closer look at the PLA in Chapter 8.

Appointed by the 17th Party Congress, Xi Jinping became Party Secretary in 2012. In the two previous party congresses, the "seven-in and eight-out" (*qishang baxia* 七上八下) rule had been established, meaning those aged 66 and below will stay, and the 68-year-olds and above will retire. But six years later, the rule was abolished, and Xi (who is now 72) became General Secretary and President for life.

Meeting under Xi's leadership in the summer of 2024, the Party's Twentieth Central Committee adopted a resolution "On Further Deepening Reform Comprehensively to Advance Chinese Modernization." The resolution laid out a strategic plan that it proposed to implement in the coming years. The plan incorporates some five dozen tasks addressing the country's polity, its economy, and its society. It is both comprehensive and ambitious in the goals it sets. The last of its tasks, it writes, is to "ensure the implementation of reforms with relentless perseverance under the Party Central Committee's centralized, unified leadership."

But achieving the ambitious goals of the 2024 plan is the task of the grid of political power in China: imperfectly formed branches of government with significantly unequal power and with no effective balance or check on one another. Within the bureaucracy, the highly specialized and vertically structured departments are incapable of communicating with one another easily. Meanwhile, the crosshatched horizontal elements of the grid- provinces, counties, and cities–though unable to defy the central government openly for long, can at least stick wrenches in its wheels and stall forward movement. Overlying everything, and active at each node, is the party, which regularly oversteps its bounds, lacks the full confidence of the people, and is utterly unwilling to submit itself to criticism, opposition, or legal regulation. And there is the problem of funding the goals. Tax revenue at both the central and local levels is dropping, having fallen more than three percent in

2024. Declining tax revenue has several causes, including deflation, plummeting land sales, falling salaries, and rising layoffs. Finally, waiting in the wings, a highly patriotic army could find itself, *faute de mieux*, holding China together if political authority were to collapse.

Far from being the well-oiled totalitarian machine it was once reputed to be, the Chinese political system is highly complex and inefficient and tends to thwart much more than foster effective governance. The central authority is meant to be ascendant over regional authority, and party authority is meant to be ascendant over government authority, yet the system operates with a substantially weakened central authority and a party whose power and legitimacy are seriously eroded. Still, we would be mistaken to think of the Chinese political system as other than authoritarian, and it is this authoritarianism that is proving increasingly counterproductive to achieving the nation's most important goal, that of promoting economic development. Unless it changes significantly and rapidly, the system will continue to lack the capacity to address and resolve the many serious problems confronting it.

Chapter 5: Politics, Power, and Protest

The paramount goal of the Chinese Communist Party over the last eighty years has been to maintain the political stability that it sees as a prerequisite for the extraordinary economic development that has taken place in China during that period. The quest for stability has relegated politics, as we know it, to a relatively marginal position.

Before we turn our attention from political structure to the process of politics in China, however, we need to take a closer look at political leadership. For all his faults of ideological rigidity and megalomania, Mao Zedong has never been repudiated or even seriously criticized since his death in 1976. In effect, however, his leadership style was thoroughly, if tacitly, repudiated by Deng Xiaoping, leader of the so-called second generation of Chinese politicians. The ultimate pragmatist, Deng is best remembered by his comment that "it doesn't matter whether the cat is black or white so long as it catches mice." Deng's legacy is mixed, however. While it was he who launched China's economic reforms in 1978 and relaunched them when they had stalled in 1992, he was also personally responsible for ordering troops to fire on student demonstrators in 1989.

Jiang Zemin, who headed the third generation of political leaders, was an eleventh-hour stand-in for two individuals who, but for the events of the spring of 1989, would have succeeded Deng. Hu Yaobang and Zhao Ziyang, the original leaders of the third generation, were known for their efforts at maneuvering carefully among the conservative elders whom they were designated to replace in order to promote political reform. But both Hu and Zhao sealed their fates by siding openly with student demonstrators against Deng: Hu in 1986; Zhao in 1989. Hu was dismissed as party general secretary in 1986 and died unexpectedly in April 1989, an event that triggered the demonstrations that culminated in the occupation of Tiananmen Square two months later. Zhao, having apologized to student demonstrators for not intervening earlier on their behalf, was dismissed as Party General Secretary in June 1989 and lived out his days under house arrest, dying in 2005.

Plucked from his position as party leader in Shanghai, Jiang Zemin became Party General Secretary in 1989, sharing power with Li Peng, who, as head of government, was tarred with the brush of what some refer to as the Beijing Massacre in 1989. A genial lightweight in the eyes of many, Jiang outlasted Li and outlived Deng to become the first leader since Mao to hold simultaneously the top positions in the party, the state, and the army. Seeking to cement his position in the pantheon of Chinese leaders, Jiang sought to make his own contribution to Chinese political ideology with his rather pathetic "theory of the three represents" a rationale for opening membership in the Chinese Communist Party to the newly emergent class of entrepreneurs. The Party was to represent "the development trend of China's advanced productive forces, the orientation of China's advanced culture, and the fundamental interests of the overwhelming majority of the Chinese people."

The fourth generation, the first to succeed to power in an orderly transition, consisted of Party General Secretary and head of state Hu Jintao and head of government Wen Jiabao. They attempted to put their stamp on Chinese political leadership with an emphasis on their relative youth (both succeeded to their offices at the age of sixty), their education (both were trained as engineers), and their attention to the needs of the grass roots.

In many respects, they closely resemble those who were designated as the fifth generation, their successors, Xi Jinping and Li Keqiang, both of them were in their late fifties when they took office in 2012. Xi is an engineer; Li has his Ph.D. in economics. If the fifth generation of central leaders possesses what we might think of as relatively progressive characteristics, these characteristics have not given rise to a commitment to democratizing the Chinese state. Warning that democracy would bring chaos to the country because of the size and political immaturity of its population, they found the idea of opposition parties contending in elections at all levels of the political system nothing short of anathema. Much more significantly, Xi decided to overturn the orderly succession of leaders that preceded him and assumed, for the first time since Mao Zedong, a lifetime hold on the positions of party and state leader.

If the central leaders can be said to be relatively forward-looking, their qualities are not mirrored in grassroots party and government leaders, particularly in the countryside. As a group, these leaders are ill-educated and likely to hold office until they reach the mandatory retirement age and then shift over to positions in the party and government for which there is no age limit. Most importantly, many of them are deeply corrupt, taking full advantage of the expanded opportunities for speculation that have accompanied the decentralization of economic decision-making in recent years. Reminiscent of the "local thugs and evil gentry" against whom Mao railed as he was organizing for revolution in the Chinese countryside of the 1920s and 1930s, the worst of local party and government leaders have been referred to by more than one observer as creating "local Mafia states" in the Chinese hinterlands.

As we look at the political process at all levels of the Chinese system, several characteristics of politics as practiced in China are especially to be noted. These characteristics are the preference for consensus and the prevalence of bargaining, networking, saving face, and corruption.

Americans seem generally comfortable with a simple majority, whether in a Supreme Court decision, a vote in Congress, or a local referendum on a school budget. Although, as individuals, we may not be satisfied with a given outcome, we tend to regard it as legitimate if a majority has decided it. The Chinese vastly prefer consensus to a simple majority, and they prefer that this consensus be achieved at the lowest possible level in the political hierarchy: if one level finds it impossible to reach a consensus, the decision is bumped up to the next level. Although strategies for building consensus are much the same as those for building a majority, it usually takes longer.

Bargaining is an almost universal characteristic of political interactions. In American political life, bargaining usually focuses on issues that will have to be voted on: "I need your vote, and this is what I'm prepared to do to get it." In the Chinese context, in which voting is less common than consensus-building, bargaining is more diffuse: "I will be more inclined to lend you my support on your issue if you agree to lend me your support on mine." Given an imperfectly developed market, exchanges of goods and services, as well as support, are also subject to political bargaining. Political bargainers in China pay careful attention to their relative rank and status, which affect both the process and the outcome. Political transactions often seem to be conducted with all the attention to protocol of an ambassadorial dinner party or a military change of command ceremony, and politicians seem to relish the bargaining. Case-by-case bargaining is almost always preferable in China to applying a uniform rule to every case.

Networking–a practice common in both American and Chinese political contexts- is also vitally important. Foreign businesspeople new to China are taught the word guanxi (关系–relationships) as though it were a powerful mantra unique to the Chinese setting. But "whom do I know who can..." is a formula that springs as quickly to the mind of a Westerner as to that of a Chinese. The difference is the degree to which it is appropriate to be proactive; a skillful practitioner of guanxi in the Chinese context actively cultivates relationships that might be helpful at some unknown point in the future. Westerners may look on someone who does them an unbidden favor with some suspicion, but a Chinese person is likely to greet the unbidden favor without surprise and to assume that a request for a quid pro quo will not be long in coming.

Students of the Chinese psyche conclude that Chinese people have a greater aversion to conflict and disorder than do Americans. And it is unquestionably true that finding oneself shamed in public is for a Chinese person an experience to be avoided if at all possible. Because open conflict is likely to result in loss of face for one of the parties, passive resistance accompanied by a perfectly opaque demeanor is the weapon of choice for the conflict-averse Chinese.

Unfortunately, three aspects of Chinese society today combine to create a climate particularly conducive to corruption, and corruption has become ubiquitous, serving to undermine the legitimacy of both party and government, and defying efforts to eliminate or at least to curb it. The first aspect is a mindset inherited from the Confucian tradition and its emphasis on understanding society as a web of mostly hierarchical relationships. As we have seen, to make one's way through this web, one is supposed to cultivate relationships that are likely to be helpful. This practice of *guanxi*, just as vital in contemporary society as it was centuries ago, lends itself all too easily to bribery and political corruption. The line between the legitimate cultivation of reciprocal friendship and the corrupt practice of bribery is difficult to draw, especially where there is the tendency to inflate the cost of the former.

A second element that encourages corruption is the experience of sixty years of socialist rule. The Yugoslav politician, theorist, and author Milovan Djilas, writing in the 1950s, was among the first Communists to describe a "new class" of privileged bureaucrats to which socialist society could give rise. Mao Zedong took up the same theme in his criticisms of the Soviet Union under Nikita Khrushchev, and he subsequently applied these criticisms to China itself on the eve of the Cultural Revolution. As managers of state resources, bureaucrats in a socialist system monopolize and misuse those resources for their own advancement. Moreover, because they control education and recruitment into the political system, they can perpetuate their personal control by favoring their own choices or, indeed, their own offspring.

Mao argued that this process of embourgeoisement–transforming corrupt proletarians into a new bourgeoisie–could be controlled only by means of a "continuing revolution" that takes power away from the privileged class. The "new bourgeoisie" in China was seriously undermined during the Cultural Revolution, though the perpetrators of that movement abused their power just as much as or more than the targets of their persecution. Many who were victimized during the Cultural Revolution then returned to power under the aegis of Deng–himself a target of the movement, and they seem to regard the comforts of their current station in life as fitting compensation for what they sacrificed during the previous thirty years. Deng and his immediate circle of senior colleagues avoided an extravagant lifestyle, but their offspring are infamous for taking advantage of their parents' positions to acquire personal wealth and influence.

A third element of Chinese society that is conducive to the growth of corruption is the economy's current state of incomplete marketization. Most decisions about allocating resources are made by the market, but decisions about allocating certain critical resources are still made by party and state officials. The sharp competition among the state, the collective, and the private sector has raised the ante in decisions about who gets what quantity of critical items in short supply, a situation rife with opportunities for corruption.

Corruption, the kudzu of contemporary China, is intractable because the legal system is not able to establish a standard against which to measure it, and the political system lacks an independent agency to attack and control it. Central authorities launch periodic anticorruption campaigns, but the agents on whom they rely to implement these campaigns are the very officials who are their most eligible targets. At best, a few scapegoats are prosecuted and lose their jobs, but the problem grows worse.

In the fall of 2006, there was a spate of arrests, trials, and convictions in high-level corruption cases involving the Shanghai party chief and two other members of the party's Political Bureau. It is unclear in retrospect whether this was a genuine move on the part of Hu Jintao to attack corruption or whether he was really motivated by a desire to secure his position with the party leadership in advance of the National Party Congress held the following year. More recently, the National Audit Office announced that officials had misused or embezzled more than $35 billion in public funds during 2009, and the mayors of Shenzhen (深圳) and Chongqing were detained as part of a graft inquiry and removed from office. All these are, no doubt, examples of the Chinese saying, "killing the chicken to scare the monkey." Observers are quick to note that anticorruption campaigns often have as much to do with settling in-party rivalries as they do with reasserting public probity.

As a result of all these characteristics, the political process in China may often seem agonizingly slow and mystifyingly obscure to Westerners. Even among Europeans, Americans have a reputation for being blunt and impatient; it is no wonder we find it hard to make sense of the actions of Chinese bureaucrats.

As we turn our attention from political process to political participation, we need to address the question of why political reform has come to be the third rail of Chinese politics. Deng Xiaoping's reform agenda focused centrally on transforming the economy. Only grudgingly did he concede that politics in China was also in need of substantial reform. To some extent, his point of view may have been shaped by the arguments of those outside China who saw a kind of inevitability to political reform when the initial steps to introduce a market economy were taken. Once granted economic freedoms, this line of reasoning goes, Chinese citizens would certainly demand an expansion of their political freedom. The entering wedge was believed to be a reform of the legal system. Economic reform could not proceed, it was argued, without a set of laws to regulate market transactions. With the introduction of the rule of law in the economic sphere, it would be sure to spread to other areas of society, including the political realm. As we noted earlier, this hypothetical sequence of reforms has proved far from inevitable in Chinese practice over the last half-century.

When Zhao Ziyang left his work in Guangdong and Sichuan to become premier and later party general secretary, he brought with him the belief that those who argued that political reform would inevitably flow from economic reform were wrong. Political reform, he argued, was necessary but not inevitable; it had to be worked at. Unfortunately, his definition of political reform was significantly different from that of Deng and his fellow elders, who held on to the reins of power throughout Zhao's tenure in office. They believed that political reform was necessary only insofar as it maintained the authority of the party. "Reform" would thus include addressing the problem of corruption on the part of party members. It might even go so far as to introduce a bit of democracy into party operations. Competition for party office might well encourage improved performance on the part of officeholders. But extending democratic practice outside the party was beyond the pale. It would inevitably result in instability–or even "chaos" –and that would disrupt the steady pace of economic growth.

There are several vehicles for political participation in the Chinese system. Among them are non-governmental organizations, elections, litigation, petitioning, and protest.

The first form of political participation we shall consider here is the formation of non-governmental organizations (NGOs) to take political action. At the 1992 UN Conference on Environment and Development in Rio de Janeiro, the Chinese delegation was asked to participate in a forum of NGOs dealing with environmental issues. Somewhat to their embarrassment, the Chinese had to admit there was no such thing as an NGO devoted to environmentalism in China. The best they could muster was one or two (and this is among my favorite acronyms) GONGOs–government-organized nongovernment organizations (an oxymoron, one would have thought).

In fact, GONGOs have a long history in the Chinese Communist Party and the People's Republic of China. Soon after its founding, the party established a series of so-called mass organizations, such as the All-China Federation of Trade Unions (founded in 1926) and the Chinese National Peasants' Association (founded in 1926 and disbanded in 1986). and the All-China Federation of Women (founded in 1949). These groups have been described as being nongovernmental organizations having "a very large national membership organized along the lines of specialized interests." In fact, they are very heavy on the "government-organized" side and very light on the "nongovernmental" side of the description of a GONGO. Their functions emphasized the "promotion of knowledge of and enthusiasm for official policy lines" and were not at all interested in channeling or promoting opposition to these policy lines.

The All-China Federation of Trade Unions (ACFTU) was founded in 1925 when the Second National Labor Congress of China convened in Canton with 277 delegates representing 540,000 workers. It is made up of ten national industrial unions, 31 provincial trade union federations, and 5.3 million grassroots trade union organizations. The membership of the ACFTU totals some 300 million; it constitutes the world's largest trade union. It is the only union recognized under the law in China. It does not take part in American-style collective bargaining over wages and benefits, but it does hold conferences between workers and management. Independent unions are illegal, and the law does not protect the right to strike.

The China National Peasants' Association was founded in 1927 and was taken up by Mao Zedong as he recruited some ten million members in Hunan Province and inaugurated what became the ultimately victorious Chinese Revolution. It was renamed the China National Poor and Lower-Middle Peasant Association in 1964. Its function was to mobilize, educate, and represent the interests of China's rural residents. It was disbanded twenty-two years later in 1986.

The All-China Women's Federation was established in 1949 and currently has 1.2 million members. It has federations at the provincial, city, county, town, and village levels across the country. It describes its main tasks as follows:

1. To organize and lead women to study and implement Xi Jinping Thought and the lines, principles, and policies of the Party, and to unite women with a shared aspiration of socialism with Chinese characteristics.

2. To unite and mobilize women to dedicate to reform and opening-up and the socialist economic, political, cultural, social, and ecological development, to give full play to women's unique roles in social and family life, and to contribute to building China into a great nation and advancing national rejuvenation.
3. To represent women to take part in the management of state and social affairs, economic and cultural undertakings, and to promote the implementation of laws and policies on the protection of women's rights and interests and the implementation of national programs for women's and children's development.
4. To safeguard the legitimate rights and interests of women and children, listen to women's opinions and voice their concerns, put forward recommendations to state organs at all levels, request and assist government departments and institutions to conduct investigations into violations of women's and children's rights and interests, and provide assistance to victims.
5. To educate and guide women to cultivate self-esteem, self-confidence, self-reliance, and self-improvement, strengthen overall competence, and realize all-around development. To promote the implementation of the fundamental national policy of gender equality, create an environment of respect and care, and support women's all-round development. To publicize and honor outstanding women role models, and nurture and recommend women's talents.
6. To educate and guide women to practice core socialist values, advocate Chinese family virtues, and lead family members in carrying forward fine traditions, conduct family education in a scientific way, and give play to the important roles of family, family education, and family virtues in community-level governance, and promote fine socialist family culture.
7. To care about women's work and life, expand access to, innovate means, and build facilities of services, and advance public welfare undertakings. To connect and guide women's

organizations and mobilize the whole society to enhance services for women, children, and the family.

8. To consolidate and expand the great unity of women of all ethnic groups and from all walks of life, as well as with overseas Chinese women and women's organizations,
9. To actively develop friendly exchanges with women and women's organizations around the world, deepen mutual understanding, enhance friendship and cooperation, and contribute to world peace and common development.

Something more closely resembling what we think of as NGOs, or social intermediary organizations, as they are often called in China, began to crop up early in the reform period and numbered as many as 200,000 in the early 1980s. Like Harriet Beecher Stowe's Topsy, they "just grow," with little or no government regulation until the mid-1980s, at which point, as we have seen, a movement opposed to corruption and in favor of political liberalization began to take shape on college campuses and in the cities in which they were located. Suddenly, the party-state paid close attention, issued new regulations, and required all existing organizations to reregister and associate themselves with appropriate government offices through a process known as "align and adopt."

A second setback to the development of NGOs came a decade later when, as we shall see shortly, *Falun Gong* (法轮功) suddenly sprang upon the scene in 1999. Falun Gong, a spiritual practice combining meditation and moral teachings, proved to be neither a CONGO nor an NGO but something far closer to an "AGO" –an anti-government organization.

These episodes pointed up two very firm rules to which the party-state adheres in dealing with NGOs: first, they must be local, not national, in scope; second, they must be apolitical in their purposes. Isolated and local political protests are one thing; organized and national protests are quite another.

Operating under the somewhat misleading slogan "big society, small government," the party-state has come in recent years to see as a necessary evil the formation of organizations that can take up some of the burden of providing social services in a newly privatized environment. Depending on how one defines NGOs, there could be as many as two million such groups across China today. That large number would include a myriad of very small local organizations that are not officially registered. Limiting the number to those registered and recognized by the Ministry of Civil Affairs, there are probably three hundred thousand. The degree to which the registered groups are genuinely independent of the government is always an open question.

Observers of Chinese NGOs both inside and outside China wonder whether they are sufficiently well organized, sufficiently effective, and sufficiently independent to be considered the beginning of a "civil society" in the country, a counterweight to the party-dominated political culture that has smothered, or attempted to smother, extra-party-political life. Intent on maintaining its monopoly on political power and justifying that intention with the argument that its monopoly is the *sine qua non* of political stability and continued economic development, the party casts a wary eye on the world of Chinese NGOs and does everything in its power to ensure that they remain small, isolated, ill-funded, and apolitical.

Despite his skepticism about the virtues of democratic practice outside party circles, Deng himself had introduced elements of democracy at the lowest levels of the political system nearly half a century ago, perhaps as a tool for rooting out corruption. Beginning in 1979, elections for members of village administrative committees were held on an experimental basis.

Village elections were sanctioned in the new election law adopted by the National People's Congress in 1998. A village committee of three to seven members is directly elected based on open nominations. While the authority of the committee is limited, voter turnout is typically high. By 2004, more than 90 percent of China's 680,000 village administrative committees were being populated by open elections, and the experiment had been extended to city neighborhoods as well.

Foreign observers of village elections have found them to be open, honest, and boisterous events. Scholars studying village elections, however, find the candidate pool in many of these elections to be dominated by party members and those favored by the party and, in villages where clans remain an important social entity, by members of the dominant clan. While one observer has called the process "creeping democratization," thus far, the party-state has prevented the electoral process from creeping above the most local levels of government. An experiment with direct election in a township in Sichuan in 1999 was squashed when the vote was declared illegal by higher authorities. Interestingly, however, the authorities allowed the elected township head to remain in office.

Another approach to grassroots politics is an experiment in deliberative democracy initiated by the Stanford University professor James Fishkin and his Australian colleague Baogang He in the township of Zeguo (泽国) in Zhejiang (浙江) Province in 2005.[3] A random sample of 275 villagers met in small groups to discuss how to spend the village's public works budget. Through

---

[3] James S. Fishkin, Baogang He, Robert C. Luskin and Alice Siu, "Deliberative Democracy in an Unlikely Place: Deliberative Polling in China, *British Journal of Political Science* 40:2 (April 2010)

several hours of deliberation, the villagers selected twelve projects from a list of thirty. Their findings were passed along to the local people's congress, which adopted the recommendation by a vote of eighty-four to eight. Several other villages and townships have undertaken similar experiments in deliberative democracy.

Despite the current leaders' adamant rejection of parliamentary democracy at any but the village and neighborhood levels, a number of important voices have expressed their dissent. In 2007, the party authorized the publication of the memoirs of Long March veteran Lu Dingyi, in which he voiced his support for the democratization of the system. More recently, the tape-recorded memoirs of Zhao Ziyang, who served as party general secretary at the time of the 1989 Tiananmen massacre and who was dismissed by Deng Xiaoping because of his support of the student demonstrators, were smuggled out of China and published in Hong Kong and the United States. Like Lu, Zhao argued that the eventual introduction of parliamentary democracy into China is inevitable. "Why is there not even one developed nation practicing any other system?" he asked.

In the absence of political parties as a meaningful avenue for expressing their opinions, dissatisfied Chinese citizens have turned to three other avenues, each with some precedents in Chinese history: petitions, protests, and litigation.

Petitioning the imperial government in Beijing to redress grievances against local authorities was a well-established practice in traditional China. Mirroring that tradition, the party-state established a Bureau of Petitions under the Central Committee and the State Council. Subordinate bureaus exist at the provincial and local levels as well. The Chinese name for these bureaus denotes the vehicles used for petitioning: they are offices for "letters and visits." A study conducted in the mid-1980s found that about half the petitions submitted contained advice on economic reforms, a third sought redress for personal grievances, and the remainder exposed cases of illicit behavior on the part of local authorities.

At the end of 2008, more than three hundred dissident intellectuals signed an open letter to the government entitled "Charter 08" that called for an end to one-party rule. The charter advocated, among other provisions, the direct election of legislators and administrative heads at all levels of the system. In addition to the arrest of those suspected of having published the charter, NPC Standing Committee chair Wu Bangguo took the occasion of his speech to the 2009 NPC meeting to denounce the dissidents and to remind his listeners that with a democratic system in place, "China would be torn by strife and incapable of accomplishing anything." In June of the same year, Liu Xiaobo, one of those who initiated the charter, was formally charged with "alleged agitation activities aimed at subversion of government and overthrowing of the socialist system." After being held incommunicado in a detention center outside Beijing for six months, Liu was tried in December 2009 and sentenced to eleven years in prison. Reflecting on the harshness of the sentence, some observers described the trial as a tipping point in the party state's treatment of dissidents.

Currently, the majority of petitioners are seeking remuneration for property seized by local governments without full compensation and redress for injuries suffered as a result of industrial pollution. Whereas in the mid-1980s the number of petitions averaged between two and three million per year, in recent years that number has risen to more than ten million. Of that number, however, the government itself recognizes the fact that fewer than one percent are adjudicated to the petitioner's satisfaction. A survey conducted in 2004 showed that only two hundredths of one percent of petitioners expressed satisfaction with the system.

The number of petitioners in Beijing reaches a high point each year in March, when the National People's Congress meets. "This is the only time when the higher-ups might pay attention to us," said one petitioner. "I knew it was dangerous, but this is the only road open to us." Of late, however, the party-state has attempted to discourage petitioners. During the NPC meeting in 2009, for example, a Heilongjiang businessman traveled to the capital to agitate for the prosecution of police corruption in his hometown. He found himself seized by the police, confined (along with forty other abducted petitioners) in a dank room in the cellar of a local hotel, beaten, deprived of food, and then bundled into an overnight train back to Heilongjiang, where guards accompanied him to his front door.

In November 2009, Human Rights Watch published a report on what it called an "extensive network" of secret jails in Beijing that are operated by provincial and municipal governments to house petitioners before shipping them home. Responding to the report, Foreign Ministry spokesman Qin Gang said, "There are no black jails in China. If citizens have complaints and suggestions about government work, they can convey them to the relevant authorities through legitimate and normal channels." But two weeks later, the semi-official publication *Outlook* published an article listing seventy-three secret detention centers in the capital that employ as many as 10,000 "retrievers." So much for the right to petition.

When petitioning fails (as it so often does), disgruntled citizens are left with the alternative of public protest. We are all aware of recent examples of mass public protest in China. It was officially encouraged and became rampant during the Cultural Revolution in the late 1960s and early 1970s. It was officially denounced and ultimately suppressed by the guns and tanks of the People's Liberation Army in 1989.

By far the most striking example of mass public protest in China was the Cultural Revolution. In the mid-1960s, Mao likened himself to a dead parent attending his own funeral: much honored with lip service and utterly unable to affect the proceedings. To rectify this situation, he launched what came to be called the Great Proletarian Cultural Revolution in late 1966. His plan was to use the younger generation as a lever for unseating the older generation of political leaders–Mao's revolutionary colleagues, whom he accused of having become a new bourgeoisie. The campaign ultimately lasted at least five years (when to date its conclusion is a matter of dispute among historians of the period), cost the lives of at least a million Chinese, and set China's economic development back at least a decade. It also gave political protest a black eye that took a decade to heal.

The Cultural Revolution went through several phases before it eventually wound down. In the first phase, young students, dubbed Red Guards, were encouraged to study snippets of Mao's writings in tiny books bound in red plastic, to take to the streets in mass demonstrations presided over by Mao himself, to criticize their teachers and later their political leaders using *dazibao* (大字报–big character posters), and ultimately to engage in violence to destroy the so-called four olds–old ideas, old culture, old customs, and old habits. Mao then directed the Red Guards' attention to the "capitalist roaders" among his colleagues, who he asserted were threatening to undo the achievements of the socialist revolution. Among the most prominent victims were the President, Liu Shaoqi, and Deng Xiaoping, who was then serving as General Secretary of the CCP

In 1968, as the movement spread to the provinces, it became clear that the Red Guards had exceeded their mandate and were out of control. Mao and his new cronies–his wife, Jiang Qing, Zhang Chunqiao, Yao Wenyuan, and Wong Hongwen, subsequently known as the Gang of Four– used two measures to cool the ardor of the young rebels. First, they launched a massive campaign of *xiafang* (下放) –exiling the Red Guards to permanent residence in the countryside to "learn from the masses." Second, Mao called on the People's Liberation Army to bring order by taking an active role in local and central governments, transformed now into Revolutionary Committees, with representation of party, army, and "revolutionary rebels." Ultimately, order was restored and the party reconstructed. When Mao's "designated successor," Marshal Lin Biao, after apparently attempting an unsuccessful *coup d'état,* was killed in an unexplained plane crash in 1971, the military withdrew from its active participation in politics.

Mao's wily colleague, Premier Zhou Enlai, survived the chaotic period largely unscathed, indeed with his standing burnished. He acquired what many argue was an undeserved reputation for having acted as a sea anchor on Mao's geriatric excesses. It was on the occasion of his death in 1976 that political protest was revived, this time directed against Mao and the Gang of Four. Thousands of people took advantage of the Chinese tradition of honoring the dead on *Qing Ming* (清明), a holiday occurring in early April, to gather in the square in front of the Tiananmen to vent their political outrage. The Tiananmen Incident was branded as counterrevolutionary and blamed on Deng Xiaoping, who was once again deposed from the offices to which he had recently been restored. Political protest retained its black eye.

Student protests had been building on China's university campuses during the late 1980s. Many university students in China were finding that the quality of their college experience was far below the high expectations generated by the very stiff competition for admission through which they had just successfully passed. Classes were large, the curriculum was unimaginative, and the level of instruction was often disappointingly low. Moreover, the quality of student housing and food was generally far below that of the homes from which the students had come. Students were housed eight to a room that would seem barely adequate to hold two in an American dormitory. Three times a day, they carried bowls to a canteen that was too small to accommodate tables and chairs. As a result, they were obliged to consume their unpalatable food on the run. The dissatisfactions generated by campus life gave rise to academic apathy and to periodic outbursts of student protest. It was very concrete complaints about university life, not abstract demands for democracy, that brought students out onto the streets of Chinese cities in a series of protest demonstrations beginning in the mid-1980s.

Meanwhile, there was a quite different set of issues disturbing residents of China's cities as the 1980s drew to a close. Whereas the average rate of inflation during the first three decades after the establishment of the People's Republic was just under two percent, in 1988 the retail price index increased by 18.5 percent. The rate of increase was significantly higher for urban residents, and it continued to mount through the first several months of 1989. City dwellers found this decline in their buying power and their real wages alarming. Their alarm turned to anger as they came to realize that officials not only were incapable of resolving the problem but were also isolating themselves from its effects through rampant corruption.

These sources of dissatisfaction combined to form a dangerous tinderbox of public opinion in China's cities in the spring of 1989. Then, in quick succession came a precedent for the events of May and June and a spark that set them off. The precedent was the declaration of martial law in response to Tibetan demonstrations in Lhasa in March 1989 demanding independence from Chinese rule. After as many as seventy-five deaths and numerous injuries in three days of rioting, the PLA entered the city to restore order. It was the first time that martial law had been declared since the founding of the People's Republic. (The newly appointed party secretary in Tibet at the time of the demonstrations was Hu Jintao, who subsequently became president and party general secretary.)

The spark took the form of the death of the deposed party general secretary Hu Yaobang. Dismissed as dangerously liberal by the party elders in 1986 and accused of having mishandled early instances of student protest, Hu had been allowed to stay on as a member of the party Politburo. He died suddenly of a heart attack at a Politburo meeting on 15 April 1989. Because of his somewhat liberal leanings and because of his membership in a faction associated with the Communist Youth League, his death triggered an outburst of student emotion, as had been the case with the death of Zhou Enlai in 1976. Two days after Hu's death, the hundred-acre square in front of Tiananmen, the largest public square in the world, began to fill with thousands of students. The students soon moved beyond honoring the fallen Hu and began to petition the party-state with seven "demands." The content of the demands provides an interesting insight into students' views about political reform in 1989:

1. Affirm Hu Yaobang's views on democracy and freedom.
2. Admit that the campaigns against progressive political ideas carried out in the early 1980s were wrong.
3. Publish information on the incomes of state leaders and their family members.
4. End the ban on privately run newspapers, and permit freedom of speech.
5. Increase funding for education, and increase intellectuals' pay.
6. End restrictions on demonstrations in Beijing.
7. Hold democratic elections to replace government officials "who made bad policy decisions."

By 21 April, the crowd of demonstrators occupying the square had grown to more than one hundred thousand, and strikes were called on virtually every college and university campus in Beijing. Two events conspired to render the situation ultimately tragic. The relatively liberal party general secretary, Zhao Ziyang, followed through on plans to travel to North Korea as the demonstrators gathered.

His premier, the cautious and conservative Li Peng, persuaded Deng and his fellow elders to describe the demonstrations as counterrevolutionary. Their actions constituted, according to an infamous editorial in *People's Daily* on 26 April, "a well-planned plot to confuse the people and throw the country into turmoil."

Meanwhile, the demonstrations had spread to nearly every major Chinese city, and many students from across the country journeyed to Beijing to join their fellow students in the square. Returning from Pyongyang, Zhao found his elder colleagues stuck in the position they had taken, unable to understand that the students' demands were to correct the errors of the party, not to overthrow it, and totally unwilling to reverse the 26 April editorial. Thwarted in their quests to present their demands to the party-state, students took advantage of a visit to Beijing by Soviet party chief Mikhail Gorbachev to launch a hunger strike. Gorbachev's presence in Beijing meant that hundreds of foreign media representatives were in the capital to cover the demonstrations; the hunger strike drew out the support of thousands of Beijing residents, who not only sympathized with the young strikers but also, as we have noted, had grievances of their own against the party-state. It was their alarm and their anger that brought them out onto the streets of eighty cities in China in opposition to their government in numbers unprecedented since 1949.

By 17 May, the demonstrators in Beijing numbered more than a million. That day, Deng convened the Politburo's Standing Committee and two of his elder colleagues at his home and decided to dismiss Zhao and declare martial law in the capital. Troops gathered on the outskirts of the city, while in cities throughout China, troops and armed police attempted to quell the mounting disturbances. Two days later, Zhao visited the students in the square. Realizing that he had lost his struggle to bring about a resolution of the stalemate between his colleagues and the demonstrators, he told the students, "We have come too late." He urged them to end their hunger strike and leave the square before they put their lives in jeopardy.

Finally, on the night of 3 June, the troops surrounding Beijing were ordered to enter the city and clear the square, by force if necessary. Beijing residents did what they could to thwart the advance of the soldiers, and student leaders, once they were aware of the situation, encouraged students to evacuate the square. Nonetheless, the confrontation did occur, PLA troops did fire on student protesters, and an unknown number lost their lives or were seriously wounded as the night wore on. Estimates of the dead ranged from the official Chinese government figure of 241 (including PLA troops) to an estimate of 7,000 contained in a NATO intelligence report.

The party-state's reaction to the tragedy of Tiananmen must be considered in the context of contemporaneous events in the Soviet Union and Eastern Europe. To party leaders living in Zhongnanhai (中南海), their office and residence complex in Beijing, it must have appeared that with the fall of the governments of the Soviet Union, its constituent republics, and its satellite states in Eastern Europe, Communist governments were suddenly and inexplicably doomed, and the People's Republic would be the next domino to fall. Their response was a relentless crackdown on dissent in China and a total refusal, lasting until the present day, to reconsider the wisdom of the decision to turn guns on the Chinese. Well-known as are the events of the Cultural Revolution and the Tiananmen massacre, foreigners are less aware of the fact that in recent years, there have been, on average, as many as 180,000 instances of protests, some of them involving tens of thousands of protesters, in cities, towns, and villages across the country.

One of the most disturbing protests, from the party-state's point of view, occurred when, on a quiet spring weekend in 1999, the sidewalks surrounding *Zhongnanhai* were quickly and quietly filled with more than ten thousand very average-looking citizens, who seated themselves and engaged in a daylong silent protest. It was the largest crowd that had assembled in the capital since students occupied Tiananmen Square ten years earlier. The protesters were members of a sect known as *Falun Gong*. Li Hongzhi, a former grain bureau clerk, had founded the movement in Chongqing in 1993, capitalizing on the popular revival of qigong (气功), traditional Chinese breathing exercises designed to focus one's energy, or *qi,* in order to heal one's body and mind. Li, who now resides in New York, claims to have as many as one hundred million followers, the majority of them in China. The protesters dispersed peacefully, and the party-state initially appeared ready to ignore this unusual event. Two months later, however, the movement was branded a "superstitious cult" and banned by the Politburo. In the crackdown that ensued, dozens were arrested and sentenced to long prison terms, and tens of thousands of others were arrested, booked, released, and often transported back to their hometowns.

There are several explanations for the severity of the reaction against the movement. First, the party-state felt seriously threatened by the discovery of an organization outside party control that claimed a membership larger than that of the party itself. Second, Jiang Zemin appears to have been particularly aggrieved by the fact that some senior party leaders not only were members of *Falun Gong* but had urged their colleagues to join the movement. Finally, there are disturbing historical analogies: dynasties in decline were often threatened, some successfully, by millenarian movements with belief systems startlingly similar to those propounded by Li Hongzhi.

The number of participants in demonstrations and protests in China, which stood at fewer than 10,000 in 1994, had reached as many as 220,000 thirty years later in 2024. Like those who petition the government, the majority of protesters are aggrieved by government corruption (particularly corrupt practices regarding the transfer of rural property), government inaction (particularly in cases of damage incurred by egregious examples of environmental pollution or the failure to pay out wages owed to workers in failing state-owned factories), and government intervention (particularly in the case of Tibetans demanding greater autonomy).

A noteworthy example of protest over government seizure of land with insufficient compensation occurred in late 2005 in the village of Dongzhou (东洲) in Guangdong Province. People's Armed Police and local militiamen opened machinegun fire on the protesters, resulting in as many as twenty deaths and scores of injuries. It was described as the deadliest use of force against protesters since the Tiananmen massacre in 1989. The commander of the government's forces was subsequently detained and disciplined, and two villagers who led the protest were given prison sentences.

The potential for environmental pollution was the issue that caused hundreds of residents of the central Chinese city of Chengdu (成都) to take to the streets in mid-2008. PetroChina had broken ground for a $5.5 billion ethylene plant in a village eighteen miles from the city center. The protest was notable on two accounts. First, the majority of protesters were members of the urban middle class, and second, the protest was largely organized through websites, blogs, and cellphone text messages.

A third example of public protest followed the devastating earthquake that hit Sichuan Province in May 2008, which claimed the lives of some eighty-eight thousand, one in eight of them a school child. Observing that schools were much more likely than the buildings that surrounded them to be seriously damaged, parents protested what they believed to be shoddy construction practices condoned by local authorities. Authorities did their best to quell the demonstrations and used cash payouts to discourage parents from traveling to Beijing to petition the government with their grievances.

Public protest was very much on the minds of Beijing authorities in the months leading up to the Beijing Olympics in 2008. They faced something of a dilemma since, with the city filled with foreign guests, they wanted, on the one hand, to avoid the spectacle of mass protests. On the other hand, the International Olympic Committee had, in part, awarded the games to Beijing in 2000 to pressure the government into expanding human rights for its citizens. The compromise solution was to designate three parks in the city as areas where protests would be tolerated. The authorities required protesters to obtain a government permit in advance for their demonstration to proceed. Those who actually applied for permits, though, were harassed or arrested, and in the end, no protests at all took place during the games.

There were two unlikely victims caught up in this web. Both women in their late seventies, both walking with canes and one legally blind in one eye, Wu Dianyuan and Wang Xiuying were arrested and sentenced to reform through labor when they applied for a permit to protest having received insufficient compensation when their homes were seized for redevelopment. The episode proved to be the *reductio ad absurdum* of the actions of a ham-handed authoritarian regime.

Of late, Chinese citizens have taken to using the Internet as a vehicle for public protest. Corrupt officials are exposed, official malfeasance is revealed, and inappropriate court verdicts are challenged. In one recent incident, a woman charged with voluntary manslaughter for fatally knifing an official who forced himself upon her had her case dismissed after some four million individuals posted their disagreement with the charge.

That the central government professes to take these many instances of public protest seriously is attested to by the adoption, by the Seventeenth National Party Congress in 2006, of a policy referred to as encouraging a "harmonious society." Recognizing citizen concerns, the policy promised to address issues of corruption, pollution, a growing gap between rich and poor, and the steady decline of health services and public education. While the new policy line has resulted in a number of initiatives that benefit, in particular, rural residents, the number of protests has only increased each year since the policy was adopted.

It is important to underscore the fact that the numerous instances of public protest across the country, many of them involving very large numbers of protesters and some of them resulting in violence, are largely isolated from one another. Unlike the Falun Gong protest of 1999, which involved a very large and well-organized national, indeed, international movement, virtually all the protests in recent years are mainly spontaneous, unorganized, and isolated. Needless to say, it is among the party-state's highest priorities to keep it that way.

Yet another method of redressing grievances is litigation. China has worked hard over the last thirty years to become a society governed by laws rather than by individuals. A consequence of this movement, and a testament to its success, is the burgeoning number of potential lawsuits aimed at redressing citizens' grievances. A 1989 law made it possible, for the first time, for Chinese citizens to sue the state. The reality, however, is that few, if any, lawsuits against the state are accepted by the courts. "The number of people wanting to sue the government is large and growing," says a People's University legal scholar. "But the number of people who succeed in filing cases against the government is minuscule. So, you could say there is a gap between theory and practice."

For example, 129 parents of children killed in the Fuxin No. 2 Primary School during the Sichuan earthquake in 2008 attempted to bring suit against the local government and a construction company, charging faulty construction of the school. Parents were seeking an apology from the potential defendants, along with additional cash compensation for their losses. The court speedily rejected the lawsuit, observing that damage from the quake was the result of a natural disaster, not human error. Indeed, the party-state has in recent months decided to curb the use of litigation as an avenue of redress by arresting public interest lawyers and closing down their firms.

Thus, despite considerable progress, "politics" in China is still a pretty feeble enterprise, particularly when one looks beyond the village and the city neighborhood. Of much more significance is the "politicking" that takes place within the party, the jockeying for position among individuals and factions that goes on at every level and that ultimately has much greater influence over the lives and livelihoods of Chinese citizens than do their opportunities to vote, petition, protest, or litigate.

Chapter 6: The Economy

In the early 1960s, an ideological controversy erupted into public view after simmering bitterly within international Communist circles for years. A year before he was overthrown, Soviet premier Nikita Khrushchev scoffed at his erstwhile Chinese allies' view of communism: "To follow their line of thinking, it transpires that if a people walks in rope sandals and eats watery soup out of a common bowl, that is communism, and if a working man lives well and wants to live even better tomorrow, that is almost tantamount to the restoration of capitalism!" Mao Zedong denounced Khrushchev as a proponent of what he sneeringly labeled "goulash communism."

Twenty years later, however, Deng Xiaoping struck a remarkably Khrushchev-like note when he described the rationale behind his economic reforms: "Socialism means eliminating poverty. Pauperism is not socialism, still less communism. The superiority of the socialist system lies above all in its ability to develop the productive forces and to improve the people's material and cultural life."

Deng's first priority was to reform the Chinese economy to improve the people's standard of living. A second priority, always at a significant distance from the first, was to reform the political system. He was not an ideologue. He often sounded more like an American pragmatist than a Chinese revolutionary. During the Cultural Revolution, the regime had denounced him as one of those who would abandon socialist goals and take China "down the capitalist road." Still needing to protect himself against such charges when he returned to a position of authority in 1977, he enunciated what he called his "four cardinal principles." They were, he said, the irreducible nucleus of what had been the full-blown (some might well argue overblown) ideology of Mao, his predecessor. Any reform measure was acceptable so long as it did not call into question the leadership of the Communist Party, the dictatorship of the proletariat, the correctness of Marxism-Leninism, or the goal of socialism.

In practice, Deng operated with just two principles that became, if anything, more fixed as he aged: reform measures were legitimate if they promoted rapid economic growth and if they did not weaken the party's control of the political system; everything else was subject to compromise. This was particularly true with respect to the "socialism" of the fourth cardinal principle, which, in Deng's hands, became "socialism with Chinese characteristics."

As it exists today, Deng's socialism with Chinese characteristics is an economy moving rapidly and sometimes painfully from central planning to market-driven decision making. It is an economy with a shrinking state-owned sector, a small collective sector, and a rapidly burgeoning private sector. Indeed, liberal use has been made of capitalist methods to jump-start and then fuel truly remarkable growth since the reforms began. Until recently, the economy grew at an unprecedented average annual rate of close to 10 percent. Whereas a tiny fraction of the workforce in 1978 was employed in private enterprises, today close to a third of the workforce is thus employed. Income distribution in China, which at the beginning of the reform period was among the most equal of industrialized economies, today ranks among the world's least equal. Through the first three decades after the founding of the People's Republic in 1949, the government owned and operated all large factories and maintained a monopoly on transportation, communications, and banking.

While much diminished in importance, the government is still an important player in the Chinese economy, with about 150,000 state-owned industrial enterprises employing a workforce of about sixty million. These enterprises operate as small, semi-independent communities within China's cities, the largest including as many as half a million people, if managers, workers, service personnel, dependents, and retirees are taken into account. These state-owned factories were all once directly controlled by one or another government ministry. In the mid-1950s, ownership of most of them was turned over to provincial or municipal governments. The central government now controls just under half the assets of the state-owned sector (the other half having been sold off in the form of stock shares) and manages these enterprises under the State Asset Supervision and Administration Commission, which was set up in 2003 to consolidate the several ministries, each devoted to a single industrial sector.

Management schemes for them have come and gone over the years. At certain points, the factory manager has been given decision-making responsibility; at other times, his authority has been eclipsed by that of the factory's party secretary. Today, as a result of reforms initiated in the mid-1980s, the factory manager is usually under contract to produce a given level of profit for a fixed period of time.

Prior to the beginning of the reforms, all profits from all state-owned enterprises reverted to the government at year's end. In cases where the enterprise had a deficit rather than a profit, the deficit would be made up with a government subsidy. With the reforms, the remittance of profit was abandoned and replaced by taxes, the rates set such as to leave a portion of the profits with the enterprises, and managers were permitted some flexibility in deciding how after-tax profits should be distributed. At the same time, the subsidies to make up deficits were replaced with bank loans on which interest was charged. These bank loans constituted a substantial percentage of the nonperforming loans that, as we shall see, put China's banking system at risk.

The rapid contraction of the state sector in recent years has come at a significant cost. Unprofitable state-owned factories have been shuttered, and their employees set adrift, sometimes with welfare payments in lieu of salaries, often with no incomes and none of the very generous health and retirement benefits they enjoyed as state employees. This has swelled the ranks of the urban unemployed and triggered serious and occasionally violent protests in those areas of the country where the development of the private sector has not been fast enough to provide sufficient new jobs.

The state sector also includes about fifteen percent of China's wholesale distributors, one in nine of the country's retail outlets, a third of its hotels, and all but a handful of banks, schools, and hospitals. Most urban housing stock, once owned and managed either by individual enterprises and units or by municipal governments, has been sold to individual homeowners. Finally, although the state sector is all but completely absent from the rural economy, about nineteen hundred state farms, employing some 3.4 million workers, account for twelve million acres—about three percent of the total land under cultivation. These farms are mostly in remote areas where land is being reclaimed for cultivation and people are being resettled, in some instances for disciplinary reasons, in others to alter ethnic balances. Despite the positive effects of the recent industrial reforms on productivity, the state sector is in trouble. So serious is the deterioration that many argue that a political and economic crisis will result if it is not effectively addressed.

The state now owns and manages about 150,000 enterprises. They are among China's largest and are clustered in the areas of energy, metallurgy, telecommunications, transportation, and military-related manufacturing. The state sector's share of industrial output is declining each year, slipping below 50 percent in 1993 for the first time in forty years, and now standing at less than 30 percent. At this point, most of the state-owned enterprises that have long operated at a loss- the so-called "zombie enterprises" –have been shuttered, and the state has taken on a portion of the financial obligations of these enterprises to their former employees. To the extent it is not fulfilling these obligations, the state is the object of widespread social protest in the country's rust belt cities

A collective enterprise, in Chinese parlance, is one owned and managed by the people who make up a *danwei*, a workplace or residential unit. Although collective enterprises have been in existence since before the founding of the People's Republic, after 1978, many of them became the vehicle for transitioning the economy from government control to market control. Indeed, there are those who argue that it was the experience of these collectives operating on the borderline between public and private ownership that, despite their neglect in periods of ideological fervor, provided the reservoir of skills needed to reintroduce private enterprise into the Chinese economy.

The largest number of collective enterprises were located in rural townships, though collectives were also found in schools, neighborhoods, and even army units. The business of the collective enterprise may be farming, manufacturing, transportation, or commerce. Resources are mobilized, the enterprise is established, and the product is produced and sold based on decisions the group makes on its own. Members are also responsible for deciding how profits are to be divided–how much will be reinvested and how much distributed as compensation. Finally, they decide how members are paid–whether based on the amount of their initial investment, the level of their skills or expertise, the amount of work they do, or the difficulty of the tasks they perform.

In legal terms, title to the assets of a state-owned enterprise is vested in "all the people" –all the citizens of the country (or province or city). Title to a collective's assets is vested in its members. The collective is licensed and taxed by the local government. It may or may not have business relations with state-owned enterprises, either buying its raw materials from or selling all or a portion of its product to them. In some cases, collectives were formed within state-owned factories to diversify their product lines, to provide work for the underemployed, or to augment sagging profits. A more radical solution to the problem of losses in state-owned enterprises is to sell off a losing enterprise to its workers or to a foreign investor.

Twenty years ago, there were as many as twenty-five million collective enterprises in China, with a workforce of some 450 million people. Some have argued that the "collective" nature of these enterprises was largely fictitious and that the term "township and village enterprises" always referred to the *location* of the enterprises, not to their *ownership.* In any event, today the vast majority of these enterprises have been transferred into some form of private ownership, leaving only about 200,000 pure collectives with a workforce of fewer than three million.

Since 1949, virtually all agricultural production in China has been collectively owned and managed, but reforms have rendered the collective nature of these arrangements ambiguous at best. More than 95 percent of cultivable land in China that is not operated by state farms is collectively owned by citizens of villages and townships where the land is located. The household responsibility system, initiated as one of Deng's first economic reforms in the late 1970s, called for leasing the right to use plots of this land to individual households according to a contract stipulating the amount of grain to be produced on the plots. Contracts were awarded based on the household's probable ability to fulfill the terms, given its size and the number of its able-bodied workers. Everything produced on the leased plot over and above the contractual amount could be disposed of by the household as it wished: sold to the state (ordinarily at a higher price than that received for the contracted grain), sold on the free market, or consumed by the family.

Contracts were initially signed for one-year terms. Contracts, including the land use rights associated with them, could be inherited, bought, and sold. To encourage farmers to invest in improving the land, the household responsibility system was replaced by straight leases. Terms of the leases were initially extended to three, five, fifteen, and eventually to as long as seventy years in some cases. Indeed, as we have seen, insufficient compensation for land acquired for constructing factories or housing developments is one of the most important grievances leading to mass protests in the Chinese countryside. With key decisions thus being made at the household level and with the distinction between use rights and ownership rights blurred as a result of the extension of leases over long periods, the "collective" nature of this economic activity becomes attenuated indeed.

The private sector in China has grown with remarkable rapidity over the last thirty years. Today, about sixty percent of China's gross domestic product is produced by privately owned businesses, and those businesses employ some 200 million workers, about a third of the economy's total workforce. Recognizing the importance of the private sector, the government enacted the Private Sector Promotion Law in April 2025. This legislation aims to bolster legal protections and foster a more favorable environment for private businesses, signaling a commitment to support their continued contribution to the economy.

Also included in the private sector for statistical purposes are the more than one million foreign joint ventures. By 2024, the cumulative total of contracted foreign investment in China had reached \$3.66 trillion, and most significantly, goods produced by foreign-invested firms account for more than one-third of China's exports.

Furniture, personal effects, and individual bank accounts are all privately owned by both rural and urban Chinese. In addition, rural residents and many urban residents own their own homes, though they have use rights, not titles, to the land they live on.

As shown in Table 6, about 34 percent of the Chinese population lives in the countryside. Among these 465 million people, there is a workforce of about 261 million, many of whom elect to seek temporary work in the city. About three-quarters of the rural workforce is employed in agriculture (including farming, forestry, fishing, and animal husbandry). There is a significant surplus of labor in Chinese agriculture; some estimate that a substantial number of rural workers could be redeployed with no reduction in agricultural output.

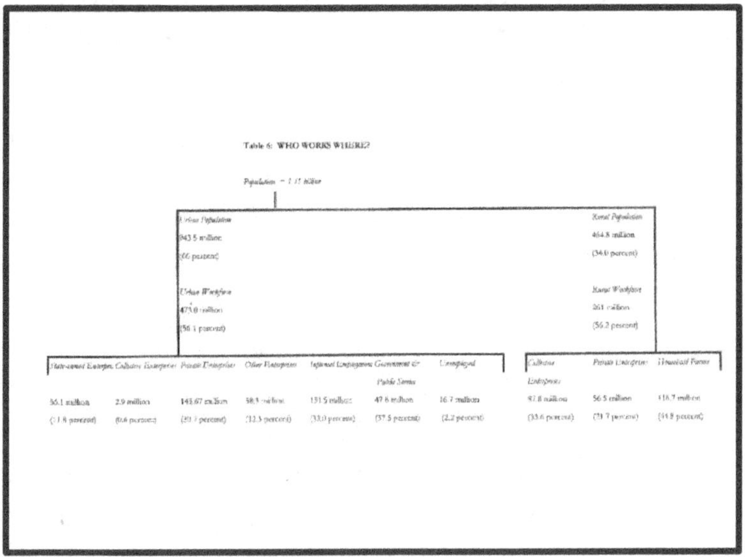

In part to absorb some of this surplus labor, in part to raise household income, and in part to boost the production of manufactured goods, reformers actively encouraged opening collective factories owned and managed or licensed by township and village governments. Known as township and village enterprises (TVEs), they experienced a peak growth in the mid-1990s, at which point they employed some 135 million workers. They tended to be small outfits with low capitalization that were thrown together quickly with little or no regard for their ill effects on air and water. Since 1996, most TVEs have been privatized, and employment in those remaining has declined to only some 15 million workers. Nonetheless, they served as an indispensable vehicle for the transition of the rural economy from public to private ownership.

Many rural households find that it makes good economic sense to keep a hand in several sectors. Holding on to the farming contract means access to fresh food and a certain amount of security, but a household's income can be significantly augmented if one or more of its members works in a TVE or a privately owned enterprise and further augmented if a family member moves to a city and, with luck, finds a job as a day laborer in construction, transportation, or a service industry.

In real terms, rural income has increased more than sevenfold since the reforms began in 1978. Urban incomes, too, have increased sevenfold, but urban income is more than three times greater than rural incomes, and in terms of spending power, the gap between city and countryside is ever more pronounced and annoying to rural residents. Moreover, rural amenities by no means match those available in the city. Rural schools are poor, and the tuition, while reasonable enough, is an expense that many find onerous. Medical care in the countryside is much less accessible than it once was and has significantly increased in cost.

Finally, very few rural residents are covered by retirement programs and must rely on their children to support them when they leave the workforce.

The remaining 594 million Chinese people are urban residents, about 294 million of them are in the workforce, and according to official figures, 10 to 15 million are unemployed. About 22 percent of urban workers work in the state sector; 25 million in state-owned industrial enterprises; another 29 million in finance and banking, education, and health care; and approximately 10 million as government and party bureaucrats. Jobs in the state sector used to be much sought after because of good pay, excellent fringe benefits, and a tenure system that made it virtually impossible to be fired. Workers receive wages based on an eight-grade pay scale set by the state; in the first two decades after the reforms began, wages were augmented by bonuses designed to reward productivity and performance, though in practice they are often given to workers regardless of their output. In addition, state-sector employees receive heavily subsidized housing, health care, primary and secondary education for their children, stipends that help offset living costs, and generous retirement packages. For most factory managers, coordinating this benefits package is as great a responsibility as overseeing the production process. In addition to supervising an assembly line, managers must oversee schools, clinics, housing blocks, and retirement communities. Covering the cost of this generous benefits package pushed many state-owned enterprises into the red.

As we have seen, responding to the deteriorating finances of enterprises in the state sector, a number of factories were simply shut down, their employees laid off, and their assets sold off. For those enterprises still manifesting a pulse, however weak, salvage measures were undertaken. A Company Law, passed by the National People's Congress in 1994, provided mechanisms by which a state-owned enterprise could transform itself into a corporation and sell ownership shares on one of China's three stock exchanges. The stock exchanges–one in Shanghai, one in Beijing, and one in the southern boomtown of Shenzhen–thus have two categories of shares, one noncirculating and one that circulates. The noncirculating shares are those retained by the state, which currently amount to about 60 percent of the shares on the markets. Circulating shares were further divided into Class A and Class B shares. Class A shares trade in Chinese currency and can be bought and sold only by Chinese citizens. Class B shares trade in foreign currency; although originally restricted to trade by foreign investors, Class B shares can now be traded by Chinese investors who hold foreign currency. Privately owned corporations are typically not listed on the Chinese stock exchanges.

At this point, about 56 million urban residents are employed in enterprises owned and managed by the state. Collective enterprises in China's cities employ about three million workers. Another 146 million work in the private sector, 60 million in other enterprises, 48 million in government and state employment, and 150 million in various forms of informal employment. Some 17 million are unemployed. Like China's "reformed" state enterprises, collective and private enterprises have considerable flexibility with respect to whom they hire or fire and how much they pay their workers, but most of these enterprises offer few if any fringe benefits, and when they do, the benefits are much less than those that state enterprises offer. To attract qualified workers, these enterprises must offer higher wages. China's social security system has been optimized since the 18th Party National Congress held in 2012, with the basic old-age insurance for enterprise employees being coordinated nationwide, and that for urban and rural residents being implemented uniformly. The number of people covered by basic old-age insurance has reached just over one billion, unemployment insurance 245 million, and work-related injury insurance 301 million.

In recent years, China's urban population has been augmented by nearly 25 percent with the arrival of as many as 375 million migrant or "floating" workers (流动人口). Until the mid-1980s, moving from the countryside to the city was virtually impossible, given a rationing system initiated in 1959 that limited access to necessities, such as grain, cooking oil, and cotton cloth. Every household had an officially registered residence, and ration coupons were issued at one's place of residence and could be redeemed only locally. When economic reform made these necessities available on the free market, the rationing system no longer worked as a means of controlling geographical mobility, and it was abolished in 1993. A relatively small but rapidly expanding labor market, in which enterprises can recruit freely, and people can choose where they work, is now in place.

Rural residents who go to China's cities in search of more lucrative employment tend to take the first jobs they find. Most employment is short-term, and although such employment is high-paying in contrast with rural wages, there is no job security and, of course, no benefits package. Moreover, the migrants are not officially city residents and hence have no claim on public services. Because they cannot live in regular housing, most of them go to squatter settlements in the suburbs. If they fall ill, they must cover the costs of their own health care. Many of them have come to the city alone; those who bring their families cannot put their children in public schools. Their presence in the cities is tolerated because they are a relatively low-cost and obligation-free labor force for the burgeoning construction projects underway everywhere, but they are potentially disruptive. When the worldwide economic downturn had its effect on Chinese exports, as many as twenty-five million of these floaters found themselves without work and were obliged to return to their rural homes.

In his pursuit of economic reform, Deng Xiaoping had an opponent with a great deal less faith in the virtues of market forces. Chen Yun, an advocate of the centrally planned economy, is famous for his description of the economic plan as a birdcage and the economy as a bird within the cage. Chen believed in enlarging the birdcage to allow the bird more room to move about, a pragmatic approach to economic problems that at key points in his career enabled him to help bring China back from the brink of economic disaster. Still, it would never have been acceptable from Chen's point of view to open the door of the cage and allow the bird to fly free.

Chen's influence was at its height during the 1950s, at which time the Chinese economy, like the Soviet one after which it was modeled, operated under a comprehensive plan. In any economy, decisions must be made about how national resources–land, raw materials, labor, and capital–are allocated. In an ideal market economy, these decisions are made based on supply and demand; in an ideal planned economy, they are based on the plan.

The Chinese economy has never been wholly governed by plan, in part because of a lack of experience and expertise, in part because of a lack of solid statistical data, in part because of a bias in favor of decentralized decision making, and in part because of a proclivity to throw the plan aside periodically in bursts of ideological fervor. Nonetheless, the State Planning Commission drew up annual, five-year, and in some cases ten-year economic plans embodying decisions about the allocation of national resources. The most recent five-year plan, the fifteenth such plan, covers the years from 2026 to 2030.

Flexibility in planning was limited by China's givens. In 1949, with the triumph of communism, the new regime found itself with a reasonable resource base and a surplus of unskilled labor, but the country had a shortage of land, capital, and skilled labor. Land, as a resource, was taken out of play in the plan, since title to all of it was vested in either the state or the rural cooperatives, and no rents were charged for it.

The principal focus of the plan was on state-owned industry, which, at the height of Chinese central planning in the late 1950s, accounted for nearly 90 percent of industrial output. The plan stipulated the amount of raw materials to be extracted and processed, the amount of energy to be generated, the amount of manufactured goods to be produced, the prices at which producer goods and products would be exchanged, the allocation and wages of the labor required to achieve these goals, and the amount and destination of investments. But agricultural production, too, was governed by national quotas, in turn divided into provincial, county, and, ultimately, commune or collective quotas: the prices at which quota grain was purchased and sold were determined by the plan; state-owned enterprises conducted the wholesale and retail trade.

Rural residents had private plots, on which they were allowed to grow goods for their own consumption or for sale on the rural free markets once they had fulfilled their obligations to produce for the state quotas. Handicrafts they produced as a sideline were either sold on the market or distributed through the collective. Rural free markets were subject to close regulation and, during the high tide of the Great Leap Forward, were shut down entirely.

Functioning on the margins of the economic plan were collective enterprises, which had gradually increased their share of industrial output from one-tenth to nearly one-quarter of the total by the late 1970s. The small private sector had been largely eliminated by the late 1950s, but it was this limited experience with private enterprise that enabled rural residents to serve as the powerful engine that launched China's economic reforms in the late 1970s.

A labor market was almost completely eliminated in China in the late 1950s. Skilled labor was scarce, and if their movement had not been subject to government regulation, workers would have bid up the cost of their services to unacceptable levels. Also, since unskilled labor was overly plentiful, particularly in the rural sector, and per capita income was consistently higher in the urban economy than in the rural economy, free movement of labor would have resulted in a massive immigration of rural workers into the already crowded cities.

The shortage of skilled labor was addressed by gradually expanding the secondary and postsecondary training facilities for scientists, technicians, and skilled workers. Through a job assignment system, graduates of these institutions were channeled into the state sector as they were needed. Once assigned, employees were given what amounted to lifetime job security, but the *quid pro quo* was that lateral moves were virtually impossible to affect. Meanwhile, the risk of urban in-migration by underemployed rural workers in search of higher pay was avoided by implementing the rationing system described above. Permission to shift one's household registration from the countryside to the city was almost never granted. Where you were born was likely to be where you spent your life; where you began working was likely to be where you retired.

This centrally planned economy was by no means a total failure in its three decades from 1950 to 1980. In fact, economic performance in China was worst during the Great Leap Forward and the Cultural Revolution, when the plan was set aside and a campaign mentality replaced it. The economy grew at an average annual rate of six percent; industrial output led this growth with an average annual rate of eight percent; agricultural output, growing more modestly, was outpaced by population growth. The end result was an abysmally low per capita gross national product and a living standard that fell far short of the expectations aroused by promises of a bright socialist future. When he launched his program of economic reforms, Deng Xiaoping proposed to expand that portion of the economy in which market forces were decisive, while keeping the central plan for the state sector. He hoped that a vibrant, rapidly growing market-driven sector would, by its success, persuade his skeptical colleagues and potential successors of its merits. China would gradually "grow out of the plan," as one economist has put it.

Agriculture was the first to experience the introduction of market forces. Deng's household responsibility system re-empowered the household, giving it the authority to decide how to use its labor and strong incentives to increase productivity. But prices and production quotas were still in government hands. Like all commodities, grain had had a very low price, limiting the exposure of the government, which supplemented the urban population's income by selling grain below cost; without quotas, this low price would have encouraged farmers to turn to more lucrative crops.

With land being withdrawn from cultivation and developed for non-agricultural purposes, and with a substantial number of rural residents moving temporarily or permanently to find work in the city, the party-state has come to place new emphasis on its long-standing goal of achieving self-sufficiency in grain production. In the early 1990s, there were experiments with allowing the market to determine grain prices and allowing prices to determine the amount produced. But this strategy resulted in a very sharp rise in the price of grain, a more than 50 percent increase in 1994, that seriously exacerbated urban inflation. Regulating grain prices helped reduce inflation, but overregulation undermines the incentive needed to increase grain production. Government-regulated prices for grain have risen very slowly, only about five percent over the last ten years, but they are supplemented by agricultural subsidies, which in 2023 amounted to some twenty billion dollars. Today, more agricultural produce is traded on the free market than in state stores. Free market prices are higher, but the quality, supply, and variety of fresh meat and produce available to city dwellers have increased markedly over the last decade.

The success of the household responsibility system in increasing agricultural output was useful to the reformers in building support for their efforts when they turned to China's cities. The straightforward solutions that had worked so successfully in the countryside were, however, ill-suited to the complex urban economy. Among the first reform steps was permission to revive the private sector. Very small, privately owned enterprises in the service sector were the first to appear: food stands, tailor shops, cigarette vendors, and the like. These small businesses gave jobs to many people returning to the cities after having been sent to the countryside during the Cultural Revolution and provided goods and services that were unavailable in state-owned stores and restaurants. At first, there was a limit on the number of nonfamily members each business was permitted to hire, though exceptions were made where needs existed that were not being filled by state-owned enterprises. But soon there were a number of very large privately owned enterprises, some of them operating under the same names and managements they had had thirty years before.

The collective sector was encouraged to expand as well. Workers in state-owned enterprises, schools, hospitals, army units, and government offices were encouraged to form collectives that, because of their smaller size and greater flexibility, could develop new product lines, employment practices, and markets. Their immediate success promoted the merits of the market to otherwise conservative skeptics and encouraged them to explore the ways the state-owned businesses could take advantage of it.

By the mid-1980s, the reform of the state-sector economy had begun in earnest. At this point, taxes replaced the remission of profits, and enterprise managers became responsible for their profits, losses, and investment decisions. These reforms were interrupted by the retrenchment measures taken to slow the overheated economy in 1988-89; efforts to revive them in the early 1990s were hindered by mounting losses. As we have seen, once undertaken under the new Company Law after 1994, the reforms included closing down the least profitable enterprises and "reforming" the more promising ones by transforming them into corporations with various forms of joint ownership.

We can see, then, that the critical decisions about allocation of land, raw materials, labor, and capital, once made by the party-state and incorporated in an economic plan, are being made, after more than forty years of reform, by the market. Contracts involving use rights to agricultural land can now be bought and sold, so there is the beginning of what amounts to a real estate market in the countryside. State-owned enterprises and governments in the cities are selling housing stock to tenants to reduce the heavy burden of providing subsidized housing. Use rights and sometimes titles to land are also involved in some joint-venture contracts. In the case of deficit producing state enterprises in which the only attractive asset of value is the land on which the factory is located, foreign investors, after signing a deal, level the factory buildings to put the land to more profitable use. In effect, the state is raising capital by liquidating some of its landholdings and, in the process, creating a real estate market for the first time in more than forty years.

The dual allocation system for raw materials–a portion allocated by the government, a portion allocated based on supply and demand–has been dismantled, and today the market determines commodity allocation. Only a few key commodities—coal, oil, and electric power–are still allocated to state-owned enterprises, and even here the prices, held artificially low to maximize industrial profits, are gradually being raised to the world market level.

Price reform is, of course, a sensitive issue in an economy as vulnerable to the effects of inflation as China's. Nonetheless, virtually all retail and capital goods prices are now market-determined, though when, in the late 1980s and early 1990s, urban inflation got out of hand, the government stepped in to regulate food prices, since the price of food accounts for as much as half the consumer price index.

The government has been reluctant to give up control of allocating labor, and a genuine labor market has been slow to develop. Nonetheless, decisions about movement in the workforce are much more likely to be made outside the government than they were thirty years ago. Though it is still very difficult for anyone to move from one job to another within the state sector (those with scarce skills or good performance records find their current employers reluctant to let them leave, and those without these qualifications are unlikely to find new employers willing to agree to their transfers), many workers have chosen to leave the security of their state-sector positions entirely and *xiahai* (下海 plunge into the sea)of private or collective enterprises. Of course, one loses the benefits package, including access to housing, a health plan, and a retirement plan, but the advantages are higher salaries and greater freedom to change jobs or even residences.

Others seek to have the best of both worlds by keeping their state-sector positions and taking second jobs in the collective or private sector. Factory workers, many of them involuntarily placed on short hours or on furlough, find part- or full-time work in private or collective enterprises; doctors with positions in hospitals or medical schools take on private patients; government employees, capitalizing on their access and connections, set themselves up as business consultants, moving, sometimes with less than perfect precision, along the fine line that divides ethical practice from corruption. Moreover, this tendency to function in several sectors is as common in the countryside as it is in the city; moonlighting has so many advantages that it would not be surprising to find that most Chinese families today have more than one employer and a foot in more than one sector.

Capital allocation is the last decision to be opened up to market forces. As a part of the urban reforms, state-owned enterprises were to be weaned from their dependence on subsidies to cover deficits or to fund expansion; government funds would continue to be available but only in the form of interest-bearing loans, for the eventual repayment of which enterprises would be held accountable.

The subsequent poor performance of most of China's state-owned enterprises and the government's unwillingness to suffer the political consequences of adding the employees of bankrupt businesses to the ranks of the disgruntled unemployed effectively rendered this reform moot. Subsidies continued to flow into state sector businesses. Nominally called loans, they accumulated as uncollectible assets in the banking system, precluding more productive use of capital. By 2001, these non-performing loans amounted to nearly a third of the portfolios of the four major state banks, according to official figures. According to foreign observers, the proportion was closer to 40 percent, or five hundred billion dollars.

A reform of the banking system aimed at addressing this problem was undertaken as early as 1993. Zhu Rongji, then serving as vice premier, was dissatisfied with its implementation, dismissed the head of the People's Bank of China, and temporarily took over its administration himself. The goals were to make the People's Bank of China a central bank and to create a series of policy banks that would direct the flow of credit away from speculative projects and toward projects that would serve the development of the overall economy.

To address the problem of uncollectible loans in the system as a whole, Zhu, now serving as premier, directed the formation, beginning in early 1999, of four asset management companies, each affiliated with one of the four major banks. Reminiscent of the Resolution Trust Corporation (RTC) established by the U.S. government to address the collapse of the American savings and loan industry in 1989 and the proposed scheme in the Emergency Economic Stabilization Act of 2008 to create "bad banks" to absorb the distressed assets in U.S. banks, the asset management companies trade debt for equity in the borrowing firms. Just as the RTC worked to sell off the real estate held by savings and loans as collateral against their non--performing loans, so the asset management companies attempted to recoup their assets by the sale or restructuring of the deadbeat firms.

Although the RTC ultimately cost the U.S. government some $450 billion, four times what was estimated at the outset, that figure amounted to only about 6 percent of gross domestic product. The $700 billion bailout bill passed by Congress in 2008 amounted to 5 percent of GDP. Nonperforming loans in the Chinese banking system amounted to a third of gross national product. Following substantial reforms of the "big four" banks, in order of size of assets, the Industrial and Commercial Bank of China, the Agricultural Bank of China, the China Construction Bank, and the Bank of China, and an infusion of some $300 billion, the banks reduced their nonperforming loans to just over 10 percent of lending.

Western economists were surprised and envious at the speed with which the Chinese economy rebounded after the onset of the world financial crisis in 2008. With demand for Chinese exports suddenly dropping, factories cut back production, unemployment (particularly among migrant workers) rose, and the rapid pace of the growth of the economy slowed for the first time in many years. The Chinese government took swift and effective action, announcing a $586 billion stimulus package in November 2008. What remains of its authoritarian approach to economic management allowed it to deploy stimulus funds very rapidly into infrastructure projects, including some $88 billion in intercity rail lines (among them a high-speed line linking Beijing and Guangzhou). By November 2009, the economy had rebounded, and economic growth for the year was more than 9.5 percent. During the course of that year, China became the largest market for cars (surpassing the United States) and the world's largest exporter of goods (surpassing Germany) and was nudging Japan out of second place among the world's economies.

The last two decades have witnessed less-than-stellar performance on the part of the Chinese economy, as demonstrated in the following graph:

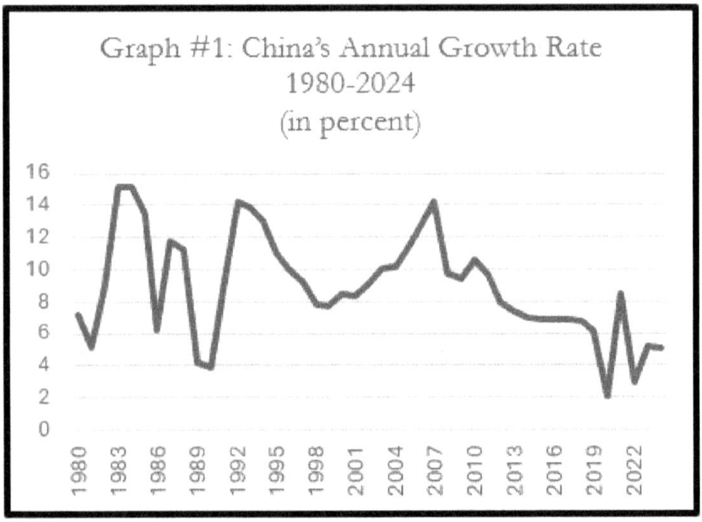

Source: www.marketoracle.co.uk

The economy was adversely affected by the global recession of 2008. A huge state investment was made to address the recession, which resulted, in turn, in inflation. Inflation in 2008 reached eight percent, the highest level in decades. Two years later, a national campaign was launched to address the problem. The economy was restructured, shifting the emphasis to expanding the domestic market, restructuring the industrial structure, upgrading products and industries toward higher quality and knowledge-based output, and offering preferential credits to selected industries. Steps were taken to expand domestic consumption, the financial sector was opened to private capital, Chinese investment in foreign countries was encouraged, and the private sector was strengthened. By 2014, growth had resumed at 7.4%, though not all provinces benefited equally. For example, while Chongqing experienced a growth rate of nearly eleven percent, Heilongjiang's economy grew at only five percent.

But the following year, the Chinese stock market crashed in June. A third of the value of A-shares on the Shanghai Stock Exchange was lost, and aftershocks occurred in July and August. The Shanghai stock market fell 30 percent over three weeks as 1,400 companies, or more than half of those listed, filed for a trading halt in an attempt to prevent further losses. Values of the stock markets continued to drop despite efforts by the government to reduce the fall. After three stable weeks, the Shanghai index fell again by 8.48 percent in August, marking the largest fall since 2007. Despite a recovery starting in February of 2016, prices were not able to reach their pre-crash highs. In fact, they went to new lows toward the end of 2018 and the very beginning of 2019. Since then, prices have recovered, but again, the recovery was less than optimal.

In 2021, China experienced a property sector crisis sparked by the default of the property developer Evergrande Group. Evergrande, along with other Chinese property developers, experienced financial stress in the wake of overbuilding and subsequent new Chinese regulations on these companies' debt limits. The crisis spread beyond Evergrande to other major property developers. Following widespread online sharing of a letter in August 2021, in which Evergrande warned the Guangdong government that it was at risk of experiencing a cash crunch, shares plunged, impacting global markets and leading to a slowdown of foreign investment in China.

The company unsuccessfully attempted to sell assets to generate money, missed several debt payments, was downgraded by international ratings agencies, and finally defaulted on an offshore bond at the beginning of December 2021. Ratings agencies declared the company to be in "restricted default." In January 2024, a Hong Kong court ordered Evergrande to be liquidated.

In 2024, the Chinese government took several steps to bolster economic growth. Income taxes were slashed and spending on social welfare, including education, social security, and retirement allowances, was increased. In addition, the central government increased transfers to local governments by 8%. Even with all these steps, annual growth in GDP was still projected to be only 5%, down from a high of more than 15% four decades earlier.

What exactly, then, is *socialist* about "socialism with Chinese characteristics"? A cold-eyed response to the question would have to be "Not much at all." The elements most commonly associated with a socialist economy are public ownership of the principal means of production, economic activity largely determined by government decision as contained in an economic plan, a heavy dose of egalitarianism, and a high level of government attention to the welfare of the working population. All these elements are in the process of being dismantled in China under the current program of economic reform. Moreover, however negative the consequences, there is little likelihood that China will return to purely socialist solutions. At this point, a better description of the Chinese economy would probably be "capitalism with Chinese characteristics," though that is not a term at all likely to gain wide currency in China today.

Thus far, our discussion of the Chinese economy has focused on the domestic side. But, since Deng first introduced the policy of *kaifang* (开放—opening up to the outside world) in 1978, China has become more and more deeply engaged in the world economy. Today, with a cumulative total of inbound contracted foreign investment amounting to $1.6 trillion, foreign exchange reserves amounting to more than three trillion (the highest foreign exchange reserves of any country, and total goods trade (imports plus exports) amounting to nearly forty percent of gross domestic product, China is inextricably linked with the world economy. We will take up the global side of China's economy in Chapter 20.

Chapter 7: The Rule of Law

From the American perspective, the single most significant obstacle to better U.S.-China relations is the Chinese government's systematic violation of its citizens' human rights, but almost as important is the absence of a fully articulated set of laws and, more fundamentally, of an understanding of the concept of the rule of law. It is with human rights and our devotion to the rule of law that many of us are least willing to make concessions for cultural differences. We believe not only that our position on these issues is correct but that it is the only correct position and thus should be universally accepted. Yet it is true that the cultural differences in this area are great.

The American political system, and to a great degree, the Western political tradition of the modern nation-state, are rooted in the concept of the rule of law, by which we mean that the law stands above individual officeholders as a neutral arbiter to which disputes are referred and based on which they are resolved. All citizens are equal before the law, and everyone, regardless of position or status, is subject to it. But China's political system is rooted in the concept of the rule of men (in recent years expanded in a limited way to include a few women), and the individual officeholder, especially the officeholder-in-chief, stands above the law and serves as the arbiter to whom disputes are referred.

These diametrically opposed concepts derive from diametrically opposed ideas about the significance of the individual. The primacy of the individual and of his or her rights and freedoms, based on philosophical traditions that go from classical Greek thought through the European Enlightenment, is the firm basis of the American economy and political system, and our legal system is designed to protect it. But the concept on which Chinese culture was based is the primacy of the family and society, and the emphasis in that tradition is on individual obligations, not on rights or freedoms. The individual has obligations to the family, and the family has obligations to society. The ruler's task is to ensure that these obligations are fulfilled.

There is a school of Chinese philosophy that supports the necessity of a fully articulated legal system. Han Fei (韓 非), a Legalist philosopher and statesman during the Warring States period whose ideas were taken up by the first Qin (秦)emperor in the third century B.C.E., asserted the principle that people are inherently evil; therefore, good behavior could be elicited only by means of carefully drafted laws backed by generous rewards and stringent punishments. Emperor Qin Shi (秦始皇) used these ideas, later known as legalism, during his brief but repressive rule, the most important accomplishment of which was the first unification of the Chinese state. But because of his brutality, legalism was discredited, and subsequent rulers looked to the very different views of Confucius (孔子) as the basis for their state ideology. Confucius, who predated Han Fei by two centuries, began with an opposite presumption about human nature. Believing that human nature is fundamentally good, he argued that good behavior was most effectively elicited by means of the ruler's example. Confucius's concept of a web of human relationships, which we considered in Chapter 3, involved mutual responsibilities: the subordinate was obliged to obey, the superior to provide a moral example, and if all went well, laws, rewards, and penalties would be superfluous. In describing the cycle of dynastic growth and decline, I have touched on the so-called right to rebel. There were, in fact, circumstances under which the obligation to obey was suspended: when the ruler failed to provide the moral example that it was his obligation to embody an official had a duty to remonstrate, but this was not a kind of embryonic freedom of speech, for the emphasis was not on the official's freedom to disagree but on his *obligation* to disagree. Carrying out this obligation might prove fatal, but the obligation stood nonetheless. Moreover, the right to rebel was granted *ex post facto* only to the successful rebel. The unsuccessful rebel was guilty of treason.

The system that emerged under the Confucian order was not devoid of written law. Although there was little in the way of written civil law, there were criminal and administrative codes, regulations for the conduct of criminal investigations, and the administration of justice. Nonetheless, the performance of the ruler or official, not the written code, was the critical element in the successful functioning of the political system.

Scholars have noted analogies between the political system constructed by the Chinese Communist Party under Mao Zedong and the Confucian political system that preceded it: Marxism-Leninism and the Confucian canon, the party cadre and the scholar-official, the core leader and the emperor. Yet the legal system as it operated under Mao Zedong only faintly resembled its Confucian antecedent. Like the Confucian past, there was no rule of law under Mao, but unlike the Confucian past, there was essentially no law at all under Mao.

When the Chinese Communists did make some effort to introduce new legal codes, as in many other areas of life in China in the 1950s, the Soviet Union was their model. The legal system was made up of three institutions: the Ministry of Public Security, which was responsible for police work; a procuracy at each level of government, which investigated and prosecuted crimes and reported to the Supreme People's Procuracy; and courts at each level of government, headed by the Supreme People's Court, which heard and decided cases and set punishments.

Despite this formal apparatus, the major political movements of the 1950s and 1960s, in which millions of landlords, bureaucrats, dissenters, intellectuals, and party officials were stripped of status, wealth, and power and sentenced to long periods of hard labor or even to death, took place without reference either to laws or to the system, which focused most of its attention on criminal cases. Civil disputes were most often resolved within the units in which conflicting parties worked: disputes between work units, by the administrative agency to which both reported, or, more informally, by party members within the contending units.

Mao believed in ideological principles, not laws. Ideological principles gave rise to a "line" of correct thinking, which in turn was translated into specific policies, each of which had implementing regulations. The regulations tended to be vague and subject to broad interpretation. Moreover, even ideological principles were subject to change. Late in life, Mao began to manipulate his ideology to serve his own purposes. At that point, the only reliable guide to action became the Chairman's gnomic "latest instruction."

Borrowing from Marx and Engels the idea that law is a tool that one social class uses to oppress another, Mao rejected the idea that the law is universally applicable: in years past, the landlord class had used Chinese law to oppress the peasantry; in a capitalist society, the bourgeoisie uses the law to oppress the proletariat, but in socialist China, the law would be used to overthrow and suppress the landlords and bourgeoisie.

By the late 1950s, these enemy classes had effectively been eliminated or rendered powerless, though not through the force of law. At that point, Mao's concept of class became more fluid. He abandoned the categories proletariat and bourgeoisie—categories that had plausible roots in the workplace—and instead began to use the broad categories "the people" and "enemies of the people."

The people were those who followed the current line; enemies of the people were those who opposed it. One set of rules (which he chose to call democracy) was to apply among the people, who, he said, constituted the vast majority of the population; another (which he termed dictatorship) applied to the small minority that made up the enemies of the people.

In the years leading up to and during the Cultural Revolution, Mao resumed the use of class labels, talking of a renewed class struggle, but this time the line between bourgeoisie and proletariat was just as fluid as the line between the people and their enemies. In both instances, the defining criteria were attitudes toward ideological principles, not economic or social relationships.

Three elements of this largely lawless system lingered on in post-Mao China. The first is the crime of counterrevolution, which, until its abandonment in 1997, served as the basis for the prosecution of political crimes. In practice, the ambiguous term *counterrevolution* was left up to the party to define, and the definition could also be changed *ex post facto*. The demonstrations in Tiananmen Square in 1976 that marked the beginning of the end of the reign of the Gang of Four were initially branded counterrevolutionary, and participants were prosecuted accordingly. After the Gang of Four fell, came a "reversal of verdicts," and first the 1976 demonstrators and subsequently a host of those persecuted during the Cultural Revolution were rehabilitated based on a new set of definitions of *revolution* and *counterrevolution*. Later, there was cautious talk among some in China of another reversal of verdicts, this time, to clear the names of those who demonstrated in Tiananmen Square in 1989.

In the mid-1990s, a few went so far as to suggest that it was time to eliminate once and for all the crime of counterrevolution from the statute books. At its meeting in March 1997, the National People's Congress approved legislation eliminating counterrevolution as a crime and substituting for it the crime of "endangering state security." While the new language is more up-to-date, it retains its ominous ambiguity.

A second carryover from the Maoist era is the concept of thought reform. Hundreds of thousands of people branded as counterrevolutionaries were executed, and many millions more were subjected to what, in its most extreme form, was brainwashing.

Its much more common form was "reform through labor" or "labor re-education." The principle behind the concept was that counterrevolution was a mistaken pattern of thought that could be changed, most effectively by indoctrination and persuasion, accompanied by a stiff regimen of physical labor. In extreme cases, persuasion was accompanied by isolation and torture. Labor reform continues to function as a court-imposed sentence of penal servitude, and labor reeducation remains among the most frequently employed sanctions available to the police, who can impose it without benefit of trial for terms of up to four years.

The third surviving Maoist element also present in its Confucian antecedent is the absence of a presumption of innocence. The criminal who was brought to trial was presumed guilty, a presumption that, wherever possible, should have been established by means of a confession. Because any profession of innocence was likely to be taken as a mistake with counterrevolutionary implications, defendants who refused to confess to the crimes of which they were accused were often subjected to all the tools of thought reform I have described. Once brought to trial, the defendant was routinely granted access to a defense lawyer, whose function was not to establish the defendant's innocence but to offer evidence in mitigation at the time of sentencing. The 1997 revisions to the criminal procedures law included at least a small step in the direction of establishing the presumption of innocence and giving defense lawyers an active role in criminal trials.

Establishing a fully functioning legal and judicial system was among the party-state's first priorities once the economic reforms were launched. The initial impetus to establish a system of laws during the reform era arose from China's rapidly expanding interaction with the world economy. Foreign firms that wanted to invest in or trade with China were reluctant to do so without laws in place that would regulate these transactions and protect all parties' interests. So, the first new laws defined the terms based on which joint ventures would be formed and trade would be conducted. Since then, the reforms themselves have created new circumstances that require regulation and adjudication, in response to which many new laws have been written and adopted by the National People's Congress.

A system of law, which the Chinese professed and continue to profess that they wish to establish, presupposes a number of elements, none of which were present in 1978. First, there needs to be clear, stable, and public laws. Second, there needs to be judges capable of adjudicating cases against the law. Finally, there needs to be lawyers who can represent defendants whose cases are brought to court. There has been a plethora of laws enacted over the last thirty years. The problem is thus not the quantity of new laws but rather their quality.

Three bodies at the level of the central government have the authority to issue laws. The National People's Congress is the principal among them, with the authority to issue what are called basic laws. Its Standing Committee, which acts in its name in the interval between its annual sessions, has the authority to promulgate and amend laws (except those enacted by the NPC). Finally, the State Council—China's cabinet, if you will—is the principal drafter of all laws and, in addition, has the power to issue administrative laws and regulations. In addition, provincial-level people's congresses are authorized to enact "local regulations." None of these responsibilities is clearly defined, and it must be remembered that all laws are subject to the review and approval of the party. Laws are thus the product of complex bureaucratic competition and reflect the compromises reached along the road to adoption. Moreover, laws drafted and approved by the party-state appear to be intentionally vague. American legal scholars attribute this to the Maoist habit of adapting experimental initiatives to diverse local conditions. The result is the use of "broad, indeterminate language" that requires officials to fit the law to specific cases.

Among the most important legal reforms were the substantial changes made to the criminal procedure law effective at the beginning of 1997. Before that, criminal cases were not brought to trial until the defendant had been proved guilty to the satisfaction of the court and the prosecutor, who worked closely together in investigating crimes. At trials, evidence was heard, and a panel of judges, some of them drawn from the local community, rendered its decision. Only at this point did the defense make its case, which was generally limited to presenting evidence in mitigation prior to sentencing. The new procedures have introduced the presumption of the defendant's innocence until proven guilty and have enhanced the role of the defense lawyer in criminal trials. Now, as before, the public is encouraged to attend most court proceedings, which are intended to provide uplifting lessons in civic behavior.

There have been reforms as well to the sanctions available to police and courts in prosecuting crimes of various sorts. With reform and growing prosperity, the opportunities for crime burgeoned in the early 1980s. The party-state retaliated with a series of "strike hard" campaigns, one result of which was to strengthen the hand of the police and to weaken the protection of the rights of the accused. Many of these measures remain in force: police are given broad discretion in incarcerating suspects as their cases are being investigated, particularly in "complex cases," whatever the police interpret that to mean. Labor reeducation is still in widespread use, as we have seen, and can be imposed without reference to the courts.

An especially odious punishment, known as shourong shencha (收容审查 shelter and investigation), was ended in 2003 by order of the newly appointed premier Wen Jiabao. The system had been under widespread use by urban police to intimidate and control the migrant worker population, once again without the benefit of legal oversight. In Guangzhou, a recent college graduate and graphic designer, Sun Zhigang, was snatched up by police and held in a shourong station because he had left his identity card behind in his room. He was held despite the intervention of his friends, and he died while in custody. Although the police attributed his death to a heart condition, an autopsy revealed he had been beaten to death. His case was taken up by a crusading newspaper, the Southern Metropolitan Daily, and investigative reporters uncovered numerous examples of police raping or beating those whom they incarcerated and extorting exorbitant sums from their relatives to secure their releases. When news of Sun's case reached the premier, he abolished the entire system by executive order.

The ultimate sanction—execution—has been massively over-used in China. For a number of years after the turn of the century, China was consistently executing more people than the rest of the world combined, as many as ten to fifteen thousand per year. For good reason, the party-state regards the number of executions it carries out as a state secret, and thus reliable statistics are not available to human rights groups monitoring the situation. But it does appear that international pressure has exerted an effect. In 2007, the Supreme People's Court reinstated its authority to review all capital sentences, an authority that had been delegated to provincial courts in 1983 to counter the mounting wave of crime in the country. The number of executions dropped close to tenfold the following year and currently stands at about 8,000 per year. Other estimates cite even lower numbers. Recently, the vice president of the Supreme People's Court wrote that the number of crimes for which the death penalty is appropriate will be significantly limited. It currently stands at 46.

As we have seen, the Supreme People's Court does not have the authority to interpret the constitution, except under very limited circumstances. That authority is vested in the Standing Committee of the NPC, and has yet to be exercised. The Supreme People's Court did for the first time overturn a provincial law in 2005, and the Standing Committee has floated the idea of a new review panel to mediate conflicts of law. While some hail this as a possible equivalent to a constitutional court, others deplore the fact that it is likely to operate behind closed doors and argue that the responsibility should belong to the courts.

As is the case with law in China today, so is the case with judges: the problem is not one of quantity but of quality. Although there are some 120,000 judges nationwide, many are demobilized PLA soldiers selected not for their intellect and judicial expertise but rather for their patriotism and their ideological correctness. The number of Chinese judges with postsecondary degrees has been growing rapidly and steadily since the reform period began. A law, enacted in 1995, requires newly appointed judges to have completed a bachelor's degree with a major in law as a minimum. Sitting judges were grandfathered in by the new law but are encouraged to pursue further study. As a result, there are many instances in which it is clear that judges are unsuccessful in grasping the subtleties of complex cases.

China's legal profession, though, has grown at an extraordinary rate. It started from a base of two law schools and about 3,000 lawyers at the beginning of the reform era. Today, there are 100 universities offering law subjects in China. Four of them offer the opportunity for students to pursue studies in the specialization of law, including international law, public law, and economic law. The country has more than 650,000 practicing lawyers, or one lawyer for every 2,150 people. (The comparable figures in the United States are 237 law schools and 1.3 million lawyers, or one lawyer for every 203 people.) But even more important than their expanding numbers is the emerging sense of independent professionalism among Chinese lawyers, who, in the past, saw themselves as no more than minor government bureaucrats.

It is this independent professionalism that the party finds deeply troubling. More than twenty cases of lawyers arrested and prosecuted in the course of their work have received prominent coverage in the international press in recent years. An example is the case of Chen Guangcheng, a blind lawyer noted for his defense of the rights of peasants in cases involving the appropriation of property and pollution of their villages. He was arrested in the summer of 2006 in Yinan County (沂南县), Shandong, charged with destroying public property and gathering a crowd to block traffic, crimes that his defenders noted would be challenging even for a sighted person to bring off. When two hundred people protested his arrest, his lawyers were detained. Sentenced to fifty-one months in prison, Chen appealed his conviction, and to the surprise of many, his conviction was overturned. Three months later, he was re-tried. His defense witnesses were prevented from entering the courtroom by what the press described as "thugs," and his sentence was reinstated. Observers interpreted the course of the case as indicative of a tug-of-war between central and local authorities. In addition, at least three major civil rights law firms have been closed down, and several dozen lawyers have had their licenses revoked. In 2006, the party-state enacted new rules requiring lawyers to submit to government supervision when representing clients in "politically delicate" cases. It would appear that, despite their professed enthusiasm for establishing a rule of law in China, party-state leaders are determined to limit the independence of the lawyers who practice that law.

This is curious in light of the fact that legal reform proceeded without interruption during the 1980s. Unlike other aspects of reform that periodically threatened to undermine the party's monopoly of political power, legal reform was a non-threatening way to create the appearance of moving toward a more modern, less arbitrary political system. But the goal was always to create a *system of laws,* never to establish the *rule of law,* a distinction that became fully evident at the end of the decade in the party's handling of the Tiananmen demonstration in 1989. As we have seen, a small group of retired leaders, feeling their backs to the wall, set aside laws, regulations, procedures, and regularly appointed officials in order to impose their disastrously misguided solution.

The events in Tiananmen Square on the night of 3 June 1989 served as a wake-up call for many thoughtful people in China. They also brought about a radical shift in American public opinion about China. Ever since Richard Nixon's visit to China in 1972, Americans had seemed to suspend judgment on the subject of Chinese politics, and many of those who called attention to the violation of human rights in the Soviet Union and Eastern Europe appeared to ignore comparable violations in the People's Republic of China. This dual standard suffered a fatal blow when tanks rumbled down the streets of Beijing.

Serious misunderstandings arise when Americans and Chinese sit down to talk about human rights. There are not only very different assumptions that the two sides bring to the table, but also very different definitions of the term *human rights* and what it encompasses. Where Americans emphasize China's failure to guarantee political and civil rights, the Chinese emphasize the American failure to acknowledge China's accomplishments in guaranteeing its citizens' economic and social rights.

A comprehensive definition of human rights would include economic, social, political, and civil categories. *Economic* rights protect the individual's access to sustenance and participation in the workforce. *Social* rights guarantee access to goods and services provided by the state, such as education, social security, and health care. *Political* rights guarantee the individual's ability to participate in the political process. *Civil* rights protect the individual from illegitimate interference by other individuals or by the state. It is true that an assessment of the protection of human rights in all four of these categories reveals both positive and negative results in China. Paradoxically, economic reforms have expanded human rights in some areas but restricted them in others.

The Chinese point with pride to the accomplishments of their state in extending the right to sustenance to the entire population. They claim that apart from the period immediately following the Great Leap Forward, when many died of starvation and hunger was widespread in much of the country, China has managed to avoid the devastating famines of the past. Output of food has increased, the distribution system has improved, and public works projects have reduced the destructive effects of natural disasters. Yet economic reform has both advanced the right to sustenance and jeopardized its future: it enhanced agricultural productivity but initially fell short in limiting population growth and reducing the amount of land under cultivation.

Prior to the initiation of economic reforms, China's planned economy provided universal employment, and though many people in the rural and urban sectors were underemployed, they all were guaranteed the right of access to the workforce. The creation of a labor market and a gradual loosening of controls over the flow of workers from job to job, place to place, and even sector to sector have given China's workers new freedom, but employment is no longer universal. Rural production team leaders are no longer at their posts, finding some kind of work for everyone. Once the fiscal crisis in the state sector began to be seriously addressed, many workers who had formerly been guaranteed jobs found themselves unemployed. If current trends persist, unemployment rates among women will be significantly higher than those among men.

With respect to social rights, the achievements of the Chinese government during its first fifty years in power are impressive. As I will show, access to public education, medical care, and retirement income have all increased substantially. The economic reforms have had mixed effects on the state's ability to guarantee these social rights, particularly to rural citizens. The household responsibility system led to an increase in the number of children leaving school before graduation, since the system's incentives encourage parents to make their children work in the fields or local factories as soon as they are old enough. While health care has improved substantially, as we will see, there are still gaps in coverage of rural areas. As for social security, the shrinking of the state sector has significantly reduced the proportion of workers with access to state-funded pensions. A new system funded directly by the government rather than by individual state-owned enterprises, with workers matching the government funds with a percentage of their wages, has begun to be implemented. But until this system is fully operative, most Chinese workers will have no access to a regular income upon retirement.

The record with respect to political rights is somewhat different. Here, although the right to participate in politics is widespread, that participation is generally devoid of significance. Elections are regularly held for executive and legislative posts, but until recently, never with more than a single candidate for each position—a candidate selected and vetted by the party. A little-publicized component of the political reforms of the 1980s, the democratization of local politics, has resulted in several candidates running for certain offices, and it is by no means always the party-endorsed candidate who wins. So, the reforms have made political participation somewhat more meaningful, if only locally.

Civil rights are the subject that Americans debate about most, and the debate is sometimes difficult for the Chinese to understand. Asked whether their lives are subject to more or less government interference than they were twenty years ago, the majority of Chinese would likely respond that they are significantly freer. They can speak relatively freely and critically about political issues, read and hear a reasonably broad range of information and opinions, and make decisions about their places of residence, careers, and leisure that were formerly made for them. But this expansion of civil rights is less the intended consequence of party or government policy than the unintended consequence of the weakening of party and government influence.

An exception is the debate within the party-state about expanding freedom of information. In this debate, it is assumed by both sides that unorthodox ideas are imported, not domestic commodities. A campaign against "spiritual pollution" was launched in 1983, and there have been sporadic rumblings since about "bourgeois liberalism." Arguing against the conservatives who advocate closing off China from undesirable foreign influences, Deng and his like-minded colleagues used an analogy: to allow fresh air into a room, one must open the windows. Along with the fresh air, flies and mosquitoes may come in, but that is not enough to justify closing the windows.

Among the most important contributors to a heightened Chinese awareness of civil rights is one of those "flies and mosquitoes" that Deng spoke about—information, that is, about civil rights in other political systems. As we will explore more fully in Chapter 16, information technology has radically expanded Chinese citizens' awareness of the outside world, despite the government's most assiduous efforts to erect firewalls to thwart its spread. Although religious belief was seen as antithetical to Marxism-Leninism and religious practices and artifacts were subject to attack by fervent Red Guards, traditional Chinese religions have enjoyed something of a revival during the five decades since the Cultural Revolution. Article 36 of the Chinese Constitution guarantees citizens of the PRC the freedom of religious belief. It goes on to state that "no state organ, public organization or individual may compel citizens to believe in, or not to believe in, any religion." While the state is assigned the responsibility to protect "normal" religious activities, individuals are precluded from using religion to disrupt public order. Finally, casting an eye on the country's past experience with external missionaries, the article states that religious affairs "are not subject to any foreign domination."

In looking at statistics about religious practice in China today, one should bear in mind that, except for the clergy, Daoism and Buddhism are not exclusive denominations. Rather, depending on one's immediate circumstances, a visit to either a Daoist or a Buddhist temple might be appropriate. Thus, when statisticians tell us that there are some four hundred million Daoists and seven hundred million Buddhists among the Chinese population, the two may well be overlapping groups. While these two religions are observed primarily by the majority Han population, Islam is observed primarily by minority populations and numbers some twenty-five million adherents nationwide.

The Falun Gong movement seriously agitates the party-state. Based on *qigong* (氣功), a traditional system of physical and mental exercise, and combining elements of Daoism and Buddhism, Falun Gong was founded by Li Hongzhi in 1992. From the party- state's point of view, the movement very clearly "disrupted public order" when ten thousand of its adherents demonstrated in front of *Zhongnanhai,* the office and residential compound of senior party leaders in central Beijing. The movement was banned, its founder fled to the United States, and its practitioners moved underground. Estimates suggest that there are tens of millions of adherents worldwide.

The party-state finds equally unacceptable those elements of Tibetan Buddhism and Islam that it believes have taken on a political, anti-state character. It is the government's position that external agitators (the Dalai Lama in the case of Tibetan Buddhism, and individuals like Rebiya Kadeer in the case of Islam in Xinjiang) are allegedly promoting "splittism" in their respective sects.

In light of the strenuous exertions of Western missionaries in China beginning with the Jesuits in the late sixteenth century and culminating in the work of both Catholics and Protestants in the late nineteenth and early twentieth centuries, it is somewhat ironic that there are significantly more active Chinese Christians today than when the missionary movement was at its height a century ago. In keeping with its constitutional concern with "foreign domination," the Chinese have authorized a domestic Catholic Church and a domestic Protestant Church. The Chinese Catholic Patriotic Association claims some six million members, and the Protestant Three-Self Patriotic Movement has some 20 million members. There are, in addition, unauthorized "house churches" in China. Many members of the Catholic house churches maintain their loyalty to the Vatican, which has, for many years, attempted without success to normalize its relationship with the government in Beijing. Estimates of those attending house churches range between forty and fifty million.

American human rights organizations and the U.S. Congress have been less interested in the rapid expansion of civil rights for the majority of Chinese people than they are in the very serious violation of the civil rights of a small minority, the individuals who have been imprisoned or sentenced to labor reeducation for their dissident political or religious views. China has the largest prison population in the world. It has some 685 prisons with around 1.5 million prisoners, including 19,000 juveniles. Another 260,000 are in slightly less harsh "reeducation through labor" prisons, but I have seen no reliable estimate of the fraction who are imprisoned for political crimes. The San Francisco-based *Dui Hua* (对话 Dialogue) Foundation keeps a database of political prisoners based on what it calls open-source material from the Chinese press and the Chinese government. At this writing, that database contains some 50,000 records. Those who have survived prolonged incarceration in the labor reform camps say that prisoners are often treated with extraordinary harshness, deprived of regular contact with their families and friends, and only under very unusual circumstances are released and allowed to return to their normal lives when their sentences expire.

Wei Jingsheng, for many years the most highly publicized political prisoner in China, was jailed in 1979 for his views on the need to democratize the Chinese political system. He was released in September 1993, six months before his fifteen-year sentence expired, in what many took to be a transparent ploy to help in China's unsuccessful bid to secure the 2000 Summer Olympics. Six months thereafter, he was rearrested and imprisoned, accused this time of illicit contact with foreign visitors and reporters. Three years later, on the eve of then-president Jiang Zemin's trip to Washington, he was released and exiled to the United States, where he currently lives, on the grounds that his health had deteriorated and that he required specialized medical attention.

Several aspects of Wei's case are worthy of note. Wei experienced particularly harsh treatment for at least two reasons: first, he was a worker, not an intellectual or a student, and the government considers disaffected workers an even greater threat to political stability than it does disaffected intellectuals or students; second, what he wrote and said seems to have aroused the personal animosity of Deng Xiaoping. As a result, his case was always dealt with at the very highest levels of the government, and favorable treatment was accorded him only with the greatest reluctance. Finally, his release from prison on both occasions came as an official response to external pressure—in the first instance, that of the International Olympic Committee, in the second, that of the U.S. State Department.

Other prominent political prisoners whose cases have been closely followed by the international community were imprisoned because of their roles in the student demonstrations of 1989. Although most of the student leaders were successfully spirited out of China after the suppression of the movement (most through Hong Kong), some were arrested, tried, and jailed. One of them, Wang Dan, was imprisoned for four years, released in 1993, and then reimprisoned in 1995. Like Wei Jingsheng, he was released for a second time on the eve of a state visit—this one, President Bill Clinton's visit to China in 1998—and he was sent to the United States for medical treatment. Wang Dan is currently living in Taiwan, where he is a member of the faculty of Tsing Hua University.

The most senior official to be arrested, tried, and imprisoned for his actions in connection with Tiananmen was Bao Tong, an aide to Zhao Ziyang, who was dismissed from his position as premier for having sympathized with the student demonstrators and placed under house arrest until his death in 2005. Released in 1997, Bao Tong disregarded the government's insistence that he refrain from airing his political opinions. He has often publicly demanded a reassessment of the Tiananmen episode and a stop to its characterization as a "counterrevolutionary incident." Bao Tong was one of the three former officials who arranged for the publication of Zhao's secretly tape-recorded memoirs. In 2005, Bao Tong and his wife were injured in attacks by more than 20 plainclothes security agents as they attempted to leave their home to pay their respects to the family of Zhao Ziyang, who died in January of that year. The authorities would only allow him access to a doctor if he removed a white flower (traditional symbol of mourning) pinned to his vest. He refused. Bao died in Beijing in 2022 at the age of 90. Thirty-five years after the Tiananmen incident, fourteen prominent participants of that movement are still behind bars for their actions in 1989.

Two more examples of high-profile cases point up the fact that while civil and political rights for many Chinese have expanded greatly, there are still hot-button issues that trigger a harsh response from the party-state. During a visit to China by President Bill Clinton in 1998, Wang Youcai attempted to register a new political party—the China Democratic Party (CDP) (*Zhongguo Minzhu Dang* 中国民主党)—at Hangzhou's city hall. The registration was rejected, and the following day, he was arrested, charged, tried (without the benefit of defense lawyers), and sentenced to eleven years in prison. On the same day, Xu Wenli, a cofounder of the CDP, was sentenced to thirteen years, like Wang, for "negating the leadership of the CCP." Xu had been an active member of the democracy movement since the time of the Democracy Wall that flourished briefly after Deng's accession to power. Wang was an active participant in the student occupation of Tiananmen in 1989. Acceding to international pressure, the party-state released the two after four and six years, respectively, and both were exiled to the United States. The hundreds of other supporters of the China Democratic Party (CDP) who were arrested were not so fortunate. Many of them remain incarcerated.

Another attempt to introduce political reform into the Chinese system resulted in the arrest and imprisonment of prominent intellectuals. In December 2008, some three thousand intellectuals signed and published a document they called "Charter 08" (零八宪章) that called for the rule of law and an end to one-party rule. As it was being published, Liu Xiaobo, a prominent reform intellectual and president of the Independent Chinese PEN Center, was arrested and placed under "residential surveillance" in a hotel in suburban Beijing. Liu was charged with "subversion of the government and overthrow of the socialist system" (counterrevolution by another name), and in December 2009, he was tried and sentenced to eleven years in prison. He died in 2017 after being treated for terminal liver cancer in a heavily guarded hospital in northeast China.

In recent years, the Chinese authorities have turned their attention to another category of intellectuals they find troublesome: Chinese who, educated abroad, have returned to China to conduct research. In at least a dozen cases, researchers, several of them naturalized U.S. citizens, have been arrested and charged with stealing state secrets and espionage. Among the more bizarre cases was that of Zhao Yan. Although not educated in the United States, Zhao was employed as a researcher for *The New York Times*' Beijing bureau. The "state secret" that he was alleged to have revealed to his employers was Jiang Zemin's intention to resign as chairman of the Central Military Commission. The "revelation" occurred two weeks in advance of the resignation's being publicly announced in the Chinese press. Zhao was arrested in September 2004, held incommunicado for six months, indicted on the state secrets charge as well as a charge of fraud, and, after the former charge was dropped, eventually tried and convicted. Despite the very substantial pressure brought to bear by the *Times* and the U.S. State Department, Zhao was released only after having completed his three-year sentence in 2007.

International human rights organizations have been very effective in compiling information on China's prisoners of conscience, tracking their cases, and putting pressure on the government to improve their treatment in prison, to give them medical attention when needed, and even, in some cases, to release them prior to the expiration of their sentences. On the basis of part of the information gathered by these organizations, the U.S. government has espoused particular cases, sometimes with positive results, in other instances less successfully.

Chinese human rights record once again came to the forefront of international attention in June 2020 when a group of nearly fifty United Nations independent experts issued a report calling on China to "abide by its international legal obligations" respecting human rights. They raised their "grave concerns" on issues ranging from the collective repression of specific communities—especially religious and ethnic minorities in Xinjiang and Tibet—in addition to disappearances of human rights defenders across the country. They also expressed alarm over allegations of forced labor in both formal and informal sectors of the economy, as well as arbitrary interferences with the right to privacy, cybersecurity laws that authorize censorship, and anti-terrorism and sedition laws applicable in Hong Kong. They called for renewed attention on the human rights situation in the country and urged China to invite civil and political rights monitors to conduct independent missions "in an environment of confidentiality and respect for human rights defenders." They encouraged the UN Human Rights Council to urgently monitor Chinese human rights practices.

Four months later, nearly 40 mainly Western countries, in a statement read at a meeting of the General Assembly's Human Rights Committee, echoed the concerns of the UN experts, criticized China's treatment of minority groups, and expressed grave concern at the impact of the new national security law on human rights in Hong Kong. They urged China "to uphold autonomy, rights and freedoms in Hong Kong and to respect the independence of the Hong Kong judiciary." Finally, they also expressed their grave concern "about the existence of a large network of 'political re-education' camps in Xinjiang where credible reports indicate that over a million people have been arbitrarily detained."

Then-Chinese Ambassador Zhang Jun rejected the statement and pushed back on any outside interference in Hong Kong, accusing the United States and others of abusing the United Nations' platform, politicizing human rights issues, and provoking "political confrontation and antagonism." "They spread false information and a political virus, smear China and interfere in Chinese affairs," he told the Human Rights Committee. "China firmly opposes and rejects that." He lashed out especially at the Trump administration, saying, "Your despicable acts are completely at odds with the trend of history. Blaming China cannot cover up your poor human rights records."

There are several points on which it is worth reflecting as we consider what Americans can do to bring about an improvement in China's human rights record. The first has to do with our assumptions about the universality of our views on law and human rights, our notion that they are appropriate standards for all societies to adopt, regardless of their possible disjunction with other traditions and cultures. The second point is often raised in Chinese rejoinders to American complaints about their human rights violations. In looking at conditions in another country, Americans often measure real conditions abroad against an idealized vision of conditions at home and thus seem blind to violations of human rights in our own society at the same time that they ferret out evidence of violations elsewhere.

A third point to bear in mind is that asking China's leaders to allow dissidents freedom of movement and expression is a lot more complicated than one might think. China's leaders understand the party's weaknesses and are well aware of the many sources of dissatisfaction within Chinese society. As they often say, political instability threatens the nation's continued economic development; more importantly, it threatens the leaders' own power, positions, and perquisites. Under these circumstances, they would regard giving free rein to dissidents as an act of national betrayal and political suicide.

The importance the Chinese attach to the question of sovereignty is a fourth point worth touching on. The Chinese interpret the history of their interaction with the outside world during the nineteenth century as a long series of painful episodes of national humiliation in which foreign powers constantly trampled on China's sovereignty. "Ours will no longer be a nation subject to insult and humiliation. We have stood up." were the words Mao chose to mark the founding of the People's Republic of China in 1949. For over three-quarters of a century, the Chinese government has been especially sensitive to incursions on its sovereignty, and it regards foreign comment on its handling of the civil and political rights of its citizens as a serious infringement. The position is not irrational; imagine the reactions of the American government if the Chinese government were to make continued American investment in joint ventures contingent on Congress enacting legislation overturning the Supreme Court's 2007 decision in *Parents Involved in Community Schools v. Seattle School District No. 1* and requiring school districts to take racial balancing into account in assigning students to schools.

Another point has to do with linking human rights with access to the American market. Frustrated by a lack of leverage in dealing with the Chinese government, members of Congress seized on China's most favored nation status (MFN) as one of the few tools available to secure compliance with demands related to human rights, and successive administrations responded with an argument about the number of American jobs that would be lost were China to retaliate by cutting back its imports from the United States. Each year, the White House proposed renewing MFN for China, and after extensive debate, Congress approved it. After thirteen years of negotiations, the U.S.-China trade agreement was signed in 1999, paving the way for China's entry into the World Trade Organization in 2001. One provision of this agreement had the United States granting China permanent "normal trade relations" (a new and more accurate term than "most favored nation"). This was a difficult decision for Congress to make, because it deprived it of the annual opportunity to act upon China's human rights practices, but the approval was coupled with new laws creating a commission that would undertake an annual assessment of human rights in China.

A final point has to do with tactics. We often seem to forget that when we deal with Chinese officialdom, we need to do so in a way that minimizes the potential for their losing face. This is problematic, for very often U.S. government actions are effective in the American political context only if they are carried out in a high-profile and public manner. Two examples—the one successful, the other much less so—serve to illustrate this point.

The American embassy in Beijing served as a safe haven for the well-known dissident astrophysicist Fang Lizhi and his wife for several months in the immediate aftermath of the Tiananmen massacre. Through quiet, protracted, and skillful negotiations, James Lilley, then the American ambassador, secured permission from the Chinese authorities for Fang and his wife to leave China unharmed. Lilley was successful because he gave the authorities a face-saving stratagem: Fang had suffered a mild heart irregularity, and when told of this, the authorities could describe his release for treatment abroad as a humanitarian gesture on their part, not as caving in to foreign pressure.

But considerably less successful, because they were carried out in the glare of full press coverage, were former Secretary of State Warren Christopher's efforts to raise human rights issues during his visit to Beijing in March 1994. The Chinese foreign minister could not afford to appear to have given ground to the United States, particularly because the National People's Congress was then assembled in Beijing. Christopher, likewise, had to take a tough position to reassure those in the United States who were arguing against the renewal of China's MFN status. No progress was made during the visit.

The most consistently successful efforts on behalf of Chinese religious and political dissidents are private, not public. They are the work of an American businessman, John Kamm, who, for several years while he was based in Hong Kong and, since 1995, from his *Dui Hua* Foundation based in San Francisco, has taken up with the Chinese authorities the causes of more than 250 dissidents on a case-by-case basis. He is effective because he understands the importance of working slowly and quietly with his Chinese interlocutors to get them to agree without their losing face.

Chapter 8: The People's Liberation Army

The current structure of the People's Liberation Army is the product of reforms initiated under Xi Jinping and endorsed by the Third Plenum of the 18th Central Committee of the CCP in 2013. The nominally civilian hand that controls the gun in China is that of the Central Military Commission (CMC). In fact, there are two CMCs- one appointed by the party and one by the state. In practice, they function as one. The seven-member party commission was chaired by Deng Xiaoping himself until 1989, when he relinquished the position to Jiang Zemin. Two years after Jiang stepped down as president and party general secretary, he resigned his chairmanship of the Central Military Commission and was succeeded by Hu Jintao. The position is currently occupied by Xi Jinping. The commission hardly constitutes civilian control, given that all its members save Xi are uniformed officers and include the minister of national defense.

Diagram #1:

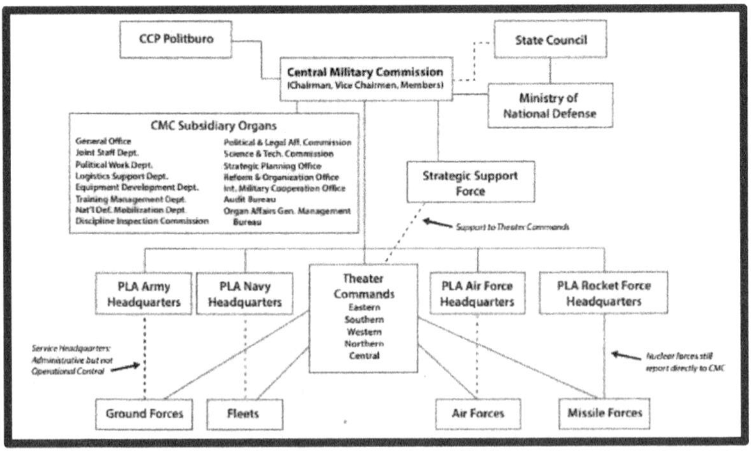

Structure of the People's Liberation Army

Source: Center for Strategic and International Studies, Chinese Strategy and Military Modernization in 2016: A Comparative Analysis (2016)

The CMC oversees the operation of four major departments: the General Office, the Joint Staff Department, the Political Work Department, and the Logistics Support Department. There are, in addition, eleven other departments under CMC supervision.

The General Office, which has operational command of the three million active troops and takes responsibility for operational planning, intelligence, and procurement; the General Logistics Department, which is responsible for finance, supply, maintenance, and transport; the General Political Department, which ensures the political correctness of the military forces, drafts regulations, and runs personnel matters, including assignment, promotion, and retirement; and the Equipment Development Department, which is responsible for weapons development and procurement. In addition, under the supervision of the CMC are the Ministry of National Defense (whose responsibilities are largely limited to overseeing the PLA's relations with foreign militaries); the Commission on Science, Technology, and Industry for National Defense (which, among other responsibilities, oversees China's space program); and three military universities. Operating under the four departments are the four branches of the PLA: the ground forces, the navy, the air force, the rocket force, and the armed police.

Also operating under the four departments are the five theater commands, each encompassing several provinces and major cities. The theater commands cover only the territory within China. Operations beyond China's borders are centrally directed by the Joint Staff Department of the CMC. The CMC remains the highest decision-making body, and the Chinese military does not have a commander-in-chief as does the United States in its president. The theater commands handle command operations, while the equipping and organizing of military units are handled by the individual services.

Source: Center for Strategic and International Studies, Chinese Strategy and Military Modernization in 2016: A Comparative Analysis (2016)

During the first seven decades of the People's Republic, there were seven military regions, the commanders of which were initially the generals whose troops had been responsible for "liberating" the areas under their command. Concurrently holding positions in local party and government organizations, they became well-connected fixtures, advantageously placed to implement, modify, or ignore central directives. But this monopoly of local power was broken by Premier Zhou Enlai, who shortly before his death in 1976 reassigned most of the regional commanders to new posts. Such reassignments have recurred periodically since then, and they reduce the resources with which the regional commanders are able to resist central directives, though not their tendency to try to do so. As in the civilian political structure, where provincial and local government officials often thwart the implementation of directives issued by the central government, regional commanders and their subordinate garrison commanders often thwart the commands issued by the central military authorities.

Naval forces serve under three fleet commands. The North Sea Fleet is based at Qingdao in Shandong Province; the East Sea Fleet headquarters are in Ningbo, near Shanghai. Finally, the South Sea Fleet is based at Zhanjiang in Guangdong Province.

All in all, the PLA, including the army, navy, and air force, has a troop of about 2.3 million men and women, just over half the size of the force level of the late 1970s, when the PLA had been increased in size in anticipation of the 1979 border war with Vietnam. Since 1985, close to 2 million troops have been demobilized, returning the army to its pre-Vietnam size. This force is somewhat less than twice the size of the U.S. military, which as of 2008 had about 1.4 million people in uniform.

Table 7: Chinese Military Troop Strength

Army	965,000
Navy	252,000
Air Force	400,000
Rocket Force	120,000
Strategic Support Force	145,000
Joint Logistics Support Force	150,000
Subtotal uniformed troops	2,035,000
People's Armed Police People's Militia	1,500,000 4,000,000
Total	**7,535,000**

Beyond the uniformed personnel, the Chinese military establishment includes about four million military dependents and several million civilian employees and workers. Finally, the People's Armed Police (PAP), administered as a branch of the

PLA and having 1,500,000 members, is the first line of defense in the case of civil unrest. It was because the PAP was so unsuccessful at this in the spring of 1989 that the PLA was called in. In the aftermath of the Tiananmen massacre, the PAP was strengthened substantially. Its budget was augmented, and its riot control equipment upgraded, and a large number of demobilized PLA troops were reassigned to the PAP.

Diagram 2:

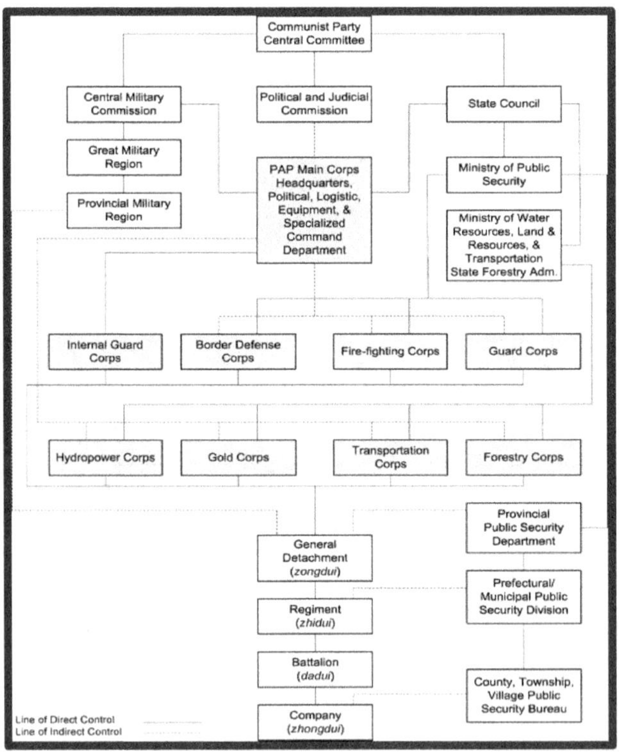

Organization of the People's Armed Police

Source: www.china.org.cn

The military establishment also includes a People's Militia of some four million members that operates under the National Defense Mobilization Commission, which is dually subordinate to the State Council and the CMC. The China Maritime Militia is a subset of the national militia and operates under the command of the PLA Navy and the China Coast Guard.

China's armed forces and the military budget that supports them are the world's largest, and the budget has been expanding rapidly. A portion of the funds has gone for new equipment from foreign suppliers, including planes, submarines, and weapons, and other Asia-Pacific powers naturally see this upgrading of the Chinese arsenal as related to a possibly aggressive and expansionist policy.

The military budget passed annually by the National People's Congress alone is insufficient to underwrite the modernization of China's armed forces, and external observers regularly calculate the country's total military expenditures as somewhere between two and four times the published budget. The official budget is thirty times larger today than it was before the reforms of the late 1970s and now stands at just over $249 billion per year. In recent years, it has stabilized at just under five percent of the total national budget.

Some have argued that the large budget increases accorded the PLA between 1989 and 1994 constituted a *quid pro quo* for services rendered when the PLA came to the aid of the party elders, but others take a longer view, seeing the expansion as compensation for the 1980s, when military budgets shrank in real terms, and for the late 1990s, when the army was stripped of control of a network of factories and enterprises, the profits from which augmented the defense budget.

The reform goal had been described as the four modernizations of agriculture, industry, science and technology, and the armed forces, and Deng told the PLA that he took the sequence in which these were listed seriously; military modernization had to wait until Chinese industry and technology could supply the needs of the PLA. Past experience, with the armed forces heavily dependent on Soviet equipment, training, and technical assistance, was not to be repeated. So, the military budgets of the 1980s reflected these priorities, first decreasing after the post-Vietnam demobilization, then averaging less than 4 percent annual growth while the national budget increased at three times that rate. Taking the effects of inflation into account, one can see that the PLA actually lost ground over the decade 1978-88; prices doubled while military expenditures increased by only 25 percent, giving a net effect of a 2.3 percent loss per year.

Another way of putting it is to say that budget increases between 1989 and 1994, which averaged a bit over 16 percent, did no more than allow the armed forces to recoup their position at the beginning of the reform period. An index of real growth in military expenditures using 1978 as 100 shows a figure of just 104 for 2025.

As one might imagine, the decline in military expenditures had a serious effect on morale, as military pay fell seriously behind civilian wages. It has since recovered. Whereas in 1988 an officer earned only a little more than half of what an average urban worker earned, today that officer earns nearly twice the wage of the urban worker. Once, the PLA had been a highly desirable avenue of advancement for rural young people, offering training, good pay, and perhaps most importantly, geographical mobility, and there had been stiff competition to get in, so recruits tended to be very capable young people. More recently, with so many lucrative employment opportunities in the countryside and the freedom to move to the city to find even better-paying work, fewer qualified young people were attracted to a military career. But the effects of the world financial crisis on China's employment opportunities have turned that situation around, and more recent college graduates are choosing to join the military.

The official military budget of $246 billion per year tells only part of the story–by far the smaller part, some argue. The "real" Chinese military budget is harder to estimate because it is not a matter of public record, and depending on the accounting practices one employs, the numbers vary from two to five times the official figure. A figure of $585 billion, roughly the midpoint between the lowest and the highest estimate, is accepted by most foreign observers. Were this figure accurate, it would place China second after the United States in military expenditure, with its military outlay at 3.2 percent of gross domestic product, a rate very nearly equal to that of the United States. For their part, Chinese officials steadfastly insist that the published military budget includes all income and expenditures.

On the expenditure side, this real budget, more than twice the official budget, includes a range of goods, services, and even salaries that are usually included in the reporting of military budgets in other countries. Among these items are expenditures on research and development, on the People's Armed Police, and on reserve forces, which currently number about 200,000 troops.

The PLA has had two major sources of income that are not reported in the official budget. The first, the sale of weapons to foreign purchasers, is estimated to have been nearly $2 billion annually in the late 1980s. With the end of the Iran-Iraq War, to both sides of which China supplied arms, and with pressure from the United States and other nations to restrict these arms sales, China has reduced the volume, but they probably continue to generate up to $800 million annually.

A second source of off-budget revenue came from a network of military-owned and operated factories and enterprises. Profits from the sale of civilian products produced in factories controlled by the military may, until recently, have contributed as much as an additional four billion dollars per year to PLA revenues. Until the late 1990s, the armed forces were responsible for some ten thousand factories that employed about seven hundred thousand workers. Most of these were administered by the General Logistics Department; others, by the General Political, General Armaments, and General Staff departments.

This network of military factories was the legacy of Mao's policy initiative to make the army self-sufficient in food and supplies and to promote the development of China's hinterlands. Locating military factories in remote areas had two advantages: the army's sources of supplies would be dispersed and thus more impervious to enemy attack, and industrialization of the hinterlands would contribute to Mao's paramount goal of egalitarian development of China as a whole. At the peak of its expansion, this so-called third line of defense-managed factories numbered thirty thousand and employed nearly three million people.

Today, enemy attack is a less than present danger, and the goal of egalitarian development has been abandoned in favor of a policy of building on the best, so the third-line factories seem more a liability than an asset. Efforts have been underway for some years to relocate them nearer lines of communication, redirect their production, restore their profitability, transform their ownership, and close those that cannot easily be transformed. During the 1980s, the central military authorities inaugurated a range of new enterprises, among them a commercial satellite-launching service. Their expanded economic activities not only augmented the lean budgets of that period but also gave work to some of the one million soldiers demobilized then.

At the beginning of the reform period, about eight percent of the output of military-managed factories was destined for the civilian economy, but by 1992 the proportion had risen to 65 percent, and before the orders to divest in 1998 and 2000, it had reached 85 percent. One estimate placed the market share of these consumer goods at 20 percent and suggested that the PLA had at one time set a 50 percent market share as its target. In addition to these state-sector factories, a plethora of collective enterprises attached to regional and local military commands and operated by uniformed troops or their dependents were spawned by the armed forces. Profits from these enterprises, impossible to calculate, generally went directly to the command under which they operated and were mostly used to augment the pay and benefits of the troops.

Finally, the PLA was not immune to the attraction of foreign joint ventures. There were, at one point, more than two dozen such foreign-invested military firms. The army's economic activity had an important unintended effect. It enmeshed the armed forces deeply in China's new market economy and its connections with the world economy, and where they were once regarded as a conservative force opposed to economic reform, many military officers would now have found their personal and professional interests seriously prejudiced were the reforms to be reversed.

There were two principal reasons underlying the party-state's decision to divest the PLA of its nonmilitary production. First, of the ten thousand PLA-managed factories, probably a third were losing money each year- a performance record significantly better than that of the rest of the state sector but still resulting in a drain on PLA coffers. Second, soldiers as economic buccaneers adversely affected combat readiness; time, energy, and thought spent managing businesses are time, energy, and thought not spent in military training. The PLA's capability to defend China's borders and its national interests was hardly strengthened by encouraging the military to augment its revenue through entrepreneurship. As one foreign observer of the Chinese military commented, "At the end of the day, this was an army that was more interested in making money than it was in being the guardian of the national interest."

With this concern in mind, in the summer of 1998, Jiang Zemin, in his capacity as chairman of the Central Military Commission, ordered the PLA to divest itself of its nonmilitary-related industrial and commercial interests. His instructions were part of a broader effort to reduce the degree to which government agencies were dabbling for profits in the fast-growing economy. The military establishment was slow to comply with Jiang's order, offloading primarily its low-end, debt-ridden enterprises onto the reluctant shoulders of local governments. Two years later, Jiang reiterated his order, and by 2009, outside observers were describing the divestiture as "mainly complete." Remaining under the control of the PLA are those industries–manufacturers of weapons, uniforms, and the like–that directly supply the needs of the army itself.

The term "praetorian rule" is sometimes used to describe a situation that results from a nation's military force seizing control from a government it regards as inept or corrupt. Under what circumstances might the PLA be tempted to establish praetorian rule in China, and how capable would it be of doing so?

The party has been very effective in preventing the emergence of any national organization that could mount strong political opposition. There is no church, no labor union, no political party in China that could do what these organizations did in Eastern Europe and the former Soviet Union when Communist Party control unraveled. The Chinese people, told that their choice is between party rule and anarchy, have reluctantly but firmly chosen party rule. But in fact, there is a third choice: the PLA could step in should the party collapse in the same fashion that the Communist Party of the Soviet Union collapsed in August 1991.

The army has a number of characteristics that lend themselves to its serving as a praetorian administration. Most important, of course, is its arms. The army has served and could certainly serve again as a backup for the People's Armed Police in quelling civil disturbance. It is also highly patriotic, and its intense patriotism could motivate it to intervene politically were there a real danger of the collapse of central authority and a breakup of the Chinese state into a state of anarchy. And the PLA enjoys credibility. While many people in China have come to question the credibility of the party, fewer question the legitimacy of the army. As a corollary, the PLA has a reputation for being less corrupt than the party.

As noted earlier, in January and February 1967, because of their personal loyalty to Mao Zedong, officers of the People's Liberation Army stepped in to take positions on Revolutionary committees, tripartite governing bodies made up of "revolutionary rebels," party cadres, and members of the PLA. The army's involvement in civil administration during the Cultural Revolution lasted until 1978, when the revolutionary committees were formally abolished. Eleven years later, in 1989, because of its commanders' personal loyalty to Deng Xiaoping, the military rallied in Beijing to enforce martial law and once again to save a regime on the brink of collapse.

It is highly unlikely that the PLA would agree to do so again on the same terms. With the possible exception of Xi Jinping, no other political leader has personal connections with the military equivalent to those that Mao and Deng used to secure its compliance, and the negative consequences of the 1989 intervention were very serious, losing the PLA's respect in the eyes of many of China's urban population and highly valued contacts with foreign military leaders as well. The next time out, it will be patriotism rather than loyalty to the party or to particular leaders that brings the military into the political arena. Although they could use New party leaders as a cover for their actions, they would function as an alternative to the existing party, not as a crutch for it.

But could the PLA succeed in restoring central authority? The PLA and the PAP have an all-but-total monopoly of armed force in Chinese society. As the legitimacy of the party and the central government has declined and the independence of local and regional governments has increased, the implicit threat of the use of this armed force has become politically more and more important. But the PLA was ill-equipped and ill-trained for what it did in the streets of Lhasa and Beijing in 1989. Upgrading the PAP in budget, equipment, and training after those episodes was intended to rectify its shortcomings in civil enforcement, but the PAP's performance in Tibet in 2008 and Xinjiang in 2009 fell short of Beijing's expectations. It is easy to imagine the 1.5-million-strong PAP, backed by the 2.3-million-strong PLA, stretched very thin were it forced to restore and maintain order over any significant portion of China.

Public respect for the party and the PLA derives from their having fought a successful revolution. Respect for the party seriously eroded over decades of disastrously counterproductive economic and social policies, but respect for the PLA suffered no such decline in the 1950s and 1960s; indeed, its reputation was enhanced by its effectiveness when the Cultural Revolution threatened anarchy.

But China's urban population lost respect for the military at the time of the Tiananmen massacre; that this loss of respect did not go beyond the cities was due to a surprisingly effective propaganda blitz about the "counterrevolutionary incident," which portrayed the PLA troops as victims rather than perpetrators. Hence, while in the cities neither party nor army is popular, in the populace as a whole, respect for the PLA almost certainly outweighs respect for the party.

From early on, this has been based in great part on the PLA's reputation for scrupulous honesty, tight discipline, and incorruptibility, especially during the revolution and civil war, but after 1949 as well. As corruption has come to taint China's politics more and more, and as politicians have failed to curb it, the PLA's reputation for honesty has frequently been called to public attention. Unfortunately, that reputation is not what it once was. During the Cultural Revolution, the PLA became deeply involved with national and local political machines, which gave it new opportunities to engage in corrupt behavior. More recently, corruption is flourishing where the political realm intersects with the economy, and the PLA's heavy involvement in entrepreneurial activity in the 1980s and 1990s was the source of most of the current perception of corruption in the ranks.

On the other hand, in some respects, the PLA is ill-suited or potentially ineffective as a praetorian force. It is a specialist organization, not an organization of generalists, and it is short on experience in civilian administration. Although it is reasonably unified, exercising the responsibilities of civil administration would very likely divide it along several fault lines. Because national defense is its mission, there is no reason to expect that its officers would be especially good at directing economic development or political and economic reform. There is no question that a military caretaker government in China would look after the interests of the armed forces, but there are serious questions about its ability to look after the national interest.

The PLA has had more experience than some armies in civil administration, but that experience is now sixty years old. One could argue that since economic issues dominate China's political agenda and since the PLA acquired considerable managerial experience in business in the recent past, it is better suited to be a caretaker than it was during the Cultural Revolution. Still, a PLA-led regime would have to depend on the technical and managerial expertise of those on whose behalf it was caretaking.

Also, within the officer corps, there are strong differences of opinion over whether the PLA should ever take on political assignments. Some of these differences of opinion correspond to the kinds of divisions found in most military forces: rivalries among the services and differences of viewpoint based on age, rank, and time in service. Finally, as we have seen, the central military authorities and the regional military commands are divided along lines parallel to those of the center and regional political divisions.

A long-standing division between so-called Reds and experts in the PLA dates from the immediate aftermath of the Korean War, when some officers began to argue for a new strategy to replace the guerrilla doctrine of the revolutionary years and for a new professionalism to accompany the transition from guerrilla band to national defense force. Mao disagreed. He argued that the strategy of drawing an invading enemy into the heartland of China and defeating it with guerrilla warfare was still appropriate. Moreover, he believed that the army was, most importantly, a paragon of political virtue to be emulated by society. To emphasize professionalism, he thought, was to undermine political correctness, for expertise was acceptable only if matched with and tempered by "redness."

The PLA's military professionalism was perforce ignored during the Cultural Revolution, when it was involved in politics for a decade. Many officers attributed its miserable performance in the border conflict with Vietnam in 1979 to that involvement. They argued that the PLA could become an effective national defense force only if it attended exclusively to training, developing a new strategy, and updating and upgrading its arsenal. Their case was strengthened during the Gulf War in 1991, when Iraqi troops were defeated with remarkable rapidity, and their equipment, some of it supplied by China, proved wholly ineffectual against American weapons. That lesson was reinforced by the NATO air war in Kosovo, where not a single NATO soldier was lost in combat. The professionals' position is that the PLA is not now combat-ready for the kinds of conflicts in which it is likely to find itself engaged. To them, any expenditure of time or money that does not directly enhance combat readiness is inappropriate, whether spent on managing a factory or doing the job of a provincial party secretary.

These professionals in the PLA are interested in defining as sharply as possible the respective roles of China's armed forces, party, and government, and working to ensure that each confine itself to its designated part. They appreciate the benefits of having contacts with the military establishments of other countries, and they are eager to maintain these, since they provide the PLA with access to technology, training, and strategic and tactical thinking; thus, they tend to be less xenophobic than some of their colleagues.

The PLA's "nonprofessionals" –for lack of a better term, certainly "reds" is no longer appropriate–take a more benign view of non-combat-related military activity. Some of them are nostalgic for the heady days when the government called in the PLA to restore order, wield political power, and pull China back together; others have a strong personal and professional interest in being economic buccaneers, and they don't mind blurring the roles of party, government, and army. Still others may well draw the lesson of the continuing relevance of Mao's theories of "people's war" from observing the United States' experiences in the deep and seemingly endless quagmires in Iraq and Afghanistan. They see more to be lost than gained by the PLA's having contact with foreign military establishments; for them, to respond to the Pentagon's request for mutual "transparency" in military affairs is to reveal state secrets in a treasonable fashion.

The professionals' hesitation to intervene politically might, in a given circumstance, be overcome by patriotism, were the situation sufficiently dire and the alternative sufficiently unsatisfactory. But any eagerness to divest themselves from political responsibility as quickly as possible would put them at odds with their more politically inclined colleagues.

To a degree, the split between professionals and nonprofessionals parallels a split among the services. Interservice rivalry, which, after all, is found in most military establishments, is encouraged to the extent it builds loyalty and enhances morale; it is played out through strategic-planning bargains and, more sharply, around the table when military appropriations are decided on. In the case of the PLA, the army is by far the largest service, with 965,000 soldiers; the air force numbers about 400,000, the navy some 252,000, the rocket force 120,000, and support forces 295,000. As one might expect, the technological level of the weapons and equipment used by the navy and air force is far higher than that of the ground forces, and so is the educational level of their soldiers and officers. Troops assigned to the ground forces are generally more conservative and less professional than their Navy and Air Force colleagues.

The current strategic doctrine in the PLA calls for rapid deployment forces capable of responding quickly to domestic or international incidents. This doctrine, relying heavily on the navy and air force, has given these two arms prominence and necessitates the upgrading of their equipment and training. Moreover, they appear to have had strong and effective spokesmen at the highest level. Admiral Liu Huaqing, once head of the PLA Navy, occupied a position on the Politburo Standing Committee and served as vice chair of the Central Military Commission until his retirement in 1997. There is no military officer currently sitting on the Politburo Standing Committee.

Divisions along lines of age, rank, and time in service are more acute in the PLA than in other, more established armed forces. For one thing, the PLA has only recently implemented a regular retirement system for senior officers, and there is a greater age spread between the oldest and youngest soldiers than in the U.S. military, for example. Also, because of the significant difference in military operations during the revolution and civil war, during the Korean War, in the border conflicts with India and Vietnam, and in the more recent attempts to intimidate Taiwan, the military "generations" in the PLA have had substantially different experiences.

The fissures between the authority of China's central military and that of the regional military commanders weaken the PLA's ability to staff any caretaker government needed in the future to help mend a regionally fractured state. The regional commanders' habit of ignoring directives that run counter to their local interests, very like the habits of civilian authorities at the provincial level, will significantly reduce the adhesive properties of the caretakers' glue. In sum, were civil authority to collapse, the PLA would very likely intervene to form a caretaker government. It would do so out of patriotism and knowing that, as the only national organization capable of taking the place of the CCP, it would have to intervene to avoid anarchy if it did not. Once in power, it would be likely to rule in the name of a purged and revivified Communist Party and to follow a policy of pursuing economic reforms and a policy of engagement with the world economy, since its officers would consider their own economic interests served by these policies. But there would be strong pressure from the professional officers to make the caretaker government a short-lived affair. The officers would consider the adverse effects on combat readiness and be sensitive to international pressure to restore civilian rule. Rebuilding confidence in China's central authority would be the major undertaking, with an effective crackdown on corruption and the equal enforcement of laws and regulations as important first steps. But apart from its possibly greater discipline, there is little to inspire confidence in the PLA as a better problem solver than those whom it would replace.

The Gulf War in 1991, the NATO bombing of Kosovo in 1999, and the U.S. wars in Afghanistan and Iraq have given rise to new strategic thinking in the PLA, though those conflicts contain contradictory lessons. "Asymmetric warfare" that makes use of "pockets of critical technology" is seen as an alternative to the all but hopeless task of across-the-board military modernization. Some even argue that the Chinese, having entered the arms race so late, are at an advantage, since they are able to pick and choose what advanced technology they acquire. Picking and choosing, however, presuppose an effective strategy that combines a close working relationship with advanced foreign military establishments–primarily that of the United States–and an ambitious program of weapons purchases, which to this point have been primarily from a cash-hungry Russia. Moreover, asymmetric warfare was a doctrine closely associated with former Secretary of Defense Donald Rumsfeld and largely discredited after "shock and awe" gave way to a protracted occupation of Iraq for which the U.S. forces were woefully ill-prepared.

U.S. policymakers are divided in their response to China's interest in what the Clinton administration called a strategic partnership between the two nations. One school of thought, noting the written work of Chinese strategists, argues that China is a potentially threatening military rival of the United States. Another school dismisses these writings as jingoistic saber-rattling and points out that the gulf in military capability between the two nations will be unbridgeable for some time to come.

George W. Bush's administration, particularly Secretary Rumsfeld, tended to characterize the Chinese as "strategic rivals" rather than potential partners. Having replaced Rumsfeld as secretary of defense in 2006, Robert Gates sought a middle ground, characterizing China as a "peer competitor" of the United States. The baker's dozen successors to Gates took a variety of positions on China. The incumbent Secretary of Defense, Pete Hegseth, has had this to say about China: "The United States is prepared to go to war with China, which is ready to fight any type of war. Those who long for peace must prepare for war. It is important to be strong."

It was in the context of this debate that widespread allegations arose that the Chinese were illicitly acquiring U.S. military technology and data through commercial technological transactions and through scholarly exchanges between technicians and scientists.

Congressional concern resulted in a select committee investigation headed by the Republican congressman Christopher Cox of California. The Cox Report, released in 1998, depicted numerous examples of lax security on the American side and an intense interest in acquiring advanced technological information by whatever means on the Chinese side. Critics of the report called its language inflammatory and its charges unsubstantiated. Nonetheless, American firms have been fined for inappropriate transfers, and there have been a series of arrests and trials of individuals on both sides who have been accused of facilitating illegal transfers of technology.

The Pentagon believes that military-to-military contacts between China and the United States can give Americans firsthand insights into Chinese military strategy and policy and avenues of communication that will help defuse tensions arising from misunderstandings. The Chinese see these contacts as a way of getting up-to-date information on U.S. strategic thinking and the deployment of military technology. Contacts began in the late 1980s, were interrupted in protest against the Tiananmen massacre in 1989, were renewed in the mid-1990s, and were interrupted again, first by Chinese military action in the Taiwan Strait at the time of the first presidential election on the island in 1996, then after the bombing of the Chinese embassy in Belgrade in 1999, for a third time after the collision of a PLA air force plane with an American reconnaissance aircraft near Hainan Island in 2001, and for a fourth time in 2008, when the Chinese side protested a round of U.S. arms sales to Taiwan. Military- to-military contacts between the two countries were renewed early in 2009 with a three-day series of Defense Policy Coordination Talks; described by both sides as "highly productive," the Pentagon argued that their value outweighs the risk involved and that it would be cautious. Contacts between the two military establishments were interrupted for a fifth time in 2010, again in protest against United States arms sales to Taiwan.

In early April 2025, U.S. and Chinese military officials held working-level meetings in Shanghai. These discussions focused on reducing unsafe and unprofessional behavior by Chinese naval and air forces, particularly in the Indo-Pacific region. The talks aimed to enhance operational safety and prevent accidental conflicts, especially around sensitive areas like Taiwan and the South China Sea. However, high-level military engagement remains strained. At the recent Shangri-La Dialogue in Singapore (May 30–June 1, 2025), Defense Secretary Pete Hegseth delivered a speech sharply critical of China's military ambitions. China's Defense Minister, Dong Jun, did not attend the summit, instead sending a lower-level delegation, which limited the potential for direct high-level dialogue. China responded to Hegseth's remarks by accusing the U.S. of promoting a "Cold War mentality" and inciting regional tensions. The Chinese delegation's participation was notably subdued, and there were no significant bilateral meetings between top defense officials from the two countries during the summit.

The PLA is actively trying to acquire foreign military hardware. During the 1980s, it was said that upgrading its equipment had to wait until China's own industries could supply the new equipment; the policy was implemented by an initial reduction in the military budget and then only very small annual increments to it, which, given the effects of inflation, did not offset the continued downsizing of the military budget. But two events at the beginning of the 1990s turned this situation around: the PLA began to augment its budget through arms sales abroad and through production for the domestic civilian market, and the collapse of the former Soviet Union put large quantities of military equipment on the market. The PLA took full advantage of this coincidence of events: it signed contracts with Russian suppliers to buy one hundred S-300 missiles, seventy-two Su-27K fighter aircraft, and four Kilo-class and two Typhoon-class submarines; conversations were also held about the purchase of SS-18 nuclear missile technology; the cost of these acquisitions is approximately five billion dollars to date, part of it paid in cash, part in barter arrangements. In addition, China has made substantial purchases of arms and equipment from Israel, including laser-guided armor-piercing warheads; electronic fire control systems; optics and cannons for tanks; night vision, communications, and radio equipment; antitank missiles; artillery ammunition; and airborne warning and control system (AWACS) equipment.

Before he retired, Admiral Liu Huaqing long sought to add aircraft carriers to the Chinese navy. In 1985, he negotiated the purchase of an Australian carrier, which was then dismantled to duplicate its design. Since even with this assistance, it was estimated that it would be many years before China is capable of building and launching its own carrier, Liu began negotiations to purchase three former carriers, including one under construction in Ukraine. His negotiations apparently came to fruition in the spring of 1998, when a Hong Kong company with connections in China acquired the carrier *Varyag* for twenty million dollars. Although the company claimed that *Varyag* would be converted to a floating hotel or resold for scrap, it was widely assumed that the ship would end up in the hands of the PLA Navy and be used for training purposes. The refitting of the *Varyag* was completed in 2011. It was renamed the *Liaoning* and was combat-ready in 2016. Since then, construction of China's first domestically produced carrier, the *Shandong*, was completed in 2018 and went into service the following year. A third, the *Fujian*, is currently undergoing sea trials, and a fourth, currently named *Type IV* and featuring nuclear propulsion, is under construction. The goal is to have six carriers by 2035.

China's own armaments industry has been rapidly adding to the PLA's arsenal. The PLA Navy has added thirty new submarines, including seven nuclear-powered vessels. According to the most recent Pentagon assessment of China's military capability, the PLA is now engaged in "the most active land-based ballistic and cruise missile program in the world." It has some 1,350 short- range ballistic missiles deployed against Taiwan and is adding a hundred missiles to that arsenal each year. In addition, it possesses a full range of land-based and submarine-launched medium- and long-range missiles.

In relation to its ever-growing missile stockpile, China is currently and rapidly developing its program for space exploration. Originally housed in the PLA's General Armaments Department (GAD), the China National Space Administration was subsequently transferred to the oversight of the Commission on Science, Technology, and Industry for National Defense (COSTIND). Both the GAD and COSTIND operate under the Central Military Commission, and the division of responsibilities between the two is far from clear.

China launched the first in a series of spaceflights, the *Shenzhou I*, in late 1999. Since then, there have been numerous subsequent launches, most recently 34 in the first half of 2025 alone. The first unmanned moon landing occurred in 2024, and a manned moon landing is projected by 2030. China's progress in developing its space program was brought inadvertently and suddenly to the world's attention when, in early 2007, American intelligence learned that the Chinese had successfully destroyed one of its own, presumably dysfunctional, satellites with a ballistic missile. Although the Chinese remained silent for twelve days, the Foreign Ministry ultimately confirmed the event.

The PLA argues that all these developments are meant simply to update its antiquated arsenal, but China's neighbors and many in the United States see evidence of expansion, not simple replacement. They relate this expansion to actions taken to strengthen China's military position outside the national borders. An agreement was signed with Burma in 1994: in exchange for sending military equipment to the Myanmar army, China would have access to naval facilities in the Bay of Bengal.

A year later, China extended its position in the South China Sea by occupying the Mischief Reef, just 135 miles off the coast of the Philippines. Alarmists saw these events as evidence of a pincer movement designed to encircle and control Southeast Asia. But the Chinese government depicts the two events as unconnected and defends the actions in the South China Sea as intended exclusively to protect Chinese territory. In 2014, Chinese and Vietnamese vessels collided in an area of the South China Sea claimed by both countries. Nine years later, China and the Philippines came to grips over territory each claimed in the sea. In March of 2021, leaders of the four states of the Quadrilateral Security Dialogue–the U.S., Japan, India, and Australia–held their first (virtual) summit meetings since the dialogue was established in 2007. Their joint statement called for a "free and open Indo-Pacific" and a "rule-based maritime order in the East and South China Seas." In September of the same year, in an in-person meeting in the White House, the four leaders sent a strong signal to Beijing by reiterating that their commitment was "undaunted by coercion."

Territorial Disputes, South China Sea

Source: Asia Times Maps 2018.

One can plausibly argue that the PLA has been engaging in these actions simply to justify an expanded military budget. But whatever its motivation, the key question is whether its actions are proceeding under a plan drawn up by civilian authorities and implemented under civilian control or whether the PLA is doing the planning and controlling. There is evidence to suggest that the latter is the case.

Just where China stands in its quest for military modernization is, of course, the subject of considerable analysis and speculation. One stark benchmark came as an unintended consequence of the

PLA's rapid and extensive efforts to stem the damage from the magnitude 7.9 earthquake that struck Sichuan Province in May 2008. While domestic and foreign observers were very favorably impressed with the scope and speed of the military relief effort, they were also struck by the primitive equipment and lack of training the soldiers brought to their rescue work.

The People's Liberation Army (PLA) is still decades away from challenging the U.S. military as a full peer competitor. While on track to rise to the challenge, the PLA currently lacks the capability for sustained forward deployment overseas that enables the American armed forces to project power globally.

Military officers who enjoyed close personal ties to Deng and his senior colleagues are now long retired, and the Chinese party-state is probably as little militarized as it has been since the establishment of the People's Republic. Nonetheless, the influence of the military remains just offstage because, as we have seen, the party-state is heavily dependent on the PLA and the PAP. Indeed, when Chinese arms purchases and sales abroad have become an international issue, the foreign minister has tried to leave the impression that he has only very indirect and ineffective control over the military corporations making these transactions.

In arguing for a larger share of the national budget, the PLA takes advantage of its position of influence within the triangle of party, government, and military authority, using the resources available to it to upgrade its arsenal, adopting a new strategy that takes account of the structure of power in East Asia and the Pacific, and lobbying effectively for a strong assertion of Chinese sovereignty broadly defined.

Chapter 9: The Centrifugal Forces of Regionalism

In our discussion of the power grid of political structures in Chapter 4, we spoke of the tension that exists between the vertical lines of authority emanating from Beijing and extending downward into the provinces, counties, townships, and cities and the horizontal thrust of the separate localities, each with its own diverse interests and its own capacities to thwart the direction of the central government. During the course of the thirty years since the reforms began, one can observe that the authority of the party and that of the national government it controls have gradually weakened, while provincial and local governments have become more assertive in advancing their interests, often at odds with those of the central government and other localities. To explore these tensions more closely, we must look particularly at the horizontal members of the power grid, whether they be individual provinces or broader regions of the country.

In Chapter 1, we saw the differences in economic opportunity among three such regions: the coast, the center, and the west. Through the reform period, Chinese policy planners have often thought in terms of these three broad regions. There has been a strategy of allowing the coast to develop first and the center next; only more recently have extensive investments been made to develop the barren, underpopulated, and ethnically diverse west. While the provinces in each of these three regions have much in common, it is also true that important interests are not shared among the provinces in each. This is perhaps most obvious along the coast, where the provinces compete for foreign investment and, in several instances, are closely linked to the economies of their principal foreign partners.

The anthropologist G. William Skinner, in a close study of the economic geography of nineteenth-century China, concluded that it was useful to consider China not as a single economic system but as nine macroregions.[4] (Skinner's macroregions are shown on the map.) These macroregions are defined by their river basins and by the mountain ranges that serve as barriers to commerce and trade. Although economic activity within each region was intense, there was relatively little economic activity across the macroregional borders. The geographical features that divided macroregions are, of course, still in place, but much has changed in the Chinese economy over the course of the century and more since the period to which Skinner's data refer. Communications links have expanded. Railroads, air routes, and highways now connect places that were once isolated, and the economy is much more unified. Through the strenuous efforts of the Nationalist government in the years leading up to World War II and, later and more successfully, of the Communist government after 1949, the economy was centralized and came to be managed under a single, unified plan. When the centralized and planned economy was subsequently decentralized once again, the units to which economic decision-making was relegated were political, not physiographic or economic.

[4] G. William Skinner, *Marketing and Social Structure in Rural China* (Ann Arbor, Michigan: Association for Asian Studies Monographs, 2010)

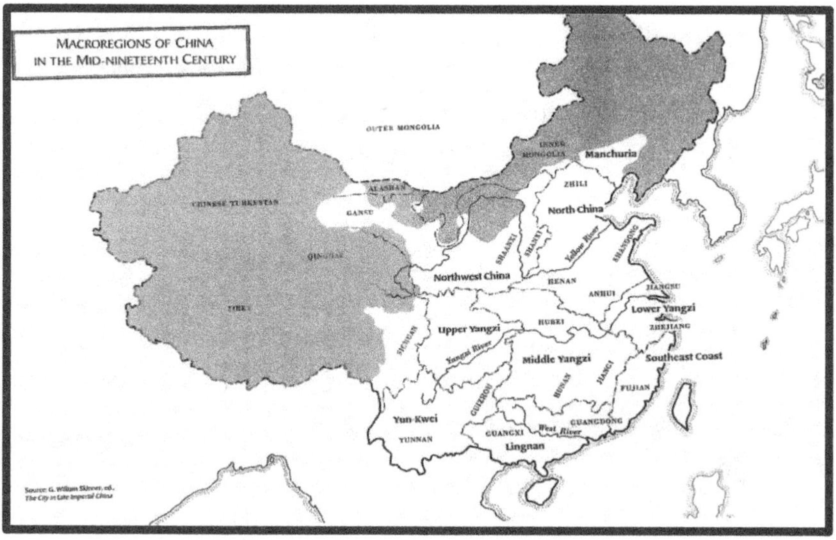

Macroregions of China in the Mid-Nineteenth Century

To gauge the realities of China's economic regions today, one would have to subject the contemporary scene to the same careful scrutiny that Skinner applied to the economic interactions of a century and a half ago. Short of this, we can speculate about the outcome of such a study. It would surely reveal additional macroregions: the far west is one, given the importance of the natural resources being explored there. A second might result from dividing North China into coastal and hinterland regions. Study of the economic activity within the latter and of its links to the Lower Yangzi region might suggest a redrawing of macroregional boundaries in central China. Apart from these adjustments, Skinner's macroregions still cohere today, despite the many changes wrought by political integration, economic development, and technological modernization. In the tug between central and local interests, provinces within these regions have much in common with one another.

As we have noted, Chinese politicians have a strong preference for *ad hoc* arrangements that are negotiated case by case over formal arrangements applied uniformly. This preference is well illustrated by the messy web of relationships that link center and region in the Chinese political system.

The American federal system was created by local governments coming together and, after careful negotiation, surrendering certain powers to the newly created central government. The U.S. Constitution provides that all powers not specifically surrendered to the federal government remain in the hands of the states.

The Chinese system, by contrast, still contains elements of the traditional division of authority between center and regions, in which provincial and local officials were supposed to serve as agents of the central government. The carefully crafted arrangement put in place to ensure that these agents did not become advocates of local interests in competition with the interests of the throne broke down when the throne was weak, threatened, and in need of the assistance of local authorities to suppress the Taiping rebels in the middle of the nineteenth century. Thereafter China experienced nearly a century of fragmentation; local interests became strong and entrenched, and the central government had little or no power over them, finding that the best it could do was to negotiate among local warlords for their cooperation in projects benefiting the nation as a whole.

In the current relationship between center and region in China, there are echoes of both Mandarins and warlords. The central government would like to think of provincial leaders as its agents, but very often it finds itself negotiating for their cooperation. Their relationship is the end product of a period of centralized decision-making authority and a subsequent one of intentional decentralization. The Chinese Communist Party and the Red

Army worked closely together to unify the country after a century and more of war, civil war, and revolution. Military and civilian authorities shared in running the territories they had captured and then, as the new government was established in Beijing, handed over control to civilian authorities in the central and provincial governments.

Military regional commanders remained actively involved in party and government affairs, however, and eventually became entrenched in the affairs of the territories under their command. To break up their strong regional identities and to stop them from forming stable long-term local interests, the party periodically reassigned commanders.

Once it had reasserted control after a century of regional fragmentation, the party began to see the disadvantages of a highly centralized political system. It was impractical and inefficient to try to manage an economy as large and diverse as China's from a single command post, and Mao was mistrustful of the bureaucracy that was being created to do this managing. Finally, as we have seen, he believed in the mass line- the idea that policy should reflect both central interests and local initiative.

He believed that decisions were best made at the level where they were most likely to express local initiative. So, beginning in the mid-1950s, the center began to devolve decision-making authority to local officials, selected for their loyalty to the interests of the central government, among other qualities. This was accomplished seldom by means of uniform provisions applying equally to all provinces or to all cities, more often by means of case-by-case negotiations, the outcome of which reflected the relative clout of the parties involved.

One of the party-state's most important levers in controlling local officials is, of course, the power of appointment, and provincial officials are, to some degree, agents of the center. On the other hand, they are most likely to be effective if they have the confidence of the local community. It used to be the case that almost all of them were outsiders brought in by and thus beholden to the center. More recently, after a long history of loyal but ineffective appointees, Beijing has been appointing to important provincial and municipal posts officials with strong local affinities.

The power to levy taxes, the second lever the center uses to control local government, expresses a very concrete aspect of the center-region relationship: who determines the local budget and how the revenue for that budget is generated. In the American fiscal system, the power to tax and the revenue generated from the tax are assigned, depending on what is being taxed, to different jurisdictions. Personal and corporate income, for example, is taxed by the federal government, by state governments, and by some cities. The sales of many goods are taxed by state and local governments, but certain items, such as alcohol, tobacco, and gasoline, are also taxed by the federal government. Personal and real property is taxed by state, county, town, and city governments. Customs duties are collected by the federal government. (Table 7 compares tax revenue by source for the American and the Chinese governments, both central and local.) States, towns, and counties must draw up expenditure budgets, the size of which is determined by their projected tax revenues. They are generally precluded from deficit spending, though they may borrow money for capital projects. The national government, however, is permitted to spend in a given year more than it takes in, and exercising that option, it has accumulated a national debt of more than $33 trillion. There are, in addition, transfers of funds from the national government to state and local governments that can amount to as much as a quarter of expenditures for the latter.

Prior to the economic reforms of the 1970s, China's party-state operated on the assumption that all government revenues were its to distribute. The largest portion of revenue is derived from state-owned enterprises. Corporate income was subject to taxation, and in addition, as we have noted, the government recouped corporate profits from state-owned enterprises in the form of transfer payments. Besides industrial and commercial taxes, the government had the revenues from customs duties on imported goods, a tax on salt, and an agricultural tax. Neither property nor personal income was subject to taxation.

Although Beijing controlled the distribution of all tax revenue, it relied on local governments to collect the revenues, and until 1994, there was no central tax collection agency. Local authorities collected taxes and corporate profits, then forwarded a pre-agreed proportion of this revenue to the central government, retaining what was needed to cover their approved annual budgets. The proportion forwarded to Beijing was subject to annual renegotiation; each province and municipality had its own negotiated rate, and these varied ·widely. For many years, the city of Guangzhou, for example, contributed only 10 percent of its municipal revenues to central coffers, while Shanghai during the same period was routinely turning over 90 percent.

Table 8: Tax Revenue by Source, China and the United States (in percentages)

	China	United States
Corporate taxes	37.8	17.4
Income tax	25.7	45.3
Value-added tax	23.7	0
Domestic consumption tax	7.4	0
Property tax	3.3	10.6
Tariffs and customs duties	1.1	0.5
Agricultural tax	1	0
Sales tax	0	15.7
Social insurance tax	0	0
Excise tax	0	10
Estate/gift tax	0	0.5

Expenditure budgets for governments at all levels were determined in a highly centralized fashion, with the budget at each level being set by the level just above it: the center set budgets for provinces and the directly administered cities; provincial authorities set budgets for their counties and cities. While some effort was made to balance revenues and expenditures at the national level, nothing related provincial, county, or city expenditures to the revenues generated in that jurisdiction. Rather, wealthy areas were expected to spend less than they took in, and Beijing used a portion of the surplus to cover the deficit in poorer areas, which routinely spent more than they could raise.

In reforming the economy, the central government looked for new sources of tax revenue, as shown in Table 8. In addition, the government began a scheme, known as "eating from separate kitchens," under which the provinces turned over a proportion of their revenues that was fixed for five years so as to allow them much-needed long-term planning; they could set their own budgets, but on the understanding that the central government would no longer cover their over budget expenditures.

Uniformity was the goal, but in practice, many different arrangements were put in place under the rubric of eating from separate kitchens. Sixteen of China's twenty-seven provinces and regions agreed to have the titles to some state-owned enterprises shifted from the central government to them. Beijing got the tax revenue from its enterprises, while provincial governments got the tax revenue from provincial enterprises. Other arrangements were made with other localities: Guangdong and Fujian provinces agreed to lump-sum transfer payments, to remain unchanged for five years; Jiangsu Province was assessed a percentage of its total revenue, fixed for five years; Beijing, Tianjin, and Shanghai were assessed percentages that were to be renegotiated annually, as in the past. The eight poorest provinces and regions, where revenues did not cover expenditures, were assigned fixed subsidies, to increase annually by 10 percent for five years.

Table 9: Chinese Government Revenue by Source, 1978 and 2023 (in billion yuan)

	1978	**2023**
Taxes:		
Individual income tax	45.1	2,774.9
Tariffs	2.9	259.0
Agricultural tax	2.8	0.0
Salt tax	1.1	0.0
Corporate income tax	0	4,110.2
Individual income tax	0	1,477.5
Value-added tax	0	7.065.1
Property tax	0	221.2
Other taxes	0	2,203.5
Revenue from enterprises	57.2	0.0
Other revenues	3	3,567.8
Total	**112.1**	**21,679.5**

Total budgetary revenue increased steadily thereafter, but an unintended consequence of eating from separate kitchens was that the central government's share of the revenue shrank from nearly 60 percent in 1978 to close to 40 percent in 1993. In transferring the titles to state-owned enterprises, the central government had kept control of strategic but not necessarily profitable factories. As its revenues declined, it shifted entire categories of expenditure from the national to local budgets, putting local governments in a bind: their revenues were fixed, but now they had to take on new expenditures. To solve this problem, they increasingly relied on extra-budgetary funds–every imaginable kind of fee, fine, levy, toll, assessment, commission, and tariff. At the beginning of the reform period, extra-budgetary funds amounted to no more than 20 percent of regular tax revenues, but by 1993, they had increased to more than 100 percent of regular tax revenues and were a particularly sore point with the people. That figure has been reduced over the last thirty years and now stands at 8.2 percent.

A second round of tax reform was put into effect on 1 January 1994. The economy was then growing with unprecedented speed, but tax revenue as a proportion of output was declining. (Whereas tax revenue amounted to about a third of the total output value of the economy in 1979, it had declined to about 20 percent by 2023. A comparable figure for Western countries is around 40 percent of output value.) Moreover, state enterprises were draining resources from the central government rather than contributing substantially to its resources, as they had been doing a decade earlier. The 1994 reform created a central government tax collection agency with local branches and set as a goal that 80 percent of all tax revenue would be collected by central government agents and only the remaining 20 percent by local collectors, which reversed the situation in which most revenue was retained by the provinces. Under the new arrangement, the central government got the lion's share of tax revenues and provided grants to the local governments where needed to cover their expenditure budgets. The scheme of distinguishing central from local government ownership of state-sector enterprises was universalized, with all enterprises paying both national and local corporate income taxes.

The most recent round of tax-related reforms was announced at the Third Plenum of the Twentieth Party Central Committee in 2024. It included provisions to implement taxation by law and standardize incentive policies, develop new business forms and deepen tax system reform, integrate the digital economy with the real economy to cultivate advanced manufacturing industries, reduce costs for manufacturing enterprises and boost their vitality, improve the tax system to promote green technology innovation, develop the reform of the individual income tax, reform the consumption tax, and deepen the reform of tax collection and administration.

As shown in Table #9, the tax reforms have raised the central government's share of tax revenues from 40 percent to 46 percent and set tax revenue as a percentage of gross domestic product at 8%.

Table 10: Central and Local Government Share of Total Revenue, China and the U.S., 2023 (%)

	China	United States
Central government revenue	45.9	52.9
Local government revenue	54.1	47.2

To counter these trends, China's interior provinces are actively courting foreign investors with bargain rates on real estate and labor, and at the same time vociferously opposing any favoritism allowed to the coastal zones in the form of tax breaks for potential investors, arguing that only if they have comparable leeway can they compete effectively. In the meantime, they are learning to turn the successes of the coastal enclaves to their own advantage, becoming major investors themselves in enterprises and property in the coastal zones. More recently, the central government took a hand once again in leveling the playing field. Between 1998 and 2001, Beijing issued more than $30 billion in bonds for infrastructure projects to stimulate economic growth. The tranche of these bonds for the year 2000 was earmarked for the western provinces. At the same time, the governor of the China Development Bank announced that 60 percent of the bank's loans would go to projects in the central and western parts of the country. As we have noted, in November 2008, the government announced a $586 billion stimulus package, comparable in size as a percentage of GDP to the U.S. stimulus package passed by Congress the following year. Many of the infrastructure projects included in this package will benefit the central and western provinces.

Having grown accustomed to a greater degree of autonomy, the provinces now tend to resist any effort by the central government to recoup its control of local affairs. The center, for its part, believes that the major problems confronting the economy—deflation, the banking crisis, and the ailing state sector—can best be addressed at the national level. Many of the issues that pit regions against the center arise from this conflict of interest. For example, the central government wants to control and direct the flow of foreign investment, while the provinces want the freedom to attract foreign investors and the authority to cut deals with them. The center sets restrictions with respect to the size and nature of investments that may be locally approved; the provincial governments then calculate how to circumvent these restrictions.

Yet another source of conflict between the center and the region is what in the United States would be called unfunded mandates. Like our own federal government, China's central government has had a habit of enacting laws and regulations that require local government action but provide no funds to cover the costs. For example, the central government, wanting to improve the quality of air and water, has put in place a full set of environmental laws and regulations, but gives little or no financial support to local governments to cover the cost of enforcing them. Similarly, as we will explore below, it is actively engaged in a program to reduce the size of the Chinese population, but vests responsibility for implementing this program in local governments and provides no funding to offset the costs involved. In education and health care, too, the central government enacts programs for expansion and improvement but relies on local governments for the funds to carry out these mandates.

Provinces and regions frequently find themselves competing with one another for the resources, benefits, and exemptions distributed by the central government, for foreign investors, and for opportunities to engage in lucrative foreign trading deals. To better their positions, they try to maximize their ability to make independent decisions, and to promote their local interests, they rival one another in lobbying the central government and currying favor with its officials.

Occasionally, competition among regions has taken the form of protectionism. Some years ago, state-owned department stores in Shandong Province, for example, launched an informal Buy Shandong campaign, agreeing to limit the stock in their stores to goods produced in Shandong and to exclude merchandise from other provinces. Similarly, when officials in Hunan Province concluded that they were on the losing end of an economic competition with neighboring Guangdong Province, where factories were buying goods from Hunan suppliers at low (regulated) prices and making finished products that they sold at high (unregulated) prices, they closed Hunan's border with Guangdong and stopped the flow of goods in both directions. Only when the central government intervened was the border reopened, and cross-border trade resumed. It was perhaps this episode that Nicholas Kristof had in mind when he wrote an article in the *New York Times* sketching out three scenarios for China's future, in one of which economic cross-border competition between Hunan and Hubei provinces erupts into a civil war that an impotent central government cannot bring under control.

There are other issues that set provinces and regions at odds with one another. Water and air pollution seldom affect only the immediate area in which the pollution occurs; provinces or regions responsible for enforcing environmental regulations find their efforts undermined by neighboring regions that are unwilling to undertake or are less responsible for enforcement. Similarly, major public works projects like the Three Gorges Dam (to which we turn shortly) or the proposed South to North Water Diversion Project (described in Chapter 17) have consequences that benefit one region while harming another. In the case of the latter, for example, the northern provinces will have more water, but the central and southern provinces not only get no extra water but also must bear the cost of the land taken out of cultivation for the right-of-way.)

Finally, with a newly mobile population, the movement of workers is a source of conflict. As noted earlier, more than 150 million people have left their original jurisdictions for distant cities. Is it the responsibility of the cities or of the rural communities from which they came to bring this population under control? A Wild West variant on this problem concerns the so-called Gold Lords, who staked out illegal mining claims in China's hinterlands, hired migrant rural workers as miners, and defended their claims against rival claimants (and local authorities) with massive arsenals. Here again, region is pitted against region. Is it the responsibility of Qinghai (where many of the claims are located) to control this "attractive nuisance" or the responsibility of the regions from which the prospectors come to give them jobs and control their movement?

The means at the disposal of a province or region for asserting and defending its interests are varied. The mildest form is the time-honored technique of persuasion through debate, jawboning, or lobbying. Local officials who think their interests are being threatened by the central government or by their neighbors will argue the case as persuasively as they can with the best-connected representative they can find. The central government seems to operate most comfortably by treating each case as *sui generis* and is least at ease when trying to enforce uniform regulations uniformly, meaning that a region or province can easily make the case for being treated as one among many exceptions to a given rule or regulation.

If this argument falls on deaf ears, local authorities can resort to the next means at their disposal for asserting their interests: passive resistance. Given the nature of China's political system, this tactic is perhaps the most effective. Paying lip service to the interests of the central government or of neighbors yet actively pursuing one's own plan is usually a highly effective way to stymie rivals. Bureaucratic practice is replete with methods for appearing to conform while not actually doing so. It is from these practices that the term "dukes" has been revived from a much earlier historical period and used to refer to powerful and recalcitrant provincial governors.

If all else fails, active resistance is possible, but this third option is a dangerous strategy because of the possibility of violent retaliation. Whether setting forth new local regulations, encouraging local practices that directly contravene central directives, failing to collect or forward tax revenues due to the central authorities, or closing one's borders to cross-border trade, a province must carefully calculate the capabilities and intentions of its opponent. Active resistance against China's central authorities has been tried only two or three times since 1949, and it has always been unsuccessful, but that was when the central authorities were strong, unified, and credible.

For some years after the 1949 revolution, China's central party and government enjoyed great credibility, central and regional interests were seen as united, and the united interests were contained in and explained by an ideology to which many were deeply committed. But much of the credibility of the party-state has now been lost, as a result in part of disastrously mistaken policies, bloated egos, pervasive corruption, and the collapse of ideology and its replacement with a shallow, self-seeking materialism. In the absence of credibility, China's central authorities have had to secure compliance with their directives by manipulation, persuasion, or coercion.

One method they use to further the cause of local compliance is to minimize the differences between central and local interests. An example of this strategy is the shift of policy after Deng's inspection trip in February 1993 to the Shenzhen special economic zone, where retrenchment policies adopted in 1988 to slow economic growth and cap inflation had been very unpopular, but where a new policy of encouraging market reform won the immediate approval and compliance of all but a handful of local authorities. Still, local interests are diverse, not uniform, and bringing central policy into conformity with the interests of one region inevitably raises difficulties with the interests of other regions.

A second strategy that the center uses to secure compliance from local governments is to bargain, since it holds a limited but significant number of chips that it can use in the game with local authorities—items that benefit the individual official, like appointments and promotions, and items that benefit the constituency, like tax waivers and public works projects. The process is akin to the pork barrel politics with which Americans are familiar, though compliance, not votes, is the operative currency in the Chinese case. It is because of the advantages it gets from bargaining that the center is so reluctant to formalize, regularize, or nationalize its policies *vis- à -vis* local governments.

Where compromise and bargaining fail, the center can always appoint or dismiss local officials. This power is somewhat limited because effective local officials need the confidence of their communities as well as that of the center; the center can replace a rebellious official, but his replacement will be a success only if he gains his constituency's cooperation. As we have seen, the center appoints people with local ties more and more frequently, but this undermines its leverage.

As a final resort, local compliance can, in theory, be secured through coercion, as it has been in the past. The center has a nominal monopoly on the instruments of coercion—that is, the People's Liberation Army and the People's Armed Police. In practice, however, it would take a very flagrant example of a local government's flouting central authority to induce the center to send in troops. Then there is the question of whether the armed forces would obey such an order. Certainly, there are reasons for military commanders to think twice before carrying it out. First, there is the issue of where a commander's loyalties lie. Despite the party's best efforts, the army itself suffers from regional divisions, and one can imagine situations in which a regional military commander might see his interests aligned with those of the region where he is stationed, not with those in distant Beijing. He might also reflect on the negative consequences for the armed forces of its having obeyed the orders of the elders in Beijing in 1989. In short, there are reasons for the army to doubt the wisdom of acting as the coercive arm of a teetering political authority.

Were the army to agree to intervene, as I believe it well might, it would do so to end an interregional conflict threatening civil war, or if it perceived that central authority had collapsed, as in the former Soviet Union in 1991. But intervening under these circumstances, it would see itself as a substitute for the paralyzed party-state, not as its agent. Given the divergence of interests between the central government and local governments in China and the relative weakness of the former, it is very likely that more and more decentralized political and economic systems will emerge.

To illustrate the way in which what we have called the power grid of Chinese politics actually operates, there is no better case than the decision to build a dam on the Yangzi River at the site of the Three Gorges, located between the cities of Chongqing and Wuhan. Damming the river at this site was initially proposed by Sun Zhongshan (孙中山–Sun Yat-sen) in 1923, but revolution, war, and civil war intervened, and the idea was shelved. The project was revived again under the aegis of Mao Zedong in the mid- 1950s, then buried in the chaos of the Cultural Revolution. In 1979, the project was revived yet again. As it has taken shape in our time, it has three objectives, each of which dictated a set of specifications and benefited a particular geographical region.

The first objective—to control flooding along the lower reaches of the Yangzi—is best served by a high dam, though it might equally well be accomplished by a series of smaller dams on the river's tributaries, and it benefits exclusively those living downriver from the dam. The second objective—to generate electrical power, a highly desirable clean alternative to coal—also points toward a high dam since the higher the dam, the more hydroelectric power can be generated. Given China's electrical grid and the topography of the area upriver, most of the power generated at the dam will go to those living downriver from the Three Gorges. The third objective—to improve navigation by deepening the river channel behind the dam to allow ships of up to ten thousand tons of displacement to get upstream as far as Chongqing—would benefit exclusively the communities upriver from the dam. (In fact, there is some possibility that downstream navigation would become more difficult, given the reduction in flow.) Navigation enhancement also imposes some very specific restrictions on the design of the dam.

Obviously, several major issues, over which opinion was deeply divided, had to be resolved before work on the dam could begin. The first was the question of whether to build a single dam or a series of smaller dams. Only a single high dam would raise the water level and improve navigation, but both hydroelectric power generation and flood control could be accomplished with smaller, safer, less costly, and technologically simpler dams. A second, highly controversial issue was the height of the dam and its effect on the people living in areas that would be inundated by the reservoir behind it. A 650-foot dam, with the capacity to produce 25,000 megawatts of electrical power, would displace, by conservative estimates, more than 1.4 million people; a 450-foot dam would produce six thousand megawatts and displace about 250,000 people.

A third set of issues concerned the cost and financing of the project. Estimates proved extraordinarily difficult, given the disagreements over objectives and varying sets of specifications. It also seemed almost impossible to do a cost-benefit analysis, since the cost bases for navigation, power generation, and flood damage differ. Moreover, the project was expected to take more than a decade to complete, during which time price reform would affect virtually every item in the budget, and future inflation rates were difficult to predict. So, project costs were a moving target. These factors help explain why published estimates of the cost of the Three Gorges project varied by a factor of eight.

The eventual financing plan was based on an official budget of $25 billion, a figure that fell well below the median cost estimate. It called for funding half the project from government revenues (a national tax on electrical power and profits from power generated at the Gezhouba Dam, downstream from the Three Gorges site). An additional 7.5 percent of the cost was to be covered by the sale of power produced at the dam once the first stage of the project was completed. The China Development Bank was tapped for loans covering a further 21 percent of the project cost, and an additional 4.5 percent was to come from loans extended by foreign providers of equipment. The World Bank indicated its unwillingness to consider a loan for the project, which the Chinese, not wanting to deal with the required environmental impact studies, would have, in any case, been reluctant to seek.

Perhaps the most serious technological issue at stake in the dam project was finding a solution for the problem of siltation. Although silt carried by the Yangzi River is only a little more than a third of that carried by the Yellow River, it nonetheless amounts to some five hundred million tons a year. Controlling the silt to protect the dam structure and to keep the upriver channel clear posed unprecedented technical problems; predicting the effect on the eroded downstream riverbed caused by a reduction in silt posed still more.

As originally conceived, the project had another seemingly insurmountable technological problem. Initial plans called for hydroelectric generators with a capacity of 1,000 megawatts, but the largest generators produced in China to date had a capacity of 300 megawatts, the largest outside China, 700 megawatts. Generator capacity technology had advanced at a rate of approximately 100 megawatts per decade. At that rate, it would have been well into the twenty-first century before big enough generators would be available for the Three Gorges. The problem was resolved by settling for 32 generators, each with a 700-megawatt capacity, and assigning their production to two Sino-foreign joint-venture companies. A quarter of the generators were constructed in China, the remainder abroad.

It is no surprise that China's political system was so deeply divided—indeed, at loggerheads—over the Three Gorges project. There were not only sharp disagreements among several regions but apparently irreconcilable divisions among central government agencies. Within the Ministry of Water Resources and Electric Power, the section responsible for water resources favored the single large dam, arguing that it was the most effective solution to the problem of flood control, while the section concerned with electrical power opposed the project on the grounds that a series of smaller dams would be a less expensive, technologically more feasible, and more reliable way to increase the country's electric power supply. The Ministry of Communication and its Yangzi River Transport Bureau opposed the large dam on the grounds that its effect on the navigability of the river downstream of the dam is highly unpredictable, and its very long construction period would disrupt existing river traffic. A third agency, the Yangzi River Planning Office, established in the mid-1950s to develop an overall plan for the Yangzi River basin, consistently advocated the high dam, primarily because of its positive effect on flood control.

Depending on the dimensions of the final plan, local governments along the Yangzi River differed substantially with respect to the costs they would bear and the benefits they would enjoy. The municipality of Chongqing was an enthusiastic booster of the project because it hoped to be able to expand its port facilities to receive bigger ships. The city government had very specific dam heights in mind: a water level of 588 feet at the dam would raise the river so that ships of ten thousand tons could reach Chongqing; if the water level were lower than this, only smaller ships could reach the new port, and if it were higher, large ships would reach a largely flooded Chongqing.

The response of the provincial government of Sichuan was mixed. Expanding the port capacity of Chongqing would greatly assist Sichuan by strengthening its links to China's rapidly developing coastal provinces, but on the other hand, Sichuan would not benefit from flood control. Moreover, relatively little of the new power would benefit the province. Yet one of the greatest costs and most vexing problems—resettling the people displaced by the reservoir—fell exclusively to Sichuan provincial authorities, a most unwelcome burden. This burden was substantially lightened when, in 1997 43 districts, cities, and counties were carved out of the province and turned over to Chongqing as it became a centrally administered city like Beijing, Shanghai, and Tianjin. Seventy percent of the 1.3 million people displaced by the reservoir were among the 30 million new residents of Chongqing.

Similarly, the township and municipal governments in the areas to be flooded were divided in their views. Some towns along the river would be eliminated entirely; others must abandon riverfront property and rebuild above the new water level. Project funds were budgeted to compensate those displaced by the resulting reservoir, a portion going to resettled people and a larger portion to the local governments responsible for building new homes and creating new job opportunities. The eventual allocation was 30 percent to individuals and 70 percent to local governments, which might well take this as a windfall. For example, the town of Wanxian, asked to draw up a relocation budget, came up with a figure of $2.9 billion. The central authorities were stunned, having budgeted only $3.5 billion for all relocation expenses. The eventual budget was in excess of $11 billion, but like all public funds of large magnitude, it was subject to misappropriation by corrupt officials, prompting stern, if not always effectual, warnings from Beijing.

The governments of Hubei and Hunan provinces were the most enthusiastic supporters of the Three Gorges project, for they were in a win-win position, being the principal beneficiaries of flood control as well as of increased power generation, and none of their residents would be displaced by the reservoir. There was less enthusiasm downriver. Jiangxi, Jiangsu, Anhui, and Shanghai would benefit from flood control and power generation, but the river channel would erode in unpredictable ways with the newly silt-free water flowing over the dam; farmland would flood, and river ports would become inaccessible.

Given this virtual gridlock of conflicting interests, it is surprising that the project was ever launched. Once launched, it appeared highly possible that the gridlock would keep it from being completed. That construction started in 1994 was largely because then-Premier Li Peng adopted the project and exerted strong pressure to get it underway. As minister of electric power in the early 1980s, he had been on record as having opposed it, but subsequently he came to see it as a monument to his personal accomplishments. Using his authority as head of government, he mobilized the various agencies supporting the project, overrode the central agencies opposed to it, and engineered a compromise in the project's scope that satisfied at least some of the conflicting objectives.

Thus, in March 1992, the National People's Congress considered a proposal to build, at an estimated cost of $10 billion, a dam just over 600 feet in height with a reservoir level of 570 feet. The generating capacity of the power plant would be 18,000 megawatts, utilizing 26 700-megawatt generators. The proposal estimated that 1.13 million people would be displaced by the reservoir and that the project would take sixteen years to complete. Responsibility for supervising the project was vested in a newly established Three Gorges Construction Committee, chaired by Li Peng. Although the proposition passed the legislature with an overwhelming majority, the level of opposition was unprecedented: of the 2,600-odd delegates, 166 voted against the project and 664 abstained.

Ground was broken in 1993, construction began in December 1994, and the sluice gates were closed in 2003. As finally built, the dam stands 331 feet high, utilizes 32 700-megawatt generators to produce 22,500 megawatts, and cost more than $25 billion. On the positive side of the ledger, the power generated at the dam is produced without the burning of soft coal.

But the negative side of the ledger also contains entries: archaeologists have reminded the Chinese government and the world that the site of the "second cradle" of Chinese civilization, as important as the first in the Yellow River basin, is being inundated. Many fish species are threatened with extinction because of the slower flow above the dam, and the upriver journey of river sturgeon to spawn is thwarted. While water quality in the growing reservoir remains stable, pollution in the tributaries flowing into the reservoir has put that quality in jeopardy.

Unanticipated landslides in the steep mountains along the riverbank appear to have been triggered by the rising water. The threats of shifting land and pollution led authorities to order the movement of another two million residents of Chongqing living near the banks of the reservoir. The 2008 earthquake in Sichuan's Wenchuan County that killed more than 80,000 people alerted the world to the fact that the reservoir is located in a geologically unstable area, and indeed, scientists studying the earthquake suggested it may have been triggered by the weight of the water in a nearby reservoir. If the Three Gorges Dam were to fail for any reason, the downstream disaster would be difficult to calculate.

As there are tensions among federal, state, and local authorities in the United States, the relationships among central, provincial, and local authorities in China are far from problem-free. Nonetheless, the example of the Three Gorges Dam project suggests that the power grid, while prone to gridlock, can on occasion be made to work on major undertakings.

Thirty years ago, it appeared to me that China's fissiparous tendencies might well cause it to "come apart at the seams," as I wrote at the time. Interregional inequities and rivalries seemed to point to the possibility that segments of the country might choose to ignore Beijing entirely and go it alone. That possibility seems much less likely today. Reducing the inequalities among coastal, central, and western provinces has been a high priority of the central government.

And, as we have seen, centralizing the collection of most tax revenues has significantly strengthened the leverage that Beijing wields over the provinces. As a testament to its newfound confidence in the center versus region dynamic, in 2004, Beijing blessed the founding of an awkwardly named Pan Pearl River Delta Regional Cooperation and Development Forum that includes the special administrative regions of Hong Kong and Macao and the nine provinces of Yunnan, Guizhou, Guangdong, Fujian, Jiangxi, Hunan, Guangxi, Hainan, and Sichuan. The purpose of the forum is described as eliminating non-tariff barriers and coordinating regional economic policy. Such a move by Beijing was described by economists in Hong Kong as having been "unthinkable" thirty years ago.

Chapter 10: Cities

Nowhere is the change in China since the beginning of the reform period so evident as in its coastal cities. Thirty years ago, China's city streets were lined with dilapidated two- and three-story buildings and filled with bicycles and buses. Stores, most of them state-owned, were stocked with garish and serviceable goods, virtually all of them domestically produced. Travelers were offered spartan and dimly lit hotel rooms with hot water available only sporadically and with little reference to the hours one generally bathes. The cities virtually closed down when the sun set: storefronts were boarded, crowds dispersed, and the sidewalks were as dimly lit as the hotel rooms.

Today, cars have taken the place to bicycles, towering office buildings and apartment blocks line the streets, and shops, many of them franchises of international chains, are filled with a myriad of goods. In fact, at the time of its opening in 2005, the Golden Resources Mall in Dongguan (东关), Guangdong, was the largest in the world. The drab blue or gray uniforms of the past have given way to brightly colored and frequently stylish apparel. Five-star hotels provide all the amenities one would expect to find in New York City or Paris. And China's major Cities, particularly Beijing, host to the 2008 Olympics, boast major structures by world-renowned architects. Street life extends well into the night hours. Neon lights and illuminated storefronts beckon. Restaurants and fast-food outlets are abundant, and their clientele is numerous. Films, most domestically produced, attract large audiences, as do discos and karaoke bars. One is reminded of Nebraska senator Kenneth Wherry's oft-cited 1940 prediction: "With God's help, we will lift Shanghai up and up, ever up, until it is just like Kansas City." Eighty-five years on, it would appear he chose the wrong target.

Mao Zedong was decidedly not a city person. Born in a small village in rural Hunan, he spent his youth deep in the Chinese countryside. Having concluded that the Communist revolution was to be won in China by mobilizing the support of the peasants, he proposed to build a peasant army and, using guerrilla tactics, seize control of the countryside; once the Japanese occupation was over and Nationalist troops had been driven out, the Red Anny would control the nation, for the cities, cut off from their sources of supply in the hinterlands, would of necessity fall to them. Having decided on this strategy, Mao and his colleagues threw in their lot with rural China for the duration of the revolution; doing so left a permanent mark on them, their party, the policies they subsequently pursued, and rural China's residents.

Mao was of the opinion that the countryside was the seat of a kind of primitive virtue, the city, by contrast, the seat of decadence and corruption. During the 1960s and 1970s, the highly disruptive and apparently irrational practice of *xiafang,* or rustication, whereby urban residents were involuntarily removed and made to live in remote rural settings, some for a short time, others for years, was based on this opinion. It was taken as an article of faith that their rural experiences would cure city dwellers of their urban flaws and instill virtue in them.

But Mao's reading of Marx presented him with a picture of urban life that conflicted with his experience. He found persuasive the idea that the proletariat was formed in the industrial workplace, a process that, despite the pain inflicted by the capitalists in control, was salutary and necessary, for only the proletariat could lead the ultimate advance toward communism. Although he had limited experience outside China, Mao understood that modern societies are urban and industrial; for China to take its place in the world, preferably at the forefront of modernity, it must first clean up, then build up its cities. So, he looked for a way to resolve these

contradictory views of the city. Bringing industry to the countryside seemed to him infinitely better than bringing the peasant to the city. The wave of rural industrialization in Mao's declining years was in effect a realization of this vision, though it was undertaken more for economic and strategic than for ideological reasons.

Reforming the urban economy in China was significantly more complex than reforming agriculture. The initial changes in the industrial workplace, begun as early as 1979, were undertaken only on an experimental basis, and full-scale urban economic reform was postponed until 1984. By that time, the successes of the household responsibility system in the countryside and the experiments in the urban sector had built a following for extending the reforms throughout the urban economy.

Reform in the countryside, as we shall see presently, had been greatly facilitated by two factors: that agricultural production as practiced in rural China is a relatively simple enterprise involving little in the way of technology or specialized expertise, and that farm households live where they work and the family operates as a production unit. These features meant that the farm household was well-suited and fully able to take on the responsibility for decisions about farming that had once been made by production team leaders. Once re-empowered, the household willingly took on this new role. Spurred on by effective incentives that soon raised household income, agricultural workers worked harder and more efficiently, and farm output increased.

Although some city families live and work in circumstances similar to those of a farming family, with all the employed family members working for the same enterprise and living in housing provided by that enterprise, for most city dwellers, the situation is very different. Family members work for different employers and are very likely to commute to their workplaces, where the labor is complex. A household lacks the qualifications to make decisions in the production process, since, except in the smallest workshops, industrial production requires collaboration, coordination, equipment, and technology.

The goal of urban reform also differed. Although no one in a position of authority in China would be rash enough to say so, the goal of the rural reforms had really been to restore private enterprise to family farms. Fictions were devised to make this goal conform to "socialism with Chinese characteristics" (for example, households were initially given use rights but not titles to the land to preserve the appearance of collective ownership), but despite these fictions, the practical effect was to privatize agricultural production and to supplement it with collectively owned industrial enterprises.

Full-scale privatization of industry was neither the spoken nor the unspoken goal of urban economic reform at the outset. Reformers encouraged the growth of private and collective enterprises to increase the supply and variety of goods and services available to city dwellers and to give them more jobs, but privatization was intended to supplement, not to supplant, a core of revivified state-owned industrial complexes. Hence, while analogies could be drawn from the agricultural reforms and applied to the urban reform process, they were only analogies, not models.

The urban reforms outlined in a document adopted by the Third Plenum of the Twelfth Central Committee in October 1984 set out to change three key relationships of state-owned enterprises, those with the state, with employees, and with customers.

The relationship between the enterprise and the state prior to the reforms was one of total dependence: the state owned the enterprise and managed it with goals and targets set in the national economic plan; the enterprise itself had no incentive to maximize its profits and minimize its losses. Profits were recouped in their entirety by the state, and operating losses were made up by state grants.

Drawing an analogy from the distinction between landownership and land use rights, the urban reform document distinguished between an enterprise's ownership, which would remain in the hands of the state, and its management, which would have full authority to run it. In the past, factories were virtual government agencies; once reformed, they would be independent legal entities with the power to transform and develop, and with the responsibility for their own profits and losses. Managers were responsible for planning, supply, production, and marketing, for appointing supervisory personnel and recruiting workers, for determining wages and rewards, and for setting prices on their products. At the same time, they were told to trim the bloated workforce and increase productivity.

To establish the economic independence of each enterprise, the state proposed that they all pay a fixed-rate corporate tax rather than turn over all profits to the state at year's end. It would be up to the manager to decide how much to reinvest and how much to put toward wages and benefits for the workforce. Similarly, the state would no longer subsidize enterprises that operated at a loss, although bank loans would be available, within limits. The responsibilities of the state were thus limited to appointing managers, levying taxes, extending credit, establishing new enterprises, and consolidating, closing, moving, or transforming enterprises that failed.

Sweeping changes were also called for in the relationship between the enterprise and its employees. Until very recently a position in a state-owned enterprise was highly coveted, since the average annual wage, though only about seventy-five dollars at the then-current rate of exchange, was better than what workers received in other sectors. Actual wages were based on seniority; there was no relation between remuneration and performance. Job security and the benefits packages were also unparalleled elsewhere in the economy, since workers in state-owned factories enjoyed lifetime tenure, popularly known as the "iron rice bowl" (*tiefanwan 铁饭碗*): once a worker was hired, it was next to impossible to dismiss him or her except in the case of a criminal conviction. The benefits package met virtually all a worker's needs: housing at a rent so low that it did not cover the cost of maintaining the housing stock, subsidies to help with food and transportation, free medical care, and China's only full retirement plan.

A word here about China's pension system. The system features three layers. The first layer includes several public pension schemes, some mandatory (the Basic Old Age Insurance and Public Employee Pensions) and some voluntary (the newly formed Resident Pension scheme that includes both urban and rural residents). The public pension systems are managed by local governments. The second layer consists of annuity programs voluntarily provided by employers; the third layer consists of household savings-based annuity insurance policies. The first layer of the system has more than 900 million participants and the total public expenditure is just short of 5 billion RMB, or about 5% of China GDP. The second and third layers are much more limited, involving only about 20 million participants.

Graph #2:

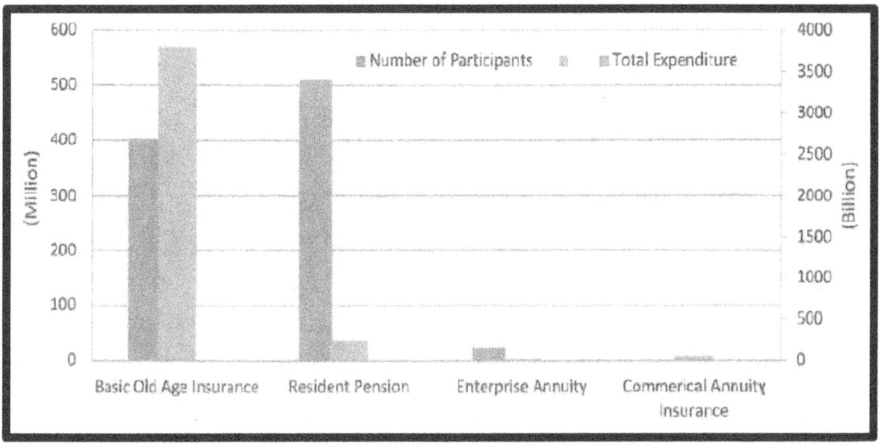

Comparison of the Various Chinese Pension Schemes

Source: China Ministry of Human Resources and Social Security, China's Statistical Yearbook of Insurance Industry (2017)

Until the costs of maintaining the benefits package became untenable, workers in the larger state-owned enterprises enjoyed what could be called, to borrow a term from American retirement homes, "total care": childcare at factory-owned creches, education at factory managed schools, medical care at factory-operated clinics, and access to tickets for entertainment and travel through factory-run procurement offices. Retired workers got pensions amounting to about three-quarters of their last wages; they might go on living in factory-owned housing, and they enjoyed virtually all the amenities provided to their working colleagues. In addition, through a system known as *dingti* (顶替–to replace someone), they could get jobs for their children as they themselves left the workforce.

The 1984 reforms sought to improve the abysmally low productivity of the industrial workforce by introducing incentives. The tenure system was phased out, and new workers were hired on limited-term contracts, renewable depending on performance.

The standardized wage scale based exclusively on seniority was replaced by one based on productivity.

To change their relationship with customers, enterprises were given new authority to determine their products' prices. The reform document described a "chaotic" system of prices, in which variation in quality of goods was ignored, the prices of producer goods, raw materials, and semi-processed goods were artificially depressed, and the state absorbed the difference between the prices that urban residents paid for food and housing and the actual cost of these items.

Creating order out of this chaos would inevitably be painful for city dwellers, so the decision was made to implement price reform piecemeal rather than all at once. Increases in living expenses were to be partially offset by wage increases and special subsidies. Price reform was a highly sensitive issue, for it could cause inflation, and inflation, the government knew, would trigger a strong reaction among city dwellers.

Reform of the urban economy was launched in earnest in the spring of 1985 and proceeded with some success for three years. The inflationary effects began to be felt in 1988, and retrenchment measures were implemented in the fall of that year. When concern over urban inflation (among other issues) brought hundreds of thousands out into the streets in protest during the spring of 1989, reform of the urban economy was put on hold. It was revived again in 1992, but the old reform program was ill-suited to the new circumstances. When the urban reforms were announced in 1984, it was noted that about a third of China's hundred thousand state-owned industrial enterprises were operating at a loss; by the early 1990s, that number had nearly doubled. Under these conditions, replacing subsidies with bank loans was impossible because the banks had all but exhausted available credit, and the state was once again in the business of subsidizing losses. Government support for state-owned enterprises amounted to nearly $50 billion in 1994, including, in addition to outright subsidies, "stability and unity loans," tax waivers, and supplementary payments to workers, a figure equivalent to half of China's total national budget.

Beyond the enterprises' profit and loss statements, the picture was even grimmer. One-third of the output of state-owned enterprises in 1994 remained unsold at year's end. In addition, those enterprises were very slow in settling their financial obligations among themselves. This so-called triangular debt among enterprises in the state sector had amounted to an additional seventy billion dollars by early 1995. Nor did the situation improve in 1996. During the first quarter of that year, losses in state-owned enterprises exceeded profits for the first time; indeed, total net losses exceeded the entire equity of China's banks. In 1996, collective, private, and joint-venture enterprises made up 99% of industrial profits, while state-owned enterprises contributed only one percent.

A major reason for the unprofitability of China's state-owned enterprises was their burden of payroll and benefits. Enterprises were, on average, about 30 percent overstaffed, yet because the tenure system was still in effect for workers hired before the reforms began, it was very difficult to downsize the workforce. Nationwide, enterprises are responsible for the pensions of some eighteen million individuals, and the number is growing. The cost of health coverage for workers and retirees is also increasing sharply. With no health insurance plans, enterprises are effectively self-insured, covering the medical costs of their employees as they are incurred; when the cost of medical care was very low, this was not onerous, but as the costs have increased, enterprises are limiting the coverage they offer. Lastly, housing was an additional financial burden, which is only increasing as housing stock ages and prices rise.

China's central government had acknowledged for some time that the state sector was in crisis. The current level of government financial support needed to keep state-sector enterprises afloat was untenable even in the short term. A logical, if drastic, solution was to allow the least successful state-owned enterprises to go out of business. With this in mind, and after extensive debate, the National People's Congress passed a bankruptcy law in early 1989. Yet fully implementing that law would have sent hundreds of thousands of workers onto the streets, unemployed and angry, and the government regarded this as equally untenable.

A major step in the process of resolving this dilemma and divesting the state of its ownership of failing firms took place with the adoption by the National People's Congress of the Company Law in 1994. The law provided the legal framework for the various forms of ownership introduced by the party-state. State-owned enterprises took on the legal status of corporations, and the corporations had a variety of ownership arrangements.

One that gained some popularity in the early 1990s was that of the enterprise group, in which a marriage would be arranged between a profitable, well-managed state-owned corporation and an unprofitable, ill-managed one, the theory being that the successful one would, with its better management and new ideas, pull the unsuccessful corporation up. In practice, the unsuccessful corporation often served as a sea anchor on its more successful partner, thereby multiplying the effects of its failure.

Another solution was divestiture: the state sold its interest in the enterprise to the employees or to outsiders in the form of equity shares, the enterprise moved from the state to the private or quasi-private sector, and its new shareholders shouldered the burdens once borne by the government. A variation on this idea was to get a foreign investor to buy out some or all the assets of an unsuccessful state-owned enterprise. But determining the value of state-owned assets was problematic for many potential investors. Some enterprises were in such bad shape that their real estate holdings turned out to be their only asset of any value. A divestiture plan was adopted at the Fifteenth National Party Congress in 1997 that called for selling off all but the five hundred largest state-owned enterprises. By the end of 1998, the number of state-owned industries had dropped by half; it has continued to decline, though more slowly, since then.

For the worst-off enterprises, bankruptcy was the only realistic alternative. A plan announced in late 1994 was designed to avoid some of the potential dangers involved in putting state firms out of business. It applied the bankruptcy law experimentally to enterprises in eighteen cities; the cities got central government funds to assist in worker outplacement and to establish municipal social security systems, giving retirement support to those put out of work. Even with these built-in safeguards, the bankruptcy program was filled with political risk for local politicians. It was also highly unpopular among those who continued to believe that a large and vibrant state sector is the *sine qua non* of a socialist economy. The outcome of the transition is shown in Table 11:

Table 11: Ownership Composition of Chinese Industrial Enterprises

	Number of firms	**Percent of output**
State-owned enterprises and enterprises controlled by the state	150,000	34.2
Joint-stock corporations	137	37.3
Foreign-invested enterprises	49,700	26.5
Collective enterprises	295,200	2.0
Totals	**495,037**	**100**

Source: China Statistical Yearbook 2024

While the immediate crisis was addressed, over the longer term, a solution had to be found for lightening the onerous burden of the benefits package once borne by the state sector. Creating a government-funded retirement program was the first step. The system that was put in place was based on worker contributions, was available only to urban workers, and was managed by local governments, not the central government. In 2000, the State Council moved to establish a national social security fund that currently covers more than 116 million urban workers, or somewhat more than a third of the workforce. In 2007, expenditures for what the budget referred to as the "social safety net and employment effort" amounted to about $80 billion of state-owned enterprise assets, 94 percent of which was funded by local governments. In the case of some foreign joint ventures, the state-owned enterprises were split into two independent corporations, one a manufacturing concern, the other a service corporation providing employee benefits. A portion of the production company's profits was earmarked as a contribution to the service company, but the service company had to find cost reduction strategies and increase employee contributions to bring its operations into some approximation of fiscal balance.

Plans are also afoot to change the housing system. First, rents have been raised on factory-owned housing at least to a level that covers construction and maintenance costs. Although rents are still remarkably low, the current average urban household expenditure on housing in 2024 was $865, accounting for 22.1 percent of total household living expenses, some sixteen times what it was in 1985. The average household budget in China is shown in Table 12.

Table 12: Average Annual Per Capita Living Expenses in China in 2024 (in dollars)

	Amount	**Percent**
Food	1,160	29.8
Transportation and communications	548	14.0
Recreation, education, and culture	440	11.3
Clothing	210	5.3
Housing	864	22.1
Health care	351	9.0
Miscellaneous goods and services	106	2.7
Household expenses	213	5.4
Other expenses	155	0.4
Totals	**4,047**	**100**

Second, the number of new employees entitled to the full package of benefits was reduced. Many of those newly employed in the state sector are hired on fixed-term contracts with limited access to benefits. And third, enterprises are selling off their housing stock to residents. This was not easy at first, since the prices were high and the quality was low. There was little incentive for tenants paying low monthly rents to increase their out-of-pocket expenses and take responsibility for maintaining their decrepit quarters. As the property market has begun to grow in China's cities, however, the possibility of getting in on the ground floor of what might be lucrative real estate investments is sweetening the deal in the minds of many tenants.

A major push to construct new housing has increased and improved the housing stock, and per capita living space in China's cities has triple over the last twenty years, but people still have just over four hundred square feet, on average, of living space. Housing is still inadequate, most apartment buildings are old and in disrepair, and most urban families live in cramped quarters and must share bathroom and kitchen facilities with their neighbors. Currently, old housing stock is being pulled down and replaced by high- rise apartments and condominiums, to the distress of residents of the courtyard houses of Beijing and the graceful neighborhoods of the former foreign concessions in Shanghai. (Historic preservation is not a high priority among China's urban planners.) Moreover, farmland on the cities' outskirts is being transformed into "California-style" housing developments with names such as Sun City and Orange County. Two-bedroom condos are selling for more than six hundred thousand dollars. In Chongqing, China's largest and fastest-growing city, economic zones are being developed around the sprawling city limits. Housing is being constructed in areas with a one-hour commute into the city; rural residents are being compensated for their land with a promise of a much-coveted urban *hukou (户口–residency status). Indeed, the current concern is that the real estate market in China's major cities is experiencing the bursting of a bubble with serious consequences for the economy as a whole.*

Those who are investing in high-end real estate and purchasing the more than thirty million cars sold in China in 2024 are members of a growing upper middle class based almost exclusively in China's cities. Approximately 6.2 million individuals in China have personal assets worth $1 million or more. More recently, the Chinese Academy of Social Sciences estimated that at least ten thousand businessmen in China have net assets that exceed ten million dollars. These numbers help us understand how China has come to have one of the world's largest gaps between rich and poor.

With the growth of an urban upper middle class has come the emergence of NIMBY (not in my backyard) social protest. Property owners in both Shanghai and Shenzhen have taken to the streets to protest the building of expressways and high-speed rail lines too near their upscale condominiums.

The official figure for unemployment in the urban sector of China's economy is a modest five percent. Many of the unemployed are young people who have yet to start full-time work. (Indeed, the Chinese term for the unemployed, *daiye* (待业), means "awaiting employment" and reflects the concerns of the group.) Finding employment for young people entering the workforce, some twenty million annually, is a major task for the government and necessitates, some estimate, a growth rate of at least seven percent in the economy. Nonetheless, were these the only urban residents whose livelihoods were at risk, China's leaders would have relatively little to worry about, particularly given the current growth rate of the urban economy.

The official figure, however, is a far from perfect guide to the employment status of the urban workforce. First, it omits workers who have been laid off from state-owned enterprises. By the beginning of 2023 that number had reached more than 35 million, only about half of whom had found new jobs. In addition, the unemployment figure does not include workers who have been put on furlough by state-owned enterprises, which, as we have seen, remained significantly overstaffed. By the late 1990s up to 10 percent of the state sector workforce, or more than fourteen million workers, had been placed on unpaid furloughs or on reduced hours and reduced pay. Laid off and furloughed workers were transferred to so-called reemployment centers run by the Ministry of Labor and Social Security, which provided them with stipends. Neither group has yet found full-time employment, and neither group is counted among the unemployed.

Second, the official unemployment figures do not mention the approximately 300 million migrants in the urban workforce. Those temporary city residents who do find work are employed only on a temporary basis, many of them work only intermittently, and millions are, for all practical purposes, unemployed. Because their legal residence is the rural communities from which they come, they are officially not city residents and have no claim on housing, health care, education, or social services. They have, in effect, slipped through the cracks of what was once a very tight system of social control. These migrants, living just beyond the long arm of the law, are purported to be major contributors to the increasing amount of urban crime. They are a current headache and a potential catastrophe for urban officials.

Some migrants are able to find work that pays reasonably well-particularly by contrast with what they would be earning in their home villages. But many others are overworked, paid only intermittently or sometimes not at all, and their workplaces and living conditions are deplorable. One migrant worker, Cai Gaoxiang, secured work assembling toys in a factory in the city of Yiwu (義烏) in Zhejiang Province. When orders for toys are high, he told a New York Times reporter, assemblers work fourteen hours a day, seven days a week, and might clear $120 in a month. More typical are $90 a month and, in a slow month, $50. "Often it's just not enough to get by on," he said. Despite these conditions, migrants are estimated to send more than $40 billion to their home villages each year.

The issues of the residency status of migrant workers and their economic and civil rights have been very much on the minds of urban officialdom of late. A set of regulations covering migrant workers was issued by the government in 1982 but never formally enacted into law. Chinese legal scholars petitioned the National People's Congress in 2003, challenging the constitutionality of the administrative regulations and citing flagrant examples of migrants being arbitrarily arrested, confined, and expelled from the cities. In response, Beijing authorities rescinded the regulations permitting the detention and expulsion of migrants without legal proceedings.

In 2001 the All-China Federation of Trade Unions signed an agreement with the United Nations International Labor Office to work on issues of job creation, a new pension plan, and unemployment insurance. Six years later the National People's Congress passed a law strengthening the state-sponsored labor union and empowering it to deal with the rights of migrant workers.

But migrant labor is necessary for the urban economy. Indeed, it is analogous in some ways to the dependence of some sectors of the U.S. economy on immigrant labor. While there is unemployment in both economies, there are jobs that are difficult to fill with non--migrant workers. As a case in point, the bulk of the construction work in preparation for the Beijing Olympics in 2008 was performed by migrants, who were then bundled unceremoniously out of town before the foreign guests arrived.

Taking all these numbers together, China's cities have as many as 100 million residents, or a quarter of their workforce, who are not fully employed and up to 150 million nonresidents who are competing with one another for short-term low-end jobs. In short, there are a disturbingly large number of people whose economic needs are not being fully met; their dissatisfactions may manifest themselves in the very political instability the party-state is trying so hard to avoid.

China's cities contained only 18 percent of the country's population in 1978; today, they contain 65 percent of the population. The cities are growing at a rate of 1.5 percent per year, and urban planners estimate that the urban population will exceed 70 percent by 2040. The question of the residency status of urban migrants has thus assumed a certain urgency. Residency status *(hukou)* included two elements. The first was based on employment and divided the Chinese population into "agricultural" and "nonagricultural." The second referred to the geographical location of an individual's permanent residency. The first step in reforming this process came in the 1990s and involved transferring the authority to change *hukou* status from the central government to local governments. A second reform of the system involved eliminating the employment categories of "agricultural" and "nonagricultural," leaving only the geographical element in place. In the mid-1990s, some cities sold urban *hukou* as a moneymaking enterprise; Shanghai, for example, established a blue card for migrant workers, providing them access to housing and city services if they met certain criteria. Although they now have the authority to alter the *hukou* status of temporary residents, all but a few city governments are very reluctant to do so, given the financial obligations the change would incur.

Immediately following the Japanese surrender in 1945, the Chinese Communists gained public support by pointing to runaway inflation in the economy and rampant corruption in the political system. They blamed the Nationalist government for both and argued that it appeared powerless to control either. The Communists promised to put in place a scrupulously honest regime that would master the problem of inflation, and they did just that upon taking power in 1949. That regime had become hopelessly mired in corruption by the early 1990s, and after three decades of nearly stable prices, inflation reappeared, the unwelcome consequence of the economic reforms and recent rapid economic growth.

The average rate of inflation during the first three decades of the People's Republic was just under two percent; retail prices rose only about 65 percent in thirty years. However, as we have seen, in 1988 the retail price index increased by 18.5 percent, and even more for urban residents, and it continued to mount through early 1989.

Graph #3:

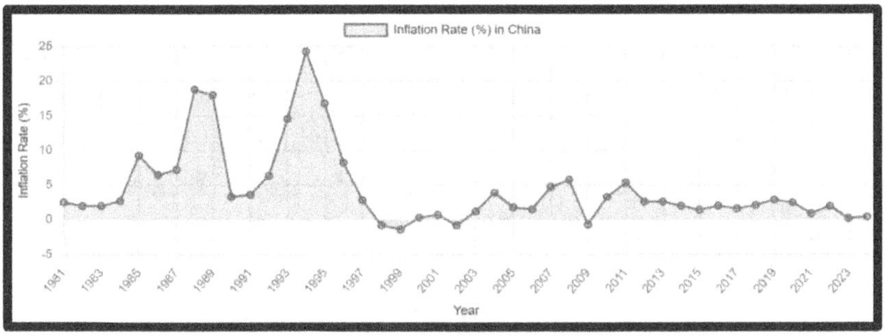

Annual Rate of Inflation in China 1981-2024

Source: http//cn.icalculator.com/current-and-historical-inflation-rates.html

The retrenchment measures the government had put in place to slow economic growth and curb inflation in late 1988 were redoubled after the demonstrations had been put down in early June 1989. As a result, the overall inflation rate was reduced from 17.8 percent in 1989 to just a little over 2 percent in 1990. It began to rise again in 1993 and reached a new high of 24.2 percent in 1994 (35 percent in the urban economy).

Until 1995, the inflation rate in China's cities consistently exceeded the rate for the economy as a whole by several percentage points. Food expenditures account for a high proportion of urban household budgets, and food prices in urban markets increased 32 percent in 1994---partly because of the effort to bring the prices paid to rural producers closer to market levels and partly because of bad weather during the growing season.

The government had difficulty meeting the targets it set each year to bring inflation under control because it was unwilling or unable to address the underlying causes. It solved its cash-flow problems by increasing the money supply, it used up bank credit to shore up the teetering state sector, and it failed to control local government speculation in property schemes. It seemed to harbor the hope that periodic wage increases would anesthetize the public to the effects of inflation.

In 1995, Zhu Rongji, then serving as vice premier, took a series of draconian measures to reverse these tendencies. Under his leadership, the government brought inflation under control, and by the end of 1997, the rate had been reduced to 2 percent. In subsequent years, indeed, deflation rather than inflation became the issue. At the beginning of 2000, the economy was experiencing its twenty-seventh straight month of a declining consumer price index, and the government was desperately seeking incentives to increase consumer spending. The inflation rate currently stands at -0.1%.

Increasing consumer spending is once again on the Chinese government's agenda, this time to absorb the effect of a sharp downturn in exports occasioned by the world financial crisis. China has one of the highest rates of personal savings in the world, reaching 39.2 percent in 2024. (The comparable figure in the United States is 5.2%.).

Graph #4:

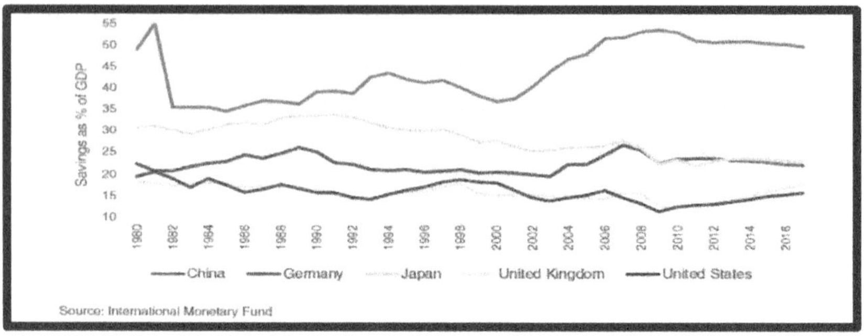

Comparative Rates of Personal Savings: China, Germany, Japan, the United Kingdom, and the United States

It is a phenomenon that dates, interestingly enough, from the beginning of the period of economic reform in 1978. As we have already seen, many of the changes to the economy have substantially reduced the degree to which the Chinese can rely on their government to supply them with goods and services, such as education, health care, and pensions, at little or no cost. As a result, amassing a substantial savings account is seen as a necessity in the current economy. Discouraging some of that saving and encouraging greater consumption are the government's current goals. It is hampered in the former task by the fact that interest rates on individual savings accounts are already very low, ranging from 1.2 to 1.6 percent.

If inflation is no longer an issue for China's urban residents, corruption is still omnipresent. China's city dwellers experience corruption in their daily lives no less than do those who live in the countryside, though differently. Rural residents are in closer touch with local government officials, and it is very often the acts of petty corruption committed by individuals whom they know, at least indirectly, that aggravate them and undermine their confidence in the party-state. China's cities are more tightly buttoned, and the opportunities for small-scale graft, bribery, and the like are relatively restricted, so urban residents experience corruption more indirectly, but on a grander scale.

Understanding the inherent dangers, Jiang Zemin responded to a petition drafted in February 1995 by twelve intellectuals that was addressed to the National People's Congress and called on that body to mount a national campaign to stamp out corruption. Jiang's campaign began with a bang. Zhou Guanwu, chairman of the massive Capital Iron and Steel Corporation and a confidant of Deng Xiaoping's, resigned suddenly and unexpectedly; shortly thereafter, his son, said to be a business partner of one of Deng's sons, was detained in relation to unspecified economic crimes. Two months later, the suicide of Wang Baosen, executive deputy mayor of Beijing, became public. He and others in the Beijing government had been accused of extracting bribes in conjunction with the granting of construction permits. Within a few weeks, Beijing Communist Party secretary Chen Xitong, tarred with the same brush, resigned under duress. An ally of Li Peng, then serving as premier, Chen was later removed from his position in the Party Politburo, dismissed from the party, and, in 1998, sentenced to sixteen years in prison.

The attack on corruption in high places then moved quickly out of the capital and into the provinces. Perhaps the most prominent case was that of Chongqing Party Secretary Bo Xilai, who was convicted of bribery, embezzlement, and abuse of power and sentenced to life imprisonment. But just as quickly, the campaign ground to a halt, for Jiang Zemin discovered that, unable to control a nationwide campaign, he risked losing supporters critical to his efforts at consolidating his position as Deng's successor. By September, the drive against corruption had all but ended.

It is a recurring pattern. Designed to stop corrupt behavior on the part of government and military officials and, as a side effect, to recover lost tariff revenue on as much as twelve billion dollars in imported goods each year, a crackdown on smuggling was announced with great fanfare in 1998. In the coastal province of Fujian, the campaign uncovered a ring of smugglers in the port city of Xiamen, and more than 150 local officials were detained. The ensuing investigation found evidence of more than ten billion dollars in smuggled goods. Lin Youfang, head of the Fujian Foreign Trade Corporation, was eventually implicated, but because Lin was the divorced wife of a Politburo member who was a close associate of Jiang Zemin's, the case against her went nowhere.

Other high-profile corruption cases have included the misappropriation of more than $40 million in flood control funds, which, had they been put to their intended use, would have saved lives and property in the extensive flooding of 1998-99. Similarly, Zhu Rongji accused local officials of misappropriating funds from the $11.2 billion budget for relocating individuals and enterprises from areas flooded by the Three Gorges Dam.

Hu Jintao and Wen Jiabao have followed in Jiang's footsteps by making public pronouncements on the need to fight corruption and by engaging in high-profile prosecutions of those accused of major instances of graft. Each year, the party-state announces the number of corruption cases it has prosecuted–855,000 in 2024–and each year, corruption continues to thrive. Chinese cynics believe that until the party-state takes the unprecedented step of creating and empowering an agency independent of both the party and the government to address the problem of political corruption, there is no hope of bringing it under control.

China's urban population has increased from 40 million to 911 million over the last fifty years, and this does not include the 150 million migrants. Shanghai's population per square mile, for example, is a third higher than that of New York City. The construction of urban infrastructure- roads, bridges, sewers, water supply systems, and like- while extensive, still lags behind population growth. Even though subway systems are under construction in more than a dozen Chinese cities, getting from place to place, whether by bicycle, public transportation, automobile, or on foot, is most often still very slow. Moreover, air and water qualities are seriously deficient in virtually all Chinese cities. Life in China's cities, as is the case with life in cities everywhere, is not easy. The pace of life and work is exhausting, the cities are crowded, all but a few residents lack economic security, and many lack any permanency in their residence status. Add to these difficulties the insecurities brought on by unemployment, underemployment, corruption, and the lack of confidence of most urban Chinese in the capability of their government officials, and you have a potent set of discontents.

For many urban residents, religion provides some solace for the difficulties of their lives. As we have seen, tens of millions of Chinese were attracted to the teachings of *Falun Gong*, despite its having been condemned by the party-state as a "superstitious cult." Although Falun Gong is by far the largest and most public movement of its kind in China, it is by no means an isolated phenomenon. This surge in religious faith is symptomatic of a widespread quest on the part of many Chinese for a belief system to replace the now discredited Marxist-Leninist-Maoist ideology of the past and the rampant self-seeking individualism of today. Some Chinese describe feeling rudderless and adrift on a fast-moving current of social and economic change. For some who are experiencing this anomie, superstition or genuine religious faith seems to offer relief. Others find the individual empowerment encouraged by the self-help aspect of a movement like Falun Gong appealing.

For its part, the party-state has advanced nationalism as a means of redirecting its citizens' discontents. Chinese nationalism first came to the fore as a reaction to Japan's incursions on Chinese sovereignty a century ago. Communists very effectively used anti-Japanese nationalism to mobilize popular support as they consolidated their position against the Nationalists in the 1930s and 1940s. Anti-Japanese sentiment is also part of the current revival of nationalism. Periodic efforts made by Japanese patriots to deny the atrocities committed by Japanese troops during what came to be known as the rape of Nanjing in 1937 evoke both official and unofficial Chinese outrage.

Anti-American nationalism, absent from the Chinese scene for thirty years, has reemerged as the United States, no longer rivaled by Russia, has undertaken what Jiang Zemin once called a "global strategy for world hegemony." When NATO bombs hit the Chinese embassy in Belgrade in May 1999, killing three staff members, tens of thousands of urban residents in China turned out in violent and very well-organized anti-American protests. Of course, the United States is also deeply implicated in another issue that the party-state has utilized to whip up nationalist fervor: the reunification with Taiwan.

But anti-American nationalism is itself a source of anguish for young Chinese. Many of those who hurled stones at the American embassy returned soon thereafter, this time to apply for visas that would permit them to study at American universities or look for jobs in Silicon Valley. Moreover, contemporary urban life in China is by no means immune from the dominant influence the United States has on popular culture worldwide. Change is unsettling, and the Chinese people, particularly those who live in the largest cities, have experienced a sustained period of extraordinary change. The revival of *qigong,* on the one hand, and of Chinese nationalism, on the other. underscores the dissatisfaction of many Chinese and the tendency to express that dissatisfaction in spontaneous and unpredictable wavs.

Chapter 11: Rural Discontents

The sheer size of China's rural population is one of its most arresting features: 500 million people, close to one and a half times the total population of the United States. During the civil war, China's rural population stood at about 450 million. Rural residents were recognized by Mao Zedong as a singular resource that could give the Communist Party the leverage it needed to defeat the city-based forces of the Nationalist Party. And so, he set aside the conventional Marxist-Leninist canon and focused his attention on peasant grievances: their desperate poverty and their concern about the depredations committed by the Japanese forces seizing and occupying so much of China's territory. Attending to these concerns, the Chinese Communists mobilized their overwhelming social force and with the help of the peasantry brought about the victory of the Communist revolution in 1949.

Graph #5:

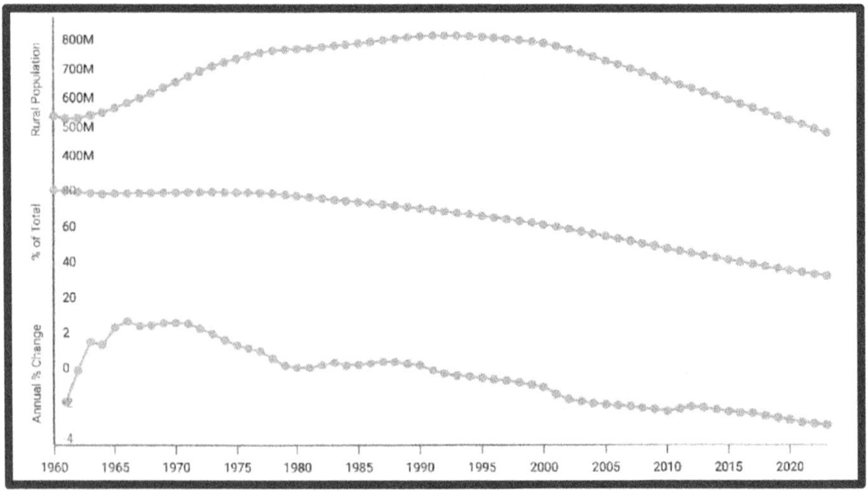

China's Rural Population, 1960-2024

Source: https://www.macrotrends.net

By means of land reform and the creation of collective farms in the years immediately following the Communist victory, rural incomes were equalized and raised. But in other ways, the exploitation of the rural population continued. Keeping the price it paid for grain artificially low, the government turned a profit at the expense of the peasantry and then used this profit as the source of capital for industrializing China's cities; city dwellers also got government subsidies for housing and food that were unavailable to the rural majority. In the thirty years prior to the reform period, per capita income in the countryside increased less than 50 percent. Moreover, it was the rural population that suffered the most serious consequences of China's disastrously misguided agricultural policies during the late 1950s, policies that resulted in more than twenty million deaths from starvation in rural villages throughout the country.

Deng Xiaoping began his economic reforms in the countryside for two reasons: he knew that reforming agriculture would be much easier than reforming industry, and if the reform of agriculture were successful, he could use that success to persuade his skeptical colleagues to take on the more complicated tasks of reforming industry.

Indispensable to the success of agricultural reform was the household responsibility system, which had originated as an experiment in the early 1960s, when Deng and his colleagues were looking for ways to alleviate the disaster brought on by the Maoist excesses of the Great Leap Forward in the late 1950s. In the experiment, land was taken out of the collective and given to households to farm; any household that produced over the quota set by the local government was permitted to sell its product on the rural free market. The experiment had been successful, but it was abandoned once the disaster abated, and Mao later denounced it as unacceptably capitalist in spirit.

The household responsibility system was resurrected in 1978, once again as an experiment in one or two locations. But almost overnight, it was adopted by farming communities throughout China. The incentives it incorporated quickly boosted productivity, output, and household income. When these increments began to slow seven years later, a further round of reform stabilized the contract system and opened the door to the proliferation of small-scale industry in the rural economy.

The combined effect of these reforms was to raise rural incomes by a factor of three over the first twelve years of the reform period. A lot of publicity was given to the first "ten thousand *kuai* ("piece," informal for *yuan*) households" (households whose annual income had reached the equivalent of $1,400). When news of this new phenomenon reached city residents, they found themselves envious of their country cousins for the first time in memory and were more than ready to see replicated in the city some of the entrepreneurial opportunities available beyond the suburbs. And given their significantly improved standard of living, China's rural residents were generally quite satisfied with their lot at the end of the 1980s. They were somewhat insulated from the inflation that loomed large in the cities, and corruption, the second most frequent complaint of city dwellers, had yet to become fully visible in rural communities. This helps explain why the slogans and speeches of students and workers who rushed into the streets of every major city in China in the spring of 1989 fell on deaf ears in the countryside, why there was so little sympathy among country folk for the demonstrators' demands, and why the demonstrators made virtually no effort to arouse the support of people living outside the cities.

During the 1990s, this quiescent satisfaction in the rural community disappeared. Urban reforms eliminated the small entrepreneurial advantages that rural residents enjoyed over their urban compatriots, and today the gap between rural and urban living standards is growing rapidly The rural majority is reacting to this situation in two ways: they are taking advantage of the relaxed restrictions on geographical mobility in record number, and, as we have seen, some 150 million underemployed workers have left their rural homes in search of temporary work in China's largest cities. Those who have stayed in the countryside are nursing their grievances and, increasingly, acting on them. Given their new attitudes and habits, it seems unlikely that they will sit on the sidelines the next time political dissatisfactions spill into China's streets.

During the first years after the Communist revolution, ownership of land and equipment and the power to make decisions about production were removed from individual households and vested in progressively larger units: first mutual assistance teams, then two stages of cooperatives, and finally communes. In this process, the size of the decision-making unit in the rural economy grew from a household to an entity encompassing, on average, more than five thousand households. Communes typically incorporated the people of what had been several villages before collectivization began. The commune was divided into brigades, each made up of a population roughly equal to that of the average village, or about two hundred households; the brigades in turn were divided into production teams of twenty to forty households. The production team or, in some cases, the brigade held title to the land and equipment for which it was responsible; members received their work assignments from the production team leader. Individual householders owned their houses (but not the land on which the houses were built) and personal effects and had use rights to a "private plot" of land on which produce or animals could he raised for home consumption or for sale on the rural free markets.

Compensation within the commune system was based on work points. Work points were assigned based on the difficulty of the task, the capability of the worker, and the amount of time spent at work. Men, who were considered more capable than women at working the land, routinely received more work points than women for performing the same task for the same amount of time. After the harvest, grain was sold to the state according to predetermined quotas, and work points were totaled; whatever amount of the team's profit it had agreed to set aside for compensation was then divided by the total number of work points earned by all the team members. This fixed the value of the work point, and team members then received compensation based on their total points. Only the largest, richest communes could offer their members retirement plans, but all of them offered medical care and primary education at nominal cost.

This compensation system gave peasant households fairly secure, if very low, incomes, but it provided no incentive to work hard or efficiently, and Chinese agricultural production was essentially stagnant. Productivity was very low, and the growth in total output did not keep up with the growth in population.

But after the failure of the Great Leap Forward, this process was reversed. Beginning in 1959, ownership and decision-making were shifted downward, first to the brigade and subsequently to the production team. The cycle was completed with the reintroduction of the household responsibility system in 1978. With it, the individual household was re-empowered and once again serves as the locus of production decision-making and *de facto* land ownership.

Village governments, which took the place of production team management groups, put the new system in place. They evaluated their land and divided it into parcels, each parcel containing non-contiguous pieces of good land and less productive land.

Households were allowed to bid for use rights on these parcels; better-off families with more able-bodied workers were rewarded with use rights to the larger, better parcels. Team implements and draft animals were sold at auction to householders.

The village authorities and successful bidders signed contracts that stipulated three "fixed items": the price the household would pay for inputs, including seed and fertilizer, which were rationed based on the size of the contracted parcels; the expected output of specific commodities, such as grain or cotton, to be produced on the parcels; and the price the state would pay for the contracted commodities. The initial contracts were written for one-year terms. Everything the household produced over and above the stipulated amount of the stipulated commodity, it was free to dispose of as it chose, whether for personal consumption, barter, or sale. Sales could be made either to the state at a price higher than that paid for contract commodities or directly to consumers on the free market.

The rural working community responded readily to this new system's incentive for hard and efficient work. The increase in grain production was modest, but total agricultural output grew significantly. The average annual increase in the total amount of grain produced from 1970 to 1977 was 3.6 percent; it rose during the seven years following the introduction of the responsibility system to 5.5 percent; comparable figures for the total income from agricultural production are 3.1 percent in 1970 and 13.9 percent in 1985. By 2013, that figure had dropped to around 4.8%. These figures reflect the fact that the contract system, which encouraged farmers to diversify their crops, led to the cultivation of fruit and vegetables, which were more profitable than grain.

Bringing industry to China's countryside was a goal that Mao pursued during the last twenty years of his life. He saw a number of advantages in doing so: peasants would be proletarianized by exposure to the industrial workplace; rusticating industry would bring factories closer to their source of supply and to the rural consumer; and China's national defense would be enhanced by making each part of the country more self-sufficient, so that the occupation or destruction of one area would not affect the economic viability of the rest of the country. Finally, opening up factories in the countryside would absorb the substantial surplus labor power in the rural economy.

The first step in introducing industrial practices into the rural community came during the Great Leap Forward with the creation of what were called "backyard steel furnaces." Rural residents, like their urban compatriots, were encouraged to collect scrap metal (along with useful tools and utensils that were declared scrap to reach the inflated goals of the campaign) and to melt it down to help increase the nation's steel output. The campaign was a failure on all counts. Few proletarianizing lessons could be learned in these *ad hoc* workplaces, and the lumps of melted metal produced in them were largely unusable.

Alongside the useless steel furnaces, however, workshops and small factories were set up that began the process of creating a "cellular" economy in rural China. During the 1960s and into the 1970s, a major effort was launched to open new factories and to make China's more than two thousand counties as self-sufficient as possible. Some of these factories belonged to the state sector, many were owned and managed by the county government, and others were owned and managed by individual communes. In the mid-1970s, rural small-scale industry was producing about 10 percent of China's total industrial output; in certain lines, such as chemical fertilizer and cement, the small-scale factories accounted for more than half the nation's total production. As we have seen, these efforts were augmented by the army, which was also active in building a "third line" of factories in remote areas.

The most recent wave of rural industrialization began in the mid-1980s, when the initial surge of growth in rural per capita income brought on by the introduction of the responsibility system had begun to slow. Reformers now encouraged a rapid proliferation of new industrial enterprises nominally under township and village ownership but actually privately financed and managed. These enterprises, the assets of the majority of them having been transferred through "insider privatization" to private hands, have a workforce of 18 million and, in 2023, had come to account for 36 percent of China's industrial output, producing both for the domestic market and for export.

Unfortunately, there are negative consequences of this otherwise promising development. The little factories occupy what was once arable land. Built with the lowest possible capitalization, very few of them conform to China's environmental protection regulations, and they contribute to air and water pollution. Local officials eager to reap the benefits of rapid industrialization put pressure on the environmental protection officials to ignore violations or to grant waivers. In the trenches where the war between economic development and environmental protection is being fought, economic development is winning most of the battles.

The household responsibility system increased farmers' productivity through monetary incentives. But the smallness of the contracted parcels- the average plot was no larger than two acres- severely limited the ultimate productivity of the agricultural sector. With the adoption of a new landownership law in the fall of 2008, the talk of rationalizing agricultural production by combining small, contracted plots into larger, more efficient farms grew louder.

Some consolidation of parcels has occurred spontaneously. In some places, households pooled their parcels, labor, tools, and animals and farmed the land as informally constituted cooperatives. The new land law effectively extends to the countryside the thriving real estate market currently functioning in the cities. With use rights contracts transferable, holders can sell their contracts and leave agriculture entirely. Others can buy up these contracts, hire a staff of farm laborers, and become large-scale agricultural producers who can realize economies of scale with respect to such inputs as chemical fertilizer and insecticides. But large, efficient farms turn under employed farm workers into unemployed ones. Their need for jobs frequently encourages local authorities to build more factories that take badly needed arable land out of cultivation, thereby reducing total production.

Chinese economists estimate that a substantial percentage of the total rural workforce is either unemployed or underemployed. This situation and environmental degradation in the countryside, about which we shall talk later, are the direct causes of the outflow of 150 million people into China's major cities as migrant laborers. As noted earlier, the conditions under which migrants work are far from ideal. Nonetheless, they send home, on average, up to $300 a year, about ten percent of the average rural household income. The social consequences of their absence from the rural communities are serious, however. There is, in effect, a missing generation in many Chinese villages, and grandparents are obliged to care for children whose parents have left for work in the city. For a year or so in 2005 and 2006, there appeared to be a shortfall of as much as 10 percent in the migrant workforce in Guangdong and Fujian, and some factory owners resorted to recruiting visits to the countryside. With the last worldwide economic downturn, however, up to 40% of factories across the country closed down, resulting in 1 in 7 migrant workers being laid off and 20 million of them returning to the countryside.

The household registration, or hukou, laws in China that classified everyone as either an agricultural worker or a nonagricultural worker rendered rural workers second-class citizens– "racial discrimination with Chinese characteristics," as Li Xiangen, an itinerant fountain pen repairman, characterized it in a letter to his local newspaper. "'Farmer' shouldn't be a label, it should be a profession like any other, which people have the freedom to leave," Mr. Li said in an interview with a New York Times reporter. As we have seen, a new law enacted in 2005 abolished the occupational categories while retaining the geographical categories and devolving to local governments the authority to grant urban residency to newcomers from the countryside, an authority they are highly unlikely to use frequently.

Once the urban economy began to rebound from its slump, rural workers returned to their urban places of employment. Looking ahead, Chinese planners have the goal in mind of shifting the rural and urban population ratio from its current 35:65 to something approaching 30:70, a ratio more typical of advanced developing countries. This they expect to accomplish only in part by enlarging the population of the country's largest cities. Much of the urbanization of the population will come as a result of transforming existing rural villages and small towns into metropolitan centers. Facilities and services will be needed for the rural residents to be relocated to these new cities. Once this plan has been implemented, rural town governments will take responsibility for administering their neighboring townships. Since there are roughly half as many towns as townships, this consolidation means that the lowest level of rural administration will be twice its current size.

The task of ensuring a sufficient food supply for the Chinese people is the first priority for those responsible for guiding China's rural economy. The task is best thought of as a fraction, with the numerator being the food supply and the denominator the population. The goal is to increase the numerator as much as possible while controlling the growth of the denominator.

The first aspect of this task is to ensure a steady increase in the production of grain, cotton, and other agricultural commodities, without which the Chinese economy would grind to a halt. The market solution, raising the price paid to farmers to encourage them to produce more, threatened to create as many new problems as it solved old ones. Under the commune system, farmers had little or no choice of what to grow, to whom to sell their produce, or at what price. Natural disasters and sloth were the only obstacles to the state's realizing its quotas each year. Natural disasters are a constant, of course; reform policies largely eliminated sloth by means of material incentives.

But these same policies created a new hurdle for the government to surmount: producing the basic agricultural commodities became a money-losing proposition for the farmers. Almost anything the rural household planted on its contracted land would yield a better income than grain, given the prevailing prices the state was willing to pay for it.

The situation is comparable to cotton production. Raising cotton on contracted land and selling it to the state at the state's artificially low price produced only about one-fifth of the income that vegetables brought in. Peasants obliged by contract to grow cotton took to selling it on the black market for three times the state's price and claiming a shortfall in the harvest when state purchasers came to claim their contracted amount. If the government had raised cotton prices, it would have increased costs for the textile plants, most of which were state-owned enterprises already teetering on the brink of bankruptcy.

As part of its package of perquisites for city dwellers, China in years past purchased grain well below market prices, then sold it in the cities at an even lower price, absorbing the difference as an expense item in the national budget. Similarly, as part of the package of subsidies for state-owned textile factories, cotton was purchased at below-market prices from the farmer and sold to factories at an even lower price. When these expense items grew, the state decided no longer to subsidize grain and cotton and to allow prices to rise to market levels: in 1994, the price of grain in city markets rose by 50 percent, and the following year another 30 percent, a major factor in driving the urban inflation rate to 25 percent in 1994 and 17 percent in 1995. Meanwhile, the price of cotton increased 60 percent in 1994 and another 30 percent in 1995, thereby exacerbating the already precarious fiscal health of the textile industry.

These radical measures (abetted by favorable weather) appear to have been effective. Grain production reached a record output of 508 million tons in 1999, and although it declined to 435 million tons in 2003, it reached a new record of 528 million tons in 2008. It currently stands at 707 million tons. Cotton production, too, has increased since 2003 at a rate of more than 10 percent per year, currently standing at 6.1 million tons. Meanwhile, the runaway inflation of the mid-1990s has been brought under control, now amounting to a mere 0.2 percent, and grain prices in the cities have stabilized.

Increasing the numerator of the food supply to population ratio is all the more difficult because of the declining supply of arable land. Every day, decisions made in rural communities reduce the already scarce amount of land available for cultivation. As we have seen, China has about 20 percent of the world's population and only about 7 percent of its arable land, currently about 108 million hectares, 87 percent of the 1990 figure. This means that over the past four decades, China has endured a net loss of about 16 million hectares despite its vigorous efforts at reclamation.

Yet land is being withdrawn from cultivation for what are, in theory, good causes. Rural factories produce goods that augment the gross national product and give jobs to workers who would otherwise leave the countryside or be unemployed. But factories occupy land that could be cultivated, and they need raw materials and markets; that means expanding the highway and rail network, eating up still more land. As rural incomes rise, people are eager to expand their living quarters, and although local regulations restrict the proportion of land in a community that can be devoted to housing, these are often stretched or violated. Land is also taken out of cultivation for uses with little or no value for economic development. Many such schemes have proliferated recently, the most egregious of which are the 310 golf courses that have been constructed in China, with many more in the pipeline.

There is another problem. Striving for grain self-sufficiency in China requires that grain be grown in areas that require extensive irrigation. The North China Plain, for example, which produces half the country's wheat, is experiencing a serious drain on its underground water. Some argue that grain production in areas like the North China Plain should be restricted to preserve China's very scarce water reserves.

In the mid-1990s, some foreign demographers and agronomists issued dire predictions about China's ability to feed its population over the next thirty years. Given the then-current growth rate of the Chinese population and its changes in diet, they estimated that it would take more than 600 million tons of grain to feed that population in 2030. Not only will there be more people to feed, but as household income increases, so does consumption of meat, poultry, and eggs. Grain production in 1998 reached what was then the record level of 486 million tons. To reach 600 million tons by 2030, production must increase annually by 3 million tons. But with land being taken out of cultivation more and more quickly in the late 1980s, conservative projections showed a drop in grain output over the next thirty-five years that would result in a grain deficit of more than 300 million tons in 2030. The total world grain surplus available for export in 1993 was only about 220 million tons, and many other countries are dependent on that surplus. "What will happen when China becomes a grain importer on a massive scale?" they asked.

The Chinese government at first ignored these dire predictions, then began to take them very seriously. A land use law that came into effect at the beginning of 1999 severely restricts the conditions under which land can be taken out of cultivation. Transfers of up to eighty acres of agricultural land to nonagricultural use are subject to approval by provincial authorities; transfers of more than eighty acres are subject to approval by the central government. Land taken out of cultivation must be compensated for by an equal amount of land reclaimed. Speaking directly to the question of China's grain self-sufficiency, Chinese agronomists pointed out that not only is the country very close to complete self-sufficiency in grain, but average annual per capita grain consumption, at 320 pounds, exceeds the world average, as does per unit grain output, at 1.8 tons per acre.

Optimists in Beijing assume that these measures to increase grain production will result in continuing growth rather than a decline in grain production over the next twenty years; state planners project an annual increase of between 2 and 3 million tons to a level of just over 600 million tons. They estimate the need for grain at some 630 million tons in 2030 and argue that imports should be relied on to make up for the shortfall of 30 million tons.

(In 2008, the Organization for Economic Cooperation and Development projected that China's grain imports would reach 12 million tons or about 4 percent of total world imports of about 284 million tons.) If the dire predictions were overly pessimistic, the new Chinese government projections seem overly optimistic, given the difficulties in enforcing the new land use law and the strong economic incentives to disobey it, as well as the lingering economic disincentives to devote land and labor to grain rather than to more lucrative crops or enterprises. In fact, China imported over 157 million metric tons of grains and soybeans in 2024.

It is important to take into account the fact that the diets of both rural and urban residents have changed in recent years. Grain and fresh vegetable consumption is down for both communities, their place in the diet being taken by meat (particularly poultry), eggs, milk, and fruit. The substantial growth in milk consumption became an issue when, in the fall of 2008, it was discovered that the milk supply, including infant formula, and some eggs were tainted with melamine, a chemical additive that mimics protein. Six infants died of kidney failure caused by the tainted milk, and more than three hundred thousand others were sickened before the milk was withdrawn from the market. The owner of the *Sanlu* Group (三鹿集团), the largest of several milk producers involved in the episode, pleaded guilty to having withheld knowledge of the scandal for more than three months and was sentenced to life in jail.

The goal of controlling the growth of the denominator of the food supply to population ratio is equally daunting. China's efforts to limit population growth to one child per family, initiated in 1980, fell short of their target. The average number of children in China's cities is very close to 1 per family, but the national average is 1.84. Rural resistance to the birth control program was attributable, on the one hand, to tradition, which dictates a preference for a male heir to carry on the family name (multiple births in one family frequently being the result of repeated attempts to have a male child), and, on the other hand, to the economics of the rural reforms. The household responsibility system rewards big families in which there are many workers. Because girls cease to contribute to their parents' exchequer once they marry and leave the household, boys are considered a better source of income. And since there are no retirement plans in the vast majority of rural collectives, a couple's only source of old-age security is a large family.

The birth control program was successful in the Chinese countryside only when it was enforced with such harsh measures as forced abortions or sterilizations, and the destruction of homes and property. But such measures further alienated the peasant community. This alienation coincided with a decline in the rate of natural increase in the Chinese population to negative numbers. The population was beginning to contract, with the possibility that it could shrink by some 200,000 people by the turn of the next century. Accordingly, the party-state abandoned the one-child policy it had inaugurated some forty years earlier and substituted a two-child policy in 2016. Five years later, it moved to a three-child policy.

Rural people have as many reasons to be dissatisfied with their government as the government has to be dissatisfied with them. They face more and more problems that local authorities are unwilling to address or unable to resolve. In some instances, the local authorities themselves are the problem.

In 1982, with the introduction of the responsibility system, a structural change in rural administration was introduced under which the township took the place of the commune as the lowest level in the government structure. On average, each township is approximately twice the size of a former commune, and its administration serves as the local government, supervising the civic life of the two dozen or so villages under its authority, and, in the early stages of rural industrialization, as a production company overseeing the half dozen or so collective enterprises in the average township. The production company is organized into agricultural and industrial departments and perhaps others with responsibility for commercial activities, transportation, and the like. With the privatization of township enterprises, the local government has assumed the role of regulating, rather than owning and managing, the elements of its non-agricultural economy.

Meanwhile, as we have seen, the countryside is the site of "creeping democratization." Beginning in the late 1990s, elections have been held on an experimental basis at the village level. A village committee of three to seven members is directly elected based on open nominations. While the authority of the committee is limited, voter turnout is typically high. Village elections were sanctioned in a new law adopted by the National People's Congress in 1998. By 2000, more than half of China's one million villages had elected committees. Today, that figure is 95 percent, and the experiment has been extended to the township level.

Among the most serious sources of dissatisfaction are excessive taxes and fees. County and township governments are seriously underfunded by the central government for the national mandates they are expected to carry out. A Central Committee document in 2005 decreed that the agricultural tax imposed on rural households, previously capped at 5 percent, would be eliminated in twenty-four provinces that year and in the remainder of the country over the next several years. That promised to return to rural household exchequers $4 billion, or about $5.60 per rural resident per year. In practice, however, the agricultural tax is the least of the fiscal burdens borne by rural residents. Local officials impose fees, tolls, fines, special levies, and charges that in most areas add up to 15 percent or more of household income, in some cases as high as 50 percent or more. Several years ago, a *New York Times* reporter described the personal finances of Li Yongrong, a peasant in Anhui Province. Li realized $700 each year from farming his four-acre plot, but local government fees absorbed $600 of that, and school fees for his two teenage children took another $300. He makes up the deficit by using his Flying Tiger pickup (purchased with $2,000 in loans and savings) to provide transport services to his neighbors.

Were this local government revenue used to pay for public services and improved infrastructure, rural taxpayers would no doubt continue to grumble, but would at least enjoy some benefit. In fact, a substantial proportion of the tax revenues goes into the personal accounts of local officials, along with their take from bribes and profiteering. All too often, this ill- gotten gain is consumed in conspicuous displays of personal excess- lavish banquets, expensive automobiles- that only inflames resentment. Indeed, this corruption is itself a potentially explosive source of rural discontent. Those who lived through the final days of the Nationalist government in the 1940s- days marked by rampant corruption- claim that the situation is worse now than it was then.

In 2004, a husband-and-wife team of investigative reporters in Anhui published *Survey of Chinese Peasants.*[5] They describe the nightmarish situation in which rural residents find themselves when they decide to protest the malfeasance of local officials. Once they travel to the township or county level to describe the illegal extortion they have experienced, they learn that officials at those levels are operating in cahoots with the local bullies, and suddenly it is the protesters who are treated as criminals and subjected to arrest and violent retribution. In what is perhaps the

---

[5]Chen Guidi and Wu Chuntao, *Survey of Chinese Peasants*, (Beijing: People's Literature Publication Company, 2003 (in Chinese)

most notorious of their stories, Grandmother Gao, an elderly resident of Gao Village, had the temerity to protest the fact that she had been double taxed on her house site. The village chief first struck the woman, then ransacked her house and furniture. Next, he took the case to his superiors, who returned to the village to arrest Grandmother Gao and ten of her supporters for tax evasion. Realizing the villagers were caught in a web of official collusion, one resident of a nearby village decided to use the vehicle of petition and took Grandmother Gao's case to Beijing twice without gaining satisfaction. The village chief remained in office, unscathed.

In addition to graft over taxes and fees, a second major bone of contention among rural residents is what amounts to the confiscation of their land with insufficient or no compensation. Until the new land law was passed in 2008, farmland could not be bought or sold. Seeking to develop the land for nonagricultural purposes, local authorities had to reclaim the land from use rights contract holders and rezone it for commercial purposes. While peasants were entitled to compensation for their contract rights, and now for the land itself, if they received compensation at all, it virtually never approached the profit the local government authorities realized from the subsequent development of the land. Some 100 million farmers have lost their land in this fashion, and some five percent of arable land has been involved in these transfers. Speaking in 2006, Premier Wen Jiabao spoke of these "land grabs" as "an historic error" that could threaten national stability.

Though perhaps not felt by rural residents in their daily lives, the gap between rural and urban incomes may be the most serious source of dissatisfaction over the long term. For a brief time in the early 1980s, economic reforms in the countryside resulted in the incomes of rural households growing much faster than those of urban households: in 1980, rural incomes were only one-third of urban incomes; by 1985, when reform of the urban economy began, they had at least grown to one-half of the average urban income. But after 1985, the gap began to widen again. Today , the gap stands at 1:5.1; in monetary terms, it is 172 times what it was in 1978. Using the Gini coefficient to measure income inequality, China currently stands at 47 (the U.S. score is 41; the lowest Gini coefficients, meaning the most equal distribution of income, are found in Denmark at 28 and Slovakia at 24).

The average urban per capita income in China's cities stands at just over $7,400 per year; the average rural per capita income is about $3,200 per year. Less than one percent of the Chinese population is living in poverty (defined by the World Bank as a per capita income of less than $784 per year), and the vast majority of these are rural residents. But the situation is very slowly getting better. The overall growth rate in the urban economy is about five percent; in the rural sector, it is about 6.5 percent.

In the past, this rural and urban gap didn't matter a great deal. The state's control over the flow of information and the almost complete absence of geographical mobility meant that much of China's rural population was ignorant of city conditions, and even if they were aware of the differences in living standards, there was nothing they could do about it. Today, the situation is very different. Information about conditions in China's most highly developed cities is trumpeted in the official media, and the vast majority of rural families have one or more members who are migrant workers temporarily living in cities. Another aspect of the rural and urban gap, of which individual farmers may be less aware but which seriously jeopardizes their long-term interests, is that the average urban per capita income in China's cities is significantly higher than that in the agricultural sector. In the early days of the People's Republic, it was very different: investment in agriculture constituted nearly a quarter of total investment in China in the late 1950s and early 1960s. By the late 1990s, however, that proportion had dropped to two percent, the rationale being that the rural collective sector, powered by reforms, was generating enough capital to allow local governments to take over agricultural investment.

The fact of the matter is, however, that this local government investment also declined precipitously during the 1980s, from nearly 40 percent of total local investment to under 10 percent by the end of the decade. Seeking a high return on each investment dollar, local governments are much more inclined to invest in new industries or even real estate development than to settle for agriculture's low return.

Recognizing the problem of insufficient investment in agriculture at all levels of government, although Xi Jinping has not specified a specific amount for investment, he has emphasized the need for strategic investments in agricultural science and technology, as well as the importance of deepening rural reform to enhance agricultural strength. The focus is on long-term stable support and innovation in agriculture to address pressing issues in rural development.

Several other problems have caused China's rural residents to lose confidence in their local governments. Environmental pollution is one of them. People in the countryside are the first to suffer when township and village industrial enterprises flout air and water pollution regulations. Until very recently, China had no grassroots "green" movement pressuring the government to address these matters, but there are signs that a citizens' movement with an interest in improving environmental quality is coming together.

Crime is on the rise throughout China, and one form of violent crime endemic in the countryside is the abduction of women and of male children, the women to be sold as wives or prostitutes, the boys to be sold to families who have not produced a male heir, and children of both sexes kidnapped to work in urban factories. About seventy thousand cases of abduction are investigated each year. Although the Public Security Ministry reports an increasing number of arrests and prosecutions in cases of kidnapping and abduction, the crime wave has sapped citizens' confidence in the local governments' ability to maintain civil order.

Compounding all this, the decline in rural health care is also a real concern. China's rural communities once benefited from one of the best rural health care systems in the developing world. That this is no longer the case is discussed in Chapter 15.

Whereas in the past the Chinese government could count on peasant acquiescence and could focus on the more volatile political behavior of workers, students, and intellectuals, today it can no longer take for granted the passivity of the peasant. As we have seen, rural China was largely inactive when students and workers in China's cities were demonstrating against the government in 1989; rural residents were generally unsympathetic with their demands for a more open, more effective government. But since 1989, as the sources of discontent described here have taken their toll on rural toleration of incompetent governance, the climate has changed. Today, there are, on average, tens of thousands of instances of public protests each year. Most of these protests take place in the countryside; most of them involve issues of graft, land grabs, and environmental pollution. Xi Jinping was prescient in his statement on the effect of these protests on national stability.

Mao's comment in 1930 on the volatile character of a discontented peasantry- "a single spark can start a prairie fire"-

vastly understates the amount of political mobilization and organizational work that it took for the Chinese Communist Party to launch the revolution that overthrew the old order in the Chinese countryside. A thousand protests (or even several tens of thousands of protests), if they are isolated from one another, do not a revolution make. On the other hand, 500 million people in rural communities who harbor serious doubts about the capability of their government to address their pressing problems pose a potentially serious challenge indeed to the central authorities in Beijing.

Chapter 12: The Autonomous Regions

The term "ethnicity" is not easy to come to grips with. People define themselves as an ethnically distinct group when they have in common a set of customs and characteristics, a language, a history, or a religion. Yet in China, people who identify themselves ethnically as Han (汉族*hanzu*), a group that makes up 92 percent of the population, or close to 1.3 billion people, not have in common, as we have seen, spoken language, customs, characteristics, or religion. Nonetheless, Han Chinese do think of themselves as ethnically distinct from the roughly 105 million people who are members of the fifty-five other ethnic groups (or minority nationalities 小数民族 *xiaozu minzu*, as the Chinese refer to them) that make up the country's population. Those groups, as we shall see, do have languages, customs, characteristics, history, and religions that separate them from one another and from the Han majority. The smallest minority nationality is the Lhoba (珞巴) ethnic group in Tibet, with only 3,680 people; the largest is the Zhuang (壮) ethnic group in the Guangxi Zhuang (广西壮) Autonomous Region, with a population of around 16 million.

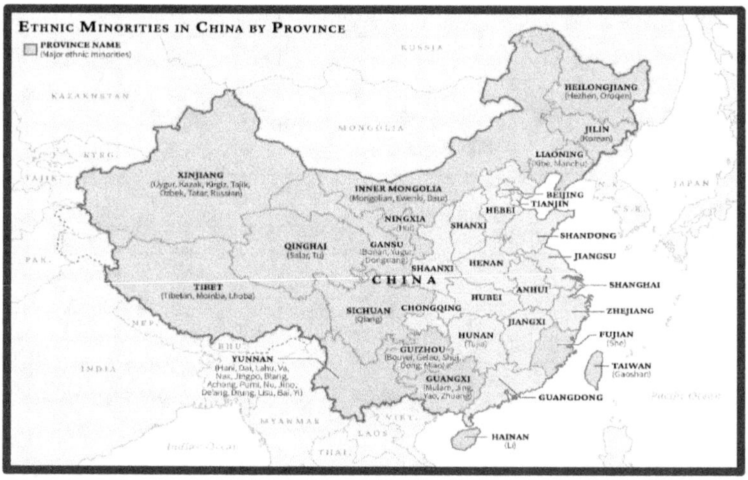

Table 13: Minority Nationalities Population (in millions)

Zhuang	16.2
Manchu	10.6
Hui	9.8
Miao	8.9
Uyghur	8.4
Tujia	8.0
Yi	7.7
Mongol	5.8
Tibetan	5.4
Buyei	2.9
Dong	2.9
Yao	2.6
Korean	1.9
Bai	1.8
Hani	1.4
Kazakh	1.2
Li	1.2
Dai	1.1
She	0.7
Lisu	0.6
Gelao	0.6
Other nationalities (34 in number)	99.3
Total minority population	105.0
As a percentage of the total population	7.5

Source: www.china.org.cn/e-groups/xiaoshu/index.hun

Four cases will serve to illustrate the way in which ethnicity presents itself as a pressing issue in China today: those of the Zhuang (壮族), the Mongolians (蒙古族), the Uyghurs (维吾尔族), and the Tibetans (藏族). These four minority nationalities all inhabit territories on China's borders. Each of the territories constitutes a province-level autonomous region—Guangxi-Zhuang, Inner Mongolia, Xinjiang, and Tibet—though in each case members of the ethnic group also live elsewhere in China. This is particularly true in the case of Tibetans, many of whom live in what is today the western third of Sichuan Province.

Although these territories are contiguous to one another (or nearly so) and some of them were linked culturally in the past, they have distinctive histories and are dissimilar today in their ethnic composition, economy, and relations with Beijing. All of them have experienced unrest inspired by ethnic separatist sentiments. Moreover, tellingly from Beijing's point of view, in each case the ethnic groups extend across China's borders and include citizens of neighboring states to the north, west, and south. Several of them have received extensive international support for their respective independence movements. Finally, they have significantly disparate economies.

Table 14: Gross Domestic Product of Four Autonomous Regions (in Dollars)

	GDP (Billion)	Populatio (millions)	Per Capita GDP	Per Capita Income ($)
Guangxi-Zhuang	380.3	503	106	7,560
Inner Mongolia	344.0	240	201	1,503
Tibet	34.2	30	160	3,493
Xinjiang	259.9	259	140	4,052
Average	356.4	258	151	3,139

With the establishment of the People's Republic in 1949, the party-state undertook the task of securing its borders and administering its border areas. Ethnic minorities were not strangers to the Chinese Communist Party. It had actively solicited their support during its protracted conflict with the Kuomintang. Indeed, during the epic Long March of 1934-35, Communist troops moved through territories inhabited by minorities, particularly Tibetans, who joined in the march and lived alongside the Red Army in its base in Yan'an.

To win their support and avoid their resistance to outside control, the minority nationalities were assured a high level of autonomy, and Beijing followed Moscow's example in establishing autonomous administrative entities at the province, prefecture, and county levels. But in fact, the term "autonomous region" was never more than a public relations gimmick designed to win the support of minority ethnicities for a party-state that was always firmly in the hands of the Han majority. Lip service was and is paid to ensuring representation of non-Hans in party and government positions, but with very few exceptions, leadership posts were and are occupied by Han Chinese. Policy toward the minority nationalities over the last 75 years has moved between the poles of autonomy and assimilation. In periods when the former has been ascendant, ethnic minorities are encouraged to use their own language in politics and education, even to the point of requiring that Han cadres learn and use the language as well, and to preserve and practice their own religion and customs.

In periods when assimilation has been ascendant, the use and teaching of local languages are abandoned, and cultural and religious practices are suppressed. More significantly, assimilation (or, perhaps better, attenuation) is accomplished by the encouragement of migration by Han Chinese into the minority areas. The effect of this in-migration is shown in the following table:

Table 15: Han Population in Autonomous Regions, 1949 And 2025

	Percent Han 1949	**Percent Han 2025**	**Percent Han Residing in Capital 2025**
Guangxi	66.0	62.0	43.7
Inner Mongolia	80.0	78.7	87.2
Tibet	0.1	8.0	17.0
Xinjiang	6.0	42.2	68.0

When challenged on their handling of the human rights of ethnic minorities, party-state leaders defend themselves by pointing to the very substantial capital investments that Beijing has made in the autonomous regions and arguing that the material quality of life of their residents has improved significantly over the years. They also point to the fact that ethnic minorities were exempted from the one-child policy from its outset, a privilege that was envied, particularly by Han Chinese living alongside minority families. In fact, this policy has made a difference: whereas China's population as a whole increased at an average rate of 1.17 percent per year between the censuses of 1990 and 2000, the minority nationality population increased at a rate of 1.65 percent per year during that period.

As the events of recent years have vividly demonstrated, China is far from having resolved the relationship ("contradiction," Mao would have said) between Han and non-Han. Knowledgeable observers of the recent outbreaks of violence in Tibet and Xinjiang point to gaping holes in Beijing's understanding of the needs and aspirations of the country's ethnic minority population. While Beijing's goals with respect to the non- Han minorities- political stability, economic development, access to raw materials, and border security- are abundantly clear, the means for achieving them are far from clear. And the fact is they are goals that, from the perspective of the ethnic minorities, benefit the Han majority more than the non-Han minority.

We shall proceed through our four cases as a tour around China's borders, beginning in the south. Our first case, the Zhuang, is an unusual one. The Zhuang are identified in the Chinese census as the country's largest ethnic minority, with more than sixteen million members. But there are two issues in identifying this group clearly. Until they were designated a minority nationality by the newly established government in Beijing, members of the Zhuang tended to identify themselves as members of much smaller ethnic groups that were often at war with one another. In addition, historians and students of the CCP's early policy toward its minorities often dismiss the Zhuang as having been too Sinified to qualify as ethnically separate from the Han.

Guangxi-Zhuang Autonomous Region

Anthropologists and historians have disagreed over whether the Zhuang are native to the area or migrated into western Guangxi and eastern Yunnan at some point. The weight of evidence currently points to there having been original inhabitants. Han Chinese arrived on the scene in 214 B.C.E. during the Win dynasty and established control of the eastern part of Guangxi. Under the Tang dynasty (618-907 B.C.E.), eastern Guangxi, Guangdong, and Hainan were combined under the name Lingnan, and the Zhuang areas of western Guangxi and Yunnan were separately administered. The province of Guangxi was established in the fourteenth century under Yuan dynasty rule, but the area, far distant and geographically cut off from the rest of the country, was largely left to its own devices.

Southern Guangxi was the site of the outbreak of the Taiping Rebellion, which came close to toppling the Qing dynasty in the mid-nineteenth century. After the dynasty fell in 1910, Guangxi became the redoubt of two generations of warlord "cliques," the Old and the New Guangxi cliques. They were finally defeated by Chiang Kai-shek in 1929, but Chiang's Nationalist government never succeeded in establishing control over the region. The CCP, meanwhile, established in the southeastern part of the province a short-lived "soviet" led by none other than the young Deng Xiaoping.

Communist forces took the province shortly after the founding of the People's Republic, and in 1958, the party-state designated the province of Guangxi as the Guangxi-Zhuang Autonomous Region. This came without significant pressure from the Zhuang themselves, but rather through an interest in consolidating Beijing's control over a border area (with the Democratic People's Republic of Vietnam) where numerous interrelated ethnic groups spill across national boundaries. These include, in addition to the Zhuang, the Buyi, Dai, Dong, Li, and Shui nationalities of China, the Thai (in Thailand), the Lao (in Laos), the Nong (in Vietnam), and the Shan (in Myanmar). *In toto,* they number more than 250 million people. Guangxi itself is home not only to the Zhuang, who occupy the western portion of the region (as well as parts of neighboring Yunnan), but also to significant numbers of the Yao and Miao ethnicities.

It is important to note in passing that the newly formed Communist government in Beijing had a complex task before it in determining what constituted a minority nationality. The CCP had first devoted its attention to the most conspicuous (and potentially most dangerous) minorities in the northwest, including the Uyghurs, the Kazakhs, and the Kirghiz (柯尔克孜族). These, together with the Mongols, were ethnic minorities that self-identified with their nationalities and had long occupied territories in which they constituted the majority of the people. When the party-state turned its attention to the south, however, it was confronted by a myriad of ethnic groupings whose self-identification was not always clear and that lived intermingled with other nationalities.

The product of the work of the government, in collaboration with the Minority Nationalities Institute, was a list of fifty-three ethnic groups (later fifty-five) that would be recognized as nationalities. They were selected based on population and the degree to which they resided together in a common geographical location. Left off the list were close to a million members of countless smaller ethnic groups that ended up with the collective (and not particularly flattering) designation of "undistinguished" minorities.

Some of these groups have been "distinguished" as belonging to one of the fifty-five recognized by the government; the rest remain unrecognized. The General Program for the Implementation of Nationality Regional Autonomy went into effect in 1952 and differentiated among three types of areas: (1) areas in which all the population belonged to the same minority nationality; (2) areas in which most inhabitants belonged to the same minority nationality but where small pockets of other nationalities existed; and (3) areas in which multiple minorities lived side by side. Based on these categories, provision was made for autonomous governments at the province, prefecture, or county level.

As is the case with each of the four autonomous regions we are considering, Beijing has two principal interests in maintaining its control: border security and natural resources. In the case of Guangxi-Zhuang, which has a 250-mile-long border with

Vietnam, border security was of paramount concern during the Sino-Vietnamese War in 1979.

Although they are not particularly well-known outside China, certainly not as well-known as the other three minority nationalities we are considering here, many Americans have been introduced to the Zhuang during their visit to the scenic region around Guilin (**桂林**), which is in the northeastern corner of Guangxi-Zhuang and which became, early on, a favored destination on package tours of China. The region is about the size of Michigan, mountainous for the most part, and home to a population of forty-nine million. Its gross regional product, close to that of Inner Mongolia, has the largest proportion of agriculture of the four regions. Living near their fields, typically in houses built on stilts, the Zhuang are heavily engaged in rice cultivation. Like the other three regions, the central government invests more in the region than is collected in regional revenue. Taiwan is the principal foreign investor in the region, with a total of close to $5 billion invested in twelve hundred joint-venture projects.

The Cultural Revolution proved especially difficult for all of China's minority nationalities, but particularly for those in Guangxi. The policies of autonomy put in place in the first fifteen years after the founding of the PRC, which included the establishment of minority nationality institutes and universities throughout the country, the recruitment of minority party members and officials, and the use of minority languages in governments and schools, were put on hold beginning in 1966. The problem arose because of the ambiguity in Mao's treatment of minority nationalities. On the one hand, he preached autonomy and assimilation; on the other hand, he insisted that ultimately, class was more important than nationality. It led his Red Guard disciples to identify minorities as class enemies. When the violent phase of the Cultural Revolution reached Guangxi, it reached a level of bloodshed well beyond that in other provinces and involved unspeakable practices in the name of revolutionary fervor.

After Deng rose to power, a so-called new era in minority nationalities policy was introduced. The priorities in this new era were to clarify the legal status of the minorities and to promote economic development in the autonomous regions to ensure economic equality with the Han majority. The product of the first policy initiative was the Law of Regional Autonomy, adopted by the NPC on 1 October 1984, the thirty-fifth anniversary of the founding of the PRC. The second policy initiative was manifested in the very substantial infusions of development capital into the autonomous regions over the last thirty years. As we shall see presently, neither legislation nor investment has succeeded in resolving the differences between Han and non-Han.

Although few Zhuang identified themselves as Zhuang prior to 1949, 75 years later, this ethnic identity has become very strong and has been used to reinforce the center and region tensions typical of the rest of the country. It manifested itself in the formation of Zhuang studies associations in both Guangxi and Yunnan. These associations in turn had the unintended consequence of sowing the seeds of Zhuang separatism, with extremists in that small movement arguing in favor of forming a Greater Tai nation that would include what are now citizens of China, Vietnam, Thailand, Laos, and Myanmar. Knowledgeable observers are highly skeptical that an active ethnic separatist movement will either thrive or turn violent in Guangxi-Zhuang.

Our second case, Inner Mongolia, is, like Guangxi, relatively benign. Both Inner Mongolia (today's Inner Mongolian Autonomous Region- *Nei Mengu Zizhi* Qu 内蒙古自治区) and Outer Mongolia (today's Mongolian People's Republic-MPR) were part of the Qing empire. Even before they established their rule over China proper, the Manchus defeated the Inner Mongols and, with their help, brought the Eastern Mongols (also known as the Khalkha—哈尔哈–-tribe) under Manchu control as well. The Western Mongols (the Dzungar– (准噶尔--tribe), by contrast, were an unruly lot never more than nominally governed from Beijing. The government set up a new office, the *Lifan Yuan* (理番院) literally, the "Barbarian Management Department," with responsibility for Mongolia, Chinese Turkestan (modern Xinjiang), and Tibet. Indeed, Mongolia was already closely linked with Tibet by religion. The branch of Tibetan Lamaism currently led by the Dalai Lama had spread to Mongolia in the mid-seventeenth century, and a succession of religious leaders known as living Buddhas were based in the city of Urga (modern Ulan Bator).

Inner Mongolia Autonomous Region

Meanwhile, Russia had expanded its influence in Asia, an expansion greatly facilitated in the latter years of the nineteenth century by the construction of the Trans-Siberian Railroad. In a 1907 agreement between Russia and Japan, spheres of influence were carved out: northern Manchuria and Outer Mongolia to Russia, southern Manchuria, and eastern Inner Mongolia to Japan. Historians draw an analogy between this assault on China's "back door" and the pressure from European powers and the United States to open treaty ports at the coastal "front door." When the debilitated Qing dynasty collapsed in 1911, Outer Mongolia declared its independence. Russia refrained from recognizing the new government as fully independent, but its tripartite formula of Chinese suzerainty, Outer Mongolian autonomy, and Russian protection amounted to the same thing. When the Mongolian People's Republic was formally established in 1924, it was recognized immediately by Moscow but not until 1952 by a reluctant Mao Zedong.

Inner Mongolia, like the rest of China, came under warlord control after the fall of the Qing and, with the backing of the Japanese in the late 1930s, declared its independence as the state of Meng Jiang (蒙疆), closely affiliated with a similar puppet regime in Manchuria. At the Japanese surrender in 1945, a provisional government was formed under the leadership of Ulanfu (乌兰夫), a Mongol who had allied himself with the Communist guerrillas. The Inner Mongolian Autonomous Region (IMAR) was established in 1947, two years before the founding of the People's Republic. By 1956, it had been expanded to include Mongol areas that had been under the administrative control of the former provincial governments of Rehe (热河), Chahar (察哈爾), Suiyuan (綏遠), and part of what is now the autonomous region of Ningxia. Although once an area closed to Chinese migration, in the declining years of the Qing, Chinese settlers had been encouraged as a counterweight to Russian influence. By 1971, Mongols had actually become a *minority* nationality even within the borders of Inner Mongolia. In 2008, only one in five of the

IMAR population was Mongol; most were engaged in raising camels and horses.

Inner Mongolia is a high plateau at about three thousand feet, roughly three times the size of California, and mostly given over to grasslands, some of which are threatened by encroaching desertification. It stretches nearly sixteen hundred miles from its northeastern border with Russia to its southwestern border with the province of Gansu. In 2025 it had a gross regional product of $344 billion, of which 45 percent was industrial production, 36 percent was from the tertiary sector—transportation, commerce, finance, and the like—and 12.5 percent derived from agriculture and animal husbandry. Like the other autonomous regions we will consider, the IMAR is heavily dependent on funds from the central government.

Interethnic relations are considerably smoother in Inner Mongolia than in Xinjiang or Tibet, at least in part because of the heavy preponderance of Han Chinese. There have been a few reported instances of separatist activities, and visitors have observed an attitude of mutual respect between Hans and Mongols in government and business settings. Pressed to define what "autonomy" means in practice in the IMAR, both Han and Mongol leaders say that in fact the term means little but is retained for "historical reasons."

Since the collapse of the Soviet Union, with which the Mongolian People's Republic had close ties, there has been considerable interest in the IMAR for cross-border trade with the MPR. China has become Mongolia's largest trading partner and source of investment. In 2023, China-Mongolia trade volume reached $16.6 billion, with China's exports to Mongolia amounting to about $3.5 billion and its imports from Mongolia—mostly timber and cashmere wool—rising to about

$13.1 billion. China has invested a total of $5.4 billion in Mongolia since 1990, accounting for 19 percent of all foreign direct investment in the country. This investment is significant in Mongolia, with over 7,543 Chinese enterprises registered in the country. A substantial international economic collaboration was proposed in the early 1990s for the Tumen River (图们江) delta in Jilin Province (吉林省). The United National Development Program project involving Mongolia, the two Koreas, China, and Japan called for a $30 billion trade and transport complex designed to expand the region's outreach to the international economy. The Asian financial crisis and ongoing problems in relations between the two Koreas stalled the project. Meanwhile, there was some concern raised in the MPR over its growing economic dependence on China. Steps have been taken to limit exports, and as a sign of its independence, Mongolia reaffirmed its historical ties to Tibet when it welcomed the Dalai Lama on a visit to Ulan Bator in 1995.

The IMAR has been relatively free of political protests. An exception occurred in May 2011 when an ethnic Mongol herdsman was struck and killed by an ethnic Han coal truck driver near Xilinhot (锡林浩特). The herdsman was obstructing a truck belonging to the Liaoning Chuncheng Industry and Trade Group that was attempting to enter the herdsman's pastureland. The protests began with more than 2,000 students and herdsmen demonstrating in Xilinhot (锡林浩特)against the herdsman's death as well as the destruction of IMAR grasslands and the integrity of the homeland of ethnic Mongols. The demonstrations then spread to the city of Tongliao (通遼) and the capital, Hohhot (青城). The authorities moved quickly to disrupt communications among the demonstrators in a successful attempt to contain further unrest.

Like Inner Mongolia and unlike Xinjiang, Tibet is geographically isolated and has historically been cut off from the outside world. Like the population of Xinjiang and unlike that of Guangxi-Zhuang and Inner Mongolia, most of Tibet's population—more than 90 percent—are non-Han. Unlike the other three, Tibet was the back door, as it were, through which Britain and the United States came to assault China. And most critically, it is virtually impossible to speak in neutral terms about Tibet. Those who think of it from the perspective of the Dalai Lama see no merit in China's position; those who sympathize with Beijing find no common cause with the Dalai Lama. The crux of the issue is the validity or invalidity of the Tibetans' claim that the territory was once independent and recognized internationally as being so.

Tibet is roughly a quarter the size of the United States, and there are also Tibetans living in portions of Sichuan, Qinghai, Gansu, and Yunnan provinces. There are three major areas in the Tibet region: the northern plain, at seventeen thousand feet, the Tsangpo River (雅鲁藏布江) valley in the south (the river is known as the Brahmaputra in India), at twelve thousand feet, and the forested slopes of eastern Tibet. Lhasa, somewhat surprisingly, lies at the same latitude as Houston. As a result of its latitude and altitude, summer days are often hot, nights are freezing, and there is little or no rainfall. In its relative isolation, Tibet borrowed and transformed Buddhism into its own idiosyncratic religion. The Yellow Hat sect of this Buddhist offshoot was established in the fifteenth century C.E. and quickly spread to Mongolia, where the reigning prince bestowed the title Dalai Lama ("all-embracing leader") on the successors of Tsongkhapa, founder of the Geluk school of Tibetan Buddhism. The Manchus also welcomed Tibetan Buddhism; their admiration took architectural form in the Qing summer residence in Chengde, modeled after the Potala palace in Lhasa, and in the stunning *Yonghegong* (雍和宫 or Lama Temple) in downtown Beijing.

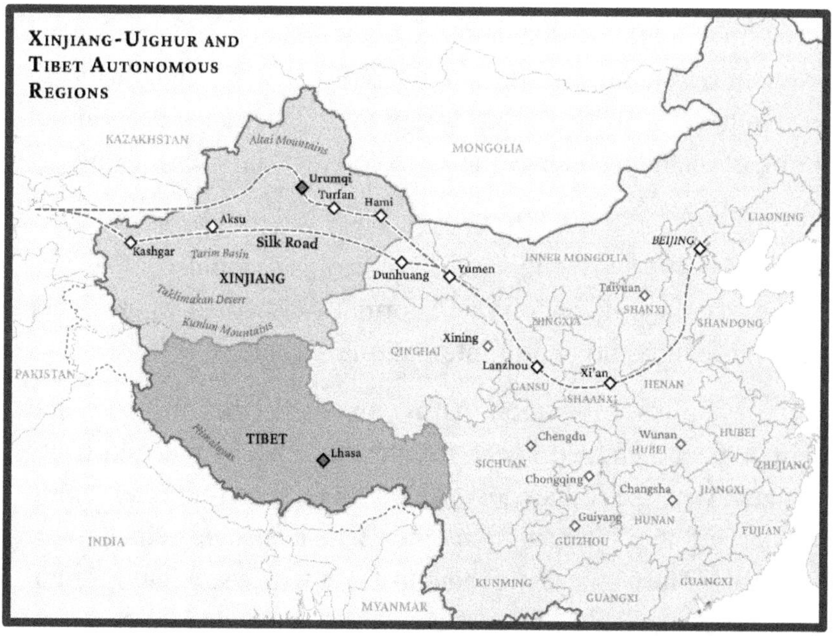

Xinjiang-Uighur and Tibet Autonomous Regions

With the support of the Mongols, the first Dalai Lama assumed temporal powers in Tibet at about the time of the founding of the Qing empire and established a tributary relationship with the Qing emperor in 1652. Qing armies intervened three times—in 1720, 1727, and 1750—reaffirming Chinese control over the territory.

Thirty years later, in 1780, the Panchen Lama, temporal ruler in western Tibet, received the first emissary from the British East India Company. This initial contact was thwarted when Gurkhas from Nepal invaded Tibet, but the Qing once again reasserted authority in 1790 and closed off Tibet from all foreign contact. Britain, meanwhile, established its presence in the northern Indian hill states and, in a series of agreements from 1886 to 1893, acknowledged Chinese suzerainty over Tibetan foreign relations but assumed responsibility for trade between India and Tibet. When Russia, the other player in the "Great Game" for ascendancy in central Asia, made contact with the thirteenth Dalai Lama in an attempt to counter British interests, the British sent an armed mission into Lhasa under the command of Francis Younghusband. The result was a British protectorate over Tibet and recognition, in 1914, of its independence (accepted on the Chinese side only by the very short-lived government of Yuan Shikai (袁世凯) in the wake of the 1911 revolution). This formula, reminiscent of that used by Russia in Mongolia and formally accepted by no other nation, has caused no end of international debate.

The People's Liberation Army invaded Tibet in 1950 and within a year subdued local resistance. Zhou Enlai skillfully negotiated with the Indian government to refrain from intervening on behalf of the Tibetans, and the British also refrained from intervening. The Chinese moved into Tibet with a soft hand at first, but by 1959, protests by Tibetans had expanded into armed rebellion. The PLA responded with force: many Tibetans were killed, and countless monasteries were destroyed. The Dalai Lama fled to a refuge in Dharamsala, India. The United States meanwhile flew Tibetan dissidents out of their country, trained them in Colorado, and repatriated them as guerrilla fighters, radio operators, and spies behind Chinese lines.

The 1960s were a difficult decade for the people of Tibet. The Chinese party-state, emboldened by its successes in suppressing the Tibetan rebellion and in its border war with India in 1962, vigorously undertook the "socialist transformation" of Tibet. Collaboration with Tibet's upper classes, which had marked Chinese policy in the 1950s, was replaced by a vigorous effort to mobilize support among Tibet's working classes. Young men were discouraged from becoming monks, and with the onset of the Cultural Revolution, most of the intact monasteries and temples were destroyed or defaced. Formal establishment of the Tibet Autonomous Region (TAR- Xizang Zizhiqu 西藏自治区) in 1965 marked, paradoxically, the destruction of the last shred of Tibetan autonomy. China claimed it had accomplished the "liberation" of an impoverished, feudal society. International human rights advocates claimed that China was engaged in a systematic effort at suppressing Tibetan religion and the human rights of the Tibetan people. Tibet had become an international *cause célèbre.*

The TAR has a population of only about three million people, very roughly the size of the population of Chicago. According to official statistics, the Han percentage is eight, but this calculation does not include the mounting number of migrant laborers who come to Tibet for work, nor does it count the PLA troops stationed there; the real number is probably four or five times that. Foreign critics accuse Beijing of a systematic effort at "Hanification" of Tibet by means of Han immigration, but the effects of this effort pale in comparison with the situation in the IMAR. Tibet's gross domestic product is a scant $498 million dollars, a third of it from industrial production, 16 percent from agriculture, and the remaining 55 percent from the service sector, much of it from the tourist trade. To enhance the latter, a seven-hundred-mile-long rail line was completed in 2005 linking Lhasa (拉萨) and Golmud (格尔木) in Qinghai at a cost of more than four billion dollars. It transported more than 1.5 million passengers to Tibet during its first year of operation.

To an even greater extent than neighboring autonomous regions, Tibet is dependent on central government funds: the regional government takes in four hundred million dollars in tax revenues while total government expenditures are close to five billion annually. Beijing argues that Tibet could not survive without support from the national coffers; Beijing's opponents argue that the support in no sense justifies the suppression of Tibetan rights.

Religion is a sensitive issue for the Chinese party-state and especially so in Tibet. The Chinese have argued that Tibetan Lamaism held thousands of young men as monks in a state of bondage equivalent to that of slavery or, at best, feudal serfdom. Beijing attacked the Panchen Lama for his opposition to its policies in the early 1960s and extended its attack to the Dalai Lama, in exile in India, for "counterrevolutionary" resistance to the party-state's authority. When the Panchen Lama died in 1989, both the Dalai Lama and China chose successors. Beijing's candidate was consecrated in ceremonies held in Xigazi (日喀则) in 1995, while the Dalai Lama's candidate (like his rival, of primary school age) is held under house arrest in Beijing.

The official Chinese press has described the situation as a "long-term, bitter, complex, you-die-I-live political battle with no possibility of compromise." The battle between Tibetan supporters of the Dalai Lama and the Chinese authorities has often taken the form of protest demonstrations. The most serious of them to date took place in the early spring of 1989, at which point the PLA was called in to restore order, a process that eventuated in the first declaration of martial law since the founding of the PRC. Thirty Tibetans were killed in that uprising; three hundred were detained by police and soldiers.

Violence broke out once again in the spring of 2008 during the run-up to the Beijing Olympics. Thousands of Tibetans took to the streets in Lhasa, and the protests quickly spread to several monasteries and throughout the Tibetan plateau, as well as Tibetan communities in neighboring Qinghai, Gansu, and Sichuan provinces. More than two hundred protests took place over the next eighteen months. In Lhasa, Han merchants were principal among the demonstrators' targets, and photographs of their ruined stores were widely circulated on television, inflaming anti-Tibetan sentiments across China. Thousands of soldiers and armed police were detached to restore order, though the government was faulted for the slow reaction of security forces during the first twenty-four hours of the rioting. Reports on casualties varied widely: Beijing claimed 22 deaths; the Tibetan government-in-exile claimed that there were 140 deaths. The Dalai Lama alleged that 400 Tibetans were killed in total.

From the party-state's point of view, the protests couldn't have come at a worse time. Pro-Tibetan and anti-Chinese protests occurred at virtually every stop on the worldwide progress of the Olympic torch. Beijing, of course, blamed the Dalai Lama for the outbreak of violence, accusing him of fomenting "cultural genocide." Tenzin Gyatso, the fourteenth Dalai Lama lives in Dharamsala with a growing flock of one hundred thousand followers. He is an international figure whose work, and praise for it, notably the Nobel Peace Prize in 1989, attracts embarrassing attention to Chinese policy in Tibet. He is now in his early nineties, and episodes of ill health have raised once again the issue of how his succession is to be determined.

Recent events in Tibet have also called into question the Dalai Lama's so-called middle way of seeking autonomy but not full independence for Tibetans in China. He would like to negotiate with Beijing to arrive at a formula for Tibet not dissimilar from those effected in Hong Kong and Macao and offered to Taiwan: that of "one country, two systems." A degree of genuine autonomy that would guarantee religious freedom and local political control would satisfy many Tibetans.

A six-day meeting of Tibetan exile leaders in Dharamsala in November 2008 led to the reaffirmation of the Dalai Lama's position, though even he, in subsequent months, has described the condition of Tibetans under Chinese rule as having become a "hell on earth." Many at the Dharamsala meeting pushed hard for a policy of total independence and international recognition of that independence. But one must ask how an independent Tibet would sustain itself, as one must ask under what circumstances the Chinese party-state would feel confident enough of itself to grant genuine autonomy to a territory that it claims to have been "always Chinese," in which Han Chinese are a small minority, and that serves as a strategic barrier between China and potentially unfriendly states to the south.

Sporadic negotiations continue between representatives of the party-state and representatives of the Dalai Lama, but little or no progress has been made. Paradoxically, then, the Dalai Lama is functioning for the moment as a damper on ethnic separatism in Tibet. An international spokesperson with an enormous and attentive audience and great religious and secular influence, he moderates the impulses of those who want to be separatists. Xinjiang has no such moderating leader, and the Zhuang and the Inner Mongolians seem not to need one.

The last case, that of Xinjiang (新疆), is far from benign. Indeed, members of the Uyghur minority appear to be the least content with their lot under the rule of the Chinese party-state, and political demonstrations—some of them very large in scope—continue to this day.

Unlike in Inner Mongolia, minority nationalities are in the majority of Xinjiang's population. The autonomous region is twice the size of Texas but has a population of only twenty million, 60 percent of which is composed of members of thirteen ethnic minorities. The population of its capital, Ulumuqi (乌鲁木齐)—or Urumqi as it is better known in the West—however, is four-fifths Han. As is shown on Map #4, Xinjiang lies athwart the Silk Road, opened in 130 B.C.E. and over which trade passed between

China and the West for centuries. The region borders on eight countries and has always been open to interactions with countless ethnic groups and foreign nationals. Unlike in Inner Mongolia, violent protests organized by ethnic separatists occurred with increasing frequency after 1985, culminating in the largest episode of ethnic violence in the history of the PRC in 2009. The two areas that make up contemporary Xinjiang, the area around the Ili River (伊犁河) in the north and the Tarim (六城) basin in the south, were brought under what historians have called a "tenuous supremacy" of the Qing dynasty in the middle of the eighteenth century. These regions are home to at least five ethnic groups: the majority Uyghurs, the Kazakhs, Kirghiz, Tajiks, and Uzbeks. All these groups are Muslim (they are Sunnis rather than Shiites), and their languages, while distinct from one another, are all variations of Turkic, a member of the Altaic family of languages (which includes Mongolian and Manchu). All these minority nationalities extend across national boundaries to the north and west into Kazakhstan, Kyrgyzstan, Tajikistan, and Uzbekistan. And increasingly, they all are subject to the appeal of Muslim fundamentalism.

The first settlement of what is now Xinjiang apparently dates to 1800 B.C.E. and was composed of Tocharians, a western Eurasian tribe of herders with Caucasoid features. Well-preserved mummies of the Tocharian settlers are on display in museums in the region. Chinese troops were garrisoned in the region beginning in the third century C.E. to guard the Silk Road trade. The Uyghurs were relatively late to arrive, migrating from Mongolia in the tenth century. In 1760 the Qing dynasty formally annexed the region known as Chinese Turkestan. Like their twenty-first-century compatriots, Qing dynasty rulers encouraged Han migration into the province, offering the incentives of free land and seed to Chinese farmers.

The tenuous hold of the Qing over Xinjiang was interrupted in the mid-nineteenth century by a Muslim rebellion in the Tarim basin led by Yakub Beg. Ten years later, when Russians occupied the Hi basin, the dynasty debated whether the campaign to recapture the territory was worth the doubtlessly daunting cost. Zuo Zongtang (左宗棠) persuaded a reluctant foreign minister to undertake the campaign in 1873, though the empire was also under assault by foreign powers on its southern littoral, and against all odds, Zuo was successful: all of eastern Turkestan was retaken, with the exception of the Russian- occupied Hi region. But the latter was recouped under the Treaty of St. Petersburg in 1880, and Chinese Turkestan became the province of Xinjiang (which translates "New Territories"), with its capital in Urumqi.

Xinjiang, like Inner Mongolia, experienced a great deal of de facto autonomy under the Qing and, subsequently, under the Nationalists. In 1944, Xinjiang followed Inner Mongolia's example and declared its independence under the name of the East Turkestan Republic, a name recently revived by Uyghur separatists. Contacts were made with Chinese Communist guerrillas, and in September 1949, the Nationalist forces there surrendered to the People's Liberation Army. In 1955, the Xinjiang-Uyghur Autonomous Region (XUAR- Xinjiang Weiwuer Zizhiqu 新疆维吾尔自治区) was formally announced. In the XUAR, ethnic minorities are in a majority in all but the capital. Special provision is made for the five (of sixteen) prefectures in Xinjiang where Uyghurs are not in the majority; they are "autonomous districts," where Kazakhs or Kirghiz outnumber Uyghurs. In the region as a whole, party and government offices are distributed in rough proportion to the ethnic balance, though Han Chinese almost always hold the top leadership positions. As in the IMAR, "autonomy" is mostly a fiction maintained for "historical reasons."

A key player in the development of the XUAR has been the Xinjiang Production and Construction Corp (XPCC). One of a number of Production and Construction Corps formed under the supervision of the PLA at the time of the founding of the People's Republic, the XPCC took primary responsibility for developing agriculture and, subsequently, new industries. All the PLA's Production and Construction Corps were disbanded in 1975, but the Xinjiang Corps was reestablished in 1982, this time under the supervision of the Ministry of Agriculture. At the end of the century, it was reassigned to the Xinjiang Military District under the Western Theater Command. The corps currently employs close to two million workers, nearly all of whom are Han; they and their dependents account for about 16 percent of Xinjiang's population, and the corps produces 20 to 25 percent of its total gross regional product (GRP). It continues to focus on agriculture but is increasingly involved in building the industrial infrastructure. Xinjiang's GRP in 2024 was $3.6 billion, of which, as is the case in the IMAR, roughly 47 per-cent derived from industry, 18 percent from agriculture, and the balance from "tertiary industry." Like the IMAR, Xinjiang served as a drain on national coffers, taking in $5.2 billion in tax revenues and expending $12.6 billion in 2024.

Relations between the Uyghur and Kazakh nationalities and the Han population in the XUAR have never achieved the level of mutual respect reported by visitors to Guangxi-Zhuang and the IMAR. The Soviet Union took advantage of this dissent to stir up trouble. In the 1950s and again at the nadir of Sino-Soviet relations in the 1960s, Russians encouraged Uyghurs and Kazakhs to immigrate to the Soviet Union. Close to a hundred thousand people did so, a decision that many of them have come to regret at a time, seventy years later, when China's western territories are relatively affluent compared with Russia's southeastern territories.

In Inner Mongolia, Pan-Mongolism attracts few supporters, but the movement in Xinjiang to establish an independent East Turkestan Republic attracts substantial support. Beginning in the 1980s, four groups were actively pursuing this goal: the East Turkestan National Salvation Committee, the East Turkestan Popular Revolutionary Front, the East Turkestan Refugee Association, and the East Turkestan Foundation, the latter two based in Istanbul. Twenty-two were killed in 1990 in an uprising in Baren triggered by the authorities' ban on the construction of new mosques. A bomb blast in the summer of 1993 destroyed part of a hotel in Kashgar (喀什) and killed three people. Four years later ten were killed in demonstrations in the city of Yining (喀什), resulting in the executions of twelve people. A month later, three bomb attacks, for which the "East Turkestan Freedom Organization" claimed responsibility, occurred in Beijing, hours after a memorial service for the deceased Deng Xiaoping: victims numbered close to a hundred. And early in 2000, when Uyghur militants and Chinese security forces clashed in Aksu (阿克苏), several militants were killed, five were sentenced to death, and eight others were given long jail sentences.

Beijing is particularly concerned about international involvement in these incidents. Chinese authorities have cited evidence that Islamic militants in Saudi Arabia, Iran, Turkey, India, Pakistan, and Afghanistan have supplied weapons to Xinjiang separatists. In an effort to address the issue of cross-border support for ethnic unrest in Central Asia, representatives from Kazakhstan, Kyrgyzstan, and Tajikistan were invited to join Boris Yeltsin and Jiang Zemin in their 1996 summit meeting in Beijing. None of the three central Asian republics supports an independent East Turkestan, and all five states regard themselves as threatened by Islamic fundamentalists; they signed an agreement to cooperate in bringing stability to the area. Five years later, at a meeting in Shanghai, attended by Jiang and Russian president Vladimir Putin, the group was expanded to include Uzbekistan, and their agreement was formalized in a treaty—the Declaration of the Shanghai Cooperation Organization—that established a "peace zone" along their common borders.

The terrorist attack on New York and Washington on 11 September 2001 and President George W. Bush's efforts to assemble a coalition against Al Qaeda brought Chinese acquiescence to the American invasion of Afghanistan. In exchange, at China's request, the U.S. government added the East Turkestan Islamic Movement (ETIM), which the Chinese claim was funded by Osama bin Laden, to the U.S. list of terrorist organizations and froze its assets. Some question whether the ETIM even exists, and spokespeople for other organizations supporting an independent East Turkestan deny any links to Al Qaeda. Human rights organizations claim that the Chinese have used the U.S. condemnation of the ETIM as a license to engage in religious persecution against Uyghurs, and in fact, the party-state has issued regulations severely limiting Muslims in their religious practices and in the use of the Uyghur language in schools and universities.

More than a dozen Uyghurs who had left Xinjiang for Afghanistan and were being trained by the Taliban were swept up by U.S. invasion forces and eventually shipped off to the U.S. prison facility at Guantanamo Bay. It soon became clear that they were no threat to U.S. interests and were eligible for release, but they were regarded as separatists by the Chinese authorities and thus would be prosecuted were they to return to Xinjiang. Under congressional pressure not to settle even the most benign of the Guantanamo detainees in the United States, the Obama administration eventually found a home for the majority of them on the tiny Pacific island of Palau, for four of them on Bermuda (whose parliament also objected to the deal), and for two in Switzerland–geographical settings about as unlike Xinjiang as one could expect to find.

As Beijing made final preparations to host the 2008 Olympics, a violent episode occurred in Kashgar (喀什) when two Uyghurs rammed a truck into a group of armed policemen, killing sixteen and injuring another sixteen. A week later a homemade bomb killed five in Kuqa (库车) County, and a month after that, three armed policemen were killed in a stabbing attack near Kashgar. Two Uyghurs were executed for their role in the Kashgar incident, and a total of eleven hundred Uyghurs were indicted in 2008 for "endangering state security."

Thus, the stage was set for a particularly deadly outbreak of ethnic violence in China. In late June 2009, some eighteen hundred miles east of Urumqi, a fight broke out in the Early Light Toy Factory in Shaoguan (韶关), near Guangzhou, between Uyghur migrant workers and their Han fellow employees over a rumor (later proved false) that a Han female worker had been raped by Uyghurs in the factory dormitory. In the melee two Uyghurs were killed and 120 injured. Word of the incident made its way back to Xinjiang, and in early July, rioters clashed with police on the streets of Urumqi and later Kashgar, resulting in more than 180 deaths and 1,000 injuries as Uyghurs attacked their Han neighbors, and then Hans retaliated against Uyghurs. Taking a hard line, Xinjiang party secretary Wang Lequan (who is simultaneously a member of the Politburo) called for an end to the violence, summoning 20,000 troops and police to restore order.

But calm was not easily restored. Protesting the military occupation, Uyghurs took to retaliating by sticking Han Chinese with hypodermic needles on crowded buses and sidewalks in Urumqi. As many as five hundred claimed to have been so wounded, though fewer than one in five had actual wounds, and rumors that the needles were contaminated with HIV proved false. Nonetheless, Han residents took to the streets to protest the party-state's failure to guarantee their security. In the aftermath of the episode, Li Zhi, Urumqi's party secretary, was dismissed from office, and two dozen Uyghurs were given death sentences for their role in the violence. In October, eleven Chinese workers in the toy factory where the episode began were tried for their roles in the melee; one was sentenced to death.

Government officials blamed the outbreak on Rebiya Kadeer, the self-styled "Mother of the Uighs," who lives in exile in Washington, D.C. Kadeer had been a model businesswoman in the late 1990s with a seat on the National People's Congress. Subsequently arrested, tried, and sentenced to an eight-year prison term for sending newspaper clippings to her husband, a Uyghur activist living in the United States, she was given an early release in 2005, when Secretary of State Condoleezza Rice visited Beijing. Kadeer denied having encouraged the outbreak of violence, but the Chinese pointed to her role as president of two Uyghur separatist organizations, both of them supported by the National Endowment for Democracy, an organization that receives its funding from the U.S. Congress.

In 2014, China faced numerous attacks by Uyghur Islamist and separatist groups. In February, a vehicle carrying explosives drove into police cars in Uqturpan County (乌什吐鲁番县) in Xinjiang, killing 11 people. In March, the train station in Kunming, capital of Yunnan Province in the southwest, was attacked by 11 knife-wielding men and women, leaving 29 civilians and four assailants dead and 140 people wounded. In April, two suicide bombers killed three people and injured 79 at a train station in Urumqi, the capital of the Xinjiang Uyghur Autonomous Region. In May, 43 persons were killed and more than 90 injured when five attackers threw dozens of explosives at customers in a busy street market in Urumqi. At the end of May, two Uyghur juvenile suspects were killed by police in Kashgar (喀什) in southern Xinjiang. The next month in Xinjiang's Kargilik County (叶城县) near the Pakistan border, a truck rammed a police station and detonated an explosive device. Thirteen attackers were shot, and several policemen were injured. In July, 37 civilians and 59 attackers were killed in Yarkand County (莎车县) in Xinjiang, in the context of a terrorist assault on government buildings. The imam of China's largest mosque in Kashgar, a supporter of the Chinese government, was stabbed to death. Later, Xinjiang saw even more violence. Altogether, close to 300 victims lost their lives.

The Chinese government responded with a year-long campaign against "violent terrorism." The Supreme People's Court reported that more than 700 individuals had been sentenced for crimes connected with terrorism and separatism over the past year. International reaction followed. In 2020 President Trump signed the Uyghur Forced Labor Prevention Act, prohibiting the import of products made with forced labor in Xinjiang. The next year the Parliament of Canada and the States General of the Netherlands both followed the United States in recognizing the Chinese persecution of Uyghurs as a genocide. That same year, nearly fifty independent United Nations human rights experts spoke out against the repression of ethnic minorities in Xinjiang, and in 2021, the European Union declared its first sanctions against China since 1989 in response to China's persecution of Uyghurs.

Uyghur separatists complain of the lack of international support for their cause, particularly when compared with international support for Tibet. When Uyghur separatists demonstrate in support of their cause in Washington or New York City, a handful of supporters join them. When Tibetans demonstrate in support of their cause, they draw crowds in the thousands, usually including celebrities. An obvious difference, of course, is that the Uyghurs have no leader to match the charisma of the Dalai Lama.

The conflict between Han and Uyghur exemplifies the cross purposes at which the party-state and China's ethnic minorities operate. Uyghurs are resentful of having become a minority in their own capital, unable to practice their religion and in danger of losing their language. Their Han neighbors find them uncouth and ungrateful. It is clear that Beijing has yet to figure out a way to resolve the impasse. Ethnicity remains a divisive, not a uniting influence in China, and the party-state appears ill-equipped to deal with it except with the ineffectual carrot of investment and the stick of military suppression.

Chapter 13: The Special Administrative Regions: Hong Kong and Macao

How the Chinese government is handling the administration of Hong Kong as a special administrative region is a matter of great moment. This vibrant financial center, which supplies about two-thirds of China's external direct investment, could become a stagnant urban backwater if badly handled. On the other hand, effectively administering Hong Kong will not only enhance the region's economic future but also demonstrate to the people of Taiwan the viability of the "one country, two systems" formula. A failure to maintain Hong Kong's political, economic, and social systems largely intact will only confirm the expectations of Taiwan's many skeptics.

The British crown colony of Hong Kong was formed based on three treaties between Britain and the Qing dynasty government of China. The Treaty of Nanjing was signed in 1842 at the conclusion of the First Opium War, fought when the Chinese imperial government tried to exclude British opium from China. By the terms of the treaty, the Chinese government ceded in perpetuity the island of Hong Kong to Great Britain. Foreign Secretary Lord Palmerston was not pleased with the work of his envoy, Charles Elliot, who negotiated the treaty, and described Hong Kong (accurately, as it happens) as "a barren island with hardly a house upon it." Eighteen years later, at the conclusion of the Arrow War in 1860, the First Convention of Beijing ceded more territory in the vicinity of Hong Kong island to Britain, including Stonecutters Island and the peninsula of Kowloon (九龙) as far north as present-day Boundary Street. Hong Kong's territory today includes a third parcel of land several times the size of the earlier ceded land: the New Territories, the subject of the Second Convention of Beijing, signed on 1 July 1898. The terms of this agreement were different: rather than cede the land outright, China leased this additional land to the British government for ninety-nine years, a lease that expired on 30 June 1997.

Taken together, the three parcels—a large peninsula at the mouth of the Pearl River on the South China Sea and a number of islands surrounding the peninsula—amount to about 419 square miles, making it roughly one-third the size of Rhode Island.

The colony got off to a slow start. Ten years after it was first established as a base for British naval and military operations in East Asia, fewer than two thousand foreigners and a little more than thirty thousand Chinese lived there. As a commercial center, it was eclipsed by Guangzhou, and by the early twentieth century, Shanghai had outpaced it as a manufacturing and financial center.

On the eve of World War II, Hong Kong's population stood at close to a million. When the Japanese occupied Hong Kong in 1941, the foreign population was imprisoned, and many Hong Kong Chinese fled to Macao, which remained neutral under Portuguese control. By the end of the war, only about six hundred thousand people were living in Hong Kong, but the number grew swiftly as Chinese fled the civil war between Nationalist and Communist forces that swept southward through the mainland; the population quadrupled in less than five years. Many of Hong Kong's new residents were businessmen and their families from Guangzhou and Shanghai, who, fleeing from the prospect of life under Communist rule, brought their skills and capital to Hong Kong.

After the founding of the People's Republic in 1949, Chinese citizens continued to enter Hong Kong, a few legally and many, many more illegally. Most came from neighboring Guangdong Province, and many risked their lives in making their escape. A significant proportion of Hong Kong's current population of about

7.5 million are people (or their descendants) who chose not to be citizens of the People's Republic of China. The economy of Hong Kong has undergone several transformations over the last seventy-five years. Through the 1950s its principal economic *raison d'être* was commerce—as a free port and as China's main economic window to the outside world—and then in the 1960s it began to industrialize. The process began with the manufacture of low-end consumer goods and gradually shifted into appliances and electronics. In the early 1970s, when Hong Kong's labor and real estate costs rose, manufacturers moved to other East Asian countries that were cheaper, and the Hong Kong economy shifted to money and banking; the city became, after Tokyo, East Asia's second financial center.

Following the inauguration of reforms in China and its opening up to the world economy, Hong Kong's focus shifted once again to manufacturing. This time, however, although the companies are owned and managed by Hong Kong residents, the factories are located across the border in Guangdong Province, in the special economic zone of Shenzhen or elsewhere. Today, some 9.6 million Guangdong residents are employed in Hong Kong-owned enterprises.

When Prime Minister Margaret Thatcher, flush from the British victory over Argentina in the Falkland Islands in 1982, visited Beijing, she had been urged to raise the issue of the future of Hong Kong with her hosts. Hong Kong businessmen, concerned over the status of their holdings once the lease on the New Territories expired in 1997, wanted to know whether the Chinese intended to renew the lease.

The existing arrangement had always worked for the benefit of the Communist government. When local leftist zealots had attempted to take advantage of the chaos of the Cultural Revolution to overthrow the Hong Kong government, Mao and his colleagues had reined them in to preserve the symbiotic relationship. By 1982 Hong Kong had come to provide 40 percent of China's foreign exchange and had become China's largest trading partner. Hong Kong firms were investing in joint ventures in Shenzhen and Guangdong and gave every indication they would continue to do so. Hong Kong issues were occasionally discussed by the Foreign Ministry and the British ambassador in Beijing, but day-to-day relations between China and the Hong Kong government were carried on by the former's unofficial emissary in the territory, the head of the New China News Agency (新华通讯社 *Xinhua Tongxun She*).

Thatcher did indeed raise the issue of Hong Kong during her meeting with Deng Xiaoping. She reminded him rather starchily that the British always honored their treaties and expected other nations to do the same. Making her remarks in this setting and framing them as she did, Thatcher simultaneously touched two raw nerves: China's view of its sovereignty and the matter of face. Questioning China's right to govern its own territory was bad enough, but she did this in such a public way that failure to respond would entail China's loss of face. Deng reminded Thatcher that the treaties to which she referred had been signed under duress by a Chinese government no longer in power. He said that Hong Kong, being Chinese territory, must be returned to Chinese sovereignty and that he hoped he lived long enough to visit the city after that occurred. He came within five months of realizing his hope.

Had Thatcher made her point in different terms and another setting, the Chinese might have considered renewing the New Territories lease. But that was now out of the question, and the British concluded that the ceded territories alone—Hong Kong Island, Stonecutters Island, and the tip of Kowloon—did not constitute an economically viable entity. Some arrangement for the transfer of sovereignty to China would have to be negotiated.

The negotiations, involving seventeen sessions over three years, resulted in the Joint Declaration on the Question of Hong Kong, signed in December 1984. The declaration set up the Sino-British Joint Liaison Group, responsible for ongoing negotiations with respect to questions that might arise between the two sides during what the British called the "run-up" to 1997. Two other bodies were constituted at the same time: the Basic Law Drafting Committee, made up of Hong Kong and PRC citizens, to draw up a constitution under which Hong Kong would be governed after 1997 as the Hong Kong Special Administrative Region (SAR–Xianggang Tebie Xingzhengqu 香港特别行政区), and the Basic Law Consultative Committee, made up of Hong Kong citizens and charged with assessing Hong Kong public opinion with respect to the provisions of the Basic Law.

Several aspects of these negotiations, not all of them perfectly clear at the time, came to be very significant as the transfer of sovereignty approached. One was a conflict over the premises of negotiations. The Chinese position was based on an offer the government had first extended to Taiwan in 1981 and then to Hong Kong in 1983: to leave their economic and political systems intact for fifty years after the transfer of sovereignty. The Chinese understood this to mean that no change would be made to Hong Kong's economic and political systems *as they existed at the time of the signing of the agreement in 1984,* while Britain presumed that it could legitimately make alterations in Hong Kong's governance, as it saw fit, prior to the transfer of sovereignty in the thirteen years leading up to 1997 and that China's offer meant Beijing would make no change to the economic and political systems of Hong Kong *as they existed at the time of the transfer of sovereignty in 1997.*

During the negotiations, both sides used the "through train" as a metaphor for the transition. Visitors to China in the 1970s will recall the ritual of boarding a train at the Kowloon station to go to mainland China and traveling on it to Lowu (羅湖), a town on the border. One got off the train at Lowu and, carrying one's luggage, walked across a bridge spanning the border. After going through customs formalities, one boarded the Chinese train on the other side at the Shenzhen station. For frequent travelers, it was a great moment when a through train was inaugurated that allowed passengers to board in Kowloon, cross the border on the train, and disembark in Guangzhou.

In the context of the negotiations, the through train meant that every effort would be made by both sides to ensure that the political system in the time just before the transfer of sovereignty would fit as closely as possible with the political system to be inaugurated after it. If the track were properly laid and the train properly built, the shift of sovereignty would require no one to disembark.

One final aspect of the negotiations proved significant: the people of Hong Kong were not represented in them, though the British had pressed at the outset for three-way negotiations among representatives of the governments of China, Britain, and Hong Kong. The Chinese rejected the idea, insisting on bilateral negotiations between Britain and China, with the Hong Kong governor seated as an observer, since the Hong Kong government, they argued, reported ultimately to the British government, and the people of Hong Kong, being Chinese, were adequately represented by the Chinese government.

But if the people of Hong Kong had been represented by their own delegates, they would certainly have made a strong case for maintaining the status quo. Polls taken in Hong Kong in the early 1980s showed that an overwhelming majority favored a continuing British presence in the territory and opposed a transfer of sovereignty to China—not surprising, given the substantial number of Hong Kong citizens who had fled Communist rule in China.

These views began to change, however, in the years immediately following the signing of the Joint Declaration. Hong Kong residents observed the rapid reform and growth in the Chinese economy and its extensive new links to the world economy. Many of them took advantage of this to establish business ties across the border. By 1989 more than two thousand factories in Guangdong were wholly or partially owned by Hong Kong interests. When one added in subcontracting agreements between Hong Kong and Guangdong firms, it was estimated that Hong Kong-related enterprises accounted for more than a million jobs in southern China. As Hong Kong business interests became linked with those of China, people began to have a personal stake in a smooth working relationship among Beijing, London, and Hong Kong. And as political reforms began to alter somewhat the character of the Chinese government, making it seem slightly less repugnant, widespread skepticism about the future was superseded by cautious optimism.

The massacre in Beijing in June 1989 was a major turning point, however, not only in public attitudes in Hong Kong but also in the relations among Beijing, Hong Kong, and London. The news from Beijing on 4 June had a devastating effect on public confidence in Hong Kong, anger and fear politicizing a large segment of a population famous for its lack of interest in politics. Millions of Hong Kong residents poured into the city streets to express their outrage. Thousands contributed in various ways to support the democracy movement and to aid its fugitives by means of a hastily constructed underground railroad to safe havens in Europe and the United States.

Several political groups that have subsequently evolved into formal political parties were founded in Hong Kong in 1989. Motivated by concern that without an effective political voice, Hong Kong citizens faced as precarious a future as did the advocates of good government in China itself. Martin Lee and Szeto Wah are the two most prominent among the many individuals who stepped forward at this time. Lee helped found the Democratic Party (*Xianggang Mínzhu Dang* 香港民主党). Pro-Beijing businessmen founded the Democratic Alliance for the Betterment and Progress of Hong Kong (DAB Minzhu Jiangang Xiehui Lianming 民主建港協進聯盟). The two continued to function as the territory's largest political parties until the Democratic Party folded in 2025. Today, there are, in addition to DAB, fifteen political parties in Hong Kong, the largest of which is the Hong Kong Federation of Trade Unions (Xianggang Gonghui Lianhehui 香港工會聯合會) with half a million members.

A comparable shift of attitude occurred in Beijing. The image of Hong Kong as an apolitical golden goose faded, and in its place, Chinese authorities saw a hotbed of pro-democratic dissent and a potential threat to their own stability. The situation seemed dangerously out of control when not only the editor of a PRC-supported newspaper in Hong Kong but even Beijing's chief spokesman in the colony, Xu Jiatun (许家屯), spoke out against their government's actions.

The British position shifted as well: Britain joined the many other nations that responded to the Beijing massacre with economic and political sanctions. The future of Hong Kong looked significantly less secure than it had during the negotiation of the Joint Declaration. With London's concurrence, the Hong Kong government announced a $17 billion proposal to develop a new airport and expand harbor facilities, a measure designed to stimulate the economy and to bolster the confidence of the Hong Kong population in Britain's intention to take positive actions on its behalf in the 13-year "run-up" under British sovereignty. Realizing that to do its best for Hong Kong, it must be in dialogue with China, London resumed its conversations with Beijing, moving to a successful negotiation of an agreement on the new airport in mid-1991.

At the same time, the Hong Kong government pushed forward with plans, initiated in 1984 and refined based on a study conducted in 1987, to democratize the territory's political system. It proposed to enlarge the functions of elected local councils and to expand the number of elected positions on the fifty-seven-member Legislative Council. Beijing agreed to these proposals in early 1990, and the election for seats on the Legislative Council was held in September 1991; this election marked the debut of political parties in Hong Kong. The United Democrats, under Martin Lee and Szeto Wah, took sixteen of the eighteen contested seats; the other two went to the Liberal Democratic Federation (*Xianggang Ziyou Minzhu Lianhui 香港自由民主聯會), a probusiness alliance; the pro-China Hong Kong Democratic Federation (Xiangang Minzhu* Lianming 香港民主聯盟) failed to capture a single seat. Despite the flurry of interest generated by the election, in a now all too familiar pattern, voter turnout was very low—only 32 percent of those eligible to participate did so. Observers describe the Hong Kong electorate as "interested spectators" who have an active interest in political issues and keep themselves well informed but are reluctant to participate.

At this point, the differences in understanding of the terms of the Joint Declaration began to emerge, for Beijing took a dim view of these developments in Hong Kong. The Chinese side, registering its disapproval, reminded Hong Kong and London that it had committed itself to preserving the political and economic status quo as of 1984. The British side, noting that it retained sovereignty over Hong Kong through 1997, reaffirmed its right to modify the form of government of the territory as it saw fit. The Chinese, therefore, stalled in negotiations over every issue that arose between the two sides, the most important being capitalization for the new airport.

Christopher Patten, appointed governor of Hong Kong in May 1992, replaced David Wilson, who had served in the post since 1987. Wilson, like many of his predecessors, had been well prepared for his job and knew the Chinese well; but after Tiananmen, understanding and sensitivity were regarded by Westerners as inappropriate, and Wilson was deemed too ready to yield to the Chinese when negotiating the many disputed issues that were obstacles to a good relationship. Patten, by contrast, was neither a Sinophile nor a Sinologue but a highly successful politician who had been head of the Conservative Party and had recently suffered an embarrassing electoral defeat in his bid to retain a seat in Parliament.

Patten's mandate was to take a strong stand with the Chinese and to proceed at full speed with democratizing the Hong Kong government. With this mandate, the through train metaphor was dropped, and in its place came talk of making Hong Kong "indigestible"—as democratic as possible in the time remaining so that, when the Chinese took control in 1997, undoing the changes would cause them the maximum possible international embarrassment. It was a mandate unlikely to endear Patten to his Chinese collocutors. He began his term with a series of extensive conversations with people in Hong Kong, probing for their views on whether and how the government should be restructured in the five years remaining. Five months after taking office, he presented proposals for political reform to the Legislative Council, based, he said, on the opinions he had gathered; they called for an accelerated expansion of representative government that would double the size of the electorate, make local governing bodies elective rather than appointive, increase the number of elected seats on the Legislative Council, and shift the balance of power from the governor and his Executive Council to the now fully representative Legislative Council.

The Chinese response to Patten's proposals was unrelentingly negative. Although Patten claimed to have hewed very closely to the letter of the newly adopted Basic Law, Beijing took the position that the proposals were fundamentally at odds with it. Were the Legislative Council and reconstituted government to adopt the Patten proposals, they said, the authority of that government would be terminated when sovereignty was transferred.

Reaction to the proposals in Hong Kong was mixed. Initially, they were supported by a strong majority, but two factors caused that support to diminish. First, the proposals were out of sync with the electorate's reluctance to participate. The political activism stirred up by reactions to the Beijing massacre was relatively short-lived, and although sizable crowds turned out to mark the anniversary of the event each year, for most of the rest of the year, the Hong Kong public was more comfortable being interested spectators than active political participants. Second, the Hong Kong business community, reacting to Beijing's opposition, was cool; with more and more Hong Kong firms dependent on links with the mainland, China found it easier to disengage the business community from support for democratization.

Before putting his proposals to a vote in the Legislative Council, Patten agreed to discuss them with China. After seventeen rounds of negotiations and no progress, he submitted his proposals to the Legislative Council in two batches, one in December 1993, the other in July 1994. The first, and relatively noncontroversial, batch passed easily; the second, and more difficult, one survived a hostile amendment by a single vote and then passed thirty-two to twenty-four.

There were adverse and perhaps unanticipated consequences of the decision by the British and Hong Kong governments to abandon the idea of a through train. Although Sino-British relations had improved enough by mid-1995 to allow for talks on issues critical to Hong Kong's future, the position of the Chinese hardened with its formation of what they called a "second kitchen," a legislature chosen by the four-hundred-member Selection Committee, which, in its wisdom, selected fifty of its own number to fill all hut ten of the seats in the new body. This made the Hong Kong government all the more a lame-duck one and, in the eyes of some observers, rendered the territory ungovernable for the remainder of the run-up.

China's policy of ignoring the Hong Kong government was strengthened by an enormous amount of ill will toward Patten. The Chinese press called him virtually every uncomplimentary name its style sheets permitted (including what Patten said was his favorite, a "tango dancer"), and for years the Chinese turned their backs on him on every possible public occasion. He was not included on the schedule of Chinese officials visiting the territory, and Chinese officials did not receive him in Beijing. This tactic effectively dissuaded Hong Kong citizens from viewing their government as efficacious.

The Chinese also tried, somewhat less successfully, to discredit Hong Kong's democratic parties. Beijing made it abundantly clear that participation in the post-1997 government by Martin Lee, Szeto Wah, or any of the other prominent and outspoken members of Hong Kong's democratic parties was unacceptable. They denounced the September 1995 elections for seats on the Legislative Council carried out under Patten's new electoral rules and gave notice that the council seated by this election would be dismissed on 1 July 1997. Paradoxically, they also campaigned actively in that same election for a slate of pro-Beijing candidates, who, in the event, were soundly defeated at the polls. Voter participation, at 35 percent, was neither much lower nor much higher than in past elections.

The dispute over the election gave rise to questions about the legality of the Beijing-appointed Provisional Council. A decision adopted by the National People's Congress (NPC) in 1990 stipulated that if the composition of the Legislative Council in June 1997 conformed with the Basic Law, it would remain in office after the transfer of sovereignty. Patten consistently argued that he had carefully crafted his electoral reforms to conform to the law, and he challenged the Chinese to show where they did not conform. Without giving details, China declared that the reforms violated the Basic Law and proceeded to create its second kitchen. Tung Chee-hwa (董建华), coming to Beijing's support soon after he was named chief executive by the selection committee in 1996, disappointed those in Hong Kong who had hoped that he would uphold the results of the territory's eleventh-hour democratization. For their part, some members of the former council threatened to mount a legal challenge to the legitimacy of the new body. Thus, whether they meant to or not, all parties involved helped undermine the new Hong Kong government's authority.

Educated in Britain, Tung Chee-hwa had worked for General Electric in Boston and San Francisco before returning to Hong Kong in 1969 to join his father's Orient Overseas shipping company. Prior to his selection, questions had been raised over the fact that in 1986, he received what the press referred to as a $120 million "bailout" from Chinese investors to save his ailing firm. Some found it unlikely that, in light of this favor, he would be able to hold his own against the importunings of the Beijing government. He has also described himself as an admirer of Singapore's Lee Kuan Yew and the "Asian values" he espoused, arousing concern among Hong Kong's democratic opposition, with which Tung had little patience.

Two factors have made Hong Kong the successful financial center it is: the free flow of information and a careful adherence to the rule of law. Because neither of these, as we have seen, is a characteristic of the People's Republic of China, both seemed in jeopardy as the transfer of sovereignty approached.

One of the most serious legal issues to arise at that time was the post-1997 composition of the Hong Kong Court of Final Appeal. The original plan was for seven justices, three from the Hong Kong legal community, three from a panel of British Commonwealth judges with experience in common law, and a chief justice. The Chinese proposed that there be only one non-Hong Kong justice, drawn from either an international or a local panel. After extensive, unsuccessful negotiations, the British agreed to this, but the Legislative Council rejected it. The Chinese subsequently conceded that more than one justice could be drawn from an international panel, but adopted a very vague definition of the court's jurisdiction that leaves many cases to be decided by the National People's Congress. Reluctantly, and after much campaigning by the Hong Kong government, the Legislative Council ratified this proposal. Nonetheless, serious doubts had been raised, within Hong Kong and in the international business community, about the future integrity of Hong Kong's legal system.

The Hong Kong government in 1991 belatedly adopted a Bill of Rights, intended to supplement protections provided in the Basic Law, but China denounced this as a violation of the Basic Law, and at its March 1997 meeting, the National People's Congress invalidated it, as well as some two dozen other laws and regulations. Here again, Tung Chee-hwa disturbed many in Hong Kong with his unhesitating endorsement of the NPC's action. Without these changes, he said, Hong Kong risked becoming an "indulgent Western society." On the eve of the transfer of sovereignty, it was hard for many to imagine that the Chinese government, as then configured, would allow Hong Kong's free flow of information, so vital to its financial life, to continue uninterrupted.

In the first moments after midnight on 1 July 1997, in a solemn ceremony presided over by Prince Charles and Jiang Zemin, Britain relinquished and China resumed sovereignty over Hong Kong, ending 155 years of British colonial rule. In many ways, the immediate aftermath of the transfer resembled the immediate aftermath of the turn of the millennium two and a half years later: despite widespread expectations of impending disaster, very little actually changed.

The first quarter- century of the integration of Hong Kong into the People's Republic brought significant changes to the former colony.

Table 16: Hong Kong, China, and the US Compared, 1997 and 2025

	HK 1997	PRC 1997	US 1997	HK 2025	PRC 2025	US 2025
GDP	$177 B	$968 B	$7,640 B	$382B	$18,943B	$27,361B
Population	6.5M	1.24 B	276.2 M	7.5M	1.40B	340.1 M
Per Capita GDP	$25,809	$800	$31,459	$49,771	$19,000	$81,695
Birth rate	4.4/1000	6.8/1000	14.6/1000	10.6/1000	6.7/1000	12.0/1000

The period opened with a financial crisis in Asia that began in March of 1997 and that had a much more detrimental effect on Hong Kong than did the transfer of sovereignty. By the end of 1998 the Hang Seng index of Hong Kong stocks had fallen by half since its peak in the summer of 1997, property values were down by as much as 60 percent, tourism—a mainstay of the Hong Kong economy in the past—was off by 25 percent, unemployment reached 6.1 percent, and gross domestic product was down 5.1 percent for the year. To stabilize its currency, the Hong Kong government resorted to the unprecedented step in September of pumping $15 billion into stocks and futures, boosting the Hang Seng index by 18 percent but shocking those who looked to the territory as the last bastion of *laissez-faire* capitalism.

The Hong Kong economy began its recovery from the Asian financial crisis very quickly; at the end of 1999, quarterly growth figures were at a respectable 4.5 percent, and per capita gross domestic product was about $30,000, the third highest in Asia (after Japan and Singapore). Its close relationship with the mainland economy, which was insulated in many respects from the financial crisis, helped contain the effects of the crisis in Hong Kong. More than 78 percent of Guangdong's external direct investment comes from Hong Kong; most of it is from Hong Kong investors, but some of it is Chinese capital channeled through Hong Kong investment companies to take advantage of special privileges accorded to external investors. Hong Kong is also the point through which most of the legal trade and investment between Taiwan and the mainland passes. Until it was recently modified, Taiwanese law required that all economic activity with mainland China take place through a third party, and in the majority of cases, Hong Kong was that third party.

Output declined at the beginning of 2001, and unemployment peaked at 7.8 percent in the summer of 2002. Property values declined rapidly, and many mortgage holders found themselves "underwater"—owing more than the sales values of their properties. Faced by declining tax revenues and increasing welfare costs, the government experienced deficits of up to nine billion dollars, or five percent of GDP. The SARS epidemic added to the economic distress. There were 1,718 cases diagnosed in the territory, 253 of them fatal. Tourism fell off, and trade with the mainland declined sharply. By 2004, the situation had begun to improve, and the economy grew at an average rate of about seven percent for the next four years, only to be hit once again, this time by the international financial crisis. Growth in output was once again negative, property values were in decline, the Hang Seng stock index lost 48 percent of its value, and unemployment was up. The government responded with a stimulus package that increased government spending by about 30 percent; Hong Kong also gained from infrastructure expenditures from Beijing's $586 billion stimulus package in its cross-border neighbors.

The trend to integrate the Hong Kong economy with that of Guangdong Province has continued to accelerate. Today, about 18 percent of Guangdong's exports go to or through Hong Kong. More than 32,000 factories in Guangdong are Hong Kong-owned. Double that number of factories operate as subcontractors for Hong Kong firms. In all, some five million people in Guangdong are employed by Hong Kong-affiliated enterprises, far in excess of the 400,000 blue-collar workers in Hong Kong itself. Driven by the very high price of the territory's real estate (the cost of living in Hong Kong exceeds that of Manhattan by 36 percent), close to 100,000 Hong Kong residents have chosen to acquire property in the suburbs of Dongguan and Shenzhen, as either primary or secondary residences. The number of Hong Kong people habitually working in the mainland is estimated to be 420,000, equivalent to 5% of Hong Kong's workforce. At the same time, there are around 268,000 mainland Chinese working in Hong Kong on a long-term basis. And in 2024, more than sixteen million mainlanders visited Hong Kong on business or as tourists.

Economic collaboration was expanded beyond Guangdong in 2004 with the formation of the Pan-Pearl River Delta (PPRD) Regional Co-operation Forum. At its opening gathering, Tung Chee-hwa had this to say about the new organization: "The PPRD encompasses nine southern provinces and the two SARs of Hong Kong and Macao—an area spanning eastern, central, and western China, with its population and gross domestic product accounting for one-third of the national total. It constitutes a significant stride towards promoting the Hong Kong-Macao-mainland economic partnership. Its object has been to discuss and decide on the direction and strategy for regional development, and to explore ways and approaches for a mutually beneficial partnership." The partnership has met annually for the last twenty years.

Hong Kong's GDP currently stands at about $382 billion. The combined gross domestic product of the now closely integrated economies of Taiwan, Hong Kong, and the mainland provinces of Guangdong and Fujian (where most Taiwanese and Hong Kong investments are situated) amounts to more than $1.2 trillion, or close to 40 percent of the total gross domestic product of China as a whole. The proposed Pan Pearl River Delta Regional Cooperation and Development Forum, as we have seen, plans to integrate further the economies of Hong Kong and Macao with nine provinces in south and south-central China. The economic interdependence that this integration has brought about will have important political consequences in the years ahead. As noted above, one consequence has been to mute some voices in Hong Kong that might otherwise be critical of Beijing. It is also safe to assume that the forum's member provinces, recognizing their dependence on a strong and viable Hong Kong economy, will continue to serve as advocates and allies of the Hong Kong SAR in its relations with Beijing.

The constitution of the People's Republic of China guarantees Chinese citizens freedom of the press, yet as we have seen, whenever the press oversteps the boundary of discourse deemed appropriate by the party, it is brought back into line. Hong Kong's Basic Law also guarantees freedom of the press and publication, and citizens are expected to believe that the phrase means something more substantial than it does in the Chinese constitution. But their confidence was not strengthened by the case of Yang Xi, a reporter for the Hong Kong newspaper *Ming Pao* (明報) who was arrested in 1994 while reporting in China and sentenced to twelve years' imprisonment for stealing and publishing state secrets, the secret in question being a change in the People's Bank of China interest rate, which Yang reported on shortly before it was officially announced. Yet the media in Hong

Kong are numerous, vibrant, and diverse, with nearly seventy daily newspapers and as many as six hundred periodicals, three television stations, two privately owned and one managed by the government, and two privately owned radio stations. People in the communications business in Hong Kong are skeptical about the extent of their freedoms under the Basic Law, and some are hedging their bets, usually with voluntary self-censorship.

Such self-censorship is often a business decision. In 1993, the British Broadcasting Corporation (BBC) produced a documentary marking the centenary of the birth of Mao Zedong. Because it was more critical of aspects of Mao's life than the Chinese Communist Party permits, the Chinese government demanded that it not be shown in Hong Kong. Rupert Murdoch's Star TV pulled it from its broadcast schedule, claiming there had been insufficient time to accommodate it; subsequently, Murdoch removed all BBC programming from the cable service he was in the process of selling mainland China and canceled publication of a memoir by Chris Patten that he thought might be offensive to Beijing For all his fawning, and some $2 billion in investments, Murdoch has been unsuccessful in penetrating the China media market.

In other cases, the decision to self-censor is less obviously business-driven. A number of Hong Kong Chinese-language newspapers, for example, have eliminated their editorial pages; owners and editors presumably believe that in the minefield of Hong Kong politics, there is no telling what might offend Chinese sensibilities and what might detonate in the future. Expressing no opinion at all is the safest course, and the loss of the editorial page has not significantly affected circulation.

Despite fears to the contrary, the Hong Kong courts over the quarter century since reversion have not functioned as the rubber stamp that Beijing might have hoped for. Their most significant departure from Chinese jurisprudence came in 2005, when the

Court of Final Appeal overturned a lower court decision in the case of eight members of *Falun Gong* who had been convicted on charges of assaulting and obstructing police officers during a protest that had occurred in 2002. The high court ruled that the defendants were entitled to constitutional protection of their rights of free speech and assembly and declared that their protest was lawful. Beijing, as we have seen, has banned the group, arrested many of its followers, and declared it an "evil cult."

As promised, Tung Chee-hwa disbanded the elected Legislative Council (Legco) upon taking office on 1 July 1997, replacing it with the Provisional Council appointed in 1996. The question of the legal standing of the Provisional Council was resolved, oddly enough, during a criminal trial over the theft of a wristwatch: a three-judge panel ruled that the SAR courts were powerless to question Beijing's decision to disband the elected legislature.

The system for elections in the special administrative region, as hammered out during the lengthy negotiations leading up to the transfer of sovereignty and enshrined in the Basic Law, richly deserves the designation "byzantine." In September 1997, the Provisional Council approved plans for the 1998 election by which it would be replaced. The new sixty-member body would have twenty members elected by a system of proportional representation, thirty members elected by "functional constituencies"—professional and trade associations—and ten members appointed by an 800-person selection committee. In subsequent elections, the ten appointed members would gradually be replaced by members elected by proportional representation. The Basic Law spoke of the possibility of the entire assembly being elected based on the principle of "one person, one vote" after 2007, ten years beyond reversion, but provided that the actual system of election would be determined at that time.

Defying their reputation as hopelessly apolitical and ignoring a daylong driving rainstorm, 53.2 percent of the 2.7 million eligible voters participated in the election the following May, exceeding the previous record participation of 39 percent in Hong Kong's first direct election.

More than 70 percent of the vote went to democratic politicians ousted with the appointment of the Provisional Council. Martin Lee, the most prominent among Hong Kong's pro-democracy politicians, took his seat in the new Legco and promptly called for speeding up the timetable leading to the direct election of all Legco members and the chief executive. Tung Chee-hwa rejected the suggestion, claiming that the Hong Kong public needed time to learn about democracy.

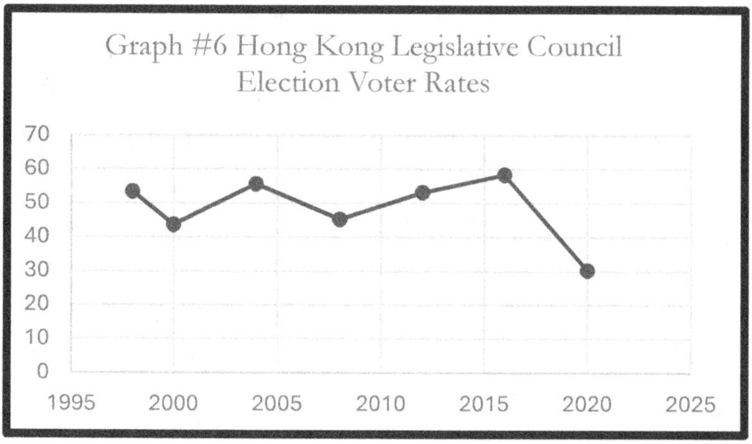

Based on the agreed-upon schedule, in the Legco elections held in September 2000, twenty-four seats in the council were open to proportional election. Whether distracted by excellent weather, political corruption, or a sense that the Legco carried little weight in determining the course of events in Hong Kong, participation in this election was only 43 percent. Pro-democracy candidates fared less well than they had in 1998, controlling twenty-two of the sixty seats on the council, and pro-Beijing candidates fared slightly better.

In the Legco election of 2004, the number of proportionally elected seats increased to thirty, or half the members of the council. All ten seats initially filled by the selection committee were now filled by election. For a while, in the run-up to the election, it looked as though prodemocracy candidates might actually secure a majority on the council, but plagued by scandal, they captured only twenty-four of the thirty elected seats and could count only on support from an additional four members elected by the functional constituencies, ending three seats shy of a majority. Voter turnout, at 56 percent, was the highest in Hong Kong's election experience. Attention now turned to the election of the chief executive, scheduled for 2006. Tung Chee-hwa had run unopposed for a second term in 2000 and had received seven hundred votes from the eight-hundred-person election committee, despite polls showing that fewer than 20 percent of Hong Kong citizens supported his continuing in office. At this point in his career, his reputation, in the words of one foreign observer, was that of "a genial if sometimes clumsy caretaker" who was careful to take his cues from Beijing. But Tung's fortunes began to decline shortly after his reelection. In 2002 , he unveiled plans to reorganize his government, adding a layer of fourteen officials to be appointed by him to oversee the operation of the civil service departments. Despite public criticism, he pushed ahead with his plan, secured Beijing's concurrence, and appointed his new team.

Later that year, Tung made public his plan for new legislation on subversion and sedition in a so-called consultation document. Because the proposal reminded people of restrictions on human rights in the PRC, opposition was intense. Tung first backed down on some of the provisions for control of the Internet, then, following a demonstration that attracted sixty thousand protesters, postponed consideration of the legislation for a second round of public consultation. When a second round of antigovernment demonstrations brought five hundred thousand out onto the streets on the fourth anniversary of the transfer of sovereignty on 1 July, Tung withdrew the legislation entirely.

He also found himself thwarted by the public in his plan to add fifty acres of landfill to the Hong Kong harbor for a new highway, waterfront park, and office and residential development. The project was opposed by two-thirds of the Hong Kong public; he put the project on hold.

Losing confidence in Tung and alarmed by the possible spillover of political unrest, Hu Jintao took the occasion of his 2004 visit to Macao for the fifth anniversary of its reversion to mainland control to publicly dress down the Hong Kong CEO, telling Tung to "sum up experiences, identify shortcomings, sharpen administrative abilities, and continue to raise the quality of governing." Two months later, Tung submitted his resignation and was replaced by his second-in-command, the chief secretary for administration, Donald Tsang (Tsang Yam-Kuen—曾蔭權). Born and educated in Hong Kong, Tsang joined the civil service in 1967. In 1982, he completed a master's degree in public administration at Harvard's Kennedy School. Because of a sartorial preference of long standing, he was popularly known as Bow-tie Tsang. Tsang was elected in July 2005 to serve out the remaining two years of Tung's term.

Tsang almost immediately turned his attention to the question of procedures for the next Legco election, procedures that had been left unresolved in the Basic Law, which had hinted at the prospect of choosing all of Hong Kong's leaders by direct election after 2007. In March, the Standing Committee of the National People's Congress issued an "interpretation" of the Basic Law. It required that the Hong Kong government consult with the committee before making any changes to the election law, but did not rule out that changes might be made in advance of the 2008 Legco election. Thousands of Hong Kong residents took to the streets to protest Beijing's intervention into what they regarded as a local question. Perhaps in response, the Standing Committee issued a second interpretation, this one ruling out direct elections for the CEO in 2007 as well as any expansion of the electorate for the Lego elections scheduled for 2008.

Tsang persevered, however, and, having secured tentative support from Beijing, put forward a compromise plan that would expand the role of elected neighborhood councilors in electing members of the selection committee and the Legco. The plan would have doubled the number entitled to vote for the CEO from eight hundred to sixteen hundred and slightly expanded the size of the Legco. Calling for a timetable for direct elections of all government officials, 250,000 demonstrators took to the streets. Tsang responded that he hoped that the territory would enjoy full direct democracy "within my lifetime" but urged support of his plan. Opposed by prodemocracy legislators, the plan went down to defeat, leaving the parties involved at an impasse. The impasse was resolved by Beijing, which ruled that direct elections for the territory's CEO would not take place until 2017 at the earliest and for Legco candidates until 2018.

Tsang was opposed for reelection in 2007 by prodemocracy candidate Alan Leong (Leong Kah-kit—梁家傑), the former chair of the Hong Kong Bar Association. In the first contested election for chief executive in the territory's history, Tsang defeated Leong by a vote of 645 to 123 in the election committee. In Legco elections the following year, pro-democracy candidates lost some ground, reducing their number from twenty-six to twenty-four legislators. The pro-Beijing Democratic Alliance (DAB) gained ground by running on a platform combining Chinese nationalism with an appeal for government aid to the poor to cope with inflation. Voter turnout returned to its earlier level of 45 percent.

Tsang stepped aside in 2012 and was replaced by Leung Chun-ying (梁振英). In the fall of 2014, protesters seeking direct elections for Hong Kong's Chief Executive laid siege to the government's headquarters. The siege came to be known as the "Umbrella Movement," named after the umbrellas used for defense against police pepper spray. The occupation covered territory in several districts of the city, including Admiralty, Causeway Bay, Mong Kok (旺角), and Tsim Sha Tsui (尖沙咀). The number of protestors reached 100,000 at a time, the majority of them students, and lasted for more than two months. Nine of the protestors were arrested and jailed. Ultimately, however, the Legislative Council rejected the government's electoral reform proposal by a vote of 28 to 8.

After the failure of the Umbrella Movement and the subsequent imprisonment of democracy activists, citizens began to fear the loss of the "high degree of autonomy provided for in the Basic Law. In 2019, protests re-emerged, this time against the government's introduction of a bill to amend the Fugitive Offenders Ordinance provision on extradition. It was the largest series of demonstrations in the history of Hong Kong, involving up to two million people. The movement was dubbed the "Water Revolution" after martial artist Bruce Lee's advice to "fight like water." As a result of the demonstrations, the Hong Kong economy slipped into recession, retail sales declined, and consumer spending decreased. Some restaurants saw their customers cancel bookings, and certain banks and shops were forced to close their doors. Ultimately, the extradition bill was withdrawn. Polls indicated that only 19% of the Hong Kong population opposed the pro-democracy demands. The Chinese government expressed its opposition to the protests, which were depicted as separatist riots. It further tightened its control in Hong Kong by replacing the head of the Liaison Office of the PRC in Hong Kong with Xia Baolong (夏宝龙). Its current head is Zhou Ji (周霁).

In the 2017 Chief Executive selection process , Carrie Lam (林鄭月娥), who had served in the Leung administration as Chief Secretary for Administration, obtained 777 votes from the 1,194-member appointed Election Committee. She was the Beijing-favored candidate and became the first female Chief Executive of Hong Kong. Her tenure has been described as a "pivotal, turbulent period." Two years into her administration, she proposed a bill that would have allowed extraditions to the mainland. It sparked massive protests that, at their peak, involved more than a million people. Protests continued throughout 2019, leading to violence and a deep political crisis. The government eventually withdrew the bill.

The following year, Beijing imposed a National Security Law on Hong Kong, bypassing the local legislature. The law criminalized secession, subversion, terrorism, and collusion with foreign forces. Under the new law, dozens of pro-democracy activists, lawmakers, journalists, and civil society leaders were arrested or forced into exile. During Lam's tenure, the Hong Kong electoral system was overhauled to ensure that only "patriots" could govern. Pro-democracy candidates were barred from running for office, and the Legislative Council was restructured to guarantee a pro-Beijing majority. Lam led Hong Kong through the COVID-19 pandemic with strict measures including quarantine, travel bans, and partial lockdowns. During her term of office, as many as 200,000 Hong Kong citizens emigrated.

Lam was succeeded in office by Hong Kong's current chief executive, John Lee (Li Jia-chao–李家超), who was elected in 2022. He is the fifth chief executive of Hong Kong; each of his four predecessors is still living. His term ends in 2027.

The issue of overpopulation of Hong Kong has come to the forefront in the years since the transfer of sovereignty. Hong Kong's current population is 7.5 million, up more than 20 percent since 1990. Paradoxically, before 1997, it was not overpopulation but rather a population drain that was of concern. Before the negotiations, Hong Kong lost an average of twenty thousand residents per year, but this was not a net loss; an equal or greater number moved into the territory each year. Once negotiations were underway, many Hong Kong residents who lacked confidence in the future of the territory emigrated in the decade preceding the transfer of sovereignty.

During the 1980s, the British government revised its policy with respect to residents in its overseas territories: a new British overseas passport entitled the bearer to visit Britain but not to take up residence there. A few Hong Kong residents were able to get regular British passports, but the vast majority could only obtain these new overseas passports, which do not qualify them as British subjects. Given this situation, many Hong Kong people who could do so decided to seek citizenship elsewhere—the United States, Canada, Australia, or New Zealand. Other countries took advantage of the situation by offering Hong Kong residents citizenship in exchange for a pledge to invest. Those who argued that Hong Kong citizens were being abandoned to an uncertain fate by the retreating colonial power brought pressure to bear on the British government after a thousand passports good for residence in Britain; up to two hundred thousand people, including dependents traveling on these passports, could be accommodated by this offer.

Most very wealthy people in Hong Kong have held foreign passports for years. Unlike the boat people who left Vietnam after the fall of their government, these "yacht people," as they are sometimes sarcastically called, have no difficulty establishing residence outside Hong Kong when and if they choose to do so. But most members of Hong Kong's working class could not afford to emigrate even if they had the papers to do so. Hence, the upper middle class was disproportionately represented among those who left in advance of the transfer of sovereignty. The mid-levels of most professions were seriously affected by the brain drain. And these well-trained and experienced emigrants from Hong Kong were replaced by immigrants, most of them from the mainland and nearly all of them less well trained and experienced. In all, some 600,000 emigrated from Hong Kong, but by 2007, thirty percent of that number had returned to the city.

Hong Kong residency is much sought-after by mainlanders. Since 1997, more than one million have secured permission to move into the territory. There is no accurate count of illegal immigration, but arrests of illegal immigrants are running just short of one thousand per year.

A potential population flood triggered the new SAR government's first major and highly controversial test of its autonomy under the "one country, two systems" formula. At issue was a court case in the spring of 1999 involving four PRC citizens whose parents were citizens of Hong Kong and who sought Hong Kong citizenship. A (a provision of the Basic Law governing the SAR states that children of Hong Kong citizens born outside Hong Kong have the rights of Hong Kong citizens. The Hong Kong Court of Final Appeal had ruled in their favor at the end of January, but Beijing immediately protested, calling the decision "a mistake [that] should be rectified." Beijing's position was that the NPC, not the Hong Kong court, has the sole authority to interpret the Basic Law. The court reviewed the case and upheld its decision, at the same time noting that it "cannot question the authority" of the NPC.

The Hong Kong government sided with Beijing against the court. Citing a figure of 1.67 million Chinese citizens who are children of Hong Kong parents and who could, in theory, take up residence in Hong Kong if the court's decision stood, the government petitioned the NPC to reverse the decision. It did so, and later the court acknowledged the final authority of the NPC to interpret the Basic Law and reversed its decision. Although the reversal met with the approval of most Hong Kong residents (who were none too eager to make way for a million new neighbors), opponents criticized it as setting a dangerous precedent with respect to the independence of the Hong Kong judicial system.

In 2001, the court ruled that a child born in Hong Kong of mainland parents had a right to residency. Although Beijing registered its disapproval, the court's ruling stood, giving rise to a very large number of pregnant mainlanders crossing the border to give birth and thereby assure their children the right to Hong Kong residency. So great was the number of these cases that the Hong Kong government instituted a new policy requiring an up-front payment of five thousand dollars for women crossing the border to deliver their children.

A different issue involving immigration and residency was also considered by the high court in 2002. It ruled that all the members of a group of more than five thousand mainlanders suing for the right to stay must leave. All the plaintiffs had arrived in the territory after the National People's Congress ruling in the 1999 case. The Hong Kong court ruled that only those living in Hong Kong before 29 January 1999 were entitled to residency. Once again, the Chinese government intervened, agreeing that the plaintiffs must return to the mainland, but moving the effective date of the right to stay back to 1 July 1997, the date of the transfer of sovereignty. More than four thousand of the plaintiffs defied the court's deadline to leave the territory, but all were eventually deported.

The civil rights record of the SAR government has been better than many expected it would be. With the transfer of sovereignty, certain civil liberties were curtailed: Hong Kong residents are now required to seek police permission before engaging in street demonstrations, and protests advocating independence for Taiwan or Tibet are forbidden. But the media remain freer from constraints than their mainland colleagues. In 1998, Xu Simin, an outspoken pro-China Hong Kong delegate to the Chinese People's Political Consultative Conference (CPPCC-*Zhongguo Renmin Zhengzhi Xieshang Huiyi*– 中国人民政治协商会议) meeting in Beijing, denounced the Hong Kong government-run radio and television network as a "remnant of colonialism" and called for Beijing's intervention. Initial reaction in Hong Kong was to denounce the CPPCC for favoring interference in the internal affairs of the region, but when both Jiang Zemin and CPPCC head Li Ruihuan warned Xu and his fellow delegates against commenting on SAR affairs in national government bodies, opposition changed to admiration for Beijing's "hands-off" approach.

A number of organizations clearly hostile to the interests of the Chinese party-state continue to operate in Hong Kong with few, if any, restrictions. For example, the Information Centre for Human Rights and Democracy, the most comprehensive source of information on dissidents and their activities, complains only that Chinese authorities thwart their efforts from time to time by jamming their beepers.

As we have seen, Hong Kong residents do not always exercise their right to go to the polls, but they certainly exercise their right to take to the streets in protest, and they did so with gusto. It is paradoxical that while young people on the mainland seem either ignorant of or apathetic about the events of the spring of 1989, every year up to 2020, protest demonstrations in Hong Kong marked the anniversary of the Tiananmen massacre; indeed, 150,000 people, the largest number since 1990, turned out for the candlelight vigil marking the twentieth anniversary in 2009. While there were no restrictions on participation, members of Hong Kong's Democratic Party have complained that they are unable to acquire visas to travel in the mainland and say that when they asked for Tung Chee-hwa's intervention to remove their names from Beijing's blacklist, he responded that they would receive more favorable treatment if they would "put the Tiananmen protests behind them." As we have seen, it was the protest on that occasion by half a million Hong Kong residents that alarmed Beijing and brought about Tung Chee-hwa's early retirement. The anniversary of the reversion, 1 July, had also become an occasion for massive protests. The Tiananmen protests were banned in 2020, citing the COVID-19 epidemic. In that same year, the national security law was imposed by Beijing. Police cordoned off Victoria Park to prevent political gatherings.

Frustrated by glitches and difficulties in an otherwise remarkably well-functioning city, Hong Kong people sometimes complain that "Hong Kong is becoming more like China every day." But the reverse of that sarcastic comment is also true: China, particularly its southern provinces, is becoming more like Hong Kong every day. The more that marketization and liberalization spread through the Chinese system, the brighter Hong Kong's future is.

Even the darkest scenario for China's future—the weakening of central control and the breakup of the country into regional satrapies—would not be the worst news for the future of Hong Kong. If the central Chinese government cannot impose its will on cities like Shanghai and Guangzhou, which have been under its close control for three-quarters of a century, why should we assume that it can do so with the Hong Kong SAR?

The key to Hong Kong's future lies in the quality of the people chosen to lead it. Optimists point to the truth that Hong Kong people have survived and thrived against what appeared to be insurmountable odds in the past: the settling of the unpromising island in the nineteenth century; the rebuilding of the colony after World War II; the dark days of the Cultural Revolution, when it seemed that sovereignty would be transferred under circumstances of violence, anarchy, and chaos. They believe it can happen again, and they may well be right.

* * *

By contrast with Hong Kong, it would not be unfair to characterize Macao (*Aomen* 澳門, or "bay gate" in Chinese) as a quiet backwater. It has a population of 710,000 and occupies some 46 square miles of territory—a small peninsula and a series of islands on the southern coast of China's Guangdong Province, thirty-six miles across the Pearl River estuary from Hong Kong, which is ten times its size. It is linked to the mainland by the Hong Kong–Zhuhai–Macao Bridge, a 55-kilometer bridge and tunnel system. It is both the longest sea crossing and the longest open-sea fixed link in the world.

The quiet Mediterranean-like enclave of Macao was first colonized as a leased territory in 1557. It was Europe's oldest colonial holding in Asia. Following the colonization of Hong Kong by Britain, Macao lost its role as a major Asian port. The Sino-Portuguese Treaty of Peking, signed in 1887, gave Portugal perpetual occupation rights. During World War II, Japan did not occupy the colony and generally respected Portuguese neutrality, though it installed a group of government "advisors" as an alternative to military occupation. Portugal tried unsuccessfully to return the colony to China twice in the past, once during the tumultuous first months of the Cultural Revolution in 1966 and again after a leftist revolution in Portugal in 1974. Portugal formally relinquished Macao as an overseas province that year and acknowledged it as a "Chinese territory under Portuguese administration." The transfer marked the end of what was once a vast European colonial empire in East Asia.

The 1987 Joint Declaration on the Question of Macao agreed to the handover of the colony in 1999, and China guaranteed Macao's political and economic systems for fifty years thereafter. The occasion was marked by ceremonies at the stroke of midnight presided over by Portugal's president, Jorge Sampaio, and China's president, Jiang Zemin. With the transfer, Macao became China's second SAR, enjoying, like Hong Kong, substantial autonomy except in foreign and military affairs.

Terms of the transfer were successfully negotiated in 1987 and formalized in the Joint Declaration signed by the Portuguese and Chinese governments; in 1993 the National People's Congress passed the Basic Law under which Macao is governed. But Portugal handled the issue of Macao residents' nationality very differently from how Britain treated residents of Hong Kong: all of Macao's residents were given the option of immigrating to Portugal with Portuguese citizenship; in fact, few took advantage of the offer.

Whereas the British government surrendered Hong Kong to Chinese sovereignty with considerable resistance and great regret, the Portuguese government seemed relieved as it received its folded flag on 20 December 1999.

China's second special administrative region has a government headed by a Chief Executive who, at the time of the turnover, was Edmund Ho (He Hou-hua 何厚鏵), a middle-aged banker whose appointment was announced by Beijing in May 1999. Ho's first priority was to control crime. The former colony was notorious as a haven for criminal gangs plagued by organized crime associated with triads, which are Asia's version of the Mafia. In the past, these gangland-style organizations have caused terror in Macao through shootings and turf wars. Although less prevalent, it is believed that triads still operate in the city's casino rooms.

The current Chief Executive—the fourth to serve—is Sam Hou Fai (Cen Haohui (岑浩輝), who was elected for a five-year term in 2024. There is a Legislative Assembly, a Court of Final Appeal, and eleven lower courts. The economy is largely based on casino gambling revenues and tourism. Macao has a GDP of approximately $54 billion, which works out to be a per capita GDP of some $89,600, placing the territory in fifth place in a 2023 ranking of the wealthiest countries and territories around the world. Macao's main exports include clothes and textiles, tobacco and wine, machinery and transport equipment, copper, watches, diamond jewelry, office machines, and telecommunication equipment. The economy relies on mainland China for food, fresh water, and energy imports, and Japan and Hong Kong for raw materials and capital goods. A very significant portion of its tax revenue derives from tourism and gambling.

A garrison of some 600 People's Liberation Army soldiers is now stationed in Macao; the first troops having arrived the day after the transfer of sovereignty. The garrison had been a point of contention before the transfer, with the Portuguese asserting that its stationing in Macao violated the terms of the Joint Declaration, but many Macanese welcomed the arrival of the troops as a further contribution to the restoration of civil order. The garrison is primarily a symbolic presence to underscore Chinese sovereignty.

Education in Macao does not have a single set of standards or curricula. Individual schools follow different educational models, including Chinese, Portuguese, Hong Kong, and British systems. Most schools are private institutions, the vast majority using Cantonese as the medium of instruction. Macao has ten universities and tertiary education institutes. The University of Macao, founded in 1981, is the territory's only public comprehensive university.

For many years, Macao has attracted visitors from Hong Kong (and, more recently, from nearby Shenzhen and Guangzhou) to its hotels, bars, and casinos. To facilitate the tourist trade, it opened an international airport in 1995 and the Hong Kong-Macao bridge and tunnel in 2018.

In recent years, Beijing has reached what some might see as a far fetched conclusion that Macao can be effective in helping cement China's relations with the Portuguese-speaking world, specifically Brazil, where China has rapidly developed trade relations. Accordingly, the teaching of Portuguese in Macao's schools was revived in 2004, five years after reversion.

The transfer of sovereignty struck observers as significantly more relaxed than that in Hong Kong. The Portuguese were not sorry to relinquish control, and most Macanese were not sorry to see them go. "As a local, I'd have to say the Portuguese didn't do a good job," said one businessman. "But in fairness," he continued, "they had their own problems and couldn't pay attention to a little spot of land on the other side of the world." It wouldn't be entirely wrong to say the same of the authorities in Beijing.

Chapter 14: Education

In American culture, the term "intellectual" carries several connotations along with its standard meaning of someone who devotes him- or herself to the life of the mind, who thinks about thinking. The other connotations are frequently uncomplimentary. Intellectuals are seen as iconoclasts. They question orthodoxy. They are assumed to be liberals—in the political sense, but more often in the sense of seeing both sides of an issue and being reluctant to come down firmly on one side or the other—spending a lot of time saying "on the one hand ..., on the other hand ..." Finally, intellectual may often be a term of disapproval. Intellectual historians point out that Americans have a long tradition of anti-intellectualism. "Pointy-headed intellectuals" are absentminded and hopelessly impractical, isolating themselves in ivory towers rather than offering practical solutions to real-world problems.

Yet American culture takes intellectual freedom very seriously indeed, the freedom that individuals, not just intellectuals, have to think, say, write, publish, and teach whatever they choose. American law offers safeguards for intellectual freedom as well as for what is called intellectual property. Moreover, American schools and universities with their tenure systems protect teachers and professors from political reprisals against what they publish or what they teach in the classroom.

In Chinese, "intellectual" is rendered *zhishi feizi* (知识分子) or *zhishizhe* (智识者). A translation from the Russian and French, it came into common use only in the early years of the twentieth century. Chinese intellectuals are aware of this Western—indeed peculiarly American—concept of the intellectual but know it to be very different from the concept of the intellectual in the Chinese tradition, *i.e.,* an individual who had mastered a particular canon.

For that, the Chinese term is *wenren* (文人) or *shidafu* (士大夫), which we usually translate as "literati."

For the literati, mastery was confirmed by one's passing an examination set by the imperial government. Once credentialed, the individual might contribute to the canon by modifying it only incrementally with interpretations or commentaries. There were, of course, critics and iconoclasts, but in general, it was not the literati's role to be openly critical or iconoclastic. Tradition and authority were to be respected, not assaulted. The goal of intellectual life was not to retreat from the world and engage in reflection but to enter public life, ideally in an official position. Public service was his obligation. Once in office, the intellectual was obliged to serve as a moral and ethical example to those whom he governed and to hold not only himself but also his colleagues, his superiors, and even his emperor to the highest standards of conduct and to criticize them when they failed to uphold these standards. Carrying out this latter obligation might cost him his job or even his life, but even under these circumstances, the obligation held.

Chinese intellectuals first became acquainted with the American concept of intellectual life in the late nineteenth century. American missionary organizations set up schools and colleges in China in which many young Chinese students were educated; some of them came to the United States, continued in colleges and universities here, and then returned to China.

The moment most frequently associated with the abandonment of the old image of the Chinese intellectual and the adoption of a new, Westernized image is the May Fourth Movement in 1919, when a protest against Japanese incursions on Chinese sovereignty at the end of World War I gave rise to a movement that marked the emergence of a new nationalism in China and the acceptance by many young Chinese intellectuals of the obligation to take a politically active and iconoclastic stance against traditional culture. Mao Zedong was part of the May Fourth generation, but he separated himself from its intellectuals. Though for a brief period as a young man he lived and worked on the fringes of their group at Beijing University, he was never fully accepted by them, presumably because they took him for something of a hick. When they began to explore the ideas of Marx and Lenin, Mao became committed to these ideas far more fervently and faithfully than they did.

He came to hold a highly contradictory view of intellectuals, perhaps because he had been bruised by their not accepting him, perhaps because he scorned their liberal tendency to equivocate in committing to a new political orthodoxy. Whatever the reason, despite the fact that Mao was in fact an intellectual—he read, he wrote, he thought, he occasionally composed poetry—he was deeply mistrustful of intellectuals and made them the target of political attack on several occasions, the anti-rightist campaign in the late 1950s and the Cultural Revolution in the mid-1960s being the most sweeping among them.

The notion of intellectual freedom—that special protection must be given to a person's right to expound his own point of view—was totally foreign to Mao's thinking. His quite different goal was to develop a new intellectual community that would be, in his words, "both red and expert." He was looking for people who were absolutely dependable in their political orthodoxy, but at the same time scientifically and technologically adept.

Chinese official attitudes toward intellectuals have changed since Mao's death. Deng Xiaoping's own record in this respect was far from admirable. Though he studied and worked in France as a teenager, Deng can scarcely be thought of as an intellectual. Indeed, he was deeply involved in the campaigns of the late 1950s, during which many Chinese intellectuals were imprisoned or denigrated. Still, he and some of his like-minded colleagues assigned a high priority to China's becoming fully modern and realized that this could not happen without the active cooperation of China's intellectuals. In part because he thought they had too favorable an attitude toward the intellectual community, Mao tarred them all with the same brush, and Deng and his colleagues suffered the same terrible fate as intellectuals did during the Cultural Revolution.

Shortly after Deng returned to power in 1977, he lent his support to a remarkable burst of public expression of dissident views. Democracy Wall, near the center of Beijing, became a place where a vigorous debate on China's recent past and its future course was permitted. It was here that Wei Jingsheng posted a manifesto critical of Deng for having failed to add democracy to his "four modernizations" (of agriculture, industry, science and technology, and the armed forces) as the critically needed "fifth modernization." But Deng's support for intellectual freedom was highly instrumental and very short-lived. He used the dissidents and their views to help him displace Hua Guofeng, Mao's designated successor, but once that was accomplished and his position was secure, he first moved the wall to a distant part of the capital and then closed it down entirely. Wei Jingsheng was arrested on a technical charge of having given state secrets to a foreign reporter and sentenced to jail. (His jail term ended, he is currently living in exile in the United States.)

Intellectuals in China today have recovered a measure of the status they lost during the Maoist era and are respected because of the contribution they can make to their country's effort to modernize. They are allowed a measure of latitude with respect to the ideas they propound, but this absolutely does not extend into the realm of political ideas. Intellectuals have not recaptured the preeminent position their forebears enjoyed in traditional society, for in today's China, that position is already occupied by the entrepreneur or the party hack.

China's preschool, elementary, and secondary schools have a total enrollment of about 250 million students. Schooling begins with prekindergarten nursery schools, widely available in China's cities, less so in the countryside. Elementary school begins with six-year-olds in kindergarten and extends through six grades. Neighborhood schools are the rule, though most cities have "key schools," where some or all the places are filled by competitive examination. Elementary education is close to universal. Secondary education begins with lower middle schools, grades seven through nine, admission into which is by examination. About four out of five elementary school students continue on to lower middle school. Students are assigned to a class of about fifty, which stays together for all their courses during the three years. Admission to upper middle schools, grades ten through twelve, is again based on examinations; depending on these and on their preferences, students are assigned to either academic or vocational high schools. Two out of five lower middle school students go on to upper middle school on average, though the figure is much higher in the cities than in the countryside.

Table 17: School Enrollment in China and the United States

	China	United States
Percent enrolled in primary school	99	99
Percent enrolled in middle school	98	98
Percent enrolled in high school	23	96
Percent enrolled in college or university	17	40
Number enrolled in graduate school	3.9 million	2.1 million

(Sources: *China Statistical Yearbook 2024* and National Center for Education Statistics)

Expanding the availability of China's postsecondary education has been a priority since the economic reforms began. Although college and university enrollment has more than tripled in the last ten years, there are still fewer than 47 million places in colleges and universities for the close to one hundred million young people of college age. Most of the colleges and universities are four-year institutions, with students admitted based on a national competitive examination taken the summer after their high school graduation. Entering students are assigned to a major field of study and take courses only in the relevant department; professional education in law, business, and medicine is offered at this level. Beginning in 1982, university departments were also accredited to admit graduate students. There are now about 1.3 million students enrolled in graduate programs leading to an M.A. or a Ph.D.

In the early years of the reform period, college graduates were guaranteed job placement. The *fenpei (分配) process was a source of great anticipation and anxiety among college seniors, as it determined their careers for them. With the marketization of the economy, the fenpei* system was disbanded, and graduates were responsible for finding their own employment.

Primary and secondary schools are tuition-free for urban residents, being financed by the municipal governments or, in some instances, by large state-owned enterprises. Parents must pay only for books and school supplies. Until 2005, schools in the countryside charged tuition. Their school budgets were met principally through tuition receipts, with only supplementary funds coming from local governments. That year, the central government announced an end to fees in rural schools. It also announced a plan to spend $2.4 billion on rural schools over the following four years for school construction, for technology, and for offsetting the loss of fees in rural schools. The amount was scarcely more than a drop in the bucket of the cost of rural schooling, and thus the central government's largesse constituted yet another unfunded mandate.

Table 18: Educational Financing in China and the United States

Amount spent on education, 2024	China $104 billion	United States $869 billion
Average annual percentage increase, 1998-2024	65	8
As a percentage of total government expenditures	14	14
As a percentage of the 2024 GNP	2	6
Per student, 2007	$346	$9,500

(Sources: *China Statistical Yearbook 2024* and National Center for Education Statistics)

Universities are operated by the central government and by provincial and municipal governments. Funding for national so-called key schools comes directly from the budget of the Ministry of Education; for other colleges and universities, from the government agency that operates them. Government funding no longer fully supports the operating costs of post-secondary institutions, which have been encouraged to devise other income-producing strategies.

Until 1992, university education was given at no cost to the student; since then, students have been charged a tuition that varies by school and discipline, currently ranging from about $1,000 to about $9,000 a year. Tuition is lower in those disciplines to which the government is interested in attracting students; teachers' colleges, for example, charge nothing at all. Scholarships are given out on a system based on financial need and academic achievement. Universities generate additional income by admitting students who failed the national qualifying examination but whose families will pay a special high tuition for their post-secondary education.

In addition to the usual forms of academic funding, most colleges and universities have established various kinds of revenue-generating operations, which run the gamut from small factories to consulting companies, and some schools lease out space on their already overcrowded campuses for shops and restaurants.

In 2022, China had 178,300 privately run schools, accounting for 34.37% of all schools across the country. The number of students attending non-state schools was 52,827,200, accounting for 18.05% of all students in China. Many of the private schools have been built with funds contributed by overseas Chinese. High tuition fees are charged at these schools; figures as high as $3,000 per academic year are not uncommon. The most recent education act passed by the National People's Congress that affects private schools recognizes online education as a teaching approach.

The substantial American influence on education in China is in part due to the many Americans who taught in and ran missionary schools there. It is also the result of the work of John Dewey, the American educator and pragmatic philosopher, who spent two years lecturing in China in the early 1920s and who supervised the work of Chinese graduate students who became influential educators in their own country.

Despite this extensive influence, one of the fundamental principles of American education—the community-based school system—was never adopted in China. Looking toward Japanese and later Russian examples, Chinese educators advocated the adoption of a uniform curriculum for the entire country. The current version of that national curriculum is fairly restrictive at the primary and secondary levels, allowing for very little local innovation. It stresses basic skills and gives short shrift to the arts and humanities. Arts training for gifted students is available in after-school programs or in special schools. English-language instruction is now almost universal in lower middle schools and at the primary level for students at the best urban schools. Methods of instruction rely heavily on rote memorization and in-class recitation. Cross-cultural studies have shown that these methods produce, as might be expected, students with excellent memory skills but weak creative and analytical skills.

In the past, American visitors to Chinese classrooms were struck. by two unexpected features. Class size was very large, sometimes numbering as many as fifty students. But classroom management—at least until recently—was never a problem. Students sat attentively in their seats with their hands tucked under their thighs and responded in unison to the instructor's questions. More recently, class size remains large, but the docile behavior of students has given way to the unruly deportment of spoiled "emperors and empresses" –single children who were overindulged by their parents from birth.

The curriculum at universities and colleges, also set by the national government, allows for more local flexibility. Because students take courses only in their major departments, a college education in China is highly specialized, and the idea of a liberal arts education, or even of imposing requirements designed to expose the student to a wider range of subject matter, is absent. Mastery of an accepted body of knowledge, not the development of critical intellectual skills, is the goal of most of China's university educators.

Many positive changes have been made in Chinese education since the reform period began. During the Maoist years, primary and secondary instruction was heavily larded with political lessons: ideological maxims figured prominently in language texts; word problems in mathematics required students to quantify and calculate the landlord's exploitation of his peasants, say. Periods of physical labor were integrated with periods of study at all levels, with a view to ensuring that intellectual lessons were not divorced from the realities of the workplace.

With the education reforms came a depoliticization of instructional materials and the end of almost all the work-study programs. Reformers believed that the earlier efforts to universalize primary education and expand the number of middle schools, notably in the countryside, had gone too rapidly and that the quality of instruction had deteriorated. They consolidated some schools, closed others, dismissed inadequately prepared teachers, and expanded and professionalized teacher-training programs. They also increased the number of vocational secondary schools. At the outset of the reform period, only one in twelve high schools offered a vocational curriculum, while the other eleven, with their equivalent of a college preparatory curriculum, were doing a disservice to their students, only a handful of whom could be accommodated in universities. Building new vocational high schools and introducing a vocational curriculum in existing high schools have expanded options for students, and specialized vocational schools now constitute some 40 percent of the total.

Post-secondary education was the level hardest hit by the Cultural Revolution, during which schools at all levels were closed down. University enrollment peaked at close to a million students in 1960, but ten years later, only forty-eight thousand students were enrolled, so expanding university education was a first priority in the reform period. In 1977 there were 625,000 spaces in colleges and universities for a college-age population of close to seventy million. In the five decades since, spaces in colleges and universities have increased to a total capacity of close to 47 million students today. Despite this, only one in five college-age young people is enrolled in school.

As colleges and universities reopened in the later stages of the Cultural Revolution, admission was based almost exclusively on a kind of affirmative action program for the politically correct. Class background and political attitude alone counted in making admissions decisions. Schools became populated by students who, in the words of one college instructor, "would have been happier somewhere else." One of the very first acts of the reform period was to re-institute the national college entrance examination (gaokao 高考) as of 1977 and to open it to a broad age range. As currently administered, the entrance examination is offered once each year, in the July following a student's high school graduation. Those who fail can take it again, but not after they reach the age of twenty-two. A record number of 34.2 million students sat for the examination in 2024. The Ministry of Education issued new guidelines for the college admissions process in 2025 that require enhanced security measures for the gaokao. The guidelines are a part of the effort to refine college enrollment policies to align with national priorities. Colleges and universities are encouraged to adjust admissions criteria based on regional and industrial needs, while enduring expanded access for students from rural and underprivileged backgrounds.

Because of Mao's mistrust of intellectuals, worker-peasant-soldier instructors were introduced into college classrooms during the 1970s. Their experience and background were considered fitting for monitors of the academic faculty, to ensure that the faculty presented ideologically correct material and to supplement excessively abstract lessons with real-world information. (Recall the problem of quantifying and calculating the landlord's exploitation of his peasants.) When political priorities changed, though it proved easy to change the composition of the student body, it was very difficult to change the faculty. Like all government employees, faculty members, including the political monitors, were virtually impossible to fire. Even today, one encounters departments in Chinese universities in which faculty members outnumber the students and in which a handful of qualified instructors carry the full course load while their less competent colleagues have no teaching responsibilities. Paying these nonfunctioning faculty members drains the already straitened university budgets.

During the Cultural Revolution, China was almost completely cut off from contact with the outside world. This had a deleterious effect on the academic community, whose members not only could not do research in China but were allowed virtually no communication with their colleagues abroad. Libraries received neither books nor journals from abroad. Scientists lost touch with the work that was being done in laboratories outside China.

The academic community immediately took advantage of the open policy that accompanied the reforms. Scholars were encouraged to travel abroad, and Chinese students enrolled in American graduate and professional schools, even a few as undergraduates. Asked during his 1979 visit to the United States whether he was worried about a brain drain, Deng was nonchalant. He would send twice as many students and scholars to the United States as were needed in China, he said. Then, when only half of them came home, China would still be adequately served.

These educational exchanges largely dried up in the wake of the Tiananmen massacre but have slowly returned to their earlier level. To date more than 8 million Chinese have studied abroad;

about half of them have been in the United States, where currently, at 278,000, they currently constitute the second largest national group (after students from India) among the international students at colleges and universities. There is a reverse flow as well. Last year, more than 256,000 foreign students were enrolled in programs at Chinese colleges and universities.

American universities reciprocated Chinese interest in educational exchange. "Sister school" relationships were established with Chinese colleges and universities, and professors and teachers were invited to China for short- and long-term teaching assignments. To take my own university as an example, Yale's ties with China date from 1854, when a student from China, Yung Wing, took an undergraduate degree at Yale College. Fifty years later, young Yale graduates formed a missionary organization that they called Yale-in-China, which eventually founded a high school, a medical school, and a teacher's college in Hunan and Hubei provinces. Severed when U.S.-China relations soured with the outbreak of the Korean War in 1950, Yale moved its China-based programs to the Chinese University of Hong Kong. Ties between the university and its schools in China were resumed immediately after the normalization of U.S.-China relations in 1979. Subsequently, the university has developed more than eighty collaborative programs with Chinese institutions in law, medicine, nursing, forestry, and other academic fields. The largest number of foreign students and scholars on the Yale campus has for many years been Chinese. Yale's former president, Richard Levin, made the university's ties with China a personal project. He traveled more than a half dozen times to China (so frequently, in fact, that an April Fool's issue of the *Yale Daily News* carried on its front page a photograph of the president in a Beijing porcelain shop under the headline "Yale Buys China"). China's then-president, Hu Jintao, made Yale his only university stop during his visit to the United States in 2006.

The most pressing issue facing China's schools is inadequate funding. With expenditures on education totaling only four percent of gross national product, China is close to the world average of 3.8 percent, yet many developing countries outspend it on their schools.

The issue of inadequate funding for school construction attracted worldwide attention at the time of the magnitude 7.9 earthquake in Wenchuan County (汶川县), Sichuan, in 2008. Some seven thousand classrooms were damaged or destroyed by the earthquake, killing between 5,300 students (the official figure) and 10,000 students (the more widely publicized estimate). Among the starkest images of the earthquake depicted schools reduced to piles of rubble surrounded by buildings that seemed to have been scarcely touched by the quake. Angry parents and residents accused officials of having scrimped on construction materials for the schools, an accusation that echoed those surrounding the collapse, six years earlier, of a school in Fangzhen (方针), north of Beijing, that killed twenty-one students and teachers. Ma Zongjin, who chaired the official committee of inquiry into the earthquake damage, acknowledged that shoddy construction was to blame for the damage to the schools and the loss of life. Six months later, however, Wei Hong, Sichuan's vice governor, perhaps mindful of the lawsuits being brought by parents seeking damages from the state, claimed that it was the magnitude of the earthquake, not shoddy construction, that was to blame.

More money for primary and secondary education would help attract and keep teachers. Because teachers' pay and prestige remain relatively low, it is hard to recruit anyone, much less highly qualified people, into the profession. University applicants who find themselves in a teacher's college will do almost anything to avoid the fate of a classroom career; entire graduating classes of teachers colleges have been known to fail to report to their assigned schools, going into the infinitely more promising private sector instead. To counteract this, some teacher's colleges have withheld the diplomas of their graduating seniors, handing them over only after they actually show up and begin their first teaching assignments.

Universities, too, suffer from a shortage of funds. The austerity of university budgets restricts the scholarship funds available for those to whom the newly instituted tuitions are an insurmountable obstacle. But the most important shortfall is in adequate space. Although they have expanded rapidly, China's colleges and universities can still turn out only twelve million graduates each year, meaning that only 19 percent of the Chinese population has a college education (as compared with 35 percent in the United States), an inadequate number to support the development to which China aspires.

Like their primary and secondary school colleagues, university teachers suffer from low pay and low status. Efforts have been made to ameliorate this situation, especially to encourage foreign-educated intellectuals to return to classrooms and laboratories in China, but many faculty members must take second jobs to make ends meet.

This has an immediate adverse effect on the quality of research and instruction. Similarly, the time and energy that faculty and administrators spend devising new moneymaking schemes to augment inadequate budgets are time and energy not spent on educational tasks. A second issue facing China's educators is the high dropout rate from rural schools and the consequent high rate of illiteracy, especially among young women. Current figures show that 46 million people, or four percent of the Chinese population, are illiterate or semiliterate; of these, the vast majority are rural residents, and a startlingly high proportion were females under the age of forty. This is precisely because rural families withdraw children, particularly girls, from school before they have completed their education.

China's government has a mandatory nine-year education policy that allows Chinese children to attend school at no cost from grades one through nine. Nonetheless, informal *ad hoc* charges can amount to as much as $500 per year, a sizable amount when the average household income is less than $5,500 per year. After completing primary school, impoverished rural children are at a much higher risk of dropping out than their urban counterparts. The income level for rural regions is three times less than that of urban regions, yet residents from both areas are expected to afford books and other educational fees. High school becomes the financial responsibility of families, but upon reaching this level, 60% of rural students have already dropped out because of the costs.

Many parents see little to be gained by paying for a high school education for a child since what the child is likely to learn seems largely irrelevant to his or her earning capabilities. This is especially so for girls, whose only chance to make money for the family is during their teen years. Only as the economy diversifies and becomes more complex will this shortsighted attitude give way to an appreciation of a high school education as an appropriate investment. Were the government to provide truly free schools in rural communities, it would help speed this change of attitude.

Statistics on university degree holders are even more stark: while some 40 percent of urban dwellers are college graduates, only five percent of rural residents hold degrees. Government-supported tuition-free rural schools will encourage families to keep their children in school, and as the rural economy develops and higher skills are required, perceptions about the value of a high school education may change. But eliminating the financial gain from putting teenagers into the workforce instead of the classroom is difficult to do.

Table 19: Gender Differences in Educational Attainment in China

	% of population age six and over	Percent Male	Percent Female
No schooling	8	28	72
Primary School	32	48	52
Middle School	40	54	46
High School	13	5	43
College or University	7	56	44

(Source: China Statistical Yearbook 2024)

Access to special education is limited for those with physical or learning disabilities. Deng Xiaoping's son, Deng Pufang, who was permanently crippled when he was pushed by Red Guards from a third-story window on the Beijing University campus during the Cultural Revolution, has devoted his life to supporting the cause of the roughly 83 million disabled people in China. Thanks to the efforts of the China Disabled Persons' Federation, of which he served as Honorary President, about three-quarters of disabled children are enrolled in public schools. In September 2023, at the age of 79, Deng Pufang retired from his work with the Federation.

As of 2023, there were 2,345 special education schools across the country. The total number of students receiving special education of all types was about 912,000. But at the higher levels of schooling, the physically disabled are generally excluded. Because it is presumed that the limited number of spaces at the college level should be reserved for the able and fit, applicants are screened by physical as well as academic examinations. An official in the Disabled People's Association in Hunan is quoted as saying, "The law stipulates that schools shouldn't reject these students because they are disabled, but the schools all emphasize 'moral, intellectual and physical development,' and they know these students are not physically perfect. So, they turn them down." University admissions officers defend the practice by pointing to the fact that disabled graduates will experience even greater difficulty in finding employment.

A third issue that has arisen in recent years is how to provide an education to children of migrant workers in China's cities. While many migrant workers choose to leave their children behind in the care of grandparents, some move to the city as a family. As we have seen, the residency status of migrant workers remains purposely vague. As a result, public schools are willing to accommodate migrant children, but only with the payment of a "nonresident" fee, which, in Beijing, ranges from $30 for primary school to $300 for secondary school. Private schools that cater specifically to migrant children and charge much less than public schools have cropped up in the cities. Nominally concerned about the quality of education in these private schools for migrants, but actually interested in increasing public school revenues, municipal officials in Beijing and Shanghai have mounted campaigns to close the private schools. A State Council law in 2003 mandating that cities provide public school education for all children within their jurisdictions only exacerbated the problem, since it came as an unfunded mandate for municipal governments.

Another concern for Chinese educators is the spread of excessive competition and examination-based education. The root of the problem is the continuing shortage of college spaces in comparison with the size of the applicant pool, which makes college entrance extraordinarily competitive, a tone that has spread downward through the whole system. It was the national college entrance examination that gave rise to a system of entrance examinations at every level. The result of this hierarchy of examinations is to make students intensely competitive in the classroom. Moreover, not unlike our own experience with standardized testing under the No Child Left Behind Act, instruction is often limited to the material students will need to master to clear their next academic hurdle.

The pressure on students is intense. Fourteen-hour high school days are not unknown, and this led Education Ministry officials to put forward a set of regulations to reduce pressure on students. Beginning in the 2000-01 school year, there are no mandatory classes during evenings, weekends, and vacations, no written homework for first and second graders, no tests for primary school students except in Chinese language and mathematics, and no entrance examinations at the middle school level.

All this competition and pressure adversely affect students' motivation once they are in college. As in other highly competitive systems—Japan's is an example—students know that a reasonably secure future is likely regardless of their performance in the college classroom. But many students in China find the quality of their college experience far below the high expectations generated by the competition that they have successfully survived. Classes are large, the curriculum is unimaginative, the level of instruction is often disappointingly low, and housing and food are deplorable.

In interviews with students conducted at the time of the ninetieth anniversary of the May Fourth Movement in 2009, *New York Times* writers found students lacking the grievances that drove the previous generation to protest. Today's students are largely apolitical, seeking party membership, if they do, for its career advantages, not for ideological reasons. If they are skeptical about the party's ability to reform, they are equally skeptical of Western-style democracy as a panacea for China's problems going forward. The dissatisfactions generated by campus life give rise to academic apathy and periodic outbursts of student protest. As noted earlier, it was very concrete complaints about university life, not abstract demands for democracy, that brought students onto the streets of China's cities in the protest demonstrations that began in the mid-1980s and culminated at Tiananmen Square in June 1989.

Finally, although Deng seemed sanguine in 1979 about the possibility of so many Chinese young people staying abroad after finishing their education, the problem is in fact more serious than he was willing to allow. Since 1979, 59 million Chinese students and scholars have gone abroad for further education, and of that number, only 60% have returned to China. In the mid-1980s, incentives were put in place to encourage them to do so, but these were only modestly successful, and the problem was aggravated by the Tiananmen massacre, after which many Chinese studying abroad took public stands against their government that made it dangerous for them to return. Foreign governments relaxed immigration regulations to take account of their situation. Although many Chinese intellectuals living abroad have gone home in recent years, they are more attracted to business opportunities than to academic careers. The Chinese government puts a good face on the situation, noting that some four thousand enterprises have been founded by returned scholars and that four out of five university presidents and Chinese Academy of Sciences members are among those educated abroad who have returned to their country. They also point out that the rate of return is increasing each year.

If your area of interest lies well outside the realm of the political, it is as good a time to be an intellectual in China as it has been since the People's Republic was founded seventy-five years ago, for despite occasional conservative rumblings that are largely ignored, the country is enjoying greater intellectual freedom than at any time since the May Fourth Movement of 1919. But unfortunately, just when the restrictions on intellectual life have been somewhat relaxed, many intellectuals find themselves wishing they were entrepreneurs.

To say that intellectual freedom has increased is not to say that the Chinese are free from all restrictions with respect to what they write, say, or teach; public expression of unorthodox political ideas is still unacceptable. Yet dissident intellectuals concern the regime less than dissident workers or dissident unemployed, and the most serious repressions have been exerted against lawyers like Chen Guangcheng and Gao Zhisheng and workers like Wei Jingsheng and Han Dongfang, whom the government believes can organize clients and fellow workers in opposition to party and government authority. This assessment of relative threats to the regime seems well-founded. Chinese intellectuals have inherited a disdain for, and thus an inability to collaborate with, the country's working population, and although their protests in 1989 were joined by workers and even government officials in eighty cities, the students and intellectuals who initiated the movement were reluctant to ally themselves with workers and actively resisted taking their movement to the rural workforce.

Dissident intellectuals everywhere have a morbid tendency to fragment their efforts, and this is true in China. Those who occupied Tiananmen Square impressed observers with their ability to organize themselves; to distribute food, information, and medical care; and to use the telephone, the fax, and the foreign and domestic press to spread word of their protests to other cities in China and to the outside world. After the massacre, numerous dissidents were spirited out of harm's way along a spontaneous and highly effective underground railroad that sprang into being. On the other hand, despite the example of the very short-lived China Democratic Party (CDP), neither the dissidents who escaped China nor those who remained could organize an effective opposition to the Chinese Communist Party.

A significant amount of money was collected in America and Europe in support of the work of the Tiananmen exiles, conferences were held, and publications were distributed. Nonetheless, individuals and groups found their differences greater than their common ground, as was manifested at a colloquium at Harvard University marking the tenth anniversary of the massacre, when public presentations by prominent dissidents gave way to private bickering. If Chinese intellectuals could outgrow their fractious tendencies and their disdain for the working classes, they might be able to join hands with the huge numbers of other people in China who have reason for discontent. Were this to occur, the regime would be obliged to take them very seriously indeed.

Chapter 15: Health Care

Medical practice has a very long history in China. According to tradition, *Huangdi (*黄帝, the "Yellow Emperor"), one of the legendary founders of Chinese civilization, wrote the canon of internal medicine called the *Huangdi Neijing* (黄帝内经, *Yellow Emperor's Inner Classic)* in the third millennium B.C.E. Most of the Chinese medical literature is founded on this book, and it is still regarded as a great authority. It described a comprehensive healing system rooted in the belief that health is achieved through the balance and free flow of energy, or *qi (*汽*),* within the body. Figuratively, *qi* is the life force that permeates and animates everything in the world. Achieving and maintaining this balance encompasses practices such as acupuncture and moxibustion.[6], cupping [7], herbal and non-herbal medicine dietary modifications, and physical exercises like *taiji* (太极) and *qigong* (汽功). Traditional Chinese medicine is still widely practiced in China, particularly in rural areas. It is also practiced extensively elsewhere in the world.

Although it is a fascinating subject, traditional Chinese medicine is not our primary concern here. Rather, we will focus on how Western medicine was introduced into China and how its practice came to dominate health care in the country beginning in the mid-nineteenth century. Four American institutions—three universities and one foundation—played a dominant role in the

---

[6] Moxibustion is a traditional Chinese medicine therapy that involves the burning of dried mugwort *(moxa)* on or near the skin's surface at specific acupuncture points. The practice is believed to stimulate circulation, promote healing, and address various health conditions.

[7] Cupping involves creating suction on the skin using a glass, ceramic, plastic or bamboo cup. The action is thought to improve the flow of energy in the body and facilitate healing.

process: Yale, Harvard, Johns Hopkins, and the Rockefeller Foundation.

Yale was the first of these institutions. Yale's relationship with China began in 1835 with the work of a remarkable man, Peter Parker (B.A. 1831, M.D. 1834). A Yale graduate, doctor, and ordained minister, Parker was responsible for a series of firsts in China. After becoming the first Protestant medical missionary to travel to China in 1835, Parker opened China's Western-style hospital, the Ophthalmic Hospital in Guangzhou, and became the first doctor to introduce modern anesthesia to China. Yale's connection to China grew rapidly over the 19th and 20th centuries. In 1854, Yung Wing graduated from Yale College and became the first person from China to earn a degree from an American college or university. In 1901, the Yale-China Association—originally known as the Yale Foreign Missionary Society—was founded by a group of Yale graduates and faculty members committed to establishing a "new kind of Christian mission" that would share Western liberal arts education and Western medicine with China. The group was nondenominational from the beginning and by the 1920s had founded one of the first Western medicine clinics in China, which became *Xiang-Ya Yiyuan* (or 湘雅医院 Hunan-Yale Hospital) as well as the *Xiangya Hushi Xueyuan* (湘雅护士学院 School of Nursing), the *Xiangya Yixue Daxue* (湘雅医学大学 Medical College), and *Yali* Zhongxue (雅莉中学 Yale High School)—all of which still exist today in the city of Changsha in Hunan Province and all of which maintain ties to Yale.

Harvard was the next to contribute to western medical education in China, establishing the short-lived Harvard Medical School of China (*Zhonggo de Huafuo Yixueyuan* 中国的哈佛医学院)

1911-1916. Johns Hopkins University's relationship with China dates from 1915, when William Welch, the first dean of the Johns Hopkins University School of Medicine, travelled there with the China Medical Board (CMB) to visit hospitals and medical schools.

By far the largest player in the field of introducing Western medicine to China was the Rockefeller Foundation. Mary Brown Bullock, in her book *An American Transplant*, describes the foundation's work in China.[8] "From its earliest years, the Rockefeller Foundation took particular interest in China, a legacy of the Rockefeller family's special interest. The CMB was created in 1914 as one of the first operating divisions of the Rockefeller Foundation. Provided with a $12 million endowment, the Board's aim was to modernize medical education and to improve the practice of medicine in China."

China was a longstanding interest of both John D. Rockefeller, Sr., and his son. For decades, they and their fellow Baptists had supported missionary work in Asia. In 1908, five years before the foundation was created, the Rockefellers funded a commission headed by Edward D. Burton, a University of Chicago professor of theology. He and other educators traveled to China to explore the potential for philanthropic work there. In its final report, the Burton Commission argued that a Western-sponsored educational program in science and medicine for Chinese students could succeed, despite a difficult political climate. The Foundation later dispatched two additional survey groups, the China Medical Commissions of 1914 and 1915, to gather more information about

---

[8] Mary Brown Bullock, *An American Transplant*: The Rockefeller Foundation and Peking Union Medical College (Berkeley, California: University of California Press, 1980)

how such an educational program could operate. Following the model established by Abraham Flexner's survey of U.S. medical education, the 1914 Commission set out to appraise medical education in both missionary and Chinese schools. It found appallingly low standards throughout the country. The report concluded that "the country is so vast, and the resources available for dealing with the problem are so limited yet that the need for outside assistance is still very great." The CMB was formed to meet these challenges, and Wallace Buttrick was named its first director.

The Foundation's approach to Chinese medical education would inevitably follow the general patterns for reforming U.S. medical education advocated in the 1910 Flexner Report and most fully embodied in the Johns Hopkins University School of Medicine. Medical education in China would be scientifically rigorous and adhere to Western standards. And, in a decision with long-term consequences, instruction would occur in English. Consequently, the school could reach only a small, elite portion of the population. In a country of 400 million people, then served by fewer than 500 well-trained doctors, such an approach was subject to criticism. Nevertheless, the CMB set out to build a medical school in China that it hoped to make the equal of Johns Hopkins.

The Rockefeller Foundation entered China with an ambitious goal: to build modern medical schools in both Beijing and Shanghai. By purchasing the Union Medical College from the London Missionary Society in 1915, the Foundation took its first steps toward that goal. Over the next six years, the Foundation assembled a faculty of 50 professors and upgraded and enlarged the facilities of what was soon called the Peking Union Medical College (PUMC). It eventually scrapped its plans for Shanghai. PUMC's initial contributions toward the improvement of medicine in China, though consequential, were inevitably limited in scale. Its graduating classes were small, in part because its standards remained high and its curriculum at the outset was exclusively in English. Between 1924 and 1943, PUMC produced only 313 doctors, more than half of whom would continue their studies abroad through CMB fellowships. Upon their return, many of these doctors ultimately became leaders in medical administration, teaching, and scientific research both before and after the Chinese revolution.

PUMC also transformed the nursing profession in China. When PUMC opened, there were fewer than 300 trained nurses in the country, many of them affiliated with various missionary organizations and most of them male. Because the Chinese had never considered nursing to be an appropriate profession for women, the task of PUMC was both to train qualified women nurses and to elevate the status of the profession.

Between 1915 and 1951, the Rockefeller Foundation and the CMB spent well over $50 million on medical initiatives in China, nearly $45 million of it to establish PUMC. Other missionary hospitals benefited from smaller Foundation contributions. Fellowships helped doctors and nurses to travel abroad for advanced training. Medical texts were translated, and medical libraries were built. PUMC is still regarded in China as an elite medical research institution. Its buildings, dedicated in 1921, still stand in the center of Beijing. The college was known for its emphasis on basic sciences, its stringent resident program, its strict academic standards for students with the elimination of unqualified ones, the full-time employment of both preclinical and clinical staff, and its facilities for research work for all senior teaching staff. These were considered Peking Union traditions and were adhered to by all medical organizations headed by PUMC men.

In 1949, apart from a few medical faculties in some multidisciplinary universities, there were altogether 22 medical colleges in the mainland of China, either run by the state or provincial government or as private enterprises, including those run by missionaries or other foreign organizations. The length of their curricula varied from four to eight years. There was no national program for medical education. The colleges that had been run by foreigners followed the educational system of their own countries, while those run by Chinese, whether national, provincial, or private, gave the type of education which their organizers had themselves received.

After its establishment, the People's Republic severed its contacts with medical institutions in the United States and Europe and replaced them with contacts with medical schools and hospitals in the Soviet Union. There, medical schools are separate from universities and offer four-year curricula of basic science and clinical courses leading to a bachelor's degree. They also offer three-year postgraduate training leading to a candidate's and a doctor of medical science degree. There is, however, little evidence that Chinese medical education was strongly influenced by the Soviet system during the period of Sino-Soviet cooperation.

Health care improved significantly in the first years of the People's Republic. Whereas the average lifespan of the population was 35 years in 1950, it had extended to 55 years by the time of Mao's death in 1976. (It is 78 years today, the same as that in the United States.) China currently has 129 medical schools; in addition, degrees in health and medicine are offered by nine universities. But access to health care was and remains uneven across the country, being high in the cities, much lower in the countryside.

Just prior to the Cultural Revolution, Mao issued a "Directive on Public Health." In it, he had this to say about rural healthcare:

> The Ministry of Public Health only works for fifteen percent of the total population of the country, and that fifteen percent is mainly composed of gentlemen, while the broad masses of the peasants do not get any medical treatment. First, they don't have any doctors; second, they don't have any medicine...
>
> Medical education should be reformed. There's no need to read so many books...[T]here is no need to accept only higher middle school graduates or lower middle school graduates into medical school. It will be enough to give three years to graduates from higher primary schools. They would then study and raise their standards mainly through practice. If this kind of doctor is sent down to the countryside, even if they haven't much talent, they would be better than quacks and witch doctors, and the villages would be better able to afford to keep them...
>
> The methods of medical examination and treatment used by hospitals nowadays are not at all appropriate for the countryside, and the way doctors are trained is only for the benefit of the cities. And yet in China, over 500 million of our population are peasants...We should leave behind in the city only a few of the less able doctors who graduated one or two years ago, and the others should all go into the countryside...
>
> In medical and health work, put the emphasis on the countryside.[9]

Hence was born what became known as the "barefoot doctor" initiative. Although there is no evidence of Soviet influence, the movement was reminiscent of Russian *feldschers* who, during the

---

[9] Mao Zedong, "Directive on Public Health," 26 June 1965 in *Selected Works of Mao Zedong* vol. 9.

nineteenth century, played a major role in rural medical systems. While the law required *feldschers* to practice under a physician's direct supervision, many were nevertheless assigned to run remote clinics on their own because of the dearth of physicians in the countryside.

The movement lasted for two decades, ending in 1985. According to one Chinese observer, "although they lacked high-quality medical skills, barefoot doctors played a significant role in informing the people of public health care service, developing public health care campaigns, planning to prevent epidemics, and treating slight injuries and diseases." In fact, barefoot doctors' achievements resulted in significant changes in the level of public health care service. The infant death rate decreased from 200 deaths per 1,000 live births to 34 deaths per 1,000 live births in 1982, while life expectancy increased from 35 to 60 years.

Seven years later, the barefoot doctors' work was replaced by the New Rural Cooperative Medical Scheme, a community-based rural health insurance system. The NRCMS is a voluntary insurance scheme designed mainly for rural residents. The scheme is financed with the cooperation of individuals and local and central governments. By the end of 2014, 99 percent of rural residents (approximately 736 million people) had joined the NRCMS. It plays a very important role in Chinese rural residents' health care, and it has improved health service quality and drug-use safety in rural China.

Graph #7:

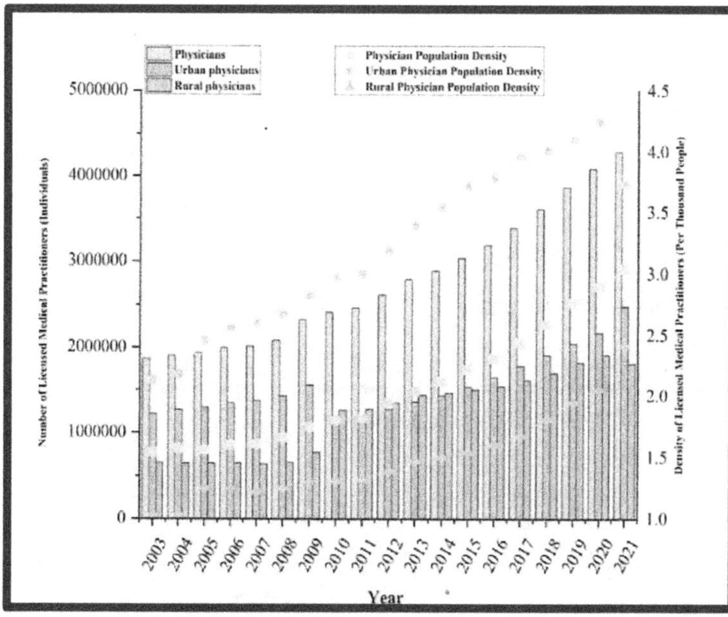

Distribution of Physicians between Urban and Rural China

Source: https://www.statista.com /statistics/

Traditional Chinese medicine remains integral to rural healthcare in China, with many relying on herbal remedies, acupuncture, and dietary therapies. Medicinal plants, often sourced locally, reflect deep-rooted knowledge passed down through generations. Traditional approaches are typically used for improving the immune system and prevention of chronic diseases, while Western medicine is used for acute diseases. While both are practiced concurrently, traditional practitioners tend to be more widely utilized in rural areas.

Today, China has nearly five million physicians and close to six million nurses. That amounts to nearly three physicians and four nurses per 1,000 people. (The comparable figures in the United States are 3.6 physicians and nine nurses.) It is still the case, however, that health care is significantly more available in China's cities than in its rural areas.

In December 2019, a massive epidemic hit China's healthcare network. It was first manifested as a cluster of mysterious pneumonia cases, mostly related to the Huanan (华南) Seafood Market in Wuhan. A new coronavirus (Severe Acute Respiratory Syndrome [SARS]-Coronavirus 2) was identified as the cause of the pneumonia. A month later, it had spread to all of China's provinces.

The government invoked a "zero-COVID" plan that involved strict lockdowns, isolation (possibly in government facilities where available), and mass testing in areas where cases were reported. Nonetheless, infection rates increased in 2022, and in April , China reported the highest single-day total of new cases since the height of the 2020 outbreak. Following nationwide protests toward the end of that year, the Chinese government relaxed many of its restrictions, effectively ending the zero-COVID policy and leading to a massive surge in cases. It was estimated that 23 Chinese cities, home to an estimated 193 million people, had implemented either full or partial lockdowns. Crowds took to the streets in several cities, crashing through lockdown barriers, protesting the restriction policies.

In December, it was estimated that more than 5,000 people were dying each day from the disease. There was a shortage of medicines and a staffing crisis in hospitals in several major cities. Ultimately, lockdowns were highly effective in reducing the spread of COVID-19, and there was a wide public consensus that the benefits outweighed the costs. In February 2023, health authorities said the country's COVID-19 epidemic had "basically" ended. China's top leaders declared a "decisive victory" over COVID, claiming the world's lowest fatality rate, although experts questioned the validity of that data.

The fact that the number of COVID cases in China and the United States were roughly equal and that the deaths from the disease were also comparable attests to the very substantial progress China has made in health care delivery in the seventy-five years since the founding of the PRC.

Chapter 16: The Flow of Information

One can imagine what Li Shulei (李书磊) dreams about when he drifts off to sleep at night. Head of the Central Committees Central Publicity [Propaganda] Department (*Zhonggong Zhongyang Xuanchuan Bu* 中共中央宣传部), Li dreams that all of China's 1.42 billion people receive their news from a single print source, *People's Daily (Renmin Ribao- 人民日报),* which is written and edited by his department. There is a single radio news broadcast carried on all the country's 3,000 radio stations. It consists of a verbatim reading of the day's issue of *People's Daily.* Similarly, there is a single television news broadcast available on China's more than 3,300 local, regional, and national television channels, and that broadcast, too, is devoted exclusively to reading, from front to back, the current issue of the paper, interspersed with carefully selected video footage. Finally, Li dreams that there is also just a single website available online; it is www.people.com.cn, the *People's Daily* website, and like the other news media, it is limited to an online version of the day's paper. Alas, Mr. Li awakens from his dream with a start and recalls that controlling information in China today is by no means as simple as he had dreamed.

Still, Mr. Li's dream is not very far from the reality of the early years of the Chinese Communist Party, when there was one newspaper—*Red China* (**红**華 *Honghua),* founded in 1931 and renamed *Liberation Daily (*解放日报 *Jiefang Ribao)* in 1941—one radio station—Yan'an's New China *(新华 Xinhua*) Radio, which went on the air in 1940— and, of course, neither television nor Internet to distract the attention of the public.

After the founding of the People's Republic, the Red China News Agency became the New China News Agency (新华通讯社

Xinhua Tongxun She), *Liberation Daily* became *People's Daily,* a network of "people's radio stations" monopolized radio broadcasting, and, as of 1958, first Beijing TV and then Shanghai TV began transmitting.

From their founding, the nascent media served as the embodiment of Mao's concept of the mass line, the idea that party policy should be based on information drawn "from the masses" and then that policy, synthesizing mass opinion with Communist ideology, should be explained "to the masses." It was the job of the press and the radio to gather information from the field, report it to party leaders, and then publicize party policy to their readers and listeners. As a result, so-called internal publications produced by the New China News Agency—publications distributed to a select audience of party and government officials—were as important as the publications they produced for the public. This continues to be a significant part of the work of the agency.

By the beginning of the Cultural Revolution in 1966, there were some forty newspapers, radio reached well over half of the population, and there were five television channels. Virtually all of them ceased operations as the movement spread, being replaced by just a handful of party-controlled media. But then there sprang up across the country a myriad of tabloid publications produced by Red Guards and "revolutionary rebels." Because of the anarchic conditions at the time, these tabloids were far more freewheeling than the strait-laced party press and contained details (whether accurate or fabricated) of the violent conflict at the local level, as well as excerpts from the previously unpublished *obiter dicta* of Chairman Mao that would not otherwise have seen the light of day.

The media had at least partially recovered from the chaos of the Cultural Revolution years by the time Deng took power in 1976. The following table will convey a sense of the mushrooming of the media during the thirty years after Deng launched his "open" policy.

Table 20: Chinese Media, 1978 AND 2024

	1978	**2024**
Print media:		
Newspapers	69	2,200
Newspaper readership	42.8 million	250 million
Magazines	930	9,468
Magazine readership	62 million	166 million
Books published	15,000	250,000
Broadcast media:		
Radio stations	460	3,000
Radio audience (percent of population)	85.0 (*est.*)	95.4
Television channels	38	3,300
Television audience (percent of population)	10.4	96.6

Source: China Journalism Yearbook 2024

Responsibility for oversight of the media lies in the hands of two administrative agencies directly under the State Council: the State General Administration of Press and Publications and the State General Administration of Radio, Film, and Television.

Oversight of the Internet is divided among the Ministry of Industry and Information Technology (which handles the physical communications infrastructure), the Internet Affairs Bureau of the State Council Information Office (which oversees Internet content and access), and the Ministry of Public Security's Cyber Police Force (for enforcement of content standards). All these government agencies operate under the watchful eye of Li Shulei.

Control of the media is exercised through a system of licenses and permits. Nothing can be published without the publisher having obtained a license, and access to the airwaves is similarly controlled through the issuing of permits. Although control over content in the media was once imposed in advance of publication or broadcasting, the proliferation of media outlets has necessitated shifting to a system of monitoring *ex post facto* what has been published and broadcast. Indeed, the party-state by no means has the capacity to review all the information disseminated to the public. Publicity Department directives are usually issued weekly and include those issues and events that are not to be covered, as well as instructions on how to treat those issues and events that will receive coverage. The censors see vagueness as a virtue in that it has the effect of promoting self-censorship among journalists.

Foreign news coverage is the exclusive purview of the New China News Agency. The agency employs more than ten thousand people, has branches in 23 provinces, Hong Kong, and Macao, offices in 50 Chinese cities, and branches in 105 countries. Despite this large capacity, as a report from Reporters Without Borders described the situation: "As far as foreign news goes, the agency is never at the origin of information. It has neither the means nor the desire to do so." Rather, it gathers news from other sources such as *Agence France-Presse* and the Associated Press and confines itself to editing and interpreting the news for consumption by Chinese readers and listeners. To the limited extent that Chinese media cover events abroad, they rely exclusively on the New China News Agency for their material. The agency also translates extensive material from the foreign press and distributes it as *Reference News (参考消息 Cankao Xiaoxi)* to a list of subscribers now numbering 3.5 million. Foreign news is also available to those possessing satellite dishes, who can pull in signals from Hong Kong and Taiwan. The party-state first moved to ban satellite dishes in 1993, then to licensing them in 1994, and finally to specifying permissible programs and viewing hours in 1995. Resisting the ban was the People's Liberation Army, the main producer of satellite dishes, which reaps a profit of 50 percent on each dish sold.

Restrictions on foreign reporters based in China have been relaxed in recent years. In the run-up to the Beijing Olympics, the requirements that foreign journalists receive permission in advance for travel away from their offices and to conduct interviews were lifted. The relaxed rules were made permanent in October 2008. One avenue of control over their access to information has not been relaxed. Chinese staff members of foreign media bureaus continue to be monitored and harassed.

Today's media operate somewhat precariously at the intersection of two opposing lines of force: the party imperative that they buttress the authority of the party and the party imperative that they operate independent of party-state subsidies. Through the early years of the PRC, the media were supported with generous contributions from central and local government budgets, together with the revenue from mandatory subscriptions. After 1976, and especially after Deng's push in favor of market forces in 1992, the subsidies and the mandatory subscriptions ended, and the commercialization of the media has proceeded apace.

To the extent that newspapers, magazines, and radio and television broadcasts serve as the mouthpiece of the party-state, bored readers, listeners, and watchers stay away in droves. To the extent that the media respond to the interests of their audiences, they risk becoming imperfect mouthpieces. Investigative reporting that uncovers official malfeasance and popular discontents attracts readers and listeners, but it risks undermining the legitimacy of the party. A case in point: as we have seen, when the *Southern Metropolitan Daily (南方都市报 Nanfang Dushi Bao)* reported on the beating death of Sun Zhigang while in police custody, it resulted in immediate and sweeping reform of the *shourong* custody system. It also resulted in the· subsequent arrest of the paper's managing editor by local authorities and his imprisonment on corruption charges. When the government moved in and replaced the paper's leading staff members, investigative coverage all but ceased, and circulation declined abruptly.

There is a third set of parties involved in media commercialization: advertisers and sponsors. Advertising revenue has grown apace since the media first started selling space, reaching some $208 billion in 2024. And, as is sometimes the case in our own media, the fine line between news coverage and infomercials is often blurred. In the most flagrant cases, advertisers pay journalists for favorable coverage, a practice that is occasionally emulated by local officials hoping to avoid having their foibles made public. Some journalists are far from passive participants in this process.

There is a clear-cut hierarchy among the media in China. At the top of the heap sit *People's Daily* and the New China News Agency, both of which enjoy the status of government ministries and whose directors are members of the Central Committee. Ranking just below is the English-language newspaper, *China Daily,* published by the Central Committee's Publicity

Department. Next comes China Central Television CCTV *(Zhonguo zhongshi dianshi tai* 中国重视电视台), which is attached to the State Administration of Radio, Film, and Television (SARFT). Also included in this category of "official" media are more specialized publications such as *Economic Daily (Jingji Ribao* 经济日报*),* operated by the State Council, and *People's Liberation Army Daily (Jiefangjun Bao* 解放军报*).* Control of the content of these front-ranking official publications is tight. To make ends meet, some of these premier institutions have formed media conglomerates that engage in a variety of undertakings. This is necessitated by the fact that most of them, not noted for their scintillating content, have lost readers in recent years. Indeed, *People's Daily* lost 50 percent of its circulation between the late 1970s and today.

Next in the hierarchy come a range of publications and broadcasters that, while affiliated with local branches of the party-state, depend for much of their income on advertising and subscriptions. Included here are provincial and municipal newspapers and television and radio stations. Control of the content in these media is somewhat looser than that of the official media. The hierarchy is maintained, however, in coverage of corruption and malfeasance. Local media cover scandals within their local areas but never neighboring areas or at higher governmental levels. Similarly, provincial media cover stories within their geographical boundaries, but not neighboring provinces, and never at the level of the central government.

A number of the media in this category are actually spin-offs or affiliates of the large central media conglomerates, and the relationship is not always perfectly harmonious. In 2005, more than one hundred journalists at Beijing News (*Xinjing Bao* 新京报) went on what appears to have been a daylong strike to protest the firing of the editor and two of his deputies. Two months later, the publication of *Freezing Point (Bingdian 冰点)*, another spin-off—this one affiliated with *China Youth Daily (Zhongquo Qingnian Bao* 中国青年报)—was suspended when it published an article criticizing the selection of middle school history textbooks that overemphasize China's "humiliations" at the hands of foreigners. Editor Li Datong was fired, and the magazine resumed publication under new management.

The censors' heavy hands are not the only problems facing newspapers in this second tier. They are also experiencing problems akin to those confronting our own newspapers. Circulation is dropping because news is available on television or the Internet, or because readers have a declining interest in news, and advertising revenue is thus more and more difficult to obtain.

The third category in the hierarchy is publications and television channels that, while of necessity affiliated (however tenuously) to the party-state, operate exclusively on a commercial basis. Perhaps most reminiscent of our grocery checkout counter tabloids, these publications are very big on sex and scandal and pay scarcely any attention at all to issues even remotely political. As a result, it is only when they run afoul of the party-state's puritanical views on pornography that they find themselves in contact with the censors. Paid journalism is an important part of the content of these magazines and papers.

There are important exceptions. *Finance and Economics (Caijing 财经)* is a widely read, highly reputable periodical reminiscent of *Fortune* that contains articles by Chinese and international contributors and a list of international advertisers that would make many American magazine publishers green with envy. It speaks frankly about issues in the Chinese economy—its coverage of the scandal over tainted milk is an example—but it also knows when to pull in its horns to ensure it stays in business.

Recently, however, a dispute arose between the magazine's editorial and business staffs and the Stock Exchange Business Council, which owns the periodical, over control of the company. The influential former editor, Hu Shuli (胡舒立), and the majority of her staff resigned in protest, putting the future of the magazine in question. She was replaced as editor by Wang Boming (王波明).

While some contend that China's media are enjoying more discretion over content than at any time since 1949, others see a post-Tiananmen relapse into censorship and oversight, particularly after the accession to office of former President Hu Jintao in 2003. Reporters Without Borders, in its annual ranking of countries based on press freedom in 2024, ranked China worst after North Korea, noting that by its count, nearly 100 journalists were serving jail terms, and 52 people had been convicted for posting political views on the Internet.

Some five hundred million Chinese, nearly 40 percent of the population, get their news from the 7:00 p.m. broadcast on CCTV, and three-fifths of them stay tuned for Focus Report (*Jiaodian Fangtan 焦点访谈), a half-hour investigative news program that has been compared with CBS's*

Sixty Minutes. Focus Report has become what one observer calls "the most influential media voice in China," notable for its strong investigative reporting. In addition to its evening news program, CCTV produces three other news programs each day, seven days a week. Roughly a third of the coverage focuses on political topics, and another third on economic issues, much of the coverage of which is drawn from local stations.

Like the publishing industry, television has become more difficult to control. Television stations, including cable, now number more than 3,500 and are growing rapidly in number. The number of television sets has doubled over the last decade, and there is now more than one television set per household in both the city and the countryside. The government owns all television stations and monitors the content of their broadcasts, but with the proliferation of stations, most of which are locally managed, the diversity of programming has increased significantly. The old, stultifying diet of official news and didactic documentaries has given way to soaps and MTV. In addition, satellite dishes and cable connections bring a range of foreign programs to some Chinese viewers. Both radio and television now feature call-in talk shows (with a built-in fourteen-second delay to allow for screening callers' comments before they hit the airwaves).

We spoke earlier of the Chinese media as a two-way transmission belt for information: information about local conditions is gathered by reporters and distributed, frequently in the form of classified publications with limited distribution, to the upper echelons of the party-state. Once properly processed, that information is disseminated back to the media (by the New China News Agency and others) and eventually finds its way into print and broadcasts. Occasionally, however, that transmission belt malfunctions, in some cases with disastrous consequences for the Chinese people. Two epidemics and a public health scandal are cases in point.

The questions of how many Chinese have been infected with the human immunodeficiency virus (HIV) and how many of them have developed autoimmune deficiency syndrome (AIDS) have been a matter of widespread speculation for many years. Until 2003, when then-Premier Wen Jiabao appeared on television news with an AIDS patient and promised that his government would take a more active role in preventing and treating the disease, the incidences of HIV and AIDS were generally treated as state secrets. Information about the epidemic no doubt reached party-state officials, but little or no information was disseminated to the public.

A particularly egregious situation in Henan Province was eventually made public, but only because of the investigative reporting of the courageous *Southern Weekend (Nanfang Zhoumo* 南方周末), a spin-off of the Guangdong Province Party Committee. Breaking the taboo on reporting on another government entity at the same level in the hierarchy, Southern Weekend in 2000 ran a series of stories detailing a cover-up initiated by the Henan authorities. Peasants in the impoverished province were encouraged by the provincial government to sell their blood as a means of supplementing their meager farm incomes. Sadly, the method for extracting the blood proved lethal. Blood from many donors was mixed together, the plasma was extracted, and the remaining red blood cells were reinjected into the donors. A case or two of HIV infection quickly multiplied into as many as a million cases. In Donghu (东 胡), a village in Xincai County (新蔡 县), as many as 80 percent of adults were HIV positive in 2001. A year later, two hundred of the village's six hundred families had one parent dead from AIDS and one parent ill. It was the world's worst incidence of AIDS in a single community. Understanding that they had a public relations problem on their hands, local government officials did their best to cover their tracks. In Chengguan (城关), in Suixian (虽岁) County, officials detained reporters attempting to interview villagers suffering from HIV. They also detained the villagers and broke up a protest by fifty villagers outside the building where their neighbors were being held.

Spurred on by the publicity generated by the *Southern Weekend* coverage, central government authorities eventually concluded that public disclosure was necessary. In the summer of

2001, then-Public Health Minister Zhang Wenkang spoke to a UN AIDS Summit and made public his ministry's figures on HIV and AIDS in China: 600,000 cases of AIDS and another 180,000 cases likely to be diagnosed in 2002. Two years later, newly appointed Premier Wen Jiabao and President Hu Jintao both made public appearances with AIDS patients and announced a doubling of AIDS prevention and treatment funding and new policies encouraging needle exchange and distribution of condoms.

Naively, one would think that the party-state would apply the maxim "Once burned, twice shy" to the outbreak of a dangerous new virus—subsequently identified as severe acute respiratory syndrome, or SARS—in Foshan (佛山) County, Guangdong, in the fall of 2002. Not so. The government delayed reporting the outbreak to the World Health Organization for two months and avoided reporting about it in the media for another six weeks. By the time a WHO team was admitted to Guangdong to investigate in early April, there were 1,200 cases in China, and seventy-five had died of the disease. As the team arrived, the Chinese media were instructed to report that SARS "is under effective control in Guangzhou." But of course, it wasn't, and it spread. One case was identified in Beijing during the National People's Congress meeting there, and no fewer than ten doctors and nurses were infected by that single patient. Once again, a cover-up was deemed to be the best response.

Only after AIDS activist and retired military physician Jiang Yanyong (蒋彦永) publicly called into question government statistics was it revealed that both the Ministry of Public Health and the Beijing municipal government had understated the number of cases of SARS, failing, among other omissions, to include patients in the city's system of military hospitals. The central government acted swiftly and decisively. The minister of public health, Zhang Wenkang (张文康), and the mayor of Beijing,

Meng Xuenong (孟学农), were peremptorily dismissed from office. At stake here were the credibility of the newly appointed president and premier and the widespread feeling that the legitimacy of the party-state was in as much jeopardy as it had been in 1989. The epidemic wound down in June with some 8,100 cases worldwide (5000 of them in China), and 775 fatalities. The full story of the failure of the media transmission belt in this instance was told in an article appearing in *Finance and Economics,* the independent and free-wheeling economic journal about which we have spoken.

Our third case is one in which information was clearly withheld, though since we have no access to the internal publications that reach the eyes of officialdom but not those of the public, we are unable to determine who was involved in the cover-up. In September 2008, after all of China's guests at the Beijing Olympics had left the country, the Ministry of Public Health announced a nationwide inquiry into the safety of infant formula. Fifty children had fallen ill after drinking the formula, and one of them had died from kidney failure. Once the full story was told later in the month, it was revealed that officials at the Foshan Group (佛山集團), a dairy products firm based in Shijiazhuang, Hebei, had begun receiving complaints from their customers in November of the previous year. Six months later, they had determined that there was, in fact, a problem with their product. Dairy farmers and milk companies supplying the Sanlu Group (三鹿集團) had been diluting their milk with water and then adding melamine, a chemical used in the production of hard plastics, which mimics a protein and makes the milk appear to be fully nutritious. The chemical damaged the kidneys of the infants who consumed the formula.

But the company waited three months to report its findings, and the report reached Beijing on the eve of the opening of the Olympics. Beijing, in turn, waited a month to announce its inquiry, and only then did Sanlu recall its contaminated product. Ultimately, three hundred thousand children were sickened as a result of consuming the formula, and six of them lost their lives. The government proposed a program to compensate parents of afflicted children; many parents, dissatisfied with the government program, turned to litigation. Tian Wenhua (田文华), Sanlu's chief executive, was convicted of the cover-up and sentenced to life in prison. Two of her colleagues were sentenced to death, and two others to life imprisonment. Once again, the full story came to light only as a result of the investigative reporting of the so-called shadow media.

Then there's the Internet. China's assiduous efforts at exerting control of that most insidious of information sources, the World Wide Web, put one in mind of those creations of Warner Brothers' Chuck Jones—the Road Runner and Wile E. Coyote. The coyote uses his (limited) wit and speed to try to catch his elusive prey, who is almost always just a few steps out of reach. When, in one episode, the coyote catches Road Runner, he finds himself so remarkably shrunken and the Road Runner so remarkably large that the coyote drops his knife and fork and holds up a sign that reads, "Now what do I do"? Of course, it may not come to that; according to the Open Net Initiative, "China's Internet-filtering regime is the most sophisticated effort of its kind in the world."

The pace of growth of Internet access in China is extraordinary. In 1996, there were between fifty thousand and a hundred thousand Internet users. In mid-2007, the number of Chinese with Internet access surpassed 253 million, the number of those with access in the United States. Today, that figure has reached 1.1 billion or 80% of the population as a whole. This very rapid growth of potential access to countless terabytes of information must be Li Shulei's worst nightmare. By contrast, it is the guiding light of those who believe that access to information will be the undoing of authoritarian government in China. It is no wonder, then, that the party-state is expending so much effort and expense to play the coyote to Chinese Internet users' desert bird.

The Internet Affairs Bureau of the State Council's Information Office is confronting two problems that have triggered the construction of what some call the Great Firewall of China: access to uncensored information, on the one hand, and the ability to communicate quickly, broadly, and freely, on the other. The first problem is being addressed by an increasingly broad and sophisticated system of filtering out unacceptable websites and Web postings. Enter "*Falun Gong*" in your favorite search engine in China, and you receive only an error message. Enter "www.nytimes.com" in your browser on certain days, and you get the same error message.

A troublesome problem for some of us is the fact that American firms are complicit in this filtering process. To enter the potentially lucrative Chinese market, Google, Yahoo, Microsoft, Cisco Systems, and other firms all agreed to abide by Chinese filtering regulations. Indeed, beyond simple compliance, Yahoo was sued by an imprisoned Chinese dissident for having provided the party-state with information that was used in his prosecution. At a congressional hearing on the issue in 2006, the companies were denounced for what House subcommittee chair Christopher Smith (R-NJ) termed "sickening collaboration."

Five years after entering the Chinese market, Google abruptly announced in early 2010 that it would no longer comply with Chinese Internet censorship rules, even if that meant it was forced to leave China entirely. The move was in retaliation for sophisticated cyber attacks on Google's computer systems that the company had reason to believe originated in China. But the announcement won widespread approbation from advocates of Internet freedom, who noted that Google had at last lived up to its motto: “Don’t be evil.”

Shortly thereafter, then-Secretary of State Hillary Rodham Clinton gave a speech in which she said, “Those who disrupt the free flow of information in our society or any other pose a threat to our economy, our government, and our civil society. Countries or individuals that engage in cyber-attacks should face consequences and international condemnation.” Though she did not mention China by name, a Foreign Ministry spokesman denounced her comments, saying that they put United States-China relations in jeopardy. The Chinese government referred to Clinton’s foreign policy stand as “information imperialism.”

A recent (and, in the view of many, the most over-the-top) addition to the Great Firewall’s tools was a computer program innocuously called Green Dam Youth Escort. Billed as a filter similar to those used by parents in the United States to block their children’s access to undesirable sites, It was suddenly announced on the Ministry of Industry and Information Technology website in 2009 that Green Dam must be installed in all computers sold in China after 1 July. It was merely a way, the website said, of protecting Chinese children from viewing pornographic images on the Internet. Three University of Michigan computer scientists saw something considerably more insidious when they analyzed the program: “We have discovered remotely exploitable vulnerabilities in the censorship software Green Dam. Any website a Green Dam user visits can take control of the PC.” Faced with a storm of domestic skepticism and international opposition, the mandatory installation of Green Dam was suspended in July and withdrawn in August. But it is highly unlikely to be Wile E. Coyote’s last stratagem.

The second problem for the Internet Affairs Bureau is the ability the Internet affords the Chinese to communicate with one another. Beginning with e-mail and moving on through chat rooms, forums, blogs, instant messaging, YouTube, Facebook, and Twitter, these modes of communicating through cyberspace have proved a challenge to keep ahead of, since currently nearly all Chinese internet users connect via mobile phones, indicating a dramatic shift away from PCs and public cafés.

Currently, more than 827 million Chinese, about three-quarters of netizens, use Internet sites that offer search engines, e-mail service, and other modes of communication. Key providers include Baidu (百度), Bing (必应), Sogou (搜狗), Haosou (好搜), Shenma (神马), Xiaohongshu (小红书–Little Red Book), and WeChat. These platforms—ranging from general web search to social and e-commerce integrated search—serve virtually all Chinese users seeking information. E-mail on these and other sites is routinely filtered. Chat rooms, forums, and blogs are monitored by an army of some thirty thousand volunteers, many of them students (believe it or not), who sift through postings, rejecting those that are inappropriate in the eyes of the authorities and, for repeat offenders, rejecting those who post them. Instant messaging and social network sites that are located abroad can relatively easily be blocked, as can domestic sites. Illustrative is the very short life of microblogging as chronicled on the China-based website danwei.com. The U.S.-based Twitter came to the attention of Chinese netizens in mid-June 2009 and quickly spawned five Chinese microblogging sites. Four short weeks later, all of them were blocked.

Text messaging poses a somewhat more complex problem. There were about one billion cell phone users in China as of 2407, nearly twice the number of landlines. The government estimated that Chinese were texting at a rate of 550 billion messages per year, a rate of 416 messages for every man, woman, and child in China, or 7,000 messages per second. The "instant crowd" phenomenon that used text messaging to gather gaggles on the streets of Manhattan and London as a prank some years ago has quickly been shown to be politically explosive when transferred to the streets of, say, Tehran in the wake of the contested 2009 election.

While shutting down an offending website is one thing, shutting down cell phone service to eliminate offensive text messages would have vastly more significant social and economic consequences. Instead, cell phone service providers are being required to install filtering equipment that monitors and deletes messages containing words, phrases, or numbers that appear on a frequently updated Publicity Department blacklist. Late in 2008, Canadian human rights activists and computer security researchers discovered that a system was in place that not only monitors and edits the text messages of customers of TOM-Skype, a joint venture between a Chinese wireless operator and eBay, which owns Skype, the online phone and text messaging service. It archives the edited messages together with information about the senders. Despite the obstacles, a 2009 study by the San Francisco-based firm NetPop Research suggested that a remarkable 97 percent of Chinese internet users make use of social media (as compared with only 76 percent of American Internet users).

It would appear that although the party-state once succeeded in slowing the flow of information among its citizens to a weak trickle, contemporary technology has restored the flow to an unprecedented volume. It remains to be seen what the result will be.

Chapter 17: Environmental Challenges

The dark side of a high standard of living in the modern style is its adverse effect on the environment. With every improvement—greater mobility, a more varied diet, more living space, and more personal possessions—attendant costs must be borne by the environment. Given the huge size of China's population, the success of its rapid economic development in raising the living standard has posed a particularly ominous threat to environmental degradation. Coping with this threat is one of the most serious problems confronting China and, because China's environment is also our environment, the rest of the world as well.

There are two conflicting interpretations of the historical relationship between the Chinese people and their environment. One suggests that the Chinese state in traditional times worked hard to preserve a delicate balance between human needs and natural resources. The central government took responsibility for mobilizing the labor needed to build and maintain a system of flood control and irrigation works, as well as a network of inland waterways. Generations of Chinese peasants perfected a system of farming that made maximal use of limited land and, by means of intensive recycling practices, preserved its fertility. There was very little profligacy in the Chinese people's use of natural resources.

Other historians question whether this delicate balance ever really existed, suggesting that the treatment of the relationship between humans and nature in Chinese philosophy was less a reflection of historical practice and more a mask for the exploitation of nature to serve human ends.

Whichever interpretation is correct, there is no question that whatever balance there may have been has been destroyed in modern times, and for several reasons. The first was a very rapid growth in the Chinese population during the eighteenth century. As we have seen, China's population remained stable at between fifty and one hundred million people for nearly sixteen centuries; then, in the early years of the Qing dynasty in the late seventeenth century, it began to grow rapidly, multiplying by a factor of five within two hundred years. Although new crops and techniques increased agricultural productivity, the fivefold increase in population was accompanied by only a 25 percent increase in the amount of land under cultivation. The delicate balance of human needs and natural resources, if it had existed, was destroyed.

A second factor contributing to the breakdown of this balance was industrialization. The Chinese had sat out the Industrial Revolution that swept Europe and the United States in the early nineteenth century; indeed, they were almost wholly ignorant of its products until Western powers used modern weaponry to force China to open its doors to trade. Weapons factories became the entry wedge of industrialization in China, and by the last years of the nineteenth century, the Chinese government had reluctantly and belatedly decided to emulate the West with full-scale industrialization.

A third factor was that China's subsequent industrialization was achieved under socialist auspices. Capitalist industrialization can hardly be said to have proceeded without environmental damage, but as we have seen in Russia and Eastern Europe, socialist industrialization seems to have been especially pernicious in its effects on the environment. This was, if anything, even more true in China. Mao Zedong rose to power with a very clear sense that nature was an enemy to be vanquished, not an ally to be cultivated, and that sense of the battle against nature became an even stronger element of his thinking as his career in power progressed.

There are several reasons why socialist development in China was incompatible with environmental protection. For one thing, with the land and its resources publicly owned, no one took responsibility for the land or represented its interests. For another, water and energy were supplied to consumers at no cost or at a heavily subsidized cost, and there was no incentive to conserve their use. Worse, the deficiencies in the quantity and quality of cultivable land, air, and water have only escalated, not been ameliorated.

We begin our discussion of China's environment by taking a careful look at its energy needs and energy resources. China is the world's largest user of coal, which accounts for 56 percent of all energy consumed in the country. Oil is currently about 20 percent, hydro, nuclear, and wind power account for about 18 percent, and natural gas is about six percent of the country's energy consumption. Comparable figures for China and the United States are shown in Table 21.

Table 21: Energy Consumption, China and the United States, 2025 (percent)

	China	**United States**
Coal	56	11
Petroleum	20	40
Hydro, nuclear, and wind power	18	11
Natural gas	6	38

Source: *Statistical Review of World Energy*

Annual coal production in China is currently running at a rate of just under five billion tons. While coal is found in many provinces and in the far western region of Xinjiang, mines in the northern tier of provinces contain coal that is more accessible and lower in sulfur and ash content. China's coal mines are highly unsafe, a situation that has been exacerbated over the last forty years with the opening of small, privately held, and largely unregulated mines to meet the growing demand to fuel China's economic growth. China has the world's worst mine safety record, with an average of close to six thousand miners killed each year between 1990 and 2000. Deaths declined sharply in 2006 and 2007 and currently stand at about two thousand per year.

The vast majority of China's coal is "soft" or bituminous, the burning of which contributes heavily to air pollution. Weaning China of its heavy dependence on soft coal is a necessary first step toward solving its serious environmental problems. There are other adverse consequences of coal extraction. In Shaanxi, a major coal producer, thousands of acres of land are sinking as a result of underground mining. Moreover, hundreds of out-of-control fires in coal mines—some started by lightning, some by mining accidents—spew carbon dioxide into the atmosphere. Chinese scientists estimate that as much as two hundred million tons of coal, more than the total coal burned in Japan in 2005, is consumed by these fires.

China is currently consuming more than sixteen million barrels of oil per day, making it the world's second-largest consumer of oil after the United States (which currently consumes just over twenty million barrels per day) and accounting for a quarter of the world's growth in oil consumption over the last decade. Since 2003, China has been the world's fastest-growing importer of oil, with imports increasing at about five percent per year. Close to fifty percent of China's imported oil comes from the Middle East.

Estimating oil reserves is a slippery business, since *proven* reserves are sometimes combined with *probable* and *possible* reserves to produce figures of very large magnitude. China's *proven* oil reserves have remained very close to five billion metric tons over the last forty years. When exploration in the Tarim basin in Xinjiang began in 1993, early estimates of the area's *possible* reserves were remarkably high, but most recent estimates of *proved* and *probable* reserves there stand at about six million tons. Additionally, it may contain over one billion tons of oil resources in ultra-deep, high-temperature, and high-pressure Cambrian[10] reservoirs. Meanwhile, offshore oil exploration undertaken with foreign assistance has been underway for more than thirty years. Assessing China's offshore reserves is complicated by a lack of reliable survey data and by issues of territorial rights; estimates of *possible* reserves have varied from a low of 37 billion barrels to a high of more than 200 billion barrels. Wisely, Chinese economic planners are using a conservative figure of 15 billion barrels as the basis for their energy projections. To put these figures into perspective, the proved oil reserves of North America are about 69.3 billion barrels, and of the Middle East, about 755 billion barrels.

In the late 1970s, when China began to interact with the world economy, Chinese planners estimated that oil production would double by the early 1990s and that revenues from oil exports would be sufficient to fund imports of Western and Japanese technology. In fact, while oil production increased by 65 percent between 1979 and 1992, the ensuing development of the economy increased domestic demand for petroleum at a rate that exceeded the rate of increase in oil production: whereas total economic growth has averaged in excess of nine percent per year, oil

---

[10] The Cambrian Period is the first geological time period of the Paleozoic Era, lasting from 541 million to 485.4 million years ago.

production has been increasing at about two percent. Thus, oil occupies about the same position in China's energy pool that it did twenty years ago, and as of 1994, China became a net importer of oil. In 2024, China was importing nearly three-quarters of the oil it consumed, and it is the world's largest importer of oil. China's crude oil imports fell two percent in 2024, the first annual decline in two decades

Electric power is China's third source of energy, providing about seven percent of the total. The existing electric power grid serves the eastern third of the country quite effectively; the western two-thirds, less so. Total electric power generation in 2024 was 9.42 trillion kilowatt-hours, but more than 80 percent of that power was generated thermally, using soft coal. Electric power generation is increasing annually at a rate of about 13 percent, and the ratio of hydroelectric power to coal-burning thermal-generated electricity has increased slowly but steadily over the last twenty years. Currently, about five percent of China's electric power is nuclear-generated.

The Three Gorges Dam project is the world's largest capacity hydroelectric power station, with 34 generators. It has a generating capacity of 22,500 megawatts (MW). Since 2003, it has generated over 1,600 terawatt-hours (TWh) of clean electricity. In theory, that should have reduced the use of coal by sixty million tons per year. But in fact, the annual electrical energy needs of eastern China alone are close to 2,000 terawatt hours, so power from the new dam has simply augmented the supply of thermal-generated electricity; it has not supplanted it.

With this in mind, the government began constructing a series of twenty smaller dams along the Yangzi. It has also begun a number of dam projects in China's southwest, along three rivers, the *Jinsha (金沙), a tributary of the Yangzi, the Nu (怒), also known as the Salween, and the Lancang (澜沧), better known as the Mekong.* These proposed projects have raised considerable opposition in China, where protesters deplore the damage that will be caused to pristine natural habitats. Beijing actually responded to protests over the Nu River development project. In 2004, then-Premier Wen Jiabao called a halt to the project, which would have flooded a UNESCO- designated World Heritage Site. Two years later, in 2006, a revised plan, reducing the number of dams from thirteen to four, was put before the State Council. The proposed dams have also raised concerns among China's Southeast Asian neighbors, who point out that a seriously depleted flow in the Salween and the Mekong would be devastating to their economies.

The most immediate problem with China's electric power generating system is its undercapacity. While progress is being made in developing the technology to build more efficient and less polluting coal-fired generating plants, the pressing demand for more power is simultaneously fostering the opening of small, highly polluting coal-fired plants.

Three additional sources of energy account for a small but growing amount of Chinese consumption. Natural gas currently supplies only about 6 percent of the country's energy needs, but as a clean-burning fuel, it is seen as a desirable alternative to the burning of coal. A ten-billion-dollar pipeline project to transport natural gas from the Tarim basin in Xinjiang to Shanghai was announced in 2002 and completed in 2016. Named the West-East Gas Pipeline Project, it involved the development of the gas field and the construction of a nearly two-thousand-mile-long pipeline that will supply Shanghai's natural gas needs for more than four decades. Simultaneously, negotiations were concluded for contracts with Australia, Indonesia, and Iran to supply some $28 billion in liquefied natural gas over the next twenty-five years.

Plans were announced in 2009 to build as many as ten thousand-megawatt nuclear power plants each year, with a goal of doubling nuclear energy's share of electric power generation by the year 2020. Construction began in 2009 on the first of these plants. It was a joint venture with the American firm Westinghouse, which received U.S. government backing for its successful bid. Meanwhile, China took a stake in a uranium mine in Kazakhstan to help provide the fuel for its nuclear expansion. In 2024, the country approved the construction of eleven new reactors at five sites, each with a power rating of at least one thousand megawatts. The total cost is estimated at $31 billion. China currently has 58 operating nuclear power plants, which supply 53 gigawatts, or five percent of the country's electric power. China now leads the world in the new construction of nuclear reactors.

Finally, over the last five years, China has come to recognize the potential for renewable energy sources, investing heavily in wind and solar power generation equipment. In 2009, China surpassed the United States as the world's largest market for wind turbines after doubling its wind power capacity in each of the last four years. The growth in the wind power industry was spurred, in part, by regulations adopted in 2007 that called on large power-generating companies to generate at least three percent of their electricity from renewable sources by 2010. By the end of 2024, China had some 890 gigawatts of cumulative installed solar capacity. Over the longer term, the Chinese have their eye on dominating the world market in renewable energy equipment, including photovoltaic solar panels and wind turbines.

With the exception of coal, then, energy is still in short supply in China. The country also has very serious shortages in arable land and water. Whereas China is home to 20 percent of the world's population, it has only ten percent of the world's arable land, and this shortfall is daily exacerbated when land is taken out of cultivation and used for factories, roads, railroad rights-of-way, housing, and other accoutrements of rural industrialization and economic development. Some estimate that China has lost more than one-fifth of its arable land since 1949 due to urbanization and industrialization. Currently, only about 10 to 15 percent of the remaining land is suitable for agriculture. Despite this, China's agricultural output is the largest in the world.

The government has had in place a plan requiring that for every acre of land taken out of cultivation for non-agricultural development, an acre of new arable land must be developed. But the regulation is more honored in the breach than in the observance. Local authorities are quick to grant waivers, particularly since they are very likely to profit personally from doing so.

Scarce farmland is also lost as an unintended consequence of deforestation. Wood and plant stalks supply about four-fifths of the energy used for cooking and heating in the countryside, and this, together with logging for lumber production, has resulted in the deforestation of nearly three hundred million acres of land over the last forty years. By 1996, China's forested land had been reduced to thirteen percent (compared with a U.S. figure of 29 percent). This deforestation, in turn, adversely affected adjacent farmland. The cutting of trees greatly increases water runoff, soil erosion, and siltation of riverbeds, raising the water level and augmenting the devastation caused by floods. Recognizing the seriousness of the situation, Premier Zhu Rongji declared a moratorium on logging in 1999, first in Sichuan, then in sixteen additional provinces. The effect of the moratorium, when accompanied by a nationwide program of afforestation, actually turned around the condition of China's forests. In 2024, government statisticians put the amount of forested land at 25 percent.

Deforestation, together with the destruction of grasslands, has resulted in some 31% of China's land being lost to desertification since 1949. Desert currently covers approximately 20 percent of the Chinese landmass, and the rate of its expansion has doubled over the last decade. Although efforts have been made to reestablish grasslands on the newly desertified lands, they have largely been unsuccessful. Creating a forest windbreak at the edge of desert regions to counteract sandstorms and slow further loss of land to the desert has also been only partially successful. Sandstorms from the new deserts are a major source of air pollution in northern China and beyond. Indeed, dust from a storm in April 2001 was carried as far afield as New England.

The water supply in China is neither adequate nor evenly distributed. Southern China, with about one-third of the arable land, has three-quarters of the water supply, while northern China has a serious water deficit. Not only is rainfall much less in the north (as shown on Map #3 above), but groundwater deposits are also much less abundant. Exacerbating the problem, the glaciers and underground water system feeding the source of the Yellow River, which supplies water to some 140 million people, are threatened by global warming.

A radical solution to this imbalance in the water supply, one originally proposed by Mao shortly after the founding of the PRC, was to transfer major quantities of water from the south of the country to the north. The South to North Water Diversion Project, begun in 2002, consists of three diversion routes. The eastern route makes use of the existing Grand Canal, the thousand-mile-long waterway linking Beijing and Hangzhou that was completed in the sixth century C.E., to divert water from the Yangzi River to reservoirs near Tianjin. Water on the eastern route reached Tianjin in 2017. The central route transfers water from the Danjiangkou Reservoir (丹江口水库) on the Han River to Beijing and was completed in 2014. The western route, which involves major engineering challenges, will divert water from the headwaters of the Yangzi to the headwaters of the Yellow River. Construction of this third route began in January 2024.

Even when a better balance has been established between water supplies in the south and those in the north, the country's total water supply will still be inadequate. China is a good deal like California, in that irrigated agriculture consumes a very high proportion—85 percent in China's case—of total water consumption. Paradoxically, then, while the move toward urbanization may adversely affect the food supply, it could favorably affect the water supply. However, industrialization and a higher living standard are ordinarily accompanied by an increase in water consumption, and indeed the consumption of tap water in China's cities has increased fivefold over the last twenty years.

More than half of China's cities currently have water shortages. In Beijing, for example, water consumption amounts to some 950 billion gallons per year; the water table around the city has dropped nearly two hundred feet since the mid-1960s. Because until very recently water was supplied free of charge to urban residents, there has been no incentive to conserve it. Unless new sources of water are located or stringent conservation measures are adopted, experts estimate that the country will face a shortfall of fifty-three trillion gallons by 2030, a figure greater than the country's current annual consumption.

The shortfall in the water supply is seriously exacerbated by the wholesale polluting of China's streams, rivers, and lakes. It is estimated that some 280 million Chinese drink impure water. China's wastewater treatment plants treat wastewater for some 98% of municipalities, but only 28% of rural areas. According to a report from the State Environmental Protection Agency, only a quarter of the country's twenty-one billion tons of wastewater is treated. The country plans to build or renovate 50,000 miles of sewage collection pipeline networks in the next few years. However, despite the strong focus on treatment, only 10% of the wastewater is recycled.

Moreover, despite the threat of fines and the more and more frequent outbursts of public protest, large and small industries regularly dump their waste directly into waterways. As New England was industrializing in the nineteenth century, factories were located near rivers, which provided them with their source of energy. As China's countryside industrialized in the twentieth century, factories were located near rivers that provided them with energy, but also with cost-free sewers for their industrial wastes.

In a particularly egregious example of the latter, an accident at the Jilin Petrochemical Factory in 2005 dumped some hundred tons of benzene and nitrobenzene into the Songhua River (松花江), creating a 50 mile band of toxic water that required closing down the water supply for the city of Harbin and threatened to do the same for the city of Khabarovsk as it moved into the Heilong River and crossed the border into Siberia. While the government spent $1.2 billion on a cleanup project, the state-owned factory was fined a mere $128,000, the maximum fine allowed under the law.

The State Environmental Protection Administration (SEPA) reported that between 70 and 90 percent of China's rivers are too polluted to use as drinking water sources, and any number of rivers and streams have water graded by SEPA as Category V—too toxic even to touch. Stomach and liver cancers, associated in some studies with water pollution, are the leading causes of death in the countryside. Riverside communities also experience abnormally high rates of spontaneous abortions, birth defects, and early deaths. The World Health Organization has estimated that 95,600 Chinese people lose their lives each year from polluted water.

In early 2010, the Ministry of Environmental Protection issued the results of its first national pollution census, including data that took more than two years to gather. The census, which was repeated in 2020, revealed that water pollution was more than twice as severe as was shown in figures released at the time. One reason for the discrepancy is that the census data includes pollution from agricultural waste that had been omitted from earlier calculations.

Air pollution is also an especially serious problem in China; according to the World Bank, sixteen of the world's twenty most polluted cities are in China. The air in 90 percent of China's cities does not meet the Chinese government's clean-air standards, which are not as stringent as Western ones. Beijing air is, on average, sixteen times more polluted than New York City air, and the city of Benxi (本溪), near Shenyang (沈阳) in Liaoning Province (辽宁省), periodically disappears from view on satellite maps because of the overlay of polluted air. Some seven hundred thousand deaths are attributable to the consequences of air pollution each year.

The principal cause of air pollution in China is the burning of soft coal. Two-thirds of China's factories are contributing to air pollution in this way, and their outdated and inefficient equipment means they are using excessive quantities of the polluting fuel. China's industrial plant currently uses a third more energy per dollar of gross domestic product than Japan's and about the same amount as that of the United States. As we have seen, dust carried on prevailing winds from the desert regions of the northwest also contributes to urban air pollution, particularly in China's northern cities.

Until recently, automobile exhaust was not a significant contributor to urban air pollution, but that has changed dramatically in recent years. There are currently about 402 million passenger vehicles on China's streets and roads—four times the 100 million passenger vehicles registered in the United States—and auto sales are up more than eightfold since 2000. China produced more than 30 million automobiles in 2024, surpassing U.S. auto production by a factor of three. Foreign manufacturers have actively competed to participate in the joint ventures that have helped China reach this level. Projections of auto production suggest that China may have as many as 607 million vehicles by 2050, a number that corresponds to somewhat more than a third of the total number of vehicles in the world today.

Mindful of the effect of the increase in motor vehicles on air quality, particularly in China's cities—Shanghai estimates that one third of its air pollution derives from automobile exhaust—the Chinese government has put forward fuel economy standards that are even more stringent than those recently adopted in the United States, and new-car emissions standards equivalent to "Euro 4"—the standards in effect in the European Union. To discourage driving, the price of gasoline and diesel fuel has been allowed to rise, though China, like the United States, continues to have very low gas prices compared with other countries. Also, unleaded fuel is being introduced as a pollution control measure.

The increase in the number of automobiles has resulted in China's cities being not only more polluted but also less navigable. Elaborate plans drawn up at the beginning of Shanghai's massive expansion twenty years ago have proved inadequate, and the city's streets and highways are clotted with traffic. More than one hundred thousand Chinese are killed in automobile accidents each year, a fivefold increase over the last two decades and more than twice the number in the United States. The decision to develop the automobile industry has sparked a lively debate in China. Government planners have published specifications for a small, fuel-efficient, and low-polluting "family car" of the future. But promoting such a car as the principal means of transportation carries with it a multitude of undesirable consequences. A quarter of a billion automobiles would pollute the air, require paving over still more acres of scarce farmland, exhaust the country's oil reserves, and render China's already congested cities unnavigable. Moreover, automobile engineers are skeptical that the features called for in the specifications can be achieved in a car that is supposed to cost no more than $10,000. Meanwhile, the electric vehicle industry in China has grown to be the largest in the world, accounting for more than half of global production of the vehicles. In 2024, China sold nearly 13 million passenger electric vehicles.

Air pollution in China reached worldwide attention as the date for the 2008 Beijing Olympics drew near. China had assured the Olympic Committee that the skies over the capital would be clear for the games, but it was able to accomplish this only by taking very stringent measures. Beginning in the year 2000, the city took steps to reduce air pollution by replacing coal with natural gas as a household and industrial fuel, cutting coal use to 15 percent of its earlier level and cutting particulate matter in the air by 50 percent, and both coal and water were placed on the price reform agenda to encourage conservation of their use. As the date of the games approached, hundreds of factories in and around Beijing and Tianjin were shut down weeks in advance, and automobile traffic was substantially reduced by limiting drivers' access to the capital's streets and roads based on their license plate numbers. The stringent measures have had a lasting effect. In 2024, the city enjoyed 144 so-called blue-sky days (days when air pollution was below 101 on a 0-to-500 pollution index) and only two days with dangerously high air pollution. During the same period, ten years earlier, there were nineteen days of dangerous pollution.

In addition to the substantial threat to public health and loss of life, air and water pollution is estimated to cost China somewhere between 8 and 12 percent of GDP each year, or some three to four hundred billion. This discouraging situation has not developed because of a lack of agencies, laws, or regulations. On the contrary, China has a reasonably complete set of environmental protection laws and regulations, and a fully articulated structure of government offices devoted to environmental matters.

The problem of environmental pollution was first addressed at a national conference on the subject in 1973, five years before the economic reforms began. Six years later, the National People's Congress passed an Environmental Protection Law, and five years after that, in 1984, the National Environmental Protection Agency (NEPA) was formed. In 1998, NEPA was promoted to ministerial level under the State Council, becoming the State Environmental Protection Administration (SEPA–Guojia Huanjing Baohu Zongju 国家环境保护总局). Revisions to the Environmental Protection Law, which were adopted by the National People's Congress in 1989, require environmental impact studies for all major construction projects and impose stiff fines for violating the pollution limits. The most recent revisions to China's Environmental Protection Law were adopted in 2023. The revised law prioritizes protection and tackling problems at their source, as well as coordinating activities on land and at sea to protect the ocean environment.

Undeniably, these conferences, new agencies, and new laws have had positive results. Among them is heightened public awareness. Many environmental groups have sprung up, and a stunning 98 percent of those surveyed in a recent government poll called for stricter environmental regulation and increased government expenditure for environmental protection.

China is currently spending annually three percent of its GDP, or $75.3 billion, on environmental protection. This puts it well above the international average expenditure as a percentage of GDP, which stands at less than one percent. Research and training in environmental sciences have developed quickly at universities and research institutes, and scholars at these institutions are well connected with their professional colleagues outside China. As is the case in other fields of academic endeavor, the hard science in these institutions is of reasonably high quality, while the social science lags behind.

Environmental issues are difficult to resolve in any political setting. Correcting one source of environmental degradation can often give rise to new and potentially more dangerous sources of pollution; action that benefits the environment in one region may have detrimental effects in a neighboring region. But environmental issues seem particularly difficult to resolve in the Chinese political system, where, as we have discussed, a clash of interests between the central government and regional authorities often ends in deadlock and inaction. Moreover, in a developing economy like that of China, environmental concerns and economic growth are most often at odds with each other. When push comes to shove, the latter always takes precedence, as it does in many circumstances around the world.

The conflict between economic development and environmental protection is worked out in the grid of China's political system, where local and national interests are often at odds. SEPA directives and regulations travel down the vertical paths of the grid and are thwarted at the horizontal local level, where the agency is represented by the provincial, municipal, or county environmental protection bureaus (EPBs). These bureaus, like other central government agencies at the local level, report not only to Beijing but also to the local government. When it is a question of developing the local economy by building a new factory, local authorities pressure the head of the local EPB to waive regulations to get the factory built as expeditiously and cheaply as possible.

Nearly half of environmental protection funding comes from the central government, the remainder being paid out by local governments. But most of the central government regulations take the form of unfunded mandates. Until quite recently, there has been insufficient funding for environmental concerns at the national level. Qu Geping (曲格平), for many years head of the National Environmental Protection Agency and until 2003 chair of the Environmental Protection and Resources Conservation Committee of the National People's Congress (全国人民代表大会环境与资源保护委员会), argued that China has a double burden: not only to reduce the damage currently being done to the environment but, like Russia and Eastern Europe, to clean up the damage caused by past excesses and omissions. To accomplish both, he estimated that at least twenty times the current level of expenditure is needed.

Thus, it is that the local government that is in compliance suffers a double blow: construction is prevented or delayed on factories that might bring it income while poisoning the local air and water, and the local government not only loses the tax revenue the factories would have generated but also must pay for the EPB officials who stand in the way. Local enforcement of environmental laws suffers from other disadvantages as well. While there is a plethora of environmental laws on the books, they tend to be vague, subject to interpretation, and thus difficult to enforce. Lawyers who are trained and experienced in handling environmental cases are few; judges who are both ill-trained and inexperienced are assigned to adjudicate these cases, and the courts are, in any event, firmly under the thumb of local party bosses. In those instances where enforcement succeeds, the fines provided by law are woefully insufficient; in most cases, it pays the offending factory to pay the fine and continue to pollute the water and the air.

There is yet another reason that rapid economic development almost always wins over environmental protection in China. In other countries, active and engaged grassroots movements have helped build public consciousness about environmental concerns. Despite heightened public concern and the emergence of NGOs concerned with environmental issues, there is no longer a "green movement" in China. As we have seen, the state is hypersensitive about groups that might become nuclei for political opposition, and this has made reviving a green movement virtually impossible.

Nonetheless, news of many grassroots protests reaches the Western press practically every month. For example, in 1993, a township-owned chemical factory in remote Gansu Province was polluting a local stream so seriously that peasants wading in the stream to fish were getting blisters on their legs. When the factory operators and township authorities ignored the protests, the residents descended on the factory, drove its operators out, and shut it down. There are numerous other examples like this one, and while many local environmental groups have sprung up in recent years, they are isolated from one another and show no signs yet of being able to form a national movement that will significantly affect the actions of local governments. Nor is Beijing, threatened as it is by any competition to the authority of the party-state, likely to permit the emergence of such a movement.

Chinese pollution has its effects on the rest of the world as well. At some point in 2008, China overtook the United States as the world's leading emitter of carbon dioxide, principal among the so-called greenhouse gases. Today, China emits 33% of the world's carbon dioxide; the United States emits 14%. Nonetheless, international pressure on China to do more with respect to the environment most often elicits a response heard elsewhere in the developing world. It is a response consistently voiced by Chinese delegations to international meetings on the environment since China attended its first such conference in 1973. Concern for the environment, this argument runs, is a pastime taken up late in life by wealthy nations, which themselves achieved economic development with little or no attention to its environmental consequences. Given this, why should poorer countries be held to new and higher standards in their economic development than the developed nations were in years past? If the West believes that developing nations should be held to these new high standards, then it should help pay for the very expensive process of meeting them. China has held to this position with some consistency over the last forty years.

The Kyoto Protocol, adopted in 1997 and in force from 2005 through 2012, limited neither of the world's two largest producers of greenhouse gas: the United States, because former President George W Bush decided not to honor the limitations imposed by the protocol, nor China, because the protocol imposed no limits on developing countries. Since then, it would appear that forward-looking Chinese leaders have begun to realize that China's pollution is hurting its economic development. As a result, they have become somewhat more open to the idea that the United States and China should work together in addressing the issue of global warming. When President Barack Obama visited Beijing in November 2009, high on the agenda was the question of the two nations' respective positions at the United Nations Climate Change Conference in Copenhagen the following month. Just prior to the conference, the Chinese put forward a proposal to reduce by 2010 the amount of carbon dioxide emitted per unit of economic output by 40 to 45 percent from 2005 levels. At the conference itself, however, the sticking point in the negotiations was China's refusal to submit to international monitoring of its emissions levels. The agreement hammered out between China, the United States, India, Brazil, and South Africa as the conference drew to a close sets a goal of limiting the global temperature rise to 2 degrees Celsius above preindustrial levels by 2050 and provides for the transfer of hundreds of billions of dollars from the developed economies to those countries most affected by climate change.

Even though China's change of Outlook—if genuine change there has been—derives less from eleemosynary and more from self-interested motives, the change will benefit us all, for the fact is we all inhabit the same planet. Chinese people may be the first to suffer from the poisoning of China's air and water, but ultimately, we all suffer. The first line of responsibility for China's extraordinarily serious environmental problems is, of course, the Chinese party-state, but in the end, the responsibility is international as well. A mutually beneficial partnership between the developed and the developing nations around these issues must be achieved.

Chapter 18: Population Pressures

The term "draconian" derives from the name of Draco, a perhaps fictitious Athenian lawyer who created a written code of law in the 7th century B.C.E. that was known for being highly extreme. Today, draconian is used to describe policies or actions that are extremely rigorous, severe, or harsh. It is certainly accurate to describe China's one-child policy as having been draconian. Our purpose here is to describe the implementation of this policy during the years 1979 to 2015 when it was in effect, and to explain how and why it was abandoned.

For many Chinese, the size of the country's population is one of its greatest problems, one that the Chinese government has acknowledged for more than seventy-five years. For others, its population is one of the country's greatest assets. Mao Zedong had highly mixed opinions on the subject. On the one hand, he often spoke of China's large population as one of its principal assets, and he actively encouraged people to have many children. "The more people we have, the stronger we are," he wrote.[11] He thought of every person added as two more hands whose work would contribute to national development and defense. Although he was known to express concern about the ratio of people to arable land, it was his general view that a large population was a national asset. For the first twenty years of the People's Republic, no effort was made to restrict births. Except during the years of recovery from the Great Leap Forward, the birthrate was well over thirty per thousand.

---

[11] Mao Zedong, "Refute Rightist Views that Population Growth Creates Difficulties" (驳关于人口增长有困难的右的观点), May 1958, in *Selected Readings from the Works of Mao Tse-tung* (毛泽东著作选读) (Beijing: People's Publishing House (人民出版社–Renmin Chubanshe), 1964.

On the other hand, Mao understood the potential contradiction between the rate of population growth and the rate of economic growth. In 1957, he stated that China needed to draw up national plans to regulate reproduction. He denounced the "anarchism" of uncontrolled births and advocated a national campaign to promote birth control. Ma Yinchu (马寅初) was a prominent Chinese economist who is regarded as the father of China's family planning efforts. Although Mao initially supported Ma's work, he eventually became unenthusiastic about family planning and concluded that the country wouldn't have a problem with overpopulation until it reached 800 million (which it eventually did in 1970). Ultimately, under Mao's leadership, the population was allowed to grow fairly freely. His policies—particularly those of the Great Leap Forward (which resulted in 45 million deaths from famine) and the Cultural Revolution (which resulted in another 1.5 million deaths) –persuaded him to favor large families.

Zhou Enlai took a different view. He came to believe that controlling population growth was a prerequisite to economic development, and he was responsible for initiating China's first national program to limit births in 1971, the goal being to reduce the birthrate to twenty per thousand by 1980. In practice, Zhou's program amounted to a two-child policy. The campaign's slogan was "Late, Sparse, and Few." Couples were encouraged to delay marrying until their late twenties, to space their children at least four years apart, and to limit themselves to two children for urban couples, three for rural families. The campaign was a success. Although by no means was every family limiting itself to two children, the birthrate in 1980, at eighteen per thousand, had been reduced by a third in a ten-year period. It was also coercive. Between 1971 and 1979, the total number of abortions performed in China increased from 3.9 million to 7.9 million, and of sterilizations from 1.7million to 5.3 million. If prohibited pregnancies were carried to term, the resulting children were denied schooling and welfare benefits.

Mao's successors saw the world quite differently. Excessive growth of the population threatened to thwart China's economic expansion. At the beginning of the reform period, the party state initiated a series of programs and regulations designed to end Mao's long-term opposition to birth control, which had produced runaway population growth that threatened to impoverish the nation and undermine party rule. Inaugurated in 1979, the "one-child policy," as these programs came to be collectively known, was surprisingly popular, enjoying the support of 75 percent of the Chinese population in a Pew Research Poll in 2008.

For those who were the targets of the policy—parents in their childbearing years—it was a somewhat different story. In the cities, it was accepted as a necessary evil; in the countryside, it met with widespread resistance. This resistance was triggered in part by a traditional preference for male children but also by the fact that the incentives and penalties of the one-child policy ran directly counter to those of the household responsibility system and the system of private farming to which it gave way. The one-child policy tried to limit population growth by rewarding families with a single child and penalizing larger ones; but the household responsibility system, in effect, rewarded large families by giving them high incomes, and in practice, the incentives to have a large family were significantly stronger than the penalties for exceeding the single-child limit.

The birth control program was yet another example of the problems in the power grid of China's political system. The party-state came up with a program it wanted implemented everywhere, but it had to rely on local authorities—indeed, government at the very lowest level of the political system—to enforce it. Moreover, like pollution control, the birth control program was an un-funded mandate. Because the program became both unpopular and unfunded, local party-state officials modified, delayed, or thwarted it.

Alarmed by local noncompliance, evidence of which surfaced in each national census, the central government pressured the localities by imposing limits and quotas. Under the gun to meet these, local authorities resorted to enforced abortions and sterilizations, practices that, of course, further alienated their constituencies, already disaffected by other grievances, and angered the central authorities, who denounced such draconian measures as illegitimate local violations of a legitimate central policy.

The birth control program was in sharp contrast with the economic reform program, the thrust of which was to remove the government from the daily lives of its citizens. The government would make fewer and fewer decisions for the Chinese people, who would find the government looking over their shoulders to monitor their political correctness less and less often. But the birth control program inserted the government into their lives in an unprecedented way, involving it in their most intimate decisions. This imposition of political authority angered many people inside as well as outside China. They regarded the one-child policy as an invasion of the most private aspect of an individual's life and a violation of a fundamental human right. Many who held this view were also unequivocally opposed to abortion. But with their own conception of national sovereignty, individual rights, and what they perceived as the magnitude of their population problem, Chinese authorities found this criticism impossible to fathom.

The long-term goals of the one-child policy were significantly closer to being realized in China's cities than in the countryside. There are a number of reasons for this success, some of them attributable to the policy, others having little to do with it. Urban couples are more removed from the influence of tradition and less likely to feel pressure from parents and relatives to produce large families and male heirs. Moreover, as we have seen, the cities are extraordinarily crowded and living space is very limited, so city residents experience the problems of a large population every day, whereas those problems can seem remote to people in the less crowded countryside. Urban couples are generally better educated, and worldwide, there is a correlation between education level (particularly of women) and the decision to limit births. In most cases, both members of an urban couple work outside the house, and because childbearing disrupts the woman's career, it is more likely to be delayed and limited. Childcare is also more expensive and often more difficult to arrange in the city than in the countryside, where grandparents are near at hand. Finally, as we have seen, many urban employees are covered at least partially by a pension system that makes them less dependent than rural workers on their children as a source of retirement support.

The one-child policy proved much more difficult to implement in the countryside, where tradition was still strong and favored male children. The birth of a son is cause for celebration; the birth of a daughter is only a "small happiness." In part, this is simple gender bias: a son carries on the family line; a daughter does not. But in part, it is based on an economic reality: when a daughter is married, she leaves her parents' home and becomes a member of her husband's family, contributing to her in-laws' family income, not to her parents'. A son's income remains in the family, and he is responsible for his parents as they retire and age. In the absence of a public pension scheme in the countryside, giving birth to a son meant providing for one's retirement security. As we have noted, the incentives of the household responsibility system undermined efforts to enforce the one-child policy in the countryside because they rewarded large families: increasing the "hand-to-mouth ratio"—that is, the number of a household's able-bodied workers in relation to the number to be fed—gave one a direct increase in household income. At the time, increased productivity was winning out over decreased fertility.

In the early years of American travel to China, after President Richard Nixon first went in 1972, a visit to a commune was obligatory on every tourist's itinerary. Directing the tour group into the production team's office, local officials would point with pride to a complicated chart on the office wall—a very public display of information on the menstrual cycles, birth control practices, and pregnancy records of every woman on the team. When the tour guide translated the explanation, foreigners would be aghast—a reaction that in turn perplexed the officials—for the birth control program, from its inception, made a public issue of what, to most foreigners, is a very private matter. Yet the results of having done this were impressive. Today, in China, information about contraception and contraceptive devices is widespread, and the Chinese government estimates that close to 85 percent of the sexually active population practices some form of contraception.

Still, abortion is a common form of limiting fertility. Recent figures show that somewhat more than seven million abortions, or one for every two live births, are performed annually. This is higher than the rate in the United States, which is one for every four live births, but lower than that in Russia and parts of Eastern Europe, where it is not uncommon to find rates of more than one abortion for each live birth. Adding to the abortion rate in China is its increasing prevalence among unmarried women. A recent study conducted in Shanghai revealed that 69 percent of women surveyed had had premarital sex.

To encourage compliance with the one-child policy, the government was prepared to offer an array of incentives. In Guang'an (广安) County, Sichuan Province, for example, these included cash rewards. Although the subsidy came to no more than a dollar a month, this constituted a 3 percent increase in the average household income there. There was also access to a pension plan, subsidized health care, additional land in the household's farming contract, a reduction in the grain tax, and, finally, tuition assistance for the one- child family. This package seemed well structured to appeal to the needs and interests of young rural couples, but in general, incentive packages like these were not enough to persuade the parents of a girl not to try once more for a boy.

When carrots failed, sticks were applied. Monetary fines, the so-called "social compensation fees," were the most widespread form of penalty for noncompliance. Fines were calculated as multiples of annual family disposable income and varied by locality. While steep, even these fines were often insufficient, since the income and family security a son would provide his parents over their lifetimes far exceeded even the stiffest fine then in place. Many farming households considered noncompliance and payment of the fine a wise investment in the family's future. That was also true of the rising upper middle class in China's cities. As is the case in so many areas of Chinese life, the collection of the social compensation fee provided an opportunity for corrupt behavior on the part of local officials, who encouraged multiple births and pocketed the fines.

Frustrated by the failure of incentives and penalties to reduce reproduction, local officials often used coercion, especially when their superiors assigned birth quotas and held them personally responsible for meeting them. Coercion ordinarily began with verbal harassment of noncompliant couples: women were urged to undergo sterilization, and pregnant women were urged to have abortions. Those who resisted were threatened. One recent account describes the work of a tough- minded local family planning official, identified only as "Mrs. Liao," who marched into a remote rural community in south- central China, lined up the village women, singled out those with the most children, and told them that unless they reported to the local clinic for sterilization, their houses would be "blown up." Mrs. Liao was not alone; there was fairly widespread evidence of the destruction of personal property in retaliation against those who ignored the one-child policy. In extreme cases, women were physically restrained and forced to undergo abortions or sterilizations against their will, though I have not found reliable evidence on which to base an estimate of how frequently this occurred. There is reason to believe that it was not common. Forcing a surgical procedure on an unwilling constituent might satisfy a superior and avoid a fine, but the local official had to live with the consequences, and given conditions in most rural communities, the last thing he was interested in was pushing his constituents to their limits.

For example, in 2007, seven towns in rural Guangxi erupted in violent protest against the imposition of heavy penalties in the case of multiple births. Some three thousand people "stormed government offices, overturned vehicles, burned documents, and confronted officials." These atrocities attracted unwelcome international attention, for forced abortions are repugnant not only to those for whom abortion under any circumstances is wrong but also to human rights activists, even when they might favor abortion undertaken as a free choice.

To avoid alienating both the rural population and the international community, China's population planning authorities relaxed the one-child policy where resistance was greatest. In fact, the policy had loopholes from the outset. Ethnic minorities had always been allowed a second child in the city and a third or even a fourth child in the countryside, on the theory that it is important to preserve their continuity as a group and because the areas they most frequently inhabit are China's least densely populated.

Eventually, the rural population as a whole was subject to a relaxed policy that, in practice, permitted one child when that child was a boy, two children when the first child was a girl or handicapped, and no third births. An exception was also made for families in which both parents were themselves single children. Parents of victims of the 2008 Sichuan earthquake were also permitted to waive the one-child rule. In a 1994 survey of couples of childbearing age, 63 percent had a single child. Somewhat more than 25 percent had a second child, and only 10 percent had three or more children. Nationwide, the average family size in 2007 was just over three members.

As with many unpopular policies, for every method of enforcement the central and local governments put in place, those determined to violate the policy thought up a way of avoiding compliance. The most straightforward of these was simply to pay the fine for over quota births, treating the expenditure as an investment in the family's future. Since the object, in the case of many families, is to produce a male heir, what was done in the unwelcome event of a "small happiness"—the conception or birth of a female? As amniocentesis and sonograms have become more widely available, they have increasingly been used to identify the gender of fetuses. When a female is identified, many women choose to have an abortion. This use of amniocentesis and sonograms has recently been made a criminal offense, but enforcing this new law is difficult. Sonogram equipment, now manufactured in China, is widely available, and there is money to be made in offering the service. Violations are described as being "in greater numbers than ever."

Once a female child was born, the simplest way of avoiding having her count against the family's quota of children was to avoid recording her birth. The gradual relaxation of social control associated with the reforms and the possibility of going away from home to give birth made it easier to conceal births from those charged with limiting their number. The widespread incidence of this practice was revealed in the 1990 census, generally regarded as the most thorough ever conducted in China, when officials assured citizens that no retroactive penalties would be imposed on unregistered births. The census showed the Chinese population to stand at 1.13 billion, a figure that exceeded projections by some 13 million. Part of the discrepancy can be accounted for by statistical flaws in the projections, but most of it was due to the number of female children whose births had gone unrecorded.

Other methods of avoidance were more serious. Some parents decided to put girl babies up for adoption or, worse, to abandon them. The vast majority of children available for adoption in China or being raised in orphanages there are either girls or boys with handicaps. There were also stories of female infanticide, even some involving medical practitioners. When girl babies' lives were terminated at birth, the deliveries were recorded as stillbirths. Other stories describe instances where infanticide was committed by parents or family members desperate to avoid having the child count against the family's one- or two-child limit, though the Chinese press emphasized that infanticide is against the law in China and that cases were prosecuted wherever they were detected.

The cumulative effect of all these methods of avoidance was a marked skewing of the gender ratio among Chinese children. Whereas the worldwide ratio of male to female births is 106 males for every 100 females, the ratio in China rose to a disturbing 111 males for every 100 females in 1990; it currently stands at 110.8 boys per 100 girls and rises to as high as 115 to 100 in some rural areas. This resulted in there being 32 million more males than females under the age of twenty. Newspaper accounts describe the plight of unmarried Chinese men unable to find spouses because of the shortage of unmarried women. Among China's small but growing number of divorced people, the gender ratio is two males for each female. (The divorce rate exceeds 30 percent in China's largest cities.) Some suggest that the one-child policy was responsible, but it is actually too recent to have had this effect. The gender ratio for the cohort now of marriageable age is very close to the worldwide norm.

When all other methods of avoidance failed, rural Chinese had another option that they chose with increasing frequency: they could leave home and migrate to a city. Although most migrant workers are single males, there was also a significant number of couples who found a way of avoiding the sharp eyes and draconian penalties of the redoubtable "Mrs. Liao" and her family planning colleagues. Migrant workers, having severed ties with rural officials and not yet been picked up by urban ones, are reluctant to legitimize their presence in the city and are in something of a limbo so far as China's system of social control is concerned. Many rural couples took advantage of this to pursue their quest for sons.

A side effect of the gender imbalance in young people is the rise in human trafficking in the Chinese countryside. Boys, many of them the sons of migrant workers with shaky legal standing, are kidnapped and sold to rural households lacking male heirs. Girls, not especially valued members of their rural households, are bought or stolen and transported, some to urban factories, some to brothels, some as brides in male-predominant rural villages. The government's figures for human trafficking are two thousand five hundred cases per year, and for abduction, fifteen thousand cases per year. Human rights advocates contend the number may be as high as hundreds of thousands.

From the perspective of the central government, the one-child policy was solving China's most pressing problem. Officials estimated that without the policy in place, the Chinese population would have been between three and four hundred million larger. But from the perspective of local officials, the situation looked somewhat different. The one-child policy, even in its relaxed form, was highly unpopular among the rural population of childbearing age. To the extent that local officials aligned themselves with the central government and enforced the policy, they alienated themselves from their constituents; when they had to resort to coercion, that alienation only deepened. Moreover, because they needed to secure the compliance of their constituents on many issues besides birth control, they were reluctant to align themselves too closely with the central government's policy.

This was all the more true because they were less well qualified than their predecessors to enforce an unpopular policy. There was a substantial turnover of local officials in the 1980s, during the course of which older officeholders retired and were replaced by younger, less experienced ones. The number of women holding public office in rural communities also declined. Some of the most effective family planning workers at the local level had been older women, now retired, whose younger, male successors found it hard to take their place.

Economic reform in the countryside also altered the authority of local officials. Today, they are significantly less pervasive a presence than were the production team and brigade leaders they replaced. As the private realm has greatly expanded everywhere in China over the last twenty years, the government's ability to control individual behavior has declined. Confronted with this decline in efficacy and seeking to ensure stringent enforcement at the local level, the central government took to making local officials personally responsible for the success of the family planning program by docking salaries or fining them for over-quota births. Some officials responded positively to this pressure and resorted to coercion, but others avoided the problem by making false statistical reports to their superiors.

Yet another problem for local officials was that the one-child policy was such an expensive, unfunded mandate. Although the state claimed that nearly one billion dollars was spent annually on implementation of the birth control program, virtually all that money came from local governments, which, already pressed to meet other financial obligations, found themselves paradoxically funding the birth control program exclusively from fines levied against those who violate it.

Demographers use three figures when discussing change in the size of a population. The first is the *birthrate,* usually expressed in births per thousand people in the population as a whole. According to Chinese government statistics, the country's birthrate in 2007 was 12.1 per thousand. (As we will see, it has subsequently dropped to 10.5 per thousand.) The birthrate differs significantly between the urban and rural populations: the rural rate some years ago was close to 4 per thousand higher than the urban rate. The second figure is the *population growth rate,* the birth rate minus the death rate. The death rate in 2007 was 6.9 per thousand, while the population growth rate was 5.2 per thousand. Expressing that figure in a percentage (as is most frequently done), the 2007 population growth rate was 0.52 percent. The third figure is the *fertility rate,* the average number of children born to women of childbearing age. China's fertility rate in 2007 was 1.7.

During the year 2001, China's population passed 1.3 billion people. Were the Chinese population to have continued to grow at its 2000 rate, we could have expected that each year about sixteen million children would be born in China and about eight million Chinese would die, for a net increase of about eight million. With that net growth, the Chinese population would have passed 1.4 billion by 2010, but it failed to hit that figure. The population growth rate had begun to decline. China's efforts to slow the population growth rate were succeeding. The population growth rate began to decline in 2014, and the total population peaked at 1.41 billion in 2021.

Table 22: Population Growth, China and the United States 2024

	United States	**China**
Population	1.41 billion	342 million
Birthrate	6.77 /1,000	12.0/1,000
Mortality rate	7.8/1,000	9.2/1,000
Net migration rate	-0.9/1,000	12.8/1,000
Population growth rate	-0.00025	0.98
Fertility rate	1.2	1.8
Life expectancy	79.0 years	79.3 year
Median age	39.5 years	38.3 years

Source: Federal Reserve Bank of St. Louis (FRED) – World Bank Indicators

To bring its population problem under control, the Chinese government set a target birthrate of 13 per thousand, which the one-child policy, as it has been modified in practice over time, was designed to achieve. According to Chinese statistics, the target has been more than met. According to external statistics, it was met in 2003, and the birthrate has continued to decline in the ensuing years, now standing at 12 per thousand. One obstacle to maintaining a low birthrate over the short term is an unusually large number of women of childbearing age (between fifteen and forty-nine)---currently nearly 325 million, or roughly a quarter of China's total population.

Attempts to limit the Chinese population growth were slow in coming, largely because of Mao Zedong's views on the subject. Although he was known to express concern about the ratio of people to arable land, it was his general view that a large population was a national asset; he thought of every person added as two more hands whose work would contribute to national development and defense. For the first twenty years of the People's Republic, no effort was made to restrict births, and the birthrate was well over thirty per thousand (except during the years of recovery from the Great Leap Forward).

Zhou Enlai took a different approach. He came to believe that controlling population growth was a prerequisite to economic development, and he was responsible for initiating China's first national program to limit births in 1971, the goal being to reduce the birthrate to twenty per thousand by 1980. In practice, Zhou's program amounted to a two-child policy. The campaign's slogan was "Late, sparse, and few." Couples were encouraged to delay marrying until their late twenties, to space their children at least four years apart, and to limit themselves to two children. The campaign was a success. Although by no means was every family limiting itself to two children, the birthrate in 1980, at eighteen per thousand, had been reduced by a third in a ten-year period.

Despite this success, projections drawn up in 1978 suggested that the Chinese population would pass the one billion mark in 1980 and would reach 1.4 billion by 2000. (In fact, it did not pass the one billion mark until 1982 and only reached 1.4 billion in 2019.) Deng Xiaoping and his reformist colleagues shared Zhou's view that economic development could not proceed unless population growth was controlled, but they were alarmed by these projections and concluded that Zhou's gradualist approach to the population problem was insufficient. Out of their alarm was born the one-child policy. Although the policy was introduced in 1979, it wasn't until 2001 that the National People's Congress adopted the Law on Population and Birth Planning. The law delegated much of the responsibility for its implementation to provincial and local governments, which were responsible for setting and enforcing birth quotas. The law also laid out rewards for compliance and penalties for failure to comply. Family planning workers are enjoined to enforce the law "in a civilized manner."

Success in limiting births exacerbated another social issue in China. With fewer young people, the median age is rising, accelerating the already rapid "graying" of China. In the 2007 census sample, the retired-age population numbered 260 million, or just over 20 percent of the population; it is estimated that by 2050, there will be more than 430 million retirees, more than a third of the population. Whereas today there is one retired person for every six people of working age, by 2050, that ratio will be very close to 1:1. We are familiar with the problem because of the debates over the funding of the social security system in our own country. Our retired age population is currently 12.5 percent of the total; that figure will grow to 20 percent by 2050. Today, we have five people in the workforce supporting each retiree. In 2050, that number will be reduced to three. China today also has about five workers for each retiree. By 2050, the number will be below two.

There are two issues complicating the situation of retirees in China. First, the retirement ages are much lower there than elsewhere in the world. For blue-collar workers, the mandatory retirement age for females is fifty, and for males it is fifty-five; for professionals, the retirement age for females is fifty-five, and for males it is sixty. Obviously, a quick solution to the problem of the shrinking ratio of employed to retirees would be to raise these mandatory retirement ages. But as we have seen, China is already struggling to find employment for those entering the workforce each year. As a result, there is no current plan to adjust upward the mandatory retirement age.

The second issue is the lack of a publicly funded safety net for the vast majority of retirees in China. Most rural residents never had and do not now have pension plans. Workers in state-owned enterprises had generous pension plans, but with the collapse of the state sector, most are left with minimal or no support in retirement. Mindful of this problem, the State Council established a national social security fund directly under its administration. Government employees and employees of the remaining state-owned enterprises are eligible to participate in this fund, and in 2003, the total number of workers covered was 116 million, or somewhat less than half the urban workforce. Writing about the nascent social security system in 2007, an American economist described it as "very much a work in progress." (Of course, it didn't help that in 2006, a government audit found that more than $900 million had been misappropriated from the $37 billion social security fund.) Not only that, but the other half of the urban workforce, like their rural compatriots, have no pension provisions at all. The government's proposed solution is to expand the program while requiring employer and employee contributions. But this solution, as we are beginning to understand in the United States, postpones but does not resolve the issue.

Family planning policy in China since the early 1970s has been based on the premise that economic growth cannot occur until population growth has been brought under control. Some argue, however, that population growth can be brought under control only when economic growth has occurred. The experience of other developing countries has shown that two factors associated with economic development–urbanization and education–result in decreased fertility, and observers mark that this is true in China as well, that is, in Chinese cities. Along this line of reasoning, revisionists argue that the one-child policy. did not significantly change the population growth rate in China, and a more relaxed policy would have achieved about the same results and avoided the widespread anger and disaffection brought on by the attempt to enforce such a stringent program.

The one-child policy touched very sensitive nerves among foreign, particularly American, observers. Any policy that interferes with personal decisions regarding childbearing is, for some, a violation of human rights, for others, not only a violation of human rights but also a sin. Still others found the one-child policy acceptable but were disturbed by enforcement measures that violated human rights.

In the fall of 1994, the Chinese government released its newly drafted Maternal and Infantile Health Care Law, initially publicized as a "eugenics law," since it addressed the problem of the ten million people in China with birth defects that, in the words of the law, "could have been prevented." The new law called for sterilizing the mentally ill and aborting the fetuses of those suffering from hereditary diseases or abnormalities. The Chinese government seemed genuinely surprised and nonplussed by the storm of criticism from abroad, and its response was not to repeal the law but to avoid using the term "eugenics" when discussing it and to emphasize the provisions for ensuring informed consent on the part of those affected by it. Eugenic provisions of the law were reaffirmed in the 2001 Law on Population and Birth Planning.

The Chinese claimed that concern over reproductive rights, like certain environmental issues, is a luxury of the rich and less populous nations of the world and contended that the magnitude of China's population problem is such that honoring individual rights with respect to reproduction endangers the rights of society as a whole. While deploring the excesses that they consider unintended consequences of their policy, they claimed that extraordinary measures are necessary for China to continue to feed and clothe its population.

Two circumstances led to the party-state's reversing course regarding family planning. First, it became increasingly clear that the policy was unpopular. Xie Yu, head of Princeton University's Center on Contemporary China, commented that "Many Chinese people have considered the one-child policy a violation of their basic human rights, and they don't like the government depriving them of their individual reproductive rights. I think the change of policy will be appreciated by most people in China." True enough, but the party-state has no history of responding to adverse public opinion. More significantly, it became clear that the growth of the Chinese population was slowing and eventually, in 2020, it would begin to shrink.

Accordingly, the party-state, now firmly under the control of Xi Jinping, began what became a four-stage process of extricating itself from the business of population control. In the first stage, in March 2013, the National Population and Family Planning Commission and the Ministry of Health created a new National Health and Family Planning Commission (*Guojia Weisheng he Jihua Shengyu Weiyuanhui* 国家卫生和计划生育委员会. Eight months later, the Commission was merged into the newly created National Health Commission (NHC– *Guojia Weisheng Jiankang Weiyuanhui* 国家卫生健康委员会). The NHC announced a second stage, a partial policy relaxation that allowed couples to have two children if one parent is an only child. Somewhat surprisingly, only about 15% of eligible couples took advantage of the policy relaxation.

A third stage was announced in October 2015 when the policy was amended to allow all couples to have two children. The final stage came six years later, when the Standing Committee of the NPC and the Central Committee of the CCP issued the "Decision on Improving the Birth Policy to Promote Long-Term and Balanced Population Development." Effective immediately, the new law allowed married couples to have three children. It also abolished the expensive "social compensation fee" that had been levied against couples who exceeded the birth limit under the previous law.

It remains to be seen whether the revised policy will succeed in stemming the reduction of the Chinese population and end the undermining of the already tenuous authority of local governments. As it turns out, Zhou Enlai's simple policy of "late, sparse, and few" may have been right all along.

Perhaps the episode suggests that we are witnessing something largely unprecedented. In Xi Jinping, we might be dealing with a leader who learns from his own and others' mistakes—a pragmatic ideologue. In "seeking truth from facts," Xi was thus following in the footsteps not only of Deng Xiaoping but also those of American pragmatist John Dewey. They were certainly not the footsteps of Mao Zedong (nor, for that matter, those of Donald Trump).

Chapter 19: Taiwan

Taiwan is an island of about 4,000 square miles in size. Sparsely inhabited by a population of Malay-Polynesian ethnic origin, Taiwan was "discovered" during the sixteenth and seventeenth centuries by Portuguese explorers, who named it *Ilha Formosa* (beautiful island). In 1624, the southern part of the island was colonized by the Netherlands, and two years later, the northern part was colonized by Spain.

With the collapse of the Ming dynasty in 1644, loyalists to the fallen house, pursued by Manchu forces, retreated across the Taiwan Strait. In 1662, the Dutch and Spaniards were driven out by the Chinese warlord Zheng Chenggong (鄭成功), better known by his title, Koxinga (*Guoxingye* 國姓爺 lit. "Lord with a Royal Surname"). Koxinga continued in power for twenty years, after which the Chinese emperor asserted his control of the island. Qing dynasty forces finally brought Taiwan under their control, and it was placed under the administration of the governor of Fujian, where it remained for two hundred years. That control of the island population was something less than wholly effective is attested to by a Taiwanese saying, "Small rebellions every three years, big ones every five." Only in 1885 did Taiwan gain its own provincial administration, and that was short-lived.

Ten years later, following China's defeat in the Sino-Japanese War of 1894-95, Taiwan was ceded in perpetuity to Japan. It remained under Japanese control for the next fifty years, administered as an agricultural colony, its principal crop being sugarcane. Japanese was adopted as its official language and was taught in the schools. Gradually, if reluctantly, Taiwan's culture began to grow away from that of mainland China under the influence of its Japanese rulers.

At the Cairo Conference in December 1943, the Allied powers agreed that Taiwan would be returned to Chinese sovereignty after the defeat of Japan. After World War II ended, it returned to the control of the Republic of China. Nationalist forces received the surrender of Japan on the island, and Taiwan began once again to be administered as a province of China, this time under the Nationalist government based in Nanjing. But on 28 February 1947, less than two years later, the local population revolted against the Nationalist forces occupying the island. The Nationalist government brutally suppressed this uprising, with the loss of many lives, and declared martial law, which was not lifted for forty years. Taiwan remained under ROC control for four years, after which the ROC government retreated to Taiwan in 1949 after the victory of the Chinese Communist Party on the mainland.

In much the same fashion as the Ming loyalists who, pursued by Manchus, had fled to Taiwan in 1644, about two million Nationalist loyalists, pursued by the Red Army, fled to Taiwan and set up residence on the island. The population of Taiwan today includes the result of these two retreats. Descendants of the seventeenth-century influx, often referred to as "the Taiwanese," make up about 85 percent of the population; the survivors and descendants of the twentieth-century influx, called "mainlanders," make up the remaining 15 percent. A very small number of the Aboriginal population remains, amounting to less than 1 percent of the total.

Taiwan is nominally a province of China, though the government on the island still calls itself the Republic of China and, until very recently, claimed sovereignty over all of China in addition to ruling the island of Taiwan, that government exercises sovereignty over three other tiny island chains: Penghu (澎湖), in the Taiwan Strait about 40 miles off the coast of Taiwan; Matsu

(Mazu 馬祖), just a few miles off the coast of the mainland near the city of Fuzhou (福州); and Quemoy (Jinmen 金門), even closer to shore near the city of Xiamen.

A little smaller than the state of Connecticut, Taiwan has a population of 23.6 million, about seven times that of Connecticut. The people of Taiwan enjoy a *per capita* gross national product of about $32,500, which is fourth in Asia after Singapore, Hong Kong, and Japan, and about 1.3 times the figure for mainland China. Its economy, now the world's fourteenth largest, is growing at less than one percent per year; inflation stands at less than three percent.

The question of the relationship between the government in Taiwan and the government in Beijing, unresolved for seventy-five years, is a source of friction in both governments' relations with the United States. In the spring of 1996, and again as the millennium began, it became a potential flash point that had many of China's East Asian neighbors concerned.

Those who believe that Taiwan should be unified with the mainland begin their argument by asserting that "Taiwan has always been an integral part of China." As we have seen, despite the frequency with which it is repeated, the statement is a myth, not a fact, and reminds one of similar assertions about Tibet. Only during the decade 1885-95 and in the four years immediately after the end of World War II was Taiwan governed as a province of China. At all other times, Taiwan has been largely independent of the control of a mainland Chinese government.

A kind of *modus vivendi* was established in Taiwan in the years following the arrival of the mainlanders. Politics, the professions, and the armed forces were controlled by mainlanders; the economy was dominated by the Taiwanese. The political system, a highly authoritarian one based on a constitution adopted by the

Nationalist forces when their Republic of China was still on the mainland, included a National Assembly and a legislature composed of representatives elected on the mainland in 1947.

The United States did not at first intend to protect Nationalist forces in Taiwan against attack from the Communist regime on the mainland. The United States did not recognize the government in Beijing, instead tacitly supporting the Nationalists' claim to be the rightful government of China. The outbreak of war on the Korean peninsula altered that policy militarily, and the U.S. Seventh Fleet was ordered to begin patrolling the Taiwan Strait, and a mutual defense treaty was signed. During the 1950s, the United States contributed some $2 billion in economic and military aid to Taiwan's postwar economic recovery and became deeply involved in the relationship between Taiwan and the mainland. Despite its best efforts to extricate itself, it remains deeply involved today. Since the founding of the PRC, reunification with Taiwan—peaceful, if possible, by force if necessary—has been an invariable and high-priority policy for the party-state in Beijing. While it could be argued that China would stand to lose economically because of reunification, as with many other issues concerning the outside world, Beijing is driven by its conception of national sovereignty and its determination to gain face and avoid losing it.

Were economic logic to govern Beijing's position in Taiwan, it would dictate maintaining the *status quo*. Taiwan is now the fourth-largest supplier of external direct investment to China, and there is a substantial two-way trade between them. It is unlikely that economic interaction could improve with reunification; indeed, there is a strong likelihood that it could deteriorate. As with Hong Kong, even if the Chinese government wanted to keep its promise to leave the capitalist system in Taiwan intact for fifty years after reunification, the likelihood that it could do so is slim. Authorities in Beijing have limited experience in allowing a capitalist system to function without excessive regulation, and the situation in Taiwan, like that in Hong Kong, is far too sensitive for the authorities to let well enough alone.

But why is the Chinese concept of national sovereignty at stake? The senior leaders in Beijing believe their own myths: they believe that Taiwan has always been an integral part of China, and that national sovereignty will be incomplete until they control the province. At one time it seemed only a handful of the oldest leaders in China took this hardline position, and it was hoped that once they departed the political stage, younger successors would adopt a more flexible view, but the armed forces have weighed in decisively on the side of early reunification, and the politicians who depend on the support of the PLA find that they cannot be flexible with respect to Taiwan. Moreover, the party-state's revival of Chinese nationalism in recent years has significantly increased the number of Chinese people of all ages for whom Taiwan is a hot-button issue.

Loss of face is a concern with respect to Taiwan in several ways. First is the long-standing conflict between Chinese Communists and Nationalists, a conflict only very recently finally declared at an end when then-Nationalist Party leader Lien Chan (连战) met with Hu Jintao in Beijing in 2005. Until that point, for the older generation in China, the revolution would be completed and face regained only when Taiwan was "liberated" from Nationalist hands. But there is also a link between reunification with Taiwan and regaining sovereignty over Hong Kong, since the "one country, two systems" arrangement negotiated with Britain for the future of Hong Kong was seen as a model for a future relationship with Taiwan. Taiwan also involves a potential loss or gain of face *vis-a-vis* the United States. Given recent history, Beijing refuses to believe that the United States can be a neutral party in the resolution of this issue, and its leaders are confirmed in their views by the public statements of many influential Americans who feel strongly that it would be wrong for the United States to be neutral: were the Chinese government to retreat from its policy on reunification, then, it would be seen as a serious loss of face to the Americans.

Yet Beijing's unequivocal and public policy in Taiwan, reaffirmed so strongly in recent years, has only escalated the intensity of the conflict. Beijing believed that Lee Teng-hui (李登辉), the former president of the government in Taiwan, was moving in the direction of independence. To discourage him from taking those steps and, at the same time, to discourage Taiwan's voters from re-electing him in March 1996, the PLA engaged in provocative military exercises, with live shells and missiles fired into the East China Sea near the coast of Taiwan.

Four years later, the situation deteriorated still further from Beijing's perspective with the election of Chen Shui-bian as Lee's successor. Chen ran as the candidate of the Democratic Progressive Party (DPP–*Minzhu Jinbu Dang* 民主进步党), whose platform's principal plank for many years had been Taiwan independence. Although Beijing refrained from engaging in military action (perhaps having learned that it was counter productive), it reasserted its intention to respond to a declaration of independence with military force. Under these circumstances, to effect reunification on mainland terms is to gain face; to accept any other arrangement is to lose face.

With this saber-rattling, the Chinese government was close to coming full circle. Thwarted in its initial effort in 1949 to cross the Taiwan Strait in pursuit of the defeated Nationalist forces, it set as a goal the eventual liberation of the island by force. China acted on this policy in 1954 and again in 1958, but it overestimated the sup-port it would receive from its Soviet allies and underestimated

American support for the Nationalists. When, in 1971, Mao decided to bring about a rapprochement with the United States, a move designed to intimidate the now wary Soviet Union, the policy toward Taiwan became that of promoting "peaceful reunification." In response, the American government "acknowledged" (the Chinese translation of the Shanghai Communique on this subject read "recognized") that "all Chinese on either side of the Taiwan Strait maintain that there is but one China and that Taiwan is a part of China." The use of force was never renounced entirely but was now seen as a backup, not a first step.

This new policy (and, by implication, the Shanghai Communique itself) was based on a second enduring myth about Taiwan, which has it that the vast majority of the people of Taiwan, as contrasted with the tiny handful of their reactionary leaders, harbor a deep desire to be governed as part of the PRC. Countless opinion polls taken in Taiwan suggest that the reverse is the case: it is only a tiny handful, not the vast majority, who favor reunification, and these opinion polls were borne out in the presidential elections of 2000 and 2004 in which the independence candidate won and was returned to office (if, in the second instance, by a vanishingly thin margin). But this has done nothing to dispel the myth.

Taiwan's former president Lee Teng-hui received his Ph.D. in agricultural economics from Cornell University in 1968. When he made a controversial visit to Cornell in the summer of 1995, the American media totally ignored one of the most stunning political transformations of the postwar period: although the Nationalists remained in power in Taiwan, the political system they controlled had been, during the previous decade, transformed from a highly authoritarian one-party state to a vibrant multiparty democracy.

Chinese culture and democracy, said to be the oil and water of political practice, turned out to be a viable mixture after all.

The rough-and-tumble of Taiwan politics, with its vociferous and often disrespectful opposition, has given rise to frequent fistfights in the legislature and occasional violent street demonstrations. It is a political style that belies several common assumptions about Chinese culture, such as its preference for harmony over chaos and its reverence for the elderly, and it elicits disdain from the starched and buttoned-down Singaporean Chinese. No doubt it also sends chills down Communist spines in Beijing.

Among the forces that led to this startling change, three stand out. The first is the person of Chiang Ching-kuo (蒋经国) himself. Son of Chiang Kai-shek, Ching-kuo was stricken with leukemia in the 1980s and given only a few years to live. He devoted himself to accomplishing two goals: democratizing Taiwan's political system and opening up contact with the mainland.

Chiang took the first step toward liberalizing his government in 1985, when he selected a Taiwanese rather than a mainland as his vice-presidential running mate: Lee Teng-hui, the American-educated agronomist who had made his career in Nationalist Party politics. The second step came the following year. Opposition parties had been outlawed in Taiwan, and opposition politicians campaigned as individuals (collectively known as *dangwai,* meaning "outside the [Nationalist] party"). In 1986, when the *dangwai* politicians organized themselves into a new opposition party, the Democratic Progressive Party (DPP) and campaigned on a party ticket, Chiang Ching-kuo decided not to prosecute them and not to disband their party, but, rather, to repeal the law that banned opposition parties.

The third step came a year later when he lifted the martial law that had been in effect in Taiwan since 1947. With this move, political rights guaranteed in the constitution but suspended by martial law were restored to the citizens of Taiwan. His fourth and final step was taken in October 1987, when he lifted the ban on traveling to mainland China. Initial visits were made under the guise of being merely *tanqin* (探亲, visits to relatives), but soon the regulations were very liberally interpreted, and many Taiwanese went to China to observe, to sightsee, and ultimately to begin to do business. Chiang died the following year, having accomplished his goals and having put his legacy in place.

Another force that helped transform Taiwan's political system was the courage and persistence of the *dangwai* politicians who, against all odds, brought about this political awakening. Harassed, beaten, imprisoned, and exiled by the authoritarian Nationalist government, they had persevered in their determination to be heard. Although Chiang's decisions were critically important, it is unlikely that he would have made them or that they alone would have had the effect they eventually did were it not for the boldness of the opposition.

Finally, a third force was the mainland government's calculated guess that the impending change of sovereignty in Hong Kong would help make Taiwan more flexible about the reunification issue. When the Joint Declaration on Hong Kong was released in 1984, and the Taiwan government's initial reaction was to say that, given its terms, the policy of no contact would apply to Hong Kong as well after 1997, Taiwan businessmen immediately responded that this was not acceptable. Contact with Hong Kong was critical to their businesses and thus to the economic health of Taiwan. The government would have to come up with a new and more flexible policy; Beijing's goad had proved successful.

Liberalizing the political system in Taiwan involved four related processes: bringing the Taiwanese majority into full political participation, legalizing a political opposition, reconstituting the government, and opening relations with the mainland.

Lee Teng-hui's election by the National Assembly as Chiang's vice president had been the culmination of a long, slow "Taiwanization" of the Nationalist Party and government. The informal division of labor between the Taiwanese majority and the mainlander minority in 1949 had largely excluded Taiwanese from politics, but over the years, Taiwanese were actively recruited for Nationalist Party membership and gradually rose to positions of leadership. Chiang's selection of Lee was taken by his mainland senior colleagues to be no more than a symbolic gesture, but to their surprise, Lee not only succeeded to the presidency upon Chiang's death but also was appointed head of the Nationalist Party. Very shortly thereafter, he was elected by the National Assembly to his own term as president, though mainlanders brought all their forces to bear against this happening, even enlisting the support of the elderly but determined Madame Chiang Kai-shek, who returned to Taiwan from her home in New York to lobby in favor of a mainlander. Their failure marked the real completion of the process of Taiwanization. Today, more than three-quarters of the Nationalist Party are Taiwanese, and they have held virtually all the leading positions in the party and, except for the 2000-08 and 2016-2024 interregnums, the government.

In the office, Lee kept to the policies of his predecessor. In legislative elections in 1991, the DPP adopted a platform plank that called for Taiwanese independence: advocating independence violates Taiwan law, and some demanded that the president arrest the leaders of the DPP and strip the party of its legal status. He refused to do so.

Reconstituting the Taiwan government was more difficult. The legitimacy of the government's claim to sovereignty over all China rested on the fact that the legislature and the National Assembly were initially made up of representatives of all of China's provinces, elected to office prior to the Nationalists' departure from the mainland. Almost fifty years later, though, these representatives were aged, ill, and infirm; supplementary elections held to increase the number of representatives from Taiwan were only a partial solution to the problem.

Shortly after he took office as president, Lee inaugurated discussions about reconstitution, and the government began a series of steps to alter the political system to conform to contemporary reality. A new, smaller National Assembly was elected in 1991. The following year, elderly legislators were forced to retire, and elections were held for the posts they vacated. In 1993 and 1994, local elections were held for once-appointed mayors and other officials. In December 1994, mayoral elections were held in Taiwan's two largest cities, Taipei (台北) and Kaohsiung (高雄), and a gubernatorial election was held for the province of Taiwan. The final stage of the process was the March 1996 election, in which the president was directly elected for the first time.

Through this process, the DPP gradually strengthened its position, and a number of new political parties emerged. When the DPP campaigned on a platform of Taiwanese independence, it tended to lose support but otherwise garnered about a third of the vote. Its support was mostly in the cities; it did not fare particularly well in small-town and rural elections.

Table 23. Results of Presidential Elections in Taiwan (%)

Date	Nationalist Party	Democratic Progressive Party	Other Parties	Elected
1996	54	21	25	Lee Teng-hui
2000	24	39	37	Chen Shui-bian
2004	49.9	50.1	32	Chen Shui-bian
2008	58	41	1	Ma Ying-jeou
2012	52	45	3	Ma Ying-jeou
2016	331	56	13	Tsai Ying-wen
2020	39	57	4	Tsai Ying-wen
2024	33	40	27	Lai Ching-te

Source: Wikipedia Commons

In the December 1994 elections, Nationalist candidates were elected to office as governor of Taiwan and mayor of the large southern city of Kaohsiung. The DPP candidate, Chen Shui-bian, won the election for the mayor of Taipei, in which position he sat *ex officio* in the cabinet of the national government, the first opposition politician to do so.

In 1991, though the Three Noes policy was technically still in force, President Lee put forward a proposal for a three-stage process of reunification with the mainland. The first stage had already begun, with the informal contacts initiated by Chiang Ching-kuo in 1987. According to Lee's plan, this stage would feature a policy he called "flexible diplomacy" to break the international isolation imposed in Taiwan by China's insistence that any government recognizing Beijing sever its ties with Taiwan.

Stage two in Lee's reunification plan would move the two sides from informal to formal state-to-state communications. This stage would require that China continue its economic reforms, renounce the use of force as a means of effecting reunification, and accept the government in Taiwan on an equal standing and as entitled to recognition in the world community. In the third, and final, stage, the two sides would engage in "long-term consultation and unification."

Informal contacts between the two sides resulted in substantial economic ties between Taiwan and China. In 2024, nearly three million Taiwan citizens visited China, and 750,000 have permanent residences on the mainland. As a result of recent negotiations, the daily cap on visits to Taiwan by citizens of China has been raised to 2,000. Taiwan investors have put more than $206 billion into mainland enterprises (most of them in Guangdong and Fujian provinces), and whole industries in Taiwan, such as shoe manufacturing, have moved their plants to China in search of inexpensive real estate and labor. Cross-strait two-way trade is now more than $166 billion each year, with a large trade surplus for Taiwan.

In 1993, Prime Minister Lien Chan of Taiwan proposed moving to the second stage of Lee Teng-hui's reunification process, though the preconditions laid down earlier had not been met. Still, some form of legal protection was needed for Taiwan's substantial mainland investments. A first step in this direction occurred at a meeting in Singapore in April 1993 between the heads of "unofficial" organizations set up by the two governments. Taiwan's Strait Exchange Foundation (SEF) and China's Association for Relations Across the Taiwan Strait (ARATS) followed up this initial Singapore meeting with subsequent meetings in Beijing and Taipei.

The talks were interrupted twice: once by Taiwan, after a group of Taiwanese tourists were robbed and murdered on a pleasure boat in Qiandao Lake (千岛湖) in Zhejiang Province, and the Taiwanese complained that the Chinese had engaged in a clumsy attempt to cover up the crime. The second time, they were interrupted by Beijing in protest against Lee Teng-hui's June 1995 visit to the United States. The two sides differed on what should be included on the agenda, in any case. The SEF had authority to discuss only economic and social matters; ARATS's mandate called for it to introduce political issues. Through 1999, the two sides negotiated an agreement on the return of hijacked aircraft, procedures for dealing with illegal immigrants, and a settlement of fishing rights in the Taiwan Strait.

The authorities in Beijing pushed to make the cross-strait talks between the SEF and ARATS more substantive with respect to political issues, but Beijing was unequivocal in its denunciation of the opposition DPP and its advocacy of Taiwan independence—particularly as DPP candidates began to capture major posts in the government and more seats in the legislature. A far greater threat from Beijing's perspective, however, was that the Nationalist Party, now firmly under the control of the Taiwanese majority, might pursue a policy of *de facto* independence. This threat elicited from the Chinese a strident response, which included conducting military exercises and weapons tests off the Taiwan coast. But Beijing's policy to intimidate Taiwanese voters backfired badly, only underscoring its *naïveté* in dealings with those whom it considers compatriots.

In the fall of 1998, Koo Chen-fu, chairman of the SEF, and Wang Daohan, chairman of ARATS, met in Shanghai; Koo subsequently met with Jiang Zemin in Beijing. The two sides agreed that Wang would go to Taiwan "at an appropriate time" and that cross-strait talks would resume on political and economic issues. This progress made it all the more startling when, the following year—near the end of his four-year term—Lee used the occasion of an interview recorded in early July for broadcast in Germany to assert that any further discourse across the Taiwan Strait must be conducted on a "state-to-state" basis. Accordingly, relations between the SEF and ARATS broke off in 1999. As we shall see, negotiations between the two organizations eventually resumed in 2008.

Meanwhile, Lee Teng-hui actively pursued his policy of flexible diplomacy to secure some form of recognition for the government in Taiwan beyond the 23 nations with which it then had diplomatic relations—a number that has subsequently dropped to 13. Adopting a plank from the opposition party's platform, his government also sought to return to membership in the United Nations, a position it lost in 1971, when the Chinese seat was taken from it and given to the mainland government. Flexible diplomacy made for a busy travel schedule, as Lee paid formal visits to the nations that still recognized his government and informal visits to others, and worked closely with a group of UN member states that, each year since 1993, have proposed that the issue of Taiwan's representation be added to the agenda of the General Assembly. In conducting this campaign, Lee formally abandoned his predecessors' fiction that the government in Taiwan speaks for the whole of China. Countering the "one country, two systems" formula, Lee used the phrase "one country, two governments," suggesting analogies with Germany and Korea. Although Taiwan has applied for UN membership seventeen times over the last seventeen years and has been turned down on every occasion, a small breakthrough occurred in 2009, when China agreed to an arrangement whereby a delegation from Taiwan attended the World Health Organization's annual conference under the name "Chinese Taipei."

Lee and the Nationalist Party for which he spoke continued to reject independence and to support reunification, but his articulation of this position was not unequivocal. He described his position as "conditional rejection" of the opposition's pro-independence stance, but mainland authorities were skeptical of the firmness of his pro-reunification stance.

Because they have benefited so much from economic ties with Taiwan, the mainland authorities have enthusiastically supported them. And there is a group of influential individuals in Taiwan who have a vested interest in maintaining good cross-strait ties. It is even possible that the Taiwan economy could become dependent on them for its continued health and growth. Indeed, shortly after his election in 1996, President Lee called for voluntary limits in Taiwan's investments on the mainland. He suggested that no more than 30 percent of Taiwan's total overseas investment be placed in China and that investments in China amount to no more than a fifth of any Taiwan firm's domestic investments. The Chinese denounced Lee's limits as creating obstacles to the free operation of market forces.

Beijing finds the policy of flexible diplomacy especially aggravating. That foreign governments should accord Taiwan or its representatives respect as anything other than a province of China is absolutely unacceptable. The applications of Taiwan and China to join the World Trade Organization were especially contentious. Applying under the name of the Customs Territory of Taiwan, Penghu, Jinmen, and Matsu, Taiwan pressed to be first, and of course, Beijing also insisted on being approved first so that it could have a voice in deciding the terms under which Taiwan was admitted. In the end, China was admitted to membership in the WTO on 11 December 2001. Taiwan followed on 1 January 2002.

Successive American administrations since 1972 have taken the position that relations between Taiwan and the mainland can be settled only by the two sides themselves, a hands-off policy that a substantial group in the U.S. Congress has from the outset found unacceptable. With the congressional elections in 1994, Taiwan's supporters were able to muster a majority—in some cases, near unanimity—on questions affecting Taiwan, but Beijing was unsympathetic to the Clinton administration's protestations that its freedom to maneuver was severely limited by Congress.

Cross-strait relations reached a low point during the period between President Lee's visit to the United States in the summer of 1995 and his election to the presidency in March 1996. China's leaders appeared to believe that, despite his statements to the contrary, Lee was a closet advocate of independence for Taiwan, and they found the contrast between the rapid expansion of democracy in Taiwan and their own hardening resistance to political liberalization highly distasteful and potentially embarrassing. As a result, Beijing actively worked to bring about Lee's defeat in the presidential election or at least to cut the size of his majority.

The official press carried blistering denunciations of him. More alarming, the PLA dropped hints to an American visitor to Beijing in December 1995 that should Lee be elected, it would conduct daily missile strikes on the island for thirty days. Fueling the rumors, the PLA moved more than 150,000 troops into Fujian

Province, opposite Taiwan, in late February 1996 and began a series of missile test firings into the Taiwan Strait in early March. A week later a series of war games involving the use of live ammunition in a large sector of the strait northwest of the island was announced. The sites of these exercises were chosen to cause disruption in the sea lanes used for shipping in and out of Taiwan's major ports and to demonstrate China's capability to interrupt the island's maritime commerce. What was particularly disturbing about these measures was that the PLA seemed to be calling the shots with very little interference from civilian authorities.

The general reaction among the Taiwan population was the opposite of that anticipated by Beijing. Although Taiwan's stock market fluctuated even more wildly than usual and there were some who laid in large supplies of rice and other staples, support remained strong for Lee and even for those advocating a more extreme anti-Chinese position than he did. The U.S. government, though it did not take seriously the threat of actual attack in Taiwan, denounced the military exercises as "unnecessarily provocative and reckless," moved a carrier group into the vicinity of the island, and agreed to the sale to Taiwan of Stinger air defense missiles, advanced targeting and navigating systems for jet aircraft, and three hundred additional M60-A3 tanks. In the Taiwan Relations Act, passed by Congress at the time of normalization of relations with Beijing, the United States agreed to "provide Taiwan with arms of a defensive character." Beijing of course believes that any sale of arms to Taiwan that strengthens its ability to resist China's use of force to accomplish reunification is unacceptable.

In the event, more than three-quarters of those eligible participated in the first direct election for the chief executive, giving Lee and Lien Chan, his vice-presidential running mate, 54 percent of the vote.

Of particular concern in Taiwan, beginning in the spring of 1997, was the public sense that crime was careening out of control and the government wasn't dealing with it. In May the legislature, citing an 18 percent rise in the crime rate and three high-profile murder cases that remained unsolved, attempted a no-confidence vote. Meanwhile, in the streets of Taipei, fifty thousand marched in protest against the government's apparent impotence in dealing with the surge in crime. A fortnight later New Party delegates interrupted Lee Teng-hui when he tried to address the National Assembly, demanding that he publicly apologize for the rapid decline in public order. Simultaneously, Ma Ying-jeou, the highly respected, Harvard-educated former justice minister in the national government, resigned from the cabinet, calling for the vice president to resign from his concurrent appointment as prime minister. Lien did resign during the summer and was replaced by Vincent Siew, but few seemed satisfied that the government had effectively dealt with the breakdown of public order.

In November 1997 and again in January 1998 popular dissatisfaction with the ruling party was manifested in local elections, in which the Nationalist Party continued to take a declining share of the vote. The stakes were much higher, however, in elections held in December 1998 for the Legislative Yuan and mayors' offices in the island's large cities. DPP candidate Chen Shui-bian, in one of his party's most important election victories, had won the Taipei slot four years earlier, as we have seen. The Nationalists found in Ma Ying-jeou a highly personable and ethical candidate who campaigned not only on issues of national policy but also on opposition to Chen's term as mayor, a term marked, Ma argued, by inefficiency and corruption.

Finding himself seriously threatened by Ma, Chen played the mainlander card during his campaign. Chen identifies himself as Taiwanese; although born in Hong Kong, Ma's family is counted among the mainlanders. With the support of President Lee, Ma claimed identity as a "new Taiwanese," observing during his campaign that after all, "I eat Taiwanese food. I drink Taiwanese water." Lee endorsed him as "the boy next door." In the end, Ma narrowly defeated Chen with 51 percent of the votes cast in an election that attracted close to 80 percent of eligible voters. It was not the last time Ma was to succeed Chen to office.

In the national legislative elections, the Nationalists took 124, or 55 percent of the 225 contested seats, up from 52 percent in the 1995 elections. The DPP's share of votes declined to 30 percent from 33 percent in 1995, and although it gained 16 seats to hold 70 of the total 225 seats, its percentage of seats declined from 33 percent to 31 percent, because the size of the legislature had been increased. The vote was appropriately interpreted as a major victory for the Nationalists, reversing their decline; nonetheless, it freed the popular Chen Shui-bian to run as a candidate for president in the national elections scheduled for 2000.

Lee's 1999 statement that any further cross-strait deliberations should be conducted on a state-to-state basis sharply clarified and radically altered the very ambiguous fictions that, as we have seen, had characterized the dialogue. Lee's confrontational move was initially interpreted as being motivated by an interest in bolstering the Nationalist Party's chances in the upcoming presidential election by shifting its position closer to that of the DPP. But Lee's move may have had less to do with domestic politics than with the triangular relationship among Taipei, Beijing, and Washington. American policy was laid out, as we have seen, in the Shanghai Communique of 1972, but after the serious glitch following Lee's visit to Cornell in 1995, the 1972 policy was subtly but importantly modified. In a 1995 letter to Jiang Zemin and then in public remarks during his visit to China in 1998, President Clinton claimed to "clarify our Taiwan policy, which is that we don't support independence for Taiwan, or two Chinas, or one Taiwan/one China." What was "acknowledged" in 1972 as the Chinese and Taiwanese position had, twenty-six years later, become the American position.

This American "Three Noes" policy, as authorities in Taiwan referred to it, was followed in the spring of 1999 by Assistant Secretary of State Stanley Roth's calling for "interim agreements...on any number of topics" between China and Taiwan. This was interpreted in Taipei as pressure to negotiate with Beijing. The Taiwan authorities also found it disturbingly reminiscent of a proposal made in Taipei by Kenneth Lieberthal, director of East Asia policy at the National Security Council. He had called for an "interim arrangement" in which the governments in Taipei and Beijing would agree to the concept of "one China" but would delay actual reunification for fifty years. Taiwan authorities thought this was tantamount to an endorsement of Beijing's "one country, two systems" solution. Indeed, in June, Roth reiterated his call for "technical agreements" on "significant issues." When, two weeks later, Lee put forward his "state-to-state" proviso to any further cross-strait talks, he might well have been responding to what he perceived as American pressure to accept China's terms for reunification.

Whatever Taiwan's motivation, the response from China was immediate and angry. It looked and sounded as if there would be a repeat of the saber-rattling that preceded Taiwan's first presidential election in 1996. Clinton, in a half-hour telephone conversation with Jiang Zemin, dissociated himself and his government from support of Lee's formulation and reiterated American backing for "one China." Perhaps influenced by this gesture from Washington and perhaps reflecting on the fact that its earlier bellicose response had only succeeded in increasing the margin by which Lee won the 1996 election, China confined itself to a barrage of angry prose.

Meanwhile, Taiwan's friends in the U.S. Congress used the summer's events as an opportunity to fish in troubled waters. They renewed the call for a theater missile defense system in East Asia that would protect Taiwan, along with Japan and South Korea, from attack. They simultaneously put forward the Taiwan Security Enhancement Act, which would have created a relationship between American and Taiwanese military establishments tantamount to a military alliance while upgrading and expanding U.S. arms sales to Taiwan. The bill was passed by a vote of 341-70 in the House, but faced with the threat of a veto, and distracted by attention to China's trade status as it moved toward WTO membership, the Senate tabled the bill.

It was against this international backdrop that Taiwan undertook its second presidential election in March 2000. The Nationalist Party's candidate was President Lee's vice president and chosen successor, Lien Chan; Lien's rival for the candidacy would have been James Soong (*Sung Chu-yu* 宋楚瑜), the popular governor of the Taiwan provincial government until it was dissolved in 1997. Shortly after Lien's nomination and Lee's broadcast, Soong left the Nationalist Party and declared himself an independent candidate. The DPP nominated Chen Shui-bian. The campaign among the three was hard fought, and the outcome was considered too close to predict. Lien proved lackluster, Soong was accused of pocketing Nationalist Party funds, and Chen took pains to dissociate himself from the DPP's independence plank. In the end, Chen won with 39 percent of the vote to Soong's 37 percent, Lien trailing behind with an embarrassing 23 percent. Angry Nationalist Party members blamed Lee for the defeat, citing his having driven Soong from the party; under attack, Lee resigned his position as party chair. In May, marking a second milestone for Chinese democracy, a peaceful transition from the long-ruling Nationalist Party to the opposition DPP took place when Chen was sworn in as Taiwan's second popularly elected president.

Chen's two terms in office proved to be a time of trouble for Taiwan, for cross-strait relations, and ultimately for him. As we look at the events of these eight years, it is important to bear in mind the ambiguous mandate with which Chen came to power. It was voter dissatisfaction with the Nationalists and the split between Soong and Lien, not an outpouring of support for the DPP's pro-independence platform, that won Chen his very narrow plurality. It is also important to bear in mind that with Lien's Nationalists and Soong's New Party members collaborating in the legislature, Chen found himself seriously limited in his ability to undertake new initiatives.

Chen inherited an economy that had ridden out the financial crisis of the late 1990s with relatively little damage. Taiwan had also survived the aftermath of a devastating earthquake (7.6 on the Richter scale) that struck in September 1999, killing 2,100, injuring 8,000, and leaving more than 100,000 homeless, a disaster estimated to have caused some $11 billion in damages. Despite these setbacks, overall economic growth for 1999 was just over 6 percent, significantly ahead of that of Hong Kong and Singapore. Although that growth continued into the following year, in 2001 the Taiwan economy actually shrank at a rate of -1.9 percent (the first full-year decline in fifty years of record keeping), and unemployment exceeded 5 percent, while across the strait, the Chinese economy grew by a healthy 8.4 percent. An observer summed up Chen's first year in office: "The economy is on life support, relations with the mainland are on hold, and the legislature is paralyzing politics." It was not an auspicious beginning.

Chen's approach to the mainland during his two terms in office can charitably be called erratic. On the one hand, he proposed in May 2002 to send an informal DPP delegation to Beijing for exploratory talks; on the other hand, three months later, he spoke publicly of the fact that "two countries" exist on either side of the Taiwan Strait and proposed a referendum on declaring Taiwan independence. Although that referendum did not come to a vote, referenda proved a favorite tool for Chen in dealing with his mainland neighbor. In 2003, he proposed another referendum, calling on China to withdraw its ballistic missiles aimed at Taiwan and to renounce the use of force in cross-strait relations. In 2007, when the UN turned down Taiwan's application for membership for the fifteenth time, Chen again proposed a referendum on the question (giving the impression he believed that Taiwan voters, not General Assembly members, would decide the question). Among others who took issue with Chen's referenda was the U.S. State Department, which referred to them as "needlessly provocative."

In fairness, Beijing was not the model of evenhandedness either. After the government extended an invitation to members of the DPP to visit the mainland soon after Chen took office, Chinese military leaders took it upon themselves to observe that "Taiwan's leaders have pushed the island toward an abyss of war," and the National People's Congress transformed the comment into public policy in 2005 with a law forbidding secession and mandating military action should any changes declaring the island's independence be made to Taiwan's constitution.

For his part, President Hu Jintao tried a different tack, inviting Lien Chan, representing the Nationalists, and James Soong, representing the People's First Party, to travel to Beijing. It was during Lien's visit, as we have seen, that the CCP and the KMT declared a symbolic end to hostilities. During Soong's visit, the two proposed a new formula that did little to combat ambiguity: "two sides of the strait, one China." Hu's audience, clearly, were Taiwan voters, to whom it was suggested that "anyone but the DPP" would make for smoother cross-strait relations.

Chen used Beijing's saber-rattling to reiterate his case for additional arms sales from the United States. As George W. Bush took office in 2001, Taiwan submitted its wish list: Aegis-equipped *Kidd-class* guided missile destroyers, P-3 Orion aircraft to detect submarines, and sophisticated command and control communications. Eventually, Bush agreed to the sale of four destroyers, twelve antisubmarine aircraft, and eight diesel submarines, but put off the sale of the more sophisticated items Taiwan had requested. Three months before his second term ended, Bush signed off on a $6 billion package of arms sales that included all the items held back in 2001. Beijing was far from pleased and canceled all military and diplomatic contacts with the United States for a time, awaiting the new administration to renew them.

If Chen thought his margin of victory was small in 2000, he found himself with a razor-thin margin of only 0.1 percent in the balloting in 2004. Chen and his vice-presidential running mate, Annette Lu (Lu Xiulian–吕秀莲), while campaigning in the city of Tainan, were fired at and slightly wounded on the eve of the election. Cynics accused them of having staged the episode to garner sympathy, and Lien Chan toyed briefly with the idea of calling for a recount before thinking better of it and conceding the election.

Chen was responsible, with representatives from the mainland, for initiating a Cross-Strait Economic, Trade and Culture Forum, which held its first meeting in April 2006. The Forum was intended to promote cross-strait economic, trade, cultural exchanges, dialogue, and integration. It met twice, ceasing to exist when a period of Sino-Taiwan rapprochement ended. Although the economy improved significantly during Chen's administration—growth rates from 2002 through 2007 averaged five percent—he continued to contend with a contrary legislature and waning public confidence. Then, in November, the Public Prosecutors' Office of Taiwan's high court formally indicted Wu Shu-chen (吴淑珍), Chen's wife, on charges of issuing fake receipts to extract $450,000 from a presidential fund to support Taiwan's diplomatic initiatives overseas. Chen admitted to submitting fake receipts but claimed he did so in the interest of national security and declined to resign from office.

A year after he retired, constrained by term limits as well as the likelihood of defeat, he was arrested and tried on charges of having taken some $30 million in bribes. His wife pleaded guilty to charges of forgery, and she, his son, and his daughter-in-law pleaded guilty to charges of money laundering. Chen was convicted and given a life sentence, and a week later, further corruption charges were brought against him. As a suggestion that his legal travails had caused him to become unhinged, he filed a lawsuit claiming that the United States controls Taiwan and should release him from prison. It was an ignominious end to what had begun as a courageous political career.

Sensing potential victory, the Nationalists put forward Ma Ying-jeou, former justice minister and popular mayor of Taipei, who had stood for the post of chair of the KMT in 2005, as its candidate for president. He was opposed by the DPP's Frank Hsieh. Ma was elected by a margin of almost three to two.

The new administration made improving cross-strait ties a first priority, followed in close succession by its efforts to counteract the effects of the international financial collapse. On the first front, Ma led off by sending his vice president-elect, Vincent Siew, to southern China for talks with "top" officials in April 2008. The following month, with Beijing's concurrence, Taiwan was permitted to send representatives to a World Health Organization conference in Geneva under observer status under the name "Chinese Taipei."

Regular talks between the Straits Exchange Foundation and the Association for Relations Across the Taiwan Strait were renewed in September 2008. Ma called for expanded economic ties, including access to the Chinese market for Taiwan's financial services, an end to investment restrictions, direct sea and air cargo links, regularly scheduled passenger flights, the drafting of common technical standards, and the establishment of a system to resolve commercial disputes.

In November, former Vice President Lien Chan met with Chinese President Hu Jintao at an Asia-Pacific Economic Cooperation (APEC) Forum meeting in Peru. They discussed "things about which we are concerned and how to direct our efforts toward peaceful development, cooperation, and a win-win situation between the two sides of the Taiwan Strait."

In its declining months in 2008, the Bush administration approved a $6 billion package of arms sales to Taiwan. Scarcely a year later, the Obama administration announced yet another $6 billion package, this one including Patriot and Harpoon missiles, Black Hawk helicopters, mine-hunting ships, and communications equipment for Taiwan's fleet of F-16 aircraft. This time, Beijing responded not only by cutting off military-to-military contacts with Washington but also by announcing sanctions against the U.S. companies supplying Taiwan with weapons. Given the many other obstacles standing in the way of improved United States-China relations, many questioned the scope and timing of the new arms sale agreement.

Premier Wen Jiabao, in his annual "state of the nation" address to the NPC in March 2009, endorsed Ma's proposals and called for the drafting of a "comprehensive agreement on economic cooperation" that could form the basis for an eventual free trade agreement between the two sides. More recent products of this dialogue were a series of agreements reached in late 2009 covering banking, insurance, and securities trading. Taiwan allowed financial investment from the PRC for the first time since 1949.

President Ma lost some ground with the public over his very rapid moves toward expanding cross-strait relations; they believed he was moving more precipitously than they were comfortable with. He also lost ground over the government's response to the devastation caused by Typhoon Morakat, which swept across the island in August 2009, killing as many as 500, leaving 7,000 homeless, and causing more than $1.5 billion in damage. Although the damage was dwarfed by that of Hurricane Katrina in Louisiana in 2005, Taiwan's government was ill-prepared and slow to respond, eliciting disbelief and anger among the typhoon's victims that was reminiscent of the reaction to the debacle in New Orleans brought about by the Bush administration's egregious ineptitude.

Six years later, in 2015, Ma Ying-jeou and Xi Jinping met in Singapore—the first such meeting between the leaders of the two sides of the Taiwan Strait since 1949. But the following year, relations deteriorated after the election of DPP leader and Taiwan's first female president, Tsai Ing-wen. Xi reminded his listeners that "the Chinese people would never tolerate separatism or Taiwan Independence." Meanwhile, in an ostentatious show of force, Beijing sent its aircraft carrier fleet through the Taiwan Strait. Chinese military aircraft frequently crossed the Strait midline and intruded into Taiwan's Air Defense Identification Zone (ADIZ). According to the Taiwanese defense minister,

Chinese planes had entered the zone 221 times, the highest number since 1990.

Meanwhile, the American Congress joined the conflict. In 2020, the Taiwan Allies International Protection and Enhancement Act (conveniently named to abbreviate nearly as TAIPEI) was signed into law, committing the U.S. to strengthening bilateral relations with Taiwan as well as Taiwan's international position. After the Taiwanese presidential election, CIA Director Michale Pompeo and other U.S. officials and politicians quickly congratulated Tsai Ing-wen on her re-election. In February, Vice President-elect Lai Ching-te visited the U.S. Another breakthrough was made in August, when Alex Azar, the U.S. Secretary of Health and Human Services, visited Taiwan, making him the first U.S. cabinet official to do so since 1979. Azar was followed by Keith Krach, Undersecretary of State, who went to Taiwan in September to attend the memorial service for former President Lee Teng-hui, who died at the age of 97 in July

Some have suggested that the accession of both sides to WTO membership provides them with another forum for dialogue on economic matters, as occurred in 2002 in Geneva, where the issue was disputes over steel trade. Others in China have proposed an even more ambitious arrangement. Delegates to the Chinese People's Political Consultative Conference (a largely powerless body often used as a sounding board for new ideas) were presented with a proposal for a "cross-straits economic zone" with Taiwan that would encompass the island and parts of four mainland Chinese provinces that face it across the Taiwan Strait, reminiscent of the Pan Pearl River Delta Regional Cooperation and Development Forum involving Hong Kong and Macao that was discussed earlier.

In sum, all these moves seem generally encouraging, on the one hand, but on the other hand, both sides appear to be papering over some very fundamental differences on the question of political sovereignty, leaving them to be resolved at some later date. Should this not occur, the Chinese armed forces have shown that they can pressure the civilian leadership to take a strong stand with respect to Taiwan.

Short of military invasion, which the PLA is still ill-equipped to carry out, there are several steps the Chinese government might choose to take if negotiations were to break down. Intimidation, such as the military exercises and tests conducted during 1995 and 1996, is one. Another might well be a reversion to the economic policy of the early 1970s, when firms doing business in Taiwan were not permitted to do business in China. A third step—well within the current capability of the PLA—might be to carry out a blockade of Jinmen and Matsu islands, very close to the mainland coast. The two island chains are guarded by a garrison of some ten thousand troops; substantial pressure could be brought to bear on the Taiwan government were these troops to be held hostage by mainland forces.

A fourth step—a considerable escalation—would be to blockade Taiwan itself. This would immediately and adversely affect the Taiwan economy, but it would also invite international intervention to keep international shipping lanes open. A last step to wring compliance from an intransigent Taiwan would be a direct missile or amphibious attack on the island, but launching such an attack would be a high-risk maneuver. Despite some progress in integrating civilian vessels with military exercises, the PLA is unlikely to have the range of amphibious landing capabilities or the over-the-shore logistics needed for a major cross-strait attack in Taiwan before at least 2030.

Taiwan is well defended. Its military budget is somewhat in excess of $13 billion per year—less than four percent of the estimated actual budget for the PLA—but, although somewhat outdated compared with the most advanced American, European, and Russian capabilities, the Taiwan air force is better equipped and better trained than the PLA air force. Though it is not clear that Taiwan could win an armed conflict with China, it would at least make it a protracted and costly war, which would seriously damage the island's economy, the strength of which is one of the most important motivations for reunification, and the economy of the coastal provinces in which it has invested most heavily.

Armed conflict between Taiwan and the mainland could also trigger international intervention, notably from two of China's major trade and investment partners that have strong economic ties to Taiwan—Japan and the United States. Indeed, Japan and the United States signed in 2005 a joint security statement declaring a peaceful Taiwan Strait as a common security objective. Many Americans would favor military action on Taiwan's behalf. Nonetheless, whether either Japan or the United States would go to war with China to defend Taiwan is highly questionable. At the very least, each country would feel compelled to adopt economic and military sanctions that would be certain to slow China's economic development.

Any of these steps is likely to have an undesirable effect on the Taiwan population. Threatened with blockade or outright attack, the people in Taiwan are likely to rally in support of their independence from the mainland. Even if beaten into submission, they would probably be at least as difficult to control from Beijing as were their Ming loyalist ancestors three centuries ago.

One reason that the Taiwan issue touches such a raw nerve in Beijing is that Taiwan's democratization is a countermodel for the political repression that China's authoritarian leaders are doing their best to keep in place. The two governments once closely resembled each other, but now Taiwan has set aside its authoritarian practices in favor of a no-holds-barred democracy, while enjoying continued economic prosperity, and this is a thorn in Beijing's side.

The Taiwan model of political liberalization starts with an autocratic party holding a monopoly over the political system and enforcing its control by a heavy reliance on armed force. The transformation of that system occurred because of the coincidence of two key factors: the emergence of courageous individuals who, risking arrest and persecution, actively campaigned against the autocratic party and the forward-looking decision by the autocrat Chiang Ching-kuo to permit a political evolution.

But there are key differences between Taiwan and mainland China that make the new Taiwan a questionable model. First and most obvious is that of scale. The people of Taiwan, for all their diversity, are a highly integrated island population of 22 million. China's people, for all their much-vaunted ethnic unity, are a highly diverse population of 1.3 billion scattered over a very large territory. A second important difference is in the levels of economic development. Taiwan's per capita GNP was about ten times that of mainland China when its political transformation began. If it is true that economic development produces a demand for political liberalization (and, as we have seen, there is good reason to question that hypothesis), then we should not expect that demand to be made in China—particularly in its poorer areas—for some time to come.

A third difference is that in mainland China, there is no single mobilizing issue. Gaining a political voice for the Taiwanese majority was an issue that united up to 85 percent of Taiwan's population, but despite all the complaints that citizens of the People's Republic have about their government, no single complaint has the potential to mobilize a comparable opposition.

External pressure affected the political evolution of Taiwan, but it is not clear whether it could do so in China. When the liberalization process was inaugurated, Taiwan was at its most isolated internationally, and democratization was a course of action that was certain to elicit international support, though that support has been a long time in coming. But since 1989, the Chinese government has dug in its heels and become more repressive and more defiant, apparently presuming that an economically burgeoning China cannot be ignored and will not long be isolated in the world economy.

Finally, there is a substantial difference between the former senior leaders on the two sides of the Taiwan Strait. Knowing death was near, Chiang Ching-kuo had the political courage and vision to open and revivify his government. Knowing death was near, Deng Xiaoping demonstrated the limits to his political courage and vision by moving in the opposite direction.

Chapter 20: China in the World

There were those who said that the collapse of the Soviet Union in 1991 marked the beginning of a new world order. There is no question that the sudden demise of the second superpower rearranged the familiar landmarks of international politics in the last half of the twentieth century, but if there is a new order in the rearrangement, it has yet to become manifest. The American position as the single, dominant superpower is now very much open to question. In the old order, China was equidistant from the two superpowers and, because of this position as a balancing force, could influence world politics out of all proportion to its national strength. Today, China's national strength has grown very substantially, and, consequently, its strategic importance has grown as well. Only very recently has China begun to acknowledge its status as a nascent superpower and to act upon that status. We are, once again, entering a bipolar world order. It is imperative that we review the lessons of our competitive relationship with the Soviet Union and avoid bringing about a second Cold War.

Foreign policy questions, like domestic ones, are subject to the power grid of the Chinese political system, though this has not always been the case. The formulation of foreign policy used to be confined to a small number of people at the apex of the party-state, and its implementation was the exclusive purview of the Foreign Ministry. But several changes during the 1980s opened the field to other players.

The first change was the increasing dominance of economic issues. When China was largely cut off from the world economy, ideological and strategic issues dominated foreign policy. With the economic reforms, strategic issues have receded somewhat, and

China's vastly expanded trade and investment, creating new links to the outside world, have become central.

A second, more recent change is the emergence of the People's Liberation Army as a major player. During the 1990s, as we have seen, the PLA developed extensive international connections of its own, many of them economic rather than military or strategic. Although the importance of these economic connections has waned, the PLA still has interests that are sometimes at variance with those of the party-state.

Finally, as the balance of power between the central government and the regions has shifted in the direction of the latter, they, too, have begun to influence foreign policy. But they do not speak with a single voice.

For all this, by far the most important player remains the party-state, and within it, divergent views are held with respect to China's foreign policy goals. A small and dwindling number of conservatives have a kind of "fortress China" mentality. Like American isolationists, they believe that Deng Xiaoping's open policy resulted in dangerous dependencies and noxious influences. In their view, the country would be far better off had it returned to economic autarky and strategic disengagement. But the opposite point of view is also represented within the party-state by those who argue that there should be no limit to China's interaction with the world economy, that new sources of investment capital and technology should be sought, that new markets for Chinese goods should be actively cultivated, and that market forces should be allowed to determine foreign economic links and drive the domestic economy. Although they might not want to say so, it is the dominant American model of international economic policy that they have in mind for China.

A third group within the party-state takes a cautious middle position. It shares the conservative minority's concern about China's becoming too dependent on foreign interests. But it is favorably impressed with the results of Japan's, South Korea's, and Singapore's government-managed industrial policy and their carefully calculated penetration of foreign economies in search of markets, raw materials, and labor. It considers this mercantilist approach to economic development to have greater potential for China than one based exclusively on free trade.

The armed forces during 1995 and 1996 began to look as though they might be the dominant voice in foreign policy, but they spoke from several different perspectives. From the perspective of its strategic concerns, the PLA aims to have enough military strength to assert China's sovereignty, to secure and defend its national borders, and to guarantee access for China to offshore energy sources and shipping lanes. From the perspective of its now somewhat curtailed economic interests, it wants to maintain open access to foreign capital and markets. From the perspective of its institutional self-interest, it is inclined to support a foreign policy that justifies military expansion—whether in the South China Sea, in Myanmar, or in dealing with Taiwan—and helps it get more and better equipment and a larger budget. Also in its self-interest, however, is access to the expertise and technology of the most advanced military establishments, particularly that of the United States, and seeking to ensure that access may dampen the PLA's expansionist tendencies.

The horizontal components in China's power grid have their own foreign policy interests too. The South China coast, for example, with its heavy concentration of Taiwan-invested enterprises, has its own point of view on relations with Taiwan. Similarly, Guangdong and its special economic zones, closely linked as they are to the Hong Kong economy, can be expected to advocate policies that foster the preservation of Hong Kong's economic viability. In like fashion, the southeastern macroregion has close links with Myanmar and the former Indochinese states, Shandong Province is closely tied to Korea, the northeastern provinces to Russia and Japan, and the western provinces to the Central Asian republics. Each regional player is likely to act as an advocate for policies that foster its external ties. Although every effort is made to ensure that the PLA speaks with a single voice and is immune to power grid politics, regional military commanders persist in cultivating local ties against these heavy odds. The connections they make with foreign powers serve both economic and military interests. In some cases, they appear to have been cultivated without the blessing of the central command.

If we take one or two steps back from the interests of specific nodes in the power grid, it is possible to discern some broad and generally accepted priorities in Chinese foreign policy in the post-Cold War world. The first priority is clearly that of pursuing policies that promote China's economic development. The second priority is that of pursuing policies that promote China's sovereignty and national security.

In recent years, China's participation in the global economy—particularly its quest for new sources of energy to fuel its growth—has come to dominate the formulation of its foreign policy. As the reform era began, the Chinese economy was being opened up to the outside world. Trade expanded rapidly, and the government actively encouraged foreign investment. China's experience in the world economy had been very limited, self-reliance having been a guiding principle and foreign trade having been closely controlled by the central government and confined, for the most part, to the socialist world. Although trade in the mid-l 950s had amounted to nearly a quarter of China's national income, the proportion had sunk to a mere 6 percent by the end of the Cultural Revolution in 1970.

The "open policy" of the reform era called at first for substantial importation of technology, which would be funded by the export of oil. When China's oil reserves proved insufficient for this, the strategy shifted to encouraging technology transfer through foreign investment in joint ventures; special economic zones were set aside where preferential regulations were put in place to attract this investment, the first four in Guangdong and Fujian provinces in 1979, the next on Hainan Island, which was designated as its own province. Similar arrangements were extended to fourteen coastal cities. Then, beginning in 1985, Beijing established seven additional "open economic zones," and in 1990 opened the Pudong area in the city of Shanghai to overseas investment. The third stage in this process was a substantial expansion of production for export, led by the foreign-invested industrial sector.

China was a late arrival in the modern global economy, but in a very short period has become a highly important contestant, deeply involved in the game. On a price-parity basis, China is the world's second-largest economy after the United States, having overtaken both Germany and Japan in recent years. Were it to maintain its current rate of growth—a questionable assumption—it would surpass the United States by 2036. The fact that China had, in a sense, "arrived" as a major player in the global economy was driven home in early 2007, when the Shanghai Stock Exchange suffered a 9 percent loss in a single day. To the surprise of many, the impact of that loss was immediately felt, not only on Asian markets but in Europe and the United States as well. It was particularly disturbing to financial analysts, given the *louche* rules under which China's stock exchanges operate.

Table 24: CHINESE INTERACTION WITH THE WORLD ECONOMY 2023: THE TOP TWELVE (in billions of yuan)

Chia Exports	Amoun t	China Imports	Amoun t	China Outwar d FDI[12]	Amoun t	China Inward FDI	Amoun t
US	351.9	South Korea	143.7	Singapor e	130.8	United Arab Emirates	22.1
Japan	110.7	Taiwan	140.2	Cayman Islands	87.3	Singapore	9.7
South Korea	104.6	US	114.9	US	69.1	Virgin Islands	6.8
India	82.7	Japan	113.1	South Africa	35.3	Taiwan	6.6
Russia	78.1	Russia	91.1	Vietnam	25.9	Netherland s	5.3
German y	70.6	Brazil	86.4	Algeria	20.9	Japan	3.8
UK	54.8	Germany	74.9	Thailand	20.1	Cayman Islands	3.5
Australi a	51.9	Malaysia	72.4	Nigeria	18.6	South Korea	3.5
Taiwan	45.1	Australia	51.9	UK	16.6	UK	3.4
Canada	31.7	Saudi Arabia	45.1	South Korea	6.6	US	3.4
Italy	31.2	Philippine s	36.7	India	6.1	Germany	2.5
Spain	27.9	Thailand	35.5	Japan	4.5	France	2.1

Source: Our World in Data

At about the same time, the point was reached at which trade among Asian nations exceeded trade between Asia and the United States, and China became the largest trading partner of almost every country in Asia. At the beginning of 2010, China and the ten

[12] FDI = Foreign direct investment

countries that make up the Association of Southeast Asian Nations (ASEAN) inaugurated a new free-trade zone, removing tariffs on 90 percent of traded goods. Trade between China and ASEAN countries amounted to $6.6 billion in 2008. The new zone encompasses some 1.9 billion people and, in terms of goods traded, is the third-largest free-trade zone after the European Economic Area and the North American Free Trade Area. As the zone was about to be launched, Chu Shulong, director of the Institute of Strategic Studies at Tsinghua (清华) University, was quoted as saying, "China is a major global economy now. That is a fundamental reality. What China says and does has an effect on international finance, international economics, and other economies."

Over the last ten years, China's foreign trade has grown at an average rate of 21 percent per year, twice the growth rate of the economy itself, and in 2010, China overtook Germany as the world's largest exporter of goods and services. The total two-way trade in 2024 was $5.6 trillion. Including investment from Hong Kong, the cumulative total contracted external direct investment totaled $1.6 trillion in 2024.

Certain constraints could prevent the Chinese economy from realizing its potential, as we have seen, notably continuing problems with the banking system, the growing demand for energy, the shortage of arable land and the limits that places on China's ability to feed its population without resorting to massive grain imports; its mixed results in slowing its population growth; the growing income inequality; and rampant and apparently uncontrollable corruption. Addressing the issue of inequality in 2013, the State Council adopted a 35-point program that included among its goals raising the minimum wage, reducing the number of people living in absolute poverty by 80 million, and limiting the incomes of government officials and enterprise managers.

Still, it is likely that China's foreign trade will continue to grow, albeit perhaps at a slower pace. Despite World Trade Organization rules to the contrary, China's trading partners will be tempted to develop protectionist measures to defend their own domestic industries against competition from less expensive Chinese products. Moreover, as production costs rise at home, Chinese products will begin to lose their early competitive lead. China is likely to continue to look to foreign capital markets as a source of investment capital, particularly as a means to fund major public works projects and to resolve the crisis in the state-owned sector of the economy.

China's economy is remarkably open in comparison with those of other Asian nations and is likely to continue to be so. Closed economies tend to restrict imports, but the Chinese import substantial quantities of goods (to the point of running up trade deficits in ten of the past thirty years), have placed few restrictions on foreign investors, and have tried to put in place regulations and incentives to encourage foreign participation in Chinese economic development. A measure of their success is the fact that exports of goods produced in foreign-invested enterprises made up 30% of China's total exports in 2023. Exports from foreign-invested firms are growing five times as fast as exports from domestically owned firms.

As it looks toward the global economy, China, like all the world's economies, looks for markets for its exports, sources for the goods it needs to import, destinations for politically and economically shrewd investment of Chinese funds, and sources of foreign investment to fuel China's growth.

The offshore components of Greater China—Taiwan, Hong Kong, Singapore—and the overseas Chinese communities in North America and Europe are likely to continue to be the most reliable and lucrative sources of investment capital, and this constrains Chinese policy on delicate issues of sovereignty. The Chinese authorities probably find rattling sabers in the Taiwan Strait and venting spleen against Hong Kong democrats highly gratifying in the short term, but soberer heads in Beijing are well aware that the continuing viability of the economies of Taiwan and Hong Kong is indispensable to the continuing economic growth of the nation.

Currently, oil is an important driver of Chinese foreign economic policy, which has led to an increased interest in African initiatives. Hu Jintao made two trips to Africa during his tenure in office and hosted a China-Africa Forum in Beijing in 2006 that attracted representatives from 48 of the 53 African countries, including 40 heads of state. China currently imports oil from Sudan, Angola, and Nigeria, and signed two deals in 2006, one allowing the China National Offshore Oil Corporation (CNOOC) to explore for oil off Kenya's coast, the other securing for the company a substantial share of a major oil field in Nigeria. The total two-way trade with African countries in 2024 amounted to $296 billion. Its foreign investment in African countries totaled $29 billion that year, and it is reported that close to 1.2 million Chinese are living and working for extended periods on the continent. China's interest in courting the government of Sudan made it reluctant to join other nations in protesting that government's role in the mass murders occurring in the Darfur region of the country in 2025, engendering the anger of those eager to mobilize all available resources to end the atrocities.

In addition to its deals in Africa, the CNOOC has negotiated agreements with Canada, Venezuela, Brazil, Russia, and Iraq to augment China's oil supplies. Although initially an enthusiastic bidder, it eventually withdrew from a highly publicized $18.5 billion bid to acquire the Union Oil Company of California (Unocal) in 2009 when members of Congress objected on national security grounds (despite the fact that 70 percent of Unocal's oil and gas reserves are in Asia and mostly under long-term contract to Asian nations like Thailand and Indonesia). China also signed agreements with Australia and Indonesia to supply liquefied natural gas over the next twenty-five years at a cost of $23 billion.

A second driver of Chinese foreign economic policy is to develop new markets for Chinese goods to balance the demand for costly imports of high-tech equipment and raw materials. It was in pursuit of this goal that China first turned its attention to the Third World. China's championing of the cause of less developed countries in Africa, Asia, and Latin America in the early 1980s was motivated in part by its interest in finding buyers for the low-end manufactured goods it turned out in such great quantity. More recently, Russia has become an avid customer. Some of this export business moves through ordinary trade channels, some of it is cross-border trade involving barter arrangements, and Chinese goods also make their way to Russian consumers via duffel bags carried on the Trans-Siberian Railroad by Russian and Chinese merchants in search of a fast profit. But Russia is likely to be only a temporary market for Chinese consumer goods, since the latter may be replaced by goods produced in Russian factories.

China has also cultivated its relationship with India. Since the late 1980s, both countries have successfully rebuilt diplomatic and economic ties. The two prime ministers—Atal Bihari Vajpayee and Wen Jiabao—exchanged visits in 2003 and 2005 and, after a series of fifteen negotiating sessions that began in 1988, signed an agreement on border issues. China has pledged to increase investment in India, and during a visit to Delhi in 2006, Hu Jintao promised to double Sino-Indian trade.

Since 2013, border disputes have reemerged to take center stage in the two countries' mutual relations. In early 2018, the two armies got engaged in a standoff at the Doklam plateau along the disputed Bhutan-China border. Starting in the summer of 2020, armed standoffs and skirmishes at multiple locations along the entire Sino-Indian border escalated. A serious clash occurred in the Galwan Valley, resulting in the death of 20 Indian soldiers and many Chinese soldiers. Both countries have steadily established military infrastructure along the border areas, including during the 2020 China-India skirmishes. Additionally, India remains wary about China's strong strategic bilateral relations with Pakistan and China's relations with separatist groups in Northeast India. Meanwhile, China has expressed concerns about Indian military and economic activities in the disputed South China Sea , as well as India's hosting of anti-China activity by Tibetan exiles. Today, the South Asian region is the premier site of intensified great power competition between China and India. Most recently, Indian Prime Minister Narendra Modi traveled to Tianjin, China, to attend the Shanghai Cooperation Organization (SCO) Summit. On 31 August 31 2025, he held a bilateral meeting with President Xi Jinping on the sidelines of the summit, discussing border stability, trade cooperation, and regional diplomacy.

A third goal of China's foreign economic policy is to continue to cultivate its traditional economic partners, including Japan, South Korea, Europe, and the United States. The Japanese were among the first to trade with the newly opened and reforming China, but they have been slow to invest there, though Japan now ranks fifth as a source of external capital. With two-way trade reaching $226 billion in 2024, China is Japan's largest trading partner, and Japan is China's third-largest trading partner. China's economic policy with respect to Japan is to encourage additional investment while trying to balance its trade.

Chinese factories are now turning out more and more high-quality, sophisticated products, for which new markets must be sought, most likely in developed countries. Expanding this market will help bring China's trade with Japan into balance, but only exacerbate the already serious problem of a trade surplus with the United States. It is also likely to elicit protectionist reactions from manufacturers within the developed world.

China's relationships with the two Koreas are complicated. Trade with South Korea has grown rapidly and now vastly outweighs its economic connections with North Korea, though because it shares a border as well as, nominally, a political ideology with North Korea, China is not interested in alienating that government. Moreover, its ability to communicate with Pyongyang is a unique asset that can be used as a bargaining chip with other nations, the United States among them. Two issues have complicated Beijing's ties with Pyongyang. First, there is the question of the 200,000 North Korean refugees (roughly one percent of the North Korean population) who are living illegally in China. Despite periodic roundups, the number remains relatively constant, and in 2001 and 2002, more than one hundred of them attempted to secure safe passage out of the country by breaking into and entering consulate and embassy compounds in Shenyang and Beijing.

More vexing are North Korea's pursuit of nuclear weapons and its willingness to export nuclear weapons technology to rogue states elsewhere in the world. The nation has conducted at least six tests of nuclear weapons over the last several years. Kim Jong Il, North Korea's leader, died in 2011 and was succeeded by his son, Kim Jong Un. China has served as an active partner in the thus far futile effort to persuade Kim Jong Un to abandon his nuclear ambitions. It is anticipated that Kim, now age 41, is likely to be succeeded by his daughter, Kim Ju Ae. The two recently made a state visit to Beijing.

Knowing that reunification of North and South Korea would divert South Korea's trade and investment potential, China has not strongly advocated a peace settlement ending the Korean War but instead has encouraged South Koreans to invest in China, particularly in neighboring Shandong Province, and has actively promoted Sino-South Korean trade.

In Europe, China finds trading partners and potential investors who are much more relaxed about difficult questions of human rights than Americans are. And while in some fields, high technology can be found only in the United States, European substitutes for American goods are usually acceptable and often much easier to acquire. There is, however, an exception to that rule. Despite recent efforts to end it, Europe has maintained alongside the United States an embargo on arms sales originally put in place in 1989.

A fourth goal of China's foreign economic policy, to curb its competition, is of longer-term significance. As China's economy develops, what are now complementary and symbiotic relationships are likely to become fraught. The relationship with Taiwan is an excellent example. China's need for investment capital and Taiwan's need for cheap labor and real estate for its manufacturing sector made for mutually beneficial relations. But with costs rising on the mainland, it became less desirable for Taiwan to locate manufacturing operations there, and as China's products have become more sophisticated, they are competing in foreign markets with goods produced in Taiwan. China's most immediate source of competition is the newly opened economy of Vietnam. Although on a much smaller scale, Vietnam, in pursuing foreign investors, has been just as aggressive as (though less successful than) China, and its production costs are, for the moment, considerably lower than those in China's coastal provinces.

It took the government of the PRC three decades to obtain the recognition of other governments. Securing representation in the United Nations was a particularly important goal, and China has taken its participation in that organization very seriously. Although it resists the incursions on its sovereignty that such participation might entail and consistently favors backstairs negotiations over public sanctions as a means of resolving international disputes, it nonetheless savors the status that derives from permanent membership on the Security Council. A measure of the importance it still accords to UN membership is the vigor with which it opposes Taiwan's participation. Within the UN, China participates as a member of the so-called Group of 77, a bloc of developing nations that, despite its name, actually includes 134 members. The bloc tends to argue that the UN should shift its focus from matters of peace and security to questions of economic and social development.

Securing membership in the World Trade Organization (WTO) was a high priority on the Chinese foreign policy agenda. China had expected to be offered membership in the General Agreement on Tariffs and Trade (GATT) before that organization became the WTO in January 1995, since it was one of the original contracting parties to GATT in 1948 (though the Nationalist government withdrew its membership four years later). Beijing began applying for membership in 1988. The United States took the lead in making the case that China should have no special treatment, and the other leading members of GATT supported this position, but China saw it as one more indication of a concerted anti-China policy. At issue were China's policies protecting state-owned enterprises and its lack of transparency in trade and investment regulations. China sought membership as a developing country; the United States and others responded that the Chinese economy was already too large and well developed for that category to be appropriate. The question of China's membership in the WTO, as we have seen, was complicated by the fact that Taiwan's application was being considered simultaneously.

Late in 1999, a crucial hurdle was crossed when, after thirteen years of negotiations and a cliff-hanging finish, China and the United States signed a trade agreement. A similar agreement with the European Union was signed the following spring, clearing the way for China's entry into the WTO. A provision of the Sino-American agreement called for extending to China permanent normal trade relations, thereby eliminating Congress's annual review under the Jackson-Yanik amendment to the Trade Act of 1974 (a provision originally written to permit the free emigration of Russian Jews) of China's eligibility for what was formerly referred to as most favored nation trade status. Although U.S. trade unions made the defeat of this initiative a high priority, business and farming organizations favored it. The initiative was carried in the House by a vote of 237-197—19 more than needed to pass, and was passed by the Senate in September 2000.

WTO membership has provided China with a vehicle for asserting its economic interests, a forum for conversations with Taiwan, and, occasionally, a curb on its buccaneering behavior. In 2002, China filed a complaint with the WTO against Washington's decision to impose tariffs of up to 30 percent on steel imports to protect U.S. steel producers. More recently, it was the target of an American complaint regarding restraints on the import of American books and media products. As a token of the importance that China assigns to its role in the WTO, the then foreign minister, Yang Jiechi, responded to the complaint with the comment "China will never seek to advance its interests at the expense of others."

WTO membership also brought with it the requirement that the Chinese banking system open up to foreign participation not later than 2007. Citibank was the first wholly foreign-owned bank to gain access to China's $120 billion in individual and corporate foreign exchange savings. Soon thereafter the Hong Kong and Shanghai Banking Corporation (HSBC) bought a 19.5% share in the China Bank of Communications; Bank of America acquired a 9% share in the China Construction Bank (it subsequently sold off a third of its holdings because of effects of the U.S. banking crisis on its bottom line); a partnership of Goldman Sachs and Allianz of Germany negotiated for a $1 billion share in the Industrial and Commercial Bank of China (China's largest bank, which, in 2009, declared itself the world's largest bank in terms of deposits); and the Royal Bank of Scotland invested $2.5 billion in the Bank of China. Currently, foreign institutions have taken equity stakes in more than 25 Chinese banks—a figure representing approved, albeit typically minority, stakes.

Two events tested China's willingness to adhere to the rules of the road in global trade. In late 2003, the Bush administration, confronted by a very substantial increase in imports of Chinese textiles, threatened to invoke clauses in its trade agreements that would permit the imposition of quotas. A year later, imports of textiles from China were up 75 percent, and one estimate suggested that as many as 12,000 jobs were lost in the United States as a result. China announced that it would "resolutely oppose" any moves to impose quotas on textile exports. Europe, too, felt the impact of a flood of Chinese textiles, and eventually Washington and the European Union negotiated an agreement with China in 2005 that limited the growth of its exports in 34 categories of textiles and clothing.

In a second episode, the Chinese government threatened the representatives of a foreign corporation with charges of espionage, throwing a chill across the international business community. China had engaged in negotiations with the Rio Tinto Group, a British and Australian mining and resources company, to invest $19.5 billion in an aluminum mine in Australia. After a series of negotiations reminiscent of the aborted Unocal deal described earlier, the Australian government rejected the Chinese offer. A month later, Rio Tinto executives working in China were detained and accused of stealing state secrets in the course of their negotiations over iron ore prices. The international response was immediate and firm: global economic interaction cannot thrive under the Damoclean sword of espionage charges. Sensing the damage their actions might have on trade and investment, the party-state backed off, reducing the charges against the four Rio Tinto officials to those of bribery and theft of trade secrets. Once again, the code of the global economy trumped the archaic code of China's state secrets law.

During the Cold War, the strategic triangle in East Asia was made up of the United States, the Soviet Union, and China. In economic and military terms, China was not in the same league with the other two (only much later did we learn that the Soviet Union wasn't either), but it served the interests of the two superpowers to use China as a makeweight against each other. Today, Japan has taken the place of the Soviet Union in the East Asian strategic triangle, and although the gaps among the world's four largest economies (Germany having edged out Japan) are narrowing rapidly, in strategic terms, the relationships are far from parity. Despite computer simulations that show China besting the United States in military conflicts under certain circumstances, the Chinese armed forces are still outmatched in equipment, training, and logistics by the Americans.

The Chinese have long voiced concern about the revival of Japanese militarism. Having borne the brunt of that militarism through much of the first half of the twentieth century, they were not persuaded that it was ended once and for all with Japan's defeat in 1945. Until very recently, the Chinese argument seemed counterintuitive: the Japanese were prevented from rearming by their constitution, which was imposed upon the country at the conclusion of World War II. Article 9 of that constitution reads as follows: "Aspiring sincerely to an international peace based on justice and order, the Japanese people forever renounce war as a sovereign right of the nation and the threat or use of force as a means of settling international disputes. To accomplish [this] aim...land, sea, and air forces, as well as other war potential, will never be maintained. The right of belligerency of the state will not be recognized." Historically, the country followed a long-standing unofficial cap of 1% of GDP for defense spending under the rubric of "self-defense forces." So long as the United States was prepared to serve as a shield for Japan, it would be economically foolish for the Japanese government to take over that responsibility; and Japanese public opinion has consistently opposed rearmament in any form.

But more recently reasons to question all these safeguards have lent credence to the Chinese view. There is talk in Japanese political circles of the need to reconsider the constitution. Some argue that it is time for Japan once again to become a "normal nation," by which is meant a nation with a full-scale defense establishment. The American shield was designed to protect Japan from Soviet aggression; but today a threat to Japan's national security is unlikely to come from Russia, and Japanese (and American) planners question whether American forces would leap reliably to Japan's defense in any other case. Moreover, the United States has for some years pressured the Japanese to bear a greater share of the cost of their defense, and recent public opinion polls show that a majority of Japanese citizens agree that it is time for their country to have a full-scale military force. In response to growing regional security challenges, Japan has shifted course.

The United States and Japan completed a joint review of the U.S.-Japan Defense Cooperation Guidelines in 1998, clarifying the noncombat support roles Japan would carry out in the event of the outbreak of hostilities in its region. Of significant concern to the Chinese were discussions between Tokyo and Washington on the subject of a proposed "theater missile defense" system to defend the United States, Japan, Taiwan, and South Korea. The Japanese government has earmarked $8 million for theater missile defense research and development. Beijing argues that the system would seriously shift the balance of power in East Asia, but its particular concern is the latitude Taiwan would enjoy if defended by a missile shield.

In December 2002 Japan's Prime Minister Fumio Kishida put forward a new defense strategy while proposing to double military spending by 2027 to implement it. It was the largest defense shake-up in decades, including openly acquiring offensive weapons and reshaping the Japanese military command structure for its expanded armed forces. The plan doubles military spending. adding $315 billion to Japan's defense budget over the next five years and making Japan's military the world's third largest, after the U.S. and China. Defense spending will escalate to 2% of gross domestic product, equal to the goal the U.S. sets for its NATO allies.

Although never revoked or amended, in recent years Article 9 has been subjected to very substantial "reinterpretation." In the summer of 2014, Prime Minister Shinzo Abe, through a cabinet decision, issued a reinterpretation of Article 9 that allowed Japan for the first time to engage in collective self-defense. The following year, legislation was adopted that enabled Japan to participate in "collective security operations." For the first time, Japanese personnel from its Self-Defense Forces (SDF) were able to engage in combat to support the United States when it is defending Japan, or to support other security partners under attack.

An outburst of anti-Japanese sentiment occurred in 2005. A number of issues with Japan continue to simmer in the Chinese collective mind. Japan's refusal to present an objective picture of its actions in China during World War II in classroom history texts is one instance. The Japanese prime minister's insistence upon regularly honoring soldiers who fell in that war by visiting a shrine devoted to their memory is another. But the party-state was complicit in stirring up anti-Japanese feelings in this instance, having mounted a public campaign to oppose granting Japan permanent membership on the UN Security Council. Public anger boiled over in public demonstrations on the streets of Beijing and Shanghai, organized by cell phone and calling for a boycott of Japanese goods. When the situation threatened to get out of control, the authorities called for an end to demonstrations, clearing the streets in advance of the anniversary of the anti-Japanese May Fourth Incident in 1919.

Japan's military expansion serves as a rationale for the expansion of the PLA. The growth of Chinese military capability, in turn, serves as an argument for those in Japan favoring it becoming a normal nation. The Sino-Japanese relationship, focused on economic issues almost exclusively since 1972, must at some point in the near-term concentrate on strategic concerns as well.

If China's goal is to reduce the possibility of the re-emergence of Japanese militarism, two steps are called for that the Chinese may find difficult to take. First, a continued U.S. presence in East Asia must be actively encouraged. Unfortunately, the Chinese have persuaded themselves that American policy makers are trying once again to encircle China and thwart its emergence as a world power. Given this mindset, Chinese strategic planners find it hard to separate what they believe are the baneful effects on China of the American presence in East Asia from its beneficial effects on Japan.

Second, China should not engage in anything that can be construed as military expansionism, since Japan would use this as a pretext for its own further military buildup. But the PLA's institutional self-interest, which is so influential in policy making, leads it to seek out external situations that will justify a larger, technologically more sophisticated military establishment.

Sovereignty and national security also figure importantly in China's relations with Russia and the other former Soviet republics. Sino-Soviet hostility reached the point of armed conflict in 1969, and the two sides did not begin the long process of reconstructing their relationship until the early 1980s. Mikhail Gorbachev's visit to China, which unexpectedly coincided with and was engulfed by the Tiananmen demonstrations in 1989, marked the culmination of that process of rapprochement. With the collapse of the Soviet Union and its Communist Party two years later, however, Russia again became an unpredictable and potentially dangerous neighbor. Once the Soviet Union was a strong and heavily armed source of Communist heterodoxy; today, Russia is a relatively weak and heavily armed source of heterodoxy.

The contested border between the two countries, once heavily armed, was finally demarcated in an agreement signed in 2004. The Russians are somewhat uncomfortable with what they perceive as a Chinese "colonization" of Siberia. The Russian side of the border has a population of some 6.2 million, whereas 132 million inhabit the Chinese side. The Russians are worried about the 250,000-odd Chinese entrepreneurs living and working in Siberia. Although it is likely that they only mean to make money and go back to the somewhat more hospitable clime of their homes, their presence seems to resurrect Russian fears of a "yellow horde" engulfing Mother Russia. During his term of office as Russia's president, Boris Yeltsin met with Jiang Zemin on eight occasions, the last one in 1999 just prior to his resignation. Both sides were eager to expand their trade relations. The Russians offered technical assistance for the Three Gorges Dam project, and the Chinese have been ready buyers of excess Russian military equipment. Vladimir Putin, while serving as president, met with both Jiang Zemin and Hu Jintao, and most recently has pushed for collaborative energy projects, including a pipeline connecting Angorsk in Siberia with the Daqing oil field in Heilongjiang.

As for the Mongol, Kazakh, and Kirghiz ethnicity minorities who live in China's far west, adjacent to their ethnic cousins in Mongolia, Russia, and the central Asian republics, the Chinese are interested **in** avoiding at all costs collaboration among ethnic separatists arguing for national self-determination. Indeed, as we have seen, during an August 1999 summit in Bishkek, Kyrgyzstan, Yeltsin and Jiang Zemin, together with representatives from Kazakhstan, Kyrgyzstan, and Tajikistan, signed agreements that resolved long-standing differences over their common borders, called for a peace zone in the area, established what came to be called the Shanghai Cooperation Organization and, in the wake of the attacks on the United States on 11 September 2001, formed the Shanghai Convention on Combating Terrorism, Separatism and Extremism.

Since he became President in 2013, Xi Jinping has met nearly fifty times with Vladimir Putin. Their most recent meeting took place in 2024 in the Kazan Kremlin, located in the capital of the Tatarstan Republic. Noting that that year marked the 75th anniversary of the establishment of diplomatic relations between China and Russia, Xi said that China-Russia relations have "forged ahead despite wind and rain in the last 75 years and found the right way for two big, neighboring countries to get along with each other, characterized by non-alliance, non-confrontation, and not targeting any third party." He also noted that 2025 would mark the 80th anniversary of the founding of the United Nations and the victory in the World Anti-Fascist War. "As permanent members of the UN Security Council and major countries in the world, China and Russia should deepen comprehensive strategic coordination, enhance communication and collaboration within multilateral frameworks such as the United Nations and the Shanghai Cooperation Organization."

He also alluded to the "BRICS Mechanism," an intergovernmental organization formed in 2009 that includes ten countries—Brazil, Russia, India, China, South Africa, Egypt, Ethiopia, Indonesia, Iran, and the United Arab Emirates—which he described as "the world's most important platform for solidarity and cooperation between emerging markets and developing countries. China highly commends Russia's great efforts as BRICS Chair for the BRICS Summit." Xi Jinping said that he "looks forward to having in-depth discussions with leaders of other BRICS countries on the future development of the BRICS mechanism to build consensus among the parties, send a positive message of solidarity and cooperation, and advance strategic coordination and practical cooperation between BRICS countries in various fields. In so doing, they can secure more opportunities for the Global South."

In 2024, Vladimir Putin and President Xi Jinping celebrated the 75th anniversary of the establishment of diplomatic relations between Russia and China. On that occasion, Putin noted that "Over the past 75 years, Russia and China have developed into comprehensive strategic partners of coordination for the new era, with bilateral relations maintaining high-level growth and setting an example for a new model of major-country relations."

Meanwhile, with Russia currently not a viable candidate for superpower status, Beijing has come to view with grave concern the lack of constraint on American power in the world arena. China raised strenuous objections to American action against Iraq in defense of the interests of the government of Kuwait in the First Gulf War, American participation in NATO attacks against Serbian forces in Kosovo, and the American wars in Afghanistan and Iraq. And China seems somewhat stymied in its search for allies that might serve as a makeweight against a single superpower. Europe and Japan seem too closely tied to Washington to serve the purpose, and Russia appears both weak and unpredictable. Something more closely resembling a proto-alliance with the United States may eventually prove to be a desirable alternative.

China's actions in the South China Sea continue to be a serious concern for its neighbors in East and Southeast Asia. The Chinese claim that the Spratly Islands chain, which lies in the South China Sea between Vietnam, the Philippines, and the island of Borneo, is Chinese territory, while the Philippines, Vietnam, Malaysia, Brunei, and Taiwan make rival claims to sovereignty over it. By its very liberal reading of the Law of the Sea Convention of 1982 (which it signed but has not ratified), China not only owns the islands but controls the twelve-mile contiguous zone and the two-hundred-mile "exclusive economic zone" around each island. Laws passed by the NPC in 1992 refer to the area as China's "territorial sea" and claim the right to "take all necessary measures" to assert and protect its sovereignty.

It has long been assumed that the principal reason for interest in the islands is the possibility that they have substantial offshore oil deposits; control over fishing rights is also at issue, though the sea has been heavily overfished. Finally, the South China Sea is regarded by other countries as a critical international maritime passage, open access to which they would be prepared to defend.

China began to enforce its claim to the islands in 1988, when it captured six atolls from the Vietnamese in the Johnson Reef area. Since then, it has established outposts on a number of the islands, and Chinese naval vessels have had frequent encounters with those of the other claimants. Pressed by Vietnam to state its intentions, China proposed that the two sides pursue a policy of "joint exploitation first" and leave awkward questions of sovereignty to be resolved later. But these intentions were called abruptly into question in the spring of 1995, when it was discovered that China had built an outpost on one island—appropriately named Mischief Reef—located only 135 miles off the Philippine coast. The boldness of this move, in the context of a substantial increase in military spending and the acquisition of much new equipment designed to strengthen the Chinese navy, raised many questions about China's intentions in the area. The initial American reaction was to say that the question must be settled between the Chinese and Philippine governments, but then Washington said it was prepared to intervene if the international right of free passage was interrupted. The issue remains unresolved between Beijing and Manila, and in 1999, the Chinese rejected a code of conduct for the island chain drafted by the Association of Southeast Asian Nations (ASEAN), arguing that it was preparing a code of its own.

A second theatre of contention is the uninhabited *Senkaku/Diaoyu* islands located some 125 miles north of Taiwan and 250 miles from the island of Okinawa. The waters there teem with fish, and the area around the island is thought to include large oil and gas reserves. Japan formally annexed the islands at the conclusion of the Sino-Japanese War of 1894-95, but the Chinese disputed the Japanese claim. The United States took over administration of the islands at the conclusion of WWII, but formally handed them over to Japan in 1972. The conflict escalated in 2013 when Japanese Prime Minister Abe Shinzo declared that Japan would take a "tough stance" regarding China's claims. Xi Jinping responded by declaring the islands to be a "core interest of China," and Chinese warships began to patrol in the area. The standoff between China and Japan over the islands continues, with Chinese coast guard vessels patrolling waters around the contested islands. Both sides claim sovereignty, and conflict is likely to escalate in the coming decade.

China's actions in the South China Sea and around the Senkaku Islands are, on their face, expansionist. There was no Chinese presence in the area in the past, and now there is. Is this a harbinger of a broader expansionist policy? Is this a policy on which there is general agreement in Beijing, or is it an initiative undertaken by the Chinese navy to strengthen its claim on scarce budget dollars?

As we have seen, China's foreign policy decisions are driven by a desire to enhance the respect that other nations show for China—to gain face—and by an equally strong desire to avoid situations in which the strength and competence of China and its political leaders are publicly called into question. Chinese citizens have grown exceedingly sensitive to these situations and have responded with periodic outbursts of antiforeign nationalism that the party-state has encouraged and then, concerned over the possible consequences, has sought to quell.

China takes its role as a regional power seriously and actively participates in several new international groupings, such as the ASEAN Regional Forum on Security. At the meeting of the regional forum in August 1995, the issue of China's actions in the South China Sea was taken up. It was a measure of Chinese respect for the forum and for its membership in it that China came to the table with a conciliatory approach, agreeing to multilateral negotiations.

A slightly different configuration of members makes up the Asia Pacific Economic Cooperation (APEC) Forum. Although the agenda of APEC forum meetings is intended to focus on Pacific Rim economic issues, its meetings ordinarily include a session of its Eminent Persons Group, the agenda for which is more far-ranging. China is also involved in a proposal to set up the East Asian Community, an Asian common market, with the European Union being the model. An East Asian Summit tasked with starting the planning for the pro-posed organization was held in Kuala Lumpur in December 2005.

The third grouping is the East Asia Summit (EAS), a regional forum held annually by leaders of, initially, 16 countries in the East Asian, Southeast Asian, South Asian , and Oceanian regions. Membership expanded to 18 countries, including Russia and the United States, at the Sixth EAS in 2011. The Summit is described as "a forum for dialogue on broad strategic, political and economic issues of common interest with the aim of promoting peace, stability and economic prosperity in East Asia."

The fourth group in which China has recently begun to participate is the so-called Group of Eight Plus Five. Originally established in 1975 as the Group of Six and limited to Europe's six largest economies, the group was subsequently reconstituted to include Britain, Canada, France, Germany, Italy, Japan, Russia, and the United States. More recently, France and Britain have pressed for the inclusion of five additional economies: Brazil, China, India, Mexico, and South Africa. The European Union is also represented at the group's annual meetings. The following table provides a way of comparing the membership of these international groups.

The fifth group is the BRICS Mechanism, formed in 2007, which has been described above. Membership in these five groups is shown in Table 24, which follows.

Table 25: International And Regional Groups in which China Participates

ASEAN Regional Forum on Security	Asian-Pacific Economic Cooperation Forum	East Asian Summit	Group of Eight Plus Five [Plus One]	BRICS Mechanism
Australia	Australia	Australia		
Bangladesh				
			Brazil	Brazil
			Britain	
Brunei	Brunei	Brunei		
Cambodia		Cambodia		
Canada	Canada		Canada	
Chile				
China	China	China	China	China
				Egypt
				Ethiopia
European Union			European Union	
			France	
			Germany	
India	India	India	India	
Indonesia	Indonesia	Indonesia		Indonesia
				Iran
			Italy	
Japan	Japan	Japan	Japan	
Laos		Laos		
Malaysia	Malaysia	Malaysia		
	Mexico			Mexico
Mongolia				
Myanmar		Myanmar		

New Zealand	New Zealand	New Zealand		
North Korea				
Pakistan				
Papua-New Guinea	Papua-New Guinea			
	Peru			
Philippines	Philippines	Philippines		
Russia	Russia	Russia	Russia	Russia
Singapore	Singapore	Singapore		
			South Africa	South Africa
South Korea	South Korea	South Korea		
Sri Lanka				
	Taiwan			
Thailand	Thailand	Thailand		
Timor-Leste				
				United Arab Republics
United States	United States	United States	United States	
Vietnam	Vietnam	Vietnam		

Chapter 21: Two Superpowers

The *Merriam-Webster Dictionary* defines the term "superpower" as "an extremely powerful nation." Its earliest known use is credited to William Fox, an American foreign policy scholar who published his book, *The Super-Powers: The United States, Britain, and the Soviet Union — Their Responsibility for Peace* in 1944, as World War II was drawing to a close.[13] He applied the term to nations that had global reach, vast military strength (especially nuclear capability), and the ability to project influence worldwide. At that time, he identified three superpowers: the United States, the Soviet Union, and the British Empire. Of course, Great Britain had fulfilled the criteria of a superpower long before the term was coined. But it was not long after the war that Britain ceased to qualify as a superpower, leaving only the United States and the Soviet Union in that category. When, in 1991, the Soviet Union fell, only the United States remained as the world's sole superpower, and so it remains today.

In 1997, when the first edition of this book was published, China's GNP stood at $927 billion, placing it seventh among the world's economies; the U.S., in first place, posted a GNP that year of $8.5 trillion. In 2025, as this fourth edition goes to press, China's GNP stands at $18.8 trillion, placing it second only to that of the United States, whose GNP is $29.8 trillion. Given the relative competence and probity of the current Chinese administration as compared to that of its American counterpart, it is well within the realm of possibility to suppose that China will surpass the United States and assume the position of preeminent

---

[13] (New York: Harcourt, Brace & Co., 1944)

superpower in the not-too-distant future. Meanwhile, there are two superpowers. This chapter explores how we arrived at this point.

As the new century began, Bill Clinton was serving as the American President, and Jiang Zemin as Chairman of the CCP. The relationship between Beijing and Washington was in reasonably good shape. The U.S. granted China Permanent Normal Trade Relations (PNTR) status that year and supported China's effort to join the World Trade Organization, which it achieved in 2001.

Despite this relatively tranquil period in U.S.-China relations, there were periodic outbursts of anti-American sentiment among the Chinese citizenry, one of the first of which occurred in May 1999, following the apparently accidental bombing of the Chinese embassy in Belgrade by NATO forces engaged in the war in Kosovo. Three Chinese citizens were killed by the bombs. Many Chinese doubted that the bombing was accidental and lashed out at the United States in a spate of angry nationalism. The American ambassador was under virtual house arrest for five days in the embassy compound in Beijing as angry crowds—first spontaneous, later orchestrated —swirled past, hurling rocks, bottles, and vitriolic slogans. Americans were stunned to find their Chinese friends utterly convinced that the bombing had been an intentional anti-Chinese act, though these friends were hard-pressed to explain what could have been the motive behind such a self-defeating action.

A second episode threatened to derail entirely the Bush administration's relations with China almost as soon as it had moved into its Washington offices. In April 2001, a U.S. reconnaissance plane collided with a Chinese fighter jet off the shore of Hainan Island, killing the Chinese pilot. The Chinese accused the Americans of violating their airspace; the Americans declared that the aircraft was in international airspace and that the

Chinese pilot, who had been observed in earlier encounters flying so close to American aircraft that the Americans were able to read his e-mail address as he held it up to his windscreen, had caused the accident. Once again, the reaction on the streets was a spate of angry anti-American nationalism.

It was a textbook instance of China's testiness about its sovereignty and need to save face. At issue in the first instance is the United Nations Convention on the Law of the Sea, to which China is a signatory, but the United States is not. The Chinese interpret the convention to preclude overflights of their two-hundred-mile "exclusive economic zone."

The U.S. plane, flying approximately seventy miles off the coast of Hainan, was well within that zone, but the United States maintains that the convention provides free access to national exclusive economic zones for all vessels and aircraft. Moreover, the Chinese accurately noted that the U.S. aircraft was spying; it was collecting electronic intelligence (ELINT) from the Chinese coast. The American side could hardly deny this charge, since the aircraft ended in Chinese hands once it landed on Hainan, but American officials claimed that the monitoring was "routine." There ensued a lengthy and delicate diplomatic minuet that resulted in the framing of a letter from Washington to Beijing that the Chinese could interpret as an apology and the Americans could interpret as a non-apology. The bilateral relationship took months to recover from this incident.

George W. Bush succeeded Clinton as president in January 2001. Four months later, on April Fools' Day, an American EP-3 spy plane flying over the South China Sea at a point roughly midway between Hainan Island and the Paracel Islands was intercepted by two Chinese J-8 fighter planes. A collision between the EP-3 and one of the J-8s caused damage to the EP-3 and the loss of the J-8 and its pilot. The EP-3 made an emergency landing on Hainan without PRC permission, and its 24 crew members were detained and interrogated by Chinese authorities until a carefully worded statement was delivered by the U.S. government. The ambiguous phrasing of the statement allowed both countries to save face and defused a potentially volatile situation.

Since that incident, a number of military encounters between U.S. and Chinese forces have occurred, as shown in the following table:

Table 26: U.S.-China Military Encounters Since 2001

March 2009	South China Sea	USNS *Impeccable* harassment: 5 Chinese ships harassed a U.S. surveillance vessel.	Raised concerns about freedom of navigation; part of a series of naval confrontations.
December 2013	South China Sea	USS *Cowpens* near-collision: Chinese amphibious dock ship cut across the bow of the U.S. cruiser near the Chinese cruiser *Liaoning*.	Narrowly avoided a collision. Highlighted risks near Chinese carrier operations.
September 2018	Spratly Islands (SCS)	USS *Decatur* incident: A Chinese destroyer came within 45 yards of a U.S. destroyer.	One of the closest near-collisions In decades, the U.S. accused China of unsafe maneuvers.
May 2022	South China Sea	Chinese fighters conducted "unsafe intercepts" of U.S. reconnaissance aircraft.	U.S. Indo-Pacific Command publicized the growing frequency of such dangerous encounters.
Dec 2022	South China Sea	A Chinese J-11 fighter came within 10 feet of a U.S. RC-135 aircraft.	The risk of collision drew international attention to PLA air tactics.
May 2023	South China Sea	Chinese fighter cut across the nose of the U.S. RC-135, forcing turbulence.	Pentagon condemned the action as "unsafe"; escalation of aerial confrontations.
June 2023	Taiwan Strait	A Chinese warship crossed 150 yards ahead of USS *Chung-Hoon* during transit.	Very close call; the U.S. said the maneuver violated maritime safety rules.
October 2023	South China Sea	Chinese J-11 fighter closed within 10 feet of a U.S. B-52 bomber at night.	The Pentagon said the risk of collision was extremely high; part of the ongoing unsafe intercept trend.

In 2003, the two sides collaborated in initiating the so-called Six-Party Talks involving China, the United States, the two Koreas, Russia, and Japan. The talks were a response to North Korea's 2003 withdrawal from the Nuclear Non-Proliferation Treaty (NPT). Six rounds of talks between 2003 and 2007 produced little progress until the third phase of the fifth round, when North Korea agreed to shut down its nuclear facilities in exchange for fuel aid and steps toward normalization of relations with the U.S. and Japan. In response to a UN statement in 2009 condemning a failed North Korean satellite launch, the DPRK declared on April 14 that it would pull out of the talks and resume its nuclear enrichment program. North Korea also expelled all nuclear inspectors, effectively ending the Six-Party Talks.

Over the next four years, tensions emerged as the U.S. criticized China's human rights record. Trade disputes erupted over intellectual property rights, counterfeiting, and currency manipulation. China's growing trade surplus became a political issue, and the U.S. Congress expressed concern over China's military modernization. Relations were further strained when the U.S. reaffirmed its support for Taiwan, including arms sales, prompting China to suspend certain military exchanges.

In their first meeting in 2009, Presidents Obama and Hu Jintao emphasized their desire for a "positive, cooperative, and comprehensive" relationship. They initiated the U.S.-China Strategic and Economic Dialogue (SED), an upgrade of the dialogue started under the Bush administration. Delegations met annually, alternating between capitals. In 2011, Obama announced a "strategic pivot to Asia," signaling increased American focus on the Asia-Pacific amid China's rising influence. In 2012, the U.S. joined Japan and the EU in filing a WTO case against China over rare earth export restrictions.

In 2013, Obama met with newly inaugurated President Xi Jinping at the Sunnylands Summit in California. They pledged to establish a "new model" of major power relations. But by 2015, the U.S. urged China to halt land reclamation and militarization activities in the South China Sea, raising regional security concerns.

In 2017, the newly inaugurated Trump administration adopted a confrontational stance toward China, emphasizing trade imbalances and intellectual property concerns. In 2018, the U.S. initiated a trade war, imposing tariffs on Chinese goods; China retaliated. The U.S. designated China a currency manipulator and enacted sanctions on firms like Huawei, citing national security risks. Though a "Phase One" trade deal was signed the following year, implementation lagged.

In 2021, Joe Biden took office as president. His administration maintained high tariffs on Chinese goods while seeking cooperation on global issues such as climate change. High-level visits to Taiwan by U.S. officials and the downing of a Chinese surveillance balloon further elevated tensions. As the Biden administration drew to a close, high-level meetings aimed at stabilizing relations resumed.

Then came Trump II. Within his first hundred days, the president levied 135% tariffs on Chinese imports, only to scale them back weeks later to 30%. Where the relationship will go in the next four years is wholly unclear at this writing.

China's foreign economic policy often moderates its leaders' natural instincts with regard to the United States. Concerns about sovereignty and face might otherwise lead to a break with American criticism, but economic interests dictate caution. It would be difficult, though not impossible, for China to find better markets or sources of capital and technology, so it is willing to make concessions to keep Sino-American links functioning. Some Chinese policymakers believe the U.S. needs Chinese markets, labor, and investment opportunities more than China needs the U.S. This group tends to highlight sovereignty and face, granting concessions only grudgingly and at the last moment.

Three major issues have complicated U.S.-China economic relations in recent years, each illustrating the shifting balance of power. The first is China's large trade surplus, currently at $103 billion. In the early 1980s, the U.S. had a modest annual trade surplus with China. This flipped in 1983, when China posted a $60 million surplus in $4 billion in two-way trade. By 1999, the U.S. reported a $60 billion deficit with China, nearly equal to its deficit with Japan. Trade calculations differed: the U.S. counted goods from China transshipped through Hong Kong as Chinese imports; China counted them as exports to Hong Kong. After Hong Kong's reintegration with the PRC, separate figures were no longer calculated, further inflating the U.S.-reported deficit.

As Taiwanese and Hong Kong manufacturers relocated to mainland China, exports from those facilities were counted as Chinese, not from Taiwan or Hong Kong. The U.S. deficit with China thus grew tenfold in six years, peaking at $290 billion in 2008. Over 90 percent of that surplus stemmed from the U.S. trade deficit with China.

Closely related to this surplus was China's reluctance to let its currency float. An undervalued yuan (some say by as much as 40%) made exports artificially cheap. Since 2005, China has allowed the *yuan* to float, but within a narrow, managed range. Unlike other major currencies, it is not freely traded. To gain monetary independence, China would need to fully liberalize its foreign exchange system.

A 2006 Morgan Stanley report claimed that in 2004, inexpensive Chinese goods saved U.S. consumers $100 billion and helped create over four million U.S. jobs. This view was not widely shared by the U.S. Treasury, whose secretaries, including Timothy Geithner (2009–2013), repeatedly urged China to revalue its currency, with little success.

More recently, China has begun pressuring the U.S. instead. Its trade surplus and currency policy have allowed it to amass $3.2 trillion in foreign reserves, much of which has been invested in U.S. Treasury notes. Concerned about global financial instability, Chinese leaders have warned the U.S. against running long-term deficits, fearing inflation and devaluation of their U.S.-based assets.

The key strategic relationship in East Asia—among China, Japan, and the United States—should be the central focus of American foreign policy. China needs assurances that it is not being isolated. A strategic understanding between China and Japan is essential, and the U.S. is in a strong position to facilitate it.

To reassure China, the U.S. must have a consistent policy and a more measured Congressional approach. When not focused on human rights or Taiwan, Congress is fixated on the trade surplus. Like the U.S.-Japan trade tensions of previous decades, this risks becoming a chronic irritant. Multilateral forums, rather than bilateral confrontations, should be used to address Chinese behavior. While many nations do not share the U.S. concern over human rights, they do share concerns over proliferation and arms sales. Regional and international pressure would be more effective than unilateral demands.

Finally, the U.S. should pursue contact at all levels of the Chinese government—especially with the PLA. Contacts developed after normalization in 1979 were disrupted after the Tiananmen massacre, resumed in the 1990s, and have been repeatedly suspended since, including after the 1996 Taiwan Strait crisis. Cutting off dialogue is counterproductive, especially given the PLA's influence and potential ambitions.

There are lessons to be learned from a century and a half of dealing with China. First, despite the increasing veneer of Westernization, Chinese culture remains fundamentally different. Second, American attempts to remake China have historically failed—whether through Christianization, democratization, or economic modeling. We are likely to fail again.

Although China is not a full democracy, grassroots participation has grown compared to the 1930s and 1940s, when American influence was strongest. Scientific and technological progress is advancing rapidly. These changes are due to Chinese initiative, not American pressure.

Finally, the U.S. must adopt a more neutral, less emotional stance. China is neither the utopia imagined in the 1970s nor the villain it is often portrayed as today. Realistic expectations will lead to fewer disappointments.

Chapter 22: Conclusion

This book set out to consider four questions: Why did our hypotheses about the inevitability of political liberalization in China prove false? What are the principal problems confronting China today? What is the capacity of the Chinese political system to address these problems successfully? And, given the problems and the government's capacity, what is the outcome likely to be?

Preceding chapters have described the formidable challenges to which the Chinese party-state must respond to restore its authority, maintain public order, and create the conditions under which continued economic development can occur. Clearly, the party-state has been seriously weakened by a lack of public confidence, a habit of corruption, and a rigidity in the face of change. Now we must ask, what is China's near-term future likely to be?

Political scientists do not have a stellar track record when it comes to predicting China's future. In fact, only two successful examples occur to me: we predicted that Mao would eventually die, and, indeed, he did. Emboldened by this success, we made the same prediction about Deng Xiaoping, and he also obligingly died. Despite this dismal track record, it may still be useful to offer one or two scenarios about China's future course. I begin by offering some scenarios that do not seem to be likely and then consider more probable ones.

Least likely of all, I believe, is more of the same. Deng Xiaoping adopted a unique method of overseeing China's entry into the modern world. Nearly seventy-five years old when he returned to power and launched his economic reforms, Deng had succession on his mind from the outset. It was his plan to avoid assuming the most senior positions in the party-state himself and to appoint individuals to them whom he thought he could trust to carry on his reform program. If the process had worked as planned, he would gradually have retired and vanished like Lewis Carroll's Cheshire Cat, "quite slowly, beginning with the end of the tail, and ending with the grin, which remained some time after the rest of it had gone."[14] But the process did not work as he planned: he did retire from office and become an *éminence grise,* whispering into his successors' ears from behind the curtain, but all too quickly he lost confidence in the men he had appointed and intervened either to replace them or to reverse what he believed was their incorrect course. This continued until the eve of his ninety-first birthday, when, emerging from a coma and stepping back from the brink of death, he is alleged to have called Jiang Zemin to his bedside for a heart-to-heart talk about Taiwan and the United States.

With his vision, his revolutionary credentials, and his clout, Deng was an indispensable element of the political machine he put in place to change China. He was also irreplaceable. None of his contemporaries possessed his special combination of qualities; all but a very few of them have followed him on his journey "to see Marx," as Mao put it, and China's political system cannot function in the same way following their deaths as it did while they were still alive.

Equally unlikely, in my view, is a reversal of course and the re-establishment of a centrally planned economy built around a strong state-owned sector cut off from the outside world. First, no one of any consequence in China advocates such a reversal. Second, decades of reform have created far too many interests vested in the growth of the Chinese economy—particularly the private sector— and in linking it to the world economy. It would take a massive turn in China's economic fortunes or in the world

---

[14] Lewis Caroll, *Alice's Adventures in Wonderland* (London: Macmillan, 1865) p. 64.

economy as a whole to make rebuilding a Soviet-style socialist economy seem sensible, and it would take a political revolution to implement that.

Also unlikely, as I have come to think in recent years, is an abrupt collapse of the party-state, similar to what happened in the Soviet Union in the summer of 1991. As we have seen, there are ample reasons in China today for popular dissatisfaction with the party-state. Inflation and corruption were the two problems that brought people into the streets in 1989, and so far, inflation has abated. The other, though, is increasing rapidly. Problems like a widening gap between rural and urban incomes, serious unrest in China's ethnic minority areas, and the devastating effects of environmental pollution also seem to be getting worse. Unlike in 1989, there is reason to believe that the level of anger among the rural population is even higher than among the urban population. Country people are showing no hesitation in taking their grievances to the village streets, even in today's repressive political atmosphere.

What is the spark that might set off the prairie fire (to use Mao's felicitous phrase) that brings down the government? Students might act as a vanguard, as they did in the late 1980s, though the reservoir of idealism and political activism in the student community seems well below the high-water mark then. Or rural protests over excess taxes or egregious examples of corruption might become even more numerous and violent. Moreover, as China's cities continue to grow, urban frustrations may also reach the boiling point. Unemployment, underemployment, the failure to honor promised pension payments, and the decidedly discriminatory treatment of migrant workers all have brought urban residents to the streets in protest. Amazingly, the tens of thousands of instances of local protest each year remain isolated and disorganized. It is hard to imagine that if this level of local protests continues, protesting groups will not link up with one another and create a substantially different problem for the party-state than it has heretofore. Controlling a nation in the streets is surely beyond the weakened party-state's capability. A rapid meltdown of the Chinese Communist Party and the government it controls is plausible under those circumstances.

But the party-state has shown a remarkable resiliency in the face of the problems it confronts. The malign fate of the party-state that seemed virtually inevitable in the heady days of May 1989 and that was reinforced by the ensuing collapse of its socialist allies looks to be a much more distant possibility thirty-five years later.

Or the process might be slower, triggered not by aggrieved citizens but by dissident regions. If we assume that the simultaneous weakening of central authority and strengthening of local authority continue, inter-regional and inter-ethnic conflicts are sure to arise, and the central government will no longer be in a position to mediate or end those conflicts. Some observers have called this situation economic warlordism, using a term meant to remind us of the period be-tween the collapse of dynastic authority and the reassertion of a strong central authority under the Chinese Communist Party in 1949. During this period, whichever warlord controlled Beijing and its environs claimed that he spoke for the government of China, but apart from receiving foreign envoys, he had no effective national power. If one wanted to do business in Shanghai or settle a claim in Guangzhou, one addressed oneself to the local warlord, not to Beijing. Disputes between warlords were settled by armed conflict between the troops loyal to each. A repeat of this collapse of civil order and central control is a possibility in the near term.

Were either of these last two sets of circumstances to come about, there is no question that the PLA would intervene, but in neither instance would it do so to prop up the incumbents of the weakened party-state. Rather, I believe, it would intervene in the name of Chinese patriotism and in defense of the Chinese national entity, resulting in a *de facto* military caretaker government. Given the strengths and weaknesses of the PLA as potential praetorians, such a government is more likely to be successful in the first set of circumstances—citizens in the streets—than with regional dissidence. It could very likely gain substantial popular support if it refused to endorse a discredited civilian leadership and set itself apart as an alternative to weakened and corrupted institutions. A promise to restore order to city streets and village roads would appeal to the people's natural distaste for anarchy and chaos.

An optimistic conclusion assumes that the PLA succeeds in restoring order, finds new and uncorrupted civilian leaders, rebuilds the power of the central government, and begins to address the nation's agenda of problems. It also assumes that military professionalism is stronger than the pleasures of politics and that the army returns to its barracks at an early date. A pessimistic conclusion assumes that the PLA, like the party, cannot restore the credibility of central authority and that personal and institutional self-interest preclude a successful political reconstitution.

Ending civil war among competing economic warlords would be a substantially more formidable challenge. The PLA would be stretched very thin, and even if some of its units were not actually involved as combatants, their own regional interests would not be easy to separate from patriotism. Chiang Kai-shek spent twenty years trying to create a national entity out of a patchwork of regional fiefdoms. In the end, he created a web of tenuous alliances among warlords, not a strong central state, which eventually came only as the result of a revolution that won popular support by its appeal to nationalism and its promise to run an honest government and improve living standards. That process can hardly be accomplished by the PLA acting on its own.

Muddling through—making incremental changes here and there to cope with the many problems confronting the Chinese political system as it moves forward in the years ahead—is a scenario that I regard as likely in the near term but ineffective over the longer term. Upholding the bargain of prosperity in exchange for stability requires a rate of growth that China's economy will be hard-pressed to realize over the long term. Muddling through also presupposes that the party-state can get a handle on the rampant corruption that plagues both mid-level and local government. It is the party's goal to substitute the accountability brought about by a viable political opposition and periodic elections for an internal accountability that restores the performance and the reputation of the Chinese Communist Party. While the party has made some progress in this direction, its recent moves against lawyers and reporters who identify examples of malfeasance and corruption render its rhetoric about establishing a rule of law ring hollow.

Taiwanization is a fifth scenario, unlikely in the near term, but it is my hope that it might be realized over the longer term. By "Taiwanization" I mean the duplication in mainland China of the political transformation that occurred in Taiwan: a relaxation of political repression, the emergence of a viable political opposition, and the reconstitution of the government so that more than one different party might become the ruling one in turn. Indispensable to this transformation are, as we have seen, a forward-looking leader with the political power to carry out his plans, courageous politicians willing to take risks to express their opposition, and an electorate interested in and enthusiastic about democracy. A fledgling democracy is often somewhat chaotic and occasionally ineffective. One needs economic prosperity and the absence of serious political challenges to allow for tranquility while a new system tries its wings.

At the moment, there are no signs in China of a visionary and powerful leader ready to launch a move toward democratization. Certainly, Xi Jinping is not that man. Nor is there a plethora of bold politicians prepared to form an opposition movement. Most of them have been imprisoned, placed under house arrest, or thoroughly intimidated. Also lacking is a strong commitment to democracy on the part of a politically aware and active public. In fact, among the politically conscious citizenry, there is widespread skepticism about democracy. Many of them argue that democracy is ill-suited to China, either because of its history and culture or because of its size and ungovernability. Others believe that democracy may be appropriate for China at some future date but not now, when China needs honest authoritarianism. Therefore, a political liberalization of the Chinese government similar to Taiwan's seems a highly unlikely scenario in the near term.

In sum, regardless of which of these or other scenarios comes to pass, China has a protracted and problematic time ahead. Particularly since the outcome of the last American presidential election, China is well-launched on the road to becoming the world's preeminent superpower. The extraordinary growth of its economy will continue, but at a slower pace during this transitional period, and China's best-endowed regions will weather this more successfully than the others. Because perceived threats from outside are always effective in creating national unity, we can expect China's national ego to be especially sensitive.

* * *

We began by noting that "understanding China" is an ongoing process, not a completed project. That ongoing process of striving to understand China is a necessity if we hope to be able to deal effectively with it during the period that lies ahead. To do so requires that we keep in the closest possible touch with a broad spectrum of Chinese people and institutions, for that is the only way to keep ourselves as well informed as we can be about the changes taking place there. It also requires sensitivity and flexibility in responding to the changes we observe. It requires that we bear in mind our past experience. We have, over the years, exerted a great deal of influence on China indirectly, rather than directly, and we have been most successful in doing so when we have taught by example, least successful when we have tried to teach through sanctions.

To understand China is not to hold it to a standard of its own and to exempt it from the standards to which we hold ourselves and other nations. It is suggested that since it had very little to do with setting those standards in the past, it may have difficulty in living up to them in the present. To understand China is not necessarily to love it, but understanding China is a prerequisite for dealing with it effectively in the years ahead. And, given its size and its potential, and the degree to which the rest of the world has become linked with it both economically and politically, there is no avoiding the necessity of our dealing effectively with China in the years ahead.

Appendix A: A Timeline of Events in 20th and 21st Century China

1911 The Qing dynasty falls, replaced by a Chinese republic nominally headed by Sun Yat-sen (Sun Zhongshan). He was succeeded the following year by Yuan Shikai, who subsequently declared himself president for life.

1912 The Kuomintang (KMT, GuomindangGurkhas, or Nationalist Party) is formed as an alliance of several small parties and succeeds in winning a majority in a newly formed bicameral parliament the following year. Sun Yat-sen takes over and reorganizes the party seven years later.

1916, Yuan dies, and control of the country falls to a collection of contending warlords, each controlling a piece of territory by military force.

1919 The student-led May Fourth Movement protested foreign incursions upon Chinese sovereignty. It is often taken to be the origin of Chinese nationalism.

1921 Mao Zedong and eleven others attend the founding congress of the Chinese Communist Party (CCP) in Shanghai.

1922 At Moscow's urging, the fledgling CCP forms an alliance with the KMT.

1925 Sun dies and is succeeded the following year by Chiang Kai-shek (Jiang Jieshi) as head of the KMT. Chiang engineers a rupture with the CCP and conducts a series of campaigns against the party, decimating its ranks.

1927 Through a series of alliances and campaigns, Chiang establishes himself as primus inter pares among the warlords and establishes his new government of the Republic of China in Nanjing. There follows a decade of nominal democratic rule and economic development under the aegis of the KMT.

1934 Threatened by the KMT, a band of some hundred thousand CCP members undertook a grueling five-thousand-mile Long March to a new base area in Yan'an in the remote province of Shaanxi.

1937 Japanese forces invaded China, precipitating a nominal revival of the CCP-KMT alliance.

1945 Following the Japanese surrender, an effort is made by the United States to mediate the dispute between the CCP and the KMT. It is unsuccessful, and there ensues a four-year civil war that culminates in the victory of the CCP and the retreat of the KMT to Taiwan.

1949 Standing atop Tiananmen in Beijing, Mao proclaims the founding of the People's Republic of China, saying, "The Chinese people have stood up."

1952 The CCP begins the socialist transformation of the Chinese economy, with nationalization of industry, finance, and commerce in the cities and land reform in the countryside.

1957 Confident in what has been achieved, Mao calls on Chinese intellectuals to critique the work of the CCP during its first eight years in power. When they respond to this Hundred Flowers Campaign with their criticisms, they are persecuted and largely silenced.

1958 Mao speeds up the process of transformation with the ill--starred Great Leap Forward, creating unwieldy and unproductive communes and seriously reducing agricultural output. Widespread famine spreads through central China over the next three years, causing an estimated twenty-five to thirty million deaths.

1961 His grandiose development scheme in shambles, Mao retreats to the second line of party leadership.

1966 Believing that the debacle brought about by the Great Leap Forward had been brought on not by his own excess of ambition but by opposition from his party colleagues (among them Deng Xiaoping), he brands them "capitalist roaders' and launches what he calls the Great Proletarian Cultural Revolution, reducing the country to widespread chaos.

1971 China's seat in the United Nations, then occupied by the Republic of China in Taiwan, was transferred to the Beijing government.

1972 Richard Nixon visits China, initiating the process of normalizing United States-China re-lations.

1976 Mao dies and is effectively succeeded by Deng Xiaoping, who launches policies of economic reform and opening to the outside world, which he refers to as the four modernizations. Although the resulting system is called "socialism with Chinese characteristics," it quickly loses any semblance of a so-cialist economy. Deng, the party general secretary Zhao Ziyang, and their colleagues are referred to as the second generation of party and state leaders, Mao having headed the first generation.

1979 The United States and China establish diplomatic relations.

1989 Following the unexpected death of the moderate Hu Yaobang, student protesters used the occasion of his memorial service to occupy Tiananmen Square. They remain in control of the square until, on the night of 3-4 June, Deng and his fellow elders order the People's Liberation Army to use tanks to clear the square. Hundreds of students and citizens are killed. Zhao Ziyang, who supported the students, was succeeded as party general secretary by Jiang Zemin. Jiang and his colleagues are referred to as the third generation of successors to Mao.

1992 Sensing that the reaction to the Tiananmen demonstrations threatened to derail his plans for reform, modernization, and opening to the global economy, Deng, now eighty-eight, took a "southern tour" of the special economic zones he had helped create. His comments during the tour serve to rein-vigorate economic reform.

1997 Deng Xiaoping dies.

1998 Zhu Rongji succeeds Premier Li Peng, who sided with the elders against the students in

1989 Zhu spearheads efforts to rein in the overheated economic reform movement.

1999 NATO bombs hit the Chinese embassy in Belgrade, Yugoslavia, killing three Chinese citizens. The Chinese government holds the United States culpable in the incident, and there are widespread anti-American demonstrations in many Chinese cities.

2001 Beijing is designated the site for the 2008 Summer Olympics, and China accedes to membership in the World Trade Organization. The two events are heralded outside China as "inevitably" bringing about democratic reform in the country.

2002 At the Sixteenth National Party Congress, Jiang Zemin steps down as party general secretary and is succeeded by Hu Jintao.

2003 Wen Jiabao succeeds Zhu Rongji as premier. Wen, Zhu, and their colleagues are referred to as the fourth generation of leaders of the party and state. It is the first "normal" succession to power since the founding of the party eighty-one years earlier.

2004 Jiang Zemin steps down as chairman of the Central Military Commission and is succeeded by Hu Jintao.

2007 The Seventeenth National Party Congress elects replacements to its leadership bodies, including Xi Jinping and Li Keqiang, who are taken to be the core leaders of the fifth generation of party and state leaders

2008 In May, an earthquake of magnitude 7.9 in Sichuan Province killed some sixty-nine thousand, many of them children, buried in shoddily constructed schools. Two months later, Beijing hosts the 2008 Summer Olympics.

2009 China, the United States, India, Brazil, and South Africa reach an agreement at the United Nations Conference on Climate Change in Copenhagen on a plan that codifies the commitments of the individual nations to act on their own to tackle global warming. The agreement falls well short of pre-conference expectations.

2010 A magnitude 7.1 earthquake strikes Yushu County in Qinghai, killing 2,698 people and leaving over 100,000 homeless. China dissident Liu Xiaobo is awarded the Nobel Peace Prize, highlighting ongoing human rights issues in China.

2011 At the invitation of Barack Obama, Hu Jintao pays a state visit to the United States. Pro-democracy protests occur across China, inspired by the Jasmine Revolution in Tunisia. The Chinese government undertakes efforts to combat an ongoing drought. A high-speed train crash in Wenzhou leads to significant protests.

2013 Xi Jinping is elected president, replacing Hu Jintao. Li Keqiang is appointed Premier.

2014 Xi launches an expanded anti-corruption campaign, garnering significant media coverage both domestically and internationally.

2016 China introduces a two-child policy, replacing the previous one-child policy.

2017 The CCP holds its 19th National Congress. President Donald Trump pays a state visit to China.

2018 The NPC approves a constitutional change that removes term limits for its leaders, granting Xi Jinping the status of President for Life. The Congress also adopts a measure writing "Xi Jinping Thought on Socialism with Chinese Characteristics for a New Era" into the Constitution. The amendment juxtaposes Xi's thought with Marxism-Leninism, Mao Zedong Thought, Deng Xiaoping Theory, the Theory of Three Represents, and the Scientific Outlook on Development as the guiding ideology for the Communist Party of China.

2019 The 70th anniversary of the founding of the PRC is marked by a major military parade on National Day.

2020 China is struck by the COVID-19 epidemic, with a death toll estimated to be in the hundreds of thousands.

2021 China announces the three-child policy, replacing the two-child policy of 2016.

2023 Li Keqiang dies of a heart attack shortly after resigning from his position as Premier. Li Qiang is appointed as his successor.

Appendix B: Further Reading

Barnett, A. Doak. *China's Far West: Four Decades of Change.* Boulder, Colorado: Westview, 1993.

Bergsten, C. Fred; Charles Freeman; Nicholas R. Lardy; and Derek J. Mitchell. *China's Rise: Challenges and Opportunities.* Washington, D.C.: Peterson Institute for International Economics, 2008.

Chen Guidi and Wu Chuntao. *Will the Boat Sink the Water?: The Life of China's Peasants,* (trans. Zhu Hong). New York: PublicAffairs, 2006.

Dai Qing. *The River Dragon Has Come! The Three Gorges Dam and the Fate of China's Yangtze River and Its People.* Armonk, New York: M. E. Sharpe, 1997.

Davis, Deborah; Richard Kraus; Barry Naughton; and Elizabeth Perry, eds. *Urban Spaces in Contemporary China: The Potential for Autonomy and Community in Post-Mao China.* New York and Cambridge, U.K.: Cambridge University Press, 1995.

Dittmer, Lowell. *China's Continuous Revolution: The Post-Revolutionary Epoch 1949-1981.* Berkeley, California: University of California Press, 1986.

Economy, Elizabeth C. *The River Runs Black: The Environmental Challenge to China's Future.* Ithaca, New York and London: Cornell University Press, 2004.

Fairbank, John King, and Goldman, Merle. *China: A New History. (Enlarged edition).* Cambridge, Massachusetts: Harvard University Press, 1992.

Gilley, Bruce. *China's Democratic Future: How It Will Happen and Where It Will Lead.* New York: Columbia University Press, 2004.

Huang Yasheng. *Capitalism with Chinese Characteristics: Entrepreneurship and the State.* New York and Cambridge, U.K.: Cambridge University Press, 2008.

Lam, Willy Lo-lap. *Chinese Politics in the Hu Jintao Era.* Armonk, New York: M. E. Sharpe, 2006.

Lardy, Nicholas. *Integrating China into the World Economy.* Washington, D.C.: Brookings Institution Press, 2002.

Li, Cheng. *China's Changing Political Landscape: Prospects for Democracy.* Washington, D.C.: Brookings Institution Press, 2008.

Lieberthal, Kenneth. *Governing China: From Revolution Through Reform.* New York: W. W. Norton, 1995.

Lubman, Stanley B. *Bird in a Cage: Legal Reform in China After Mao.* Stanford, California: Stanford University Press, 1999.

Naughton, Barry. *The Chinese Economy: Transitions and Growth.* Cambridge, Massachusetts: Massachusetts Institute of Technology Press, 2007.

O'Brien, Kevin J., and Li Lianjiang. *Rightful Resistance in Rural China.* New York and Cambridge, U.K.: Cambridge University Press, 2006.

Pan, Philip P. *Out of Mao's Shadow: The Struggle for the Soul of a New China.* New York: Simon & Schuster, 2008.

Pei Minxin. *China's Trapped Transition: The Limits of Developmental Autocracy.* Cambridge, Massachusetts: Harvard University Press, 2006.

Schell, Orville and Delury, John. *Wealth and Power: China's Long March to the Twenty-first Century.* New York: Penguin Random House, 2013.

Schurmann, Franz. *Ideology and Organization in Communist China.* Berkeley, California: University of California Press, 1966.

Shambaugh, David. *Modernizing China's Military: Progress, Problems and Prospects.* Berkeley, California: University of California Press, 2002.

Siu, Helen and Stern, Zelda. *Mao's Harvest: Voices from China's New Generation.* Oxford: Oxford University Press, 1983.

Solinger, Dorothy J. *Contesting Citizenship in Urban China: Peasant Migrants, the State, and the Logic of the Market*. Berkeley, California: University of California Press, 1999.

Spence, Jonathan D. *The Search for Modern China.* New York: W. W. Norton, 1990.

Tsang, Steve. *Modem History of Hong Kong.* London: I. B. Tauris & Co., Ltd., 2005.

Tyler, Patrick. A Great Wall: Six Presidents and China: An Investigative History. New York: Century Foundation, 1999.

Wakeman, Frederic. *The Fall of Imperial China.* New York: Simon and Schuster, 1976

Wasserstrom, Jeffrey. China in the Twenty-first century: What Everyone Needs to Know. Oxford: Oxford University Press, 2010.

White, Lynn T., III. *Unstately Pow*er. Vol. 1: *Local Causes of China's Economic Re-forms*. Vol. 2: *Local Causes of China's Intellectual, Legal and Governmental Reforms*. Armonk, New York: M. E. Sharpe, 1998.

Yang, Dali L. *Remaking the Chinese Leviathan: Market Transition and the Politics of Governance in China.* Stanford, California: Stanford University Press, 2004.

Zhang Liang. *The Tiananmen Papers,* ed. Andrew J. Nathan and Perry Link. New York: PublicAffairs, 2001.

Zhao Yuezhi. *Media, Market and Democracy in China: Between the Party Line and the Bottom Line*. Chicago, Illinois: University of Illinois Press, 1998.

Index

www.ingramcontent.com/pod-product-compliance
Lightning Source LLC
LaVergne TN
LVHW052211200926
848481LV00001B/75

9798295578984